RICHARD GOODWIN KEATS

A TREASURE TO THE SERVICE

First published in Australia in 2021.

Copyright © 2023 by Peter Hannah

Second Edition

All rights reserved. No part of this publication may be reproduced, distributed, or transmitted in any form or by any means, including photocopying, recording, or other electronic or mechanical methods, without the prior written permission of the publisher, except in the case of brief quotations embodied in critical reviews and certain other non-commercial uses permitted by copyright law.

 A catalogue record for this work is available from the National Library of Australia

Disclaimer

Reasonable effort has been made to trace the ownership of all copyrighted material included in this volume. Any omissions or errors that have occurred are inadvertent and will be corrected in subsequent editions provided notification is sent to the publisher and author in written form.

Hannah, Peter (author)

Richard Goodwin Keats - A Treasure To The Service

ISBN 978-1-923088-03-0

https://greenhillpublishing.com.au/

Front Cover Paintings - Portrait: oil on canvas, John Jackson 1817, NMM BHC2975 ©National Maritime Museum, Greenwich London
The Moonlight Battle off Cape St. Vincent, 16 January 1780; Richard Paton, NMM BHC0429 ©National Maritime Museum, Greenwich London
Back Cover Photo by Author

Cover and book design by Green Hill Publishing

A TREASURE TO THE SERVICE

The Historical Memoirs And
A Biography Of
Admiral Sir Richard Goodwin Keats GCB

Second Edition

PETER HANNAH

Vice Admiral Sir Richard Keats shown wearing the sash and star of the GCB and captain's medal from San Domingo, oil on canvas, John Jackson 1817, NMM BHC2975 ©National Maritime Museum Greenwich, London

"My dear Keats...nothing, I do assure you, would give me greater pleasure than to have you at all times near me; for without a compliment, I believe your head is as judicious as your heart is brave, and neither I believe, can be exceeded."

Nelson to Keats, 24 August 1805

Contents

Introduction 01

MEMOIRS

1. Early Years 07
2. American Revolutionary Wars 13
3. Post-Captain, The Western Squadron 25
4. HMS *Superb* 61
5. Second Battle Of Algeciras 67
6. In The Mediterranean With Nelson 95
7. Diplomacy On The Barbary Shores 103
8. Pursuit Of Villeneuve 113
9. The Trafalgar Battle Plan 129
10. Battle Of San Domingo 143
11. Return To The Channel 161
12. The Baltic – Second Battle Of Copenhagen 173
13. Repatriation Of A Division Of Spanish Troops 193
14. The Walcheren Expedition 231
15. Cádiz – The Peninsula War 243
16. In The Mediterranean With Pellew 261
17. Governor Of Newfoundland 267
18. Board Of Longitude 285
19. Governor Of The Royal Hospital Greenwich 289
20. A Diversity Of Interests 303
21. Captain Warner's Inventions 313
22. The Man 317
23. Funeral 331
24. Conclusion 339

MAPS

1. English Channel 32
2. Algeciras 70
3. Western Mediterranean 114
4. North Atlantic 145
5. Bay Of Biscay 163
6. Approaches To The Baltic Sea 183
7. The Scheldts; Walcheren, Flushing, Antwerp 235
8. Cádiz 251

Contents

APPENDICES

I Career by rank, promotions and honours 347
II Captains Orders For HMS *Superb* 1803-4 351
III Narrative of the services of HMS *Superb*, 74, on the night of 12 July 1801
    and the two following days 363

ILLUSTRATIONS

Portrait, Vice Admiral Keats GCB, John Jackson... IV
Portrait, Vice Admiral Keats, William Ward, engraving from John Jackson 05
HRH Prince William Henry 15
The Moonlight Battle off Cape St Vincent, Richard Paton..18
King George III Reviews the Fleet in HMS *Southampton*, W. Elliot..............................27
HMS *Galatea*, Thomas Whitcombe 35
The action off Isle de Groix, E Godefroy..40
The Passage du Raz 51
Line plans of HMS *Superb*..62
HMS *Superb* in action off Cape Trafalgar, on the night of July 12 1801, J. Brenton 77
Battle off Cabrita Point, July 12 1801, Thomas Whitcombe..88
Positioning of the fleet at San Domingo...150
Battle of San Domingo, drawn as at 10am..152
Battle of San Domingo, second position...153
Admiral Duckworth's Action off San Domingo, 6 February 1806, Nicholas Pocock......155
Danish shallop gun-boat 188
Marquis de la Romana supervises the embarkation of Spanish troops to waiting British warships, Juan Rodriguez-Jimenez...208
A convoy passing Reefness, W.A Knell 215
Keats's crests and arms 219
Presentation pistols, gift from General Romana...221
Portrait, Rear Admiral Keats, K.B, Stratford, J. Stipple engraving................................229
Arrival of the English off Ter Veere, Walcheren, J Groenewoud..................................234
Plan of HMS *Devastation*, bomb vessel...246
HMS *Implacable*, stern gallery..248
HMS *Bellerophon* off the coast, W.F. Mitchell..270
View of the entrance to St Johns Harbour, M. le Geyt...278
Royal Hospital Greenwich, W.P. Kay...290
The Embarkation of George IV, Greenwich, J.T. Serres..299
Plans of Greenwich Hospital barge..301
Yachts of the Cumberland Fleet racing on the Thames, W Havell................................308
Marble bust of Admiral Keats, by Chantry, Royal Chapel, Greenwich........................333
Monument, Royal Hospital, Greenwich..337
HMS *Keats*, Captain class frigate, 1943..349

The Historical Memoirs
And A Biography of
Admiral Sir Richard Goodwin Keats GCB

In the study of whose character we were forcibly reminded
of some lines in Longfellow's Psalm of Life:

> In the world's broad field of battle,
>   In the bivouac of Life,
> Be not like dumb, driven cattle!
>   Be a hero in the strife!
>
> Lives of great men all remind us
>   We can make our lives sublime,
> And, departing, leave behind us
>   Footprints on the sands of time;
>
> Footprints, that perhaps another,
>   Sailing o'er life's solemn main,
> A forlorn and shipwrecked brother,
>   Seeing, shall take heart again.
>
> Let us, then, be up and doing,
>   With a heart for any fate;
> Still achieving, still pursuing,
>   Learn to labour and to wait.

The Shipwrecked Mariner, *Distinguished Admirals*, 1868[1]

Introduction

Learning his craft in the American Revolutionary Wars, honing his skills as a frigate captain, and as captain of a ship of the line almost singlehandedly achieving victory over a combined French and Spanish fleet at the conclusion of the French Revolutionary Wars, Keats won a reputation as one of the stars in the period of sea wars that proved to be of unparalleled intensity and duration.[2] He had few equals as seaman, navigator, ship handler and planner of operations.

The following includes the transcription of a memoir, handwritten, probably in 1826 during his time as Governor of the Royal Hospital, Greenwich, which led to the publication of memoirs in almost identical terms by Ralfe in his *Naval Biography* in 1828.[3] Sections relating to Nelson include wording identical to that in Clarke & M'Arthur's *Life of Nelson* published in 1809[4], so the question of authorship is moot. The original volume of handwritten memoirs is now lodged with the National Maritime Museum at Greenwich. Earlier drafts written in the first person are held at the Somerset Records Office.[5]

Here, the original text of the memoirs appears in contrasting type from various annotations, comments and additional information from other sources.

There are many places where the memoirs compress into one sentence events which might otherwise fill a whole book: "Captain Keats consequently proceeded with his lordship to the West Indies in search of the enemy, but failing in their object, returned to England" is but one example. A double-crossing of the Atlantic, under full sail day and night in an unseaworthy ship, is dismissed as barely worthy of comment. Others describe it as a miracle.

The memoirs gloss over the 1797 mutinies and similarly ignore the controversial question of whether, by waiting for his musicians to arrive from another ship, Admiral Duckworth delayed

Keats's arrival off Cádiz to the extent he missed the Battle of Trafalgar, where he was otherwise to have been Nelson's second.

Fortunately, Keats kept well-ordered papers that have been retained. It was practice to reproduce dispatches in the newspapers, and there were several publications commenting on local and international events. In combination these sources allow events not fully recorded in the memoirs to be explored more fully.

Examined more fully in the following pages are his surprisingly energetic periods as Governor of Newfoundland; Governor of the Royal Hospital Greenwich; Commissioner of the Board of Longitude; and in society generally after recurring health issues forced his retirement from service at sea.

Despite prominent displays of talent and gallantry, Keats is not so well known in wider circles. A concentration upon the Battle of Trafalgar and Nelson has resulted in other actions and Nelson's companions, including Keats, receiving less acclaim in history than in justice ought to be the case.

It would be a mistake to think of Trafalgar as cementing English victory or ending the war. Napoleon still held ambitions regarding Britain and his fleets were still at large. There was just one subsequent major fleet action in the Age of Sail. That was the Battle off San Domingo in early 1806, in which Keats played a prominent part, and which resulted in the destruction of an entire French squadron. After those defeats no foreign navy had the appetite to meet the British at sea. Even so, although thereafter changed in character, the conflict grew in intensity and ensued for another ten years as a war of attrition centred around trade and economics. The navy continued to be engaged in the arduous task of blockading the ports of France and her allies, denying the enemy and their merchants access to ports, ships, shipyards, and resources, and preventing their ships of war getting to sea. Most importantly they sought to prevent the French gaining control of the Channel. If that had occurred for even the briefest period, it would have enabled Napoleon's Grande Armée to launch an invasion of England. Additionally, British ships were engaged in convoy duty across vast areas, protecting British merchants and trade routes from predation.

The navy was called upon to exercise its superiority at sea as an arm of national policy. Powerful expeditionary forces were deployed on missions to neutralise, capture or destroy enemy fleets in their home ports. In these years victory was not to be achieved by great set-piece battles at sea. Rather, intensity and variety of experience were interspersed between ceaseless day-to-day activities of patrol and escort. Figures such as Gambier, Saumarez, Hood, and Keats may lack the romantic dash and recognition of Nelson, but they participated in – and excelled at – all these activities as men of courage, talent and determination who made their own significant contributions to Britain's final triumph.[6]

Keats's career was fettered by persistent ill health, probably rheumatism, in the closing years of the war. This forced his retirement from duty at sea in 1812, when it might be observed he was otherwise at the peak of his talents and abilities, and led to the question as to whether those talents were ever called into full play.[7]

Another area left incomplete by the memoirs is that of his personality and character. Eulogisers are called upon to paint the best picture. They described him as a "smart and strict officer but at the same time a kind, intelligent, moral and generous man having a shrewd and penetrating discrimination",[8] and as one of the "bravest, most correct and most skilful Admirals that ever graced the lists of [the] Navy, possessed of all the attributes of the polished gentleman."[9]

Where possible, personal accounts and anecdotes have been added despite, or indeed because of, their various biases, to help paint a more complete picture of the character of the subject, not so apparent from an official memoir or eulogies.

Where some historians have identified a tendency in Keats towards unnecessary self-criticism, others have seen an intelligent officer who could be trusted with independent command.[10] All appear to agree he was possibly the best seaman of his generation.[11] Contemporary accounts found him prickly, rarely jocose, cool, firm and collected. He always strived to live up to his own Ship's Instruction, to have a steady attention to what was going on and "not suffer the most trifling thing to be done with indifference".[12]

The more one delves into the historical record, the more complex and interesting Keats becomes. That was true in life as well. The better one got to know him and broke through a natural reservedness the more interesting he became. The various threads were identified and summarised by Nelson who said:

> *Keats...is a most valuable officer, and does honour to your friendship. Every day increased my esteem for him, both as an officer and as a man.... I hope to be allowed to call Keats my friend. He is very much recovered and cheerful; he is a treasure to the service.*[13]

Admiral Sir Richard Goodwin Keats
Knight Grand Cross of the Most Honourable Military Order of the Bath
Admiral of the White
Major-General of His Majesty's Royal Marines
Commissioner for the Discovery of the Longitude at Sea
Governor and Commander in Chief of Newfoundland
Governor of the Royal Hospital at Greenwich
Director, Royal Sailing Society
Vice-Patron, Royal Thames Yacht Club
Honorary Member, The Royal Yacht Squadron
Vice President British & Overseas Temperance Society
Vice-President London Vaccine Institution
Vice-President Episcopal Floating Church Society
Vice-President Royal Navy Charities Society
Engraving, stipple, by William Ward, from John Jackson, circa 1825, NMM PW3551 ©National Maritime Museum, Greenwich London

ADMIRAL SIR RICHARD GOODWIN KEATS, G.C.B.
Governor of the Royal Hospital Greenwich

Historical Memoirs of
Admiral Sir Richard Goodwin Keats, GCB

Early Years

It has long been the opinion of the world, at least of that part of it which is called the learned, that real talents and abilities are given but to few, and in contemplating the records of those illustrious for qualities which entitle them to immortality, it has been remarked by some writers, that every age has been distinguished by a peculiarity, from which it has derived its characteristic appellation; that particular periods appear to have been destined to the production of men of abilities; that they have not flourished in a continued series, but in a body that, "instead of moving in a regular orbit, as the planets, their course is lawless as the comets" and the reigns of Augustus, Charles and Anne are instanced as affording proof of the assertion. A host of names, standing high in literary fame, are then given, and those periods are designated with the title of the learned ages. If this be true in letters, why not in arms? Without endeavouring to prove the truth of this position by historical records, we shall merely instance the reign of George the Third, which, according to the above opinion, may be styled the age of heroes; for though virtue, in whatever profession, in this most distinguished and comprehensive degree must, like all prodigies, appear but seldom, we believe there are more instances to be found during that period, and in the British navy, than are recorded during the same space of time, in the history of the whole world, and it is certainly a pleasing part of a writer's duty to detail the services of men of eminence, more especially of those who profess that modesty and diffidence which usually accompany merit. No opportunity of this kind ought to be omitted, and it is therefore with great pleasure we give to the world a statement of the services performed by Sir Richard Goodwin Keats, who, besides possessing the first qualities of the heart and understanding, was favoured by many contingencies which no abilities can command.

Sir Richard is the son of the Rev. Richard and Elizabeth Keats and was born on the 16th of January 1757, at the village of Chalton, in Hampshire, of which his father was at that time curate, and from whom he received the first rudiments of his education.

Reverend Keats later became Headmaster of Blundell's School at Tiverton in Bideford, Devon, and Vicar of Kings Nympton. On retirement he was admitted to the Rectory of Bideford. He was, for a period, from 1804 appointed the Domestic Chaplain to His Royal Highness, the Duke of Clarence. Reverend Keats and his wife Elizabeth are buried in the Church at Kings Nympton, where Sir Richard erected a handsome memorial. The Keats family can be traced in Berkshire and Gloucestershire three generations before 1620, William Keats having fled Hagbourne in Berkshire to Cornwall to avoid the persecutions of Queen Mary. His grandson, Ralph, was buried in St Ervan's churchyard near Padstow in 1636, although their principal residence was at nearby Bosworgey, in St. Columb Major.[14]

Richard Goodwin Keats had one brother and five sisters who survived past infancy. His brother, William, born in 1759, became a Captain[15] in the Royal Marines, and died aged 37. Richard placed a memorial tablet in St Michael's Church, Bristol. William's son, William Abraham Keats, joined the navy where he served for some years with his uncle.[1] Richard's sisters included: Martha, born in

---

1   William Abraham Keats was born early in 1795. His father died before he reached school age. He arrived at Blundell's School, Tiverton, on 15 August 1803, aged eight, remaining until the autumn of 1805, when his uncle, the subject of this memoir, took him aboard HMS *Superb* as a 1st Class volunteer where he remained for nearly four years, seeing action at San Domingo and in the Baltic.

Discharged in 1809 into HMS *Puissant* (74) at Spithead, he served in her as a supernumerary until June 1810, then became a midshipman in HMS *Menelaus* (38). In July 1810 he re-joined his uncle in the Mediterranean and followed him, generally in the rate of midshipman, as Admiral Keats moved his flag from HMS *Implacable* (74) to HMS *Milford* (74) and then to HMS *Hibernia* (110) until September 1812, when Admiral Keats returned home due to illness and William was transferred to Admiral Pellew's flagship, HMS *Caledonia* (120).

Passing his examination for lieutenant in August 1813, he was commissioned in the sloop *Partridge* (18) in the Mediterranean and served aboard her until October 1814 and the conclusion of the war with France. He was next flag lieutenant to his uncle aboard *Salisbury* (50) at Newfoundland. He was then shifted to *Albion* (74), the flagship at Sheerness, from December 1815 until April 1816. He was promoted to commander on 17 April 1816 and was then unemployed for six-and-a-half years before being given command of the brig-sloop *Cherokee* (10), whose station varied between Leith and Cork. On a mission to ascertain the practicability of taking certain observations at sea in January 1823, she became the first warship to pass through the locks of the Caledonian Canal from Inverness. Promoted to post-captain on 27 March 1826, he was not afterwards employed at sea, although he held a coastguard appointment at Babbacombe, Devon.

His wife, Catherine Jane Pitman, died only two months after they were married when she along with her sister Diana and a boatman drowned following the capsize of a small open boat, when sailing with William off Babbacombe on 8 June

1753, wife of firstly George Stucley Buck from a family of ship owners and merchants with extensive land holdings in Bideford including Affeton Castle and Hartland Abbey and in Virginia. Their son Richard also joined the navy, and for some time served with his uncle. Another son, Lewis, was a long-time member of Parliament for Devon, and, for a period, Sherriff. George Buck died in 1794 and in 1801 Martha married Lieutenant Colonel James Kirkman of the 52nd Regiment of Infantry. Elizabeth born in 1762 died unmarried in 1831. Mary born in 1764 became the wife of William Griffiths, a surgeon of considerable eminence. Ann born in 1770 married Reverend William Walter, rector of Abbotsham, and Silvester, born in 1774 married Kent, a London surgeon.

In 1768 he was received into Winchester College, on the Wykehamist foundation:[16] but his inclinations did not lead that way and this circumstance proved how necessary it is to pay particular attention to the natural turn of a youth's genius and give full scope to the bent of nature. "A shoot when grafted on ungenial stock, will fade and lose its original beauty: whereas when nature is consulted by the skilled botanist and admitted to share in an operation on which she alone has the power of conferring success, the alien shoot derives additional strength from the nutritive powers of a state congenial to its own." Mr. Keats was but little addicted to study, and spurning the trammels of scholastic education, he eagerly embraced an opportunity of going to sea, under the patronage of the Earl of Halifax; and on the 25th of November 1770, he was entered and embarked onboard the *Bellona* of 74 guns, Captain John Montagu.

Although the memoir mentions only the Winchester School, Keats was initially admitted to the New College School at Oxford in 1766. This school was established in 1379 by Bishop William of Wykeham, Chancellor of England, to prepare young boys for his New College at Oxford University. Keats attended New College School for two years before transferring to Winchester College, Winchester, established by the Bishop of Wykeham in 1393 for a similar purpose. He attended this institution for a further two years. Given the proximity of both Chalton and Winchester to Portsmouth it is not far-fetched to suggest the views from the Portsdown Hills across Portsea to the busy Spithead anchorage may have inspired the young Keats's interest in going to sea.

1833. He managed to save one sister, Louisa. He married Augusta Maria Lyford on 6 July 1835. Their son Rochfort Keats predeceased his father, dying in 1872 aged 35. William lived until the age of 79 and, through his longevity, was promoted on seniority to rear admiral (1854), vice admiral (1860), and full admiral (1864). He died on 2 May 1874 at the family estate, Porthill House, Bideford, Devon.

His first captain, John Montagu was cousin to the Earl of Sandwich, sometime first Lord of the Admiralty. *Bellona* acted as a guard-ship (that is a warship in permanent commission kept on anchor in the port) at Portsea, from whence the thirteen-year-old Keats was rapidly removed to another guard-ship, the *Yarmouth* (60), under Captain Weston Varlo. She was to take troops to Gibraltar, but was found unfit and paid off. Keats was transferred to the *Cambridge* (80), Captain Thomas Graves, a guard ship at Plymouth where he remained until April 1771 at which time he again benefited from the patronage of the Montagu family.

Captain Montagu having soon afterward obtained the rank of rear admiral, and chief command of the North American station Mr. Keats accompanied him into the flagship, the *Captain* of 74 guns, which sailed for that station in June 1771.

Soon after their arrival in Boston, the rendezvous of the commander-in-chief, Mr. Keats was removed into the *Halifax (10)* schooner, and afterwards into the *Kingfisher (14)* sloop, Captain James Montagu (the son of the Admiral), and from thence, with the same captain, into the *Mercury* of 20 guns.

**Historical Memoirs of
Admiral Sir Richard Goodwin Keats, GCB**

American Revolutionary Wars

The situation of the North American colonies then rising into, and soon arriving at, open resistance to the mother country, occasioned a great variety of service, in which Mr. Keats fully participated. He was employed in cruising, in boat service, and on shore; was present at several skirmishes, and at an attack made upon the American post at Great-Bridge in Virginia. He also commanded two armed tenders, cruised and took several prizes; was actively employed at the burning of Norfolk, and at an attack on Hampton, in Virginia. He was also present at the taking of New York, Fort Washington, and Rhode Island.[17]

Soon after the latter event took place [in December 1776], Mr. Keats was removed into the *Romney*, the flag-ship of Rear Admiral Montagu, commander-in-chief at Newfoundland, and having returned to England, was, on the 7th April 1777, promoted by the Lords of the Admiralty to the rank of Lieutenant, and appointed to the *Ramillies* of 74 guns, Commodore M'Kenzie, at that time commanding in the Downs, who being soon after promoted to the rank of rear admiral, he was succeeded in the *Ramillies* by Captain Robert Digby. The *Ramillies* was then employed on the home station, cruised much in the Bay of Biscay, and, in company with the *Terrible*, fell in with a valuable French convoy from Martinique, of which they took seven, dispersing the remainder, most of which were captured by other English cruisers. In the action of the 27th of July 1778, the *Ramillies* led the fleet on the larboard tack, in which she sustained a loss of 12 killed and 16 wounded.

This was the first Battle of Ushant (Map 1), the action fought by Admiral Keppel against D'Orvilliers. It was Keats's first taste of a fleet action and one where his ship suffered damage as well as crew injured and killed. Although the outcome of the action itself was said to be inconclusive it can be deduced in light of subsequent events that Keats's conduct during the encounter was sufficiently striking to bring him to the Captain's particular attention.

In the succeeding year, Captain Digby having been promoted to the rank of rear admiral, Lieutenant Keats followed him into his flagship, the *Prince George* of 98 guns, in which ship Prince William Henry (now [1826] Duke of Clarence), embarked in the same year to commence his naval career; and during his whole service with Admiral Digby, which exceeded three years, Lieutenant Keats had the honour of being junior or senior officer of the watch in which His Royal Highness was placed. The intimacy that here commenced between them has since continued uninterruptedly, and His Royal Highness subsequently acknowledged the debt of gratitude he owed to Lieutenant Keats, for the naval tuition he received whilst onboard the *Prince George*.[2]

As Duke of Clarence William wrote to Reverend Keats by letter dated St James's Palace, 18 November 1801, describing his son as the one "to whom I owe <u>all my</u> professional knowledge", and noted that if he may one day be placed in the Admiralty or lead the Fleet against the enemy, he would be happy in either situation to have the abilities and friendship of Keats with him.[18] He could well have required someone of Keats's abilities beside him in such situations, as the consensus would be that even though well-intentioned and popular with the men, the Duke was said to have lacked the skills and temperament required for command of a fleet.[19] He was nevertheless appointed Lord High Admiral in 1827. He subsequently ascended to the throne as King William IV of England from 1832. During the whole of their respective careers he and Keats maintained a close relationship that proved mutually beneficial.

It was rumoured that on one occasion on the *Prince George* Keats, often regarded as a rigid disciplinarian, mast-headed the young prince for some minor breach of duty. They both denied this, saying the misconception grew out of an incident during a stormy night. As a gale increased Keats, to make all snug, ordered the topmen aloft to close reef the top-sails. The Prince unseen was mounting the ratlines with the seamen when recognised by Keats, who called there was no need for His Highness to go aloft in such weather at night. The Prince knowing it was the duty of midshipmen to accompany the men unhesitatingly replied to the effect that 'where the men go, I go'.[20] There was no excess of discipline.

---

2   Clarke and McArthur (letter 18 November 1801, note 16)

In the winter of 1779 the *Prince George* accompanied Sir George Rodney to the relief of Gibraltar and assisted at the capture of the Spanish Caracas fleet, and the defeat of Langara, in which action the *San Julien* of 74 guns struck to the *Prince George*.

Prince William Henry, in the uniform of a Midshipman in HMS Prince George. For three years Keats was lieutenant of his watch. Aquatint and etching, January 1782, West, Benjamin, NMM PAH5531 ©National Maritime Museum, Greenwich London.

Rodney's defeat of the Spanish in January 1780, known as the Moonlight Battle, Keats's second experience of fleet action, is most probably the night battle experience Keats subsequently referenced in addressing his crew before the Battle of Algeciras in 1801 when he presciently identified the risks and advantages to be faced in launching a night-time engagement.

Seeing Britain distracted in conducting a war on the far side of the Atlantic, France and Spain proclaimed support for the new United States of America and declared war on Britain. Both countries sought to recover territories lost to Britain in the Seven Years War (1755 to 1763). Spain hoped to recover several islands in the Caribbean and the Mediterranean, including the island of Minorca and the territory of Gibraltar (Map 3). France was bound by the Convention of Aranjuez, made in April 1779, not to accept any peace with Britain until Gibraltar was restored to Spain. Spanish troops and ships began a blockade of Gibraltar in July 1779. The British garrison comprised some five thousand troops with around four hundred guns. As they were denied access by land, supplies of food began to run low towards the end of 1779.

On 1 October 1779, Admiral Sir George Rodney was appointed to command the Royal Navy Leeward Islands Station in the West Indies. He was to journey to his new appointment with four or five ships of the line, travelling down the coast of France, Spain and Portugal, before crossing the Atlantic to the West Indies.

The opportunity was taken for his ships to escort vessels conveying supplies for the relief of Gibraltar and Minorca, as well as protecting the supply and merchant vessels bound for the West Indies as they passed the hazardous French and Spanish coasts. A large convoy of over one hundred merchant vessels was assembled at Spithead, outside Portsmouth. A section of the Royal Navy's Channel Fleet was put under Rodney's command for the first part of the voyage, giving him some thirty ships. Squadrons within the fleet were commanded by Rear Admiral Sir John Lockhart-Ross in the *Royal George* (100), and by Rear Admiral Robert Digby in the *Prince George* (98).

On 7 January 1780, Rodney's fleet was 300 miles west of Cape Finisterre, the north-western most point of Spain, whereupon the West Indies merchant vessels together with escorting frigates left the convoy to sail across the Atlantic. At dawn on 8 January the British caught sight of twenty-two Spanish ships to the northeast. They immediately gave chase and caught them in a few hours. The fleet included fifteen merchant ships of the Royal Guipuzcoan Company of Caracas and seven escorts under the command of Don Juan Augustin de Yardi en route from San Sebastian to Cádiz, carrying naval stores and other goods for the Spanish fleet in Cádiz. Outnumbered, the Spanish ships surrendered, with only token resistance. The flagship was renamed '*Prince William*' in honour of the Prince's presence at the capture. As some of the goods would be of use to Gibraltar a number of the vessels were added to the convoy and the rest escorted back to England. On resuming its course towards Gibraltar Rodney's fleet received news of a different Spanish squadron off Cape St. Vincent. The British warships were warned to expect action.

This Spanish squadron comprised nine ships of the line and two frigates commanded by Admiral Don Juan de Langara. On sighting the enemy, Rodney ordered his ships into line abreast, advancing under a press of canvas. After initially having been misled by a spy into believing his squadron would be facing only a small convoy escort, Langara soon realised he was confronting a powerful Royal Naval force and turned to make for port.

Rodney ordered a 'General Chase', which gave his ships the discretion to break line and pursue the Spanish with as much speed as each ship could make. As all the British ships were faster than each of the Spanish ships, (graphically illustrating the benefits of copper sheathing as an anti-fouling measure) it was only a matter of time before disaster engulfed Langara's squadron. As a British ship came into action, the others were to pass and pursue the remaining Spaniards. The chase took place over several hours, leading to a battle that continued through the night. Despite the fact a substantial and increasing storm blew up, with heavy rain, the approaching night was lit by a strong moon, giving rise to the description; the *Moonlight Battle*.

Edgar fired a broadside into the Spanish ship, *San Domingo*, as she forged past. HMS *Bienfaisant* came up behind, engaging her with her bow chasers, and at 4.40pm, *San Domingo* blew up, causing the loss of her entire crew, bar one survivor. *Ajax* and *Marlborough* next came up on the *Princesa (70)*, disabling her before resuming the chase. At around 7.30pm, British ships overtook Langara's flagship, *Fenix*. The attack was continued by *Prince George* and *Bienfaisant* until the Spanish ship lost her mizzen and main topmast and surrendered. *Culloden* and *Prince George* moved on to the *San Julian* and bombarded her into striking her colours at around 1am.

The Moonlight Battle off Cape St. Vincent, 16 January 1780; Paton, Richard. The Spanish ship San Domingo is seen blowing up ahead of the British flagship, HMS Sandwich. Donated to the Naval Gallery, Royal Hospital Greenwich, by William Tennant, through Governor Keats in 1829, NMM BHC0429 ©National Maritime Museum, Greenwich London

The surrendered Spanish ships not wrecked on the shore were brought away from the coast and taken by British crews into Gibraltar. The garrison was re-supplied, and the squadron finally continued to the West Indies on 13 February 1780.

Sir George having proceeded to the West Indies, Admiral Digby returned to England with the prizes, and on the passage captured the *Prothee* of 64 guns, and two valuable ships under her convoy, with naval and military stores, bound to the East Indies. The *Prince George* was then attached to the Channel Fleet, commanded by Sir Charles Hardy and Lieutenant Keats, for the first and only time in his life, had subsequently the mortification to witness (to the westward of the Lizard) a hostile force, consisting of sixty-seven sail of the line, threatening the shores of Britain; whilst the force under the British Admiral, being only thirty-eight sail of the line, prevented him from making any immediate attempt to vindicate the honour of his country.

In March 1781, the *Prince George* was again involved in a relief of Gibraltar which was still under Spanish siege. This time Keats, having severe labour in the boats, delivered some seven thousand tons of provisions and two thousand barrels of gunpowder with other stores, all amid a severe cannonade from the enemy.[21] The *Prince George* being detached to the Leeward Islands station under Rear Admiral Hood, Keats followed Admiral Digby into the *Lion* (64), Captain Fooks.

In 1781, Lieutenant Keats accompanied Admiral Digby to the North American station, where he had been appointed commander-in-chief. In the winter of that year he was entrusted by the Admiral with the command of the naval (whilst Captain, the late Sir George Beckwith, commanded the military) part of an expedition fitted out for the destruction of numerous formidable boats, from which the trade of New York suffered considerable loss and annoyance. The enemy had usually their rendezvous at New-Brunswick, about fourteen miles up a tide-river [the Raritan] in the Jerseys. Notwithstanding the weather was very severe, and the wind, which was strong, kept the tide out, the troops were landed at the appointed time and place in a storm; the town was completely surprised, and every boat and vessel taken or destroyed that was found at the wharfs. This arduous service being performed, the expedition returned, but not without sustaining some loss during the re-embarkation and the passage down the River. The whole, however, was conducted with such skill and intrepidity, that Lieutenant Keats was on the 18th January 1782, promoted to the rank of commander, and appointed by Admiral Digby to the *Rhinoceros* a large ship fitted with a floating battery at New York. In May following he was removed to the *Bonetta* sloop of 16 guns, in which he continued until the peace of 1783.

In the course of her patrols regulating trade with New York the *Bonetta* took a number of prizes including the Spanish merchant *San Joseph* carrying a valuable cargo of salt, raisins and fruit from Cádiz taken in February, and the Massachusetts privateer *Heyder Ally* (2) taken in July 1782.

In the September preceding that event [the peace of 1783], being attached to a small squadron[3] the *Bonetta* (at that time detached) fell in with, and was chased for a few hours by, two French frigates, *L'Aigle* of 40 guns and *La Gloire* of 36.

The *Bonetta* managed to evade her pursuers through the night. After continuing towards Delaware Bay (Map 4) the French were seen the next morning by the brig *Racoon* (14), Lieutenant Nagle, who had departed company with the squadron some time earlier and who unfortunately failed to identify them as enemy ships until too late. After receiving raking fire, he was forced to surrender.

That same morning Keats re-joined the squadron and reported his encounter the previous evening advising the vessels were French men of war. The squadron sailed in chase of the ships which could now be seen in the distance to windward. At this time a third ship was seen standing across from the east flying unrecognised colours. She was chased by the *Warwick* and *Bonetta* until at noon she hoisted French colours and soon after struck, resulting in the capture of the newly constructed French ship, *Sophie* (22) which had been following the frigates and, it was discovered, had onboard the mistress of the French Commander, La Touche. From interrogating the crew it was learnt that the frigates were carrying high ranking officers and a considerable sum of money to fund the French army in America. The British attempts to capture the *Aigle* and *Gloire* took on a heightened significance. The *Lion* and frigate *Vestal* (28), Captain Fox, were ordered to the mouth of the Delaware (Map 4) to prevent the enemy entering. On 13 September they found the French vessels and their prize, *Racoon* anchored off the Cape Henlopen Light at the entrance. Being cut off from the proper channel, the French commodore determined to run in among the shoals, called the Shears. In the absence of a pilot familiar with the river and the waters being too constricted for the larger ships, it was thought the enemy had made good their escape. However, Keats in the *Bonetta* volunteered to continue with the *Vestal* and *Sophie* each being of light draught and the latter now being crewed by men from the *Warwick*, in pursuit of the enemy seeking passage through the shallows.

On the following morning Captain Keats had the good fortune (the enemy still in sight) to re-join the British squadron, when the enemy became the pursued and were chased into the Delaware. The capture of the *Racoon* sloop of war, in sight of the British squadron, supplied the enemy with a pilot (of questionable loyalty) for the Delaware, and as the British squadron was deprived of that advantage, the chase was after some risks and

---

3 *Warwick* 50 guns, *Lion* 64, *Vestal* 28 and *Bonetta* 16

perseverance given up; but Captain Keats, with his usual zeal for the service, having offered his services in the *Bonetta* to endeavour to find a passage up to the enemy, then at anchor several leagues higher up the river, it was accepted, and the pursuit was in consequence resumed.

The exertions of Captain Keats on this occasion were highly important and attended with so much success, that, after a pursuit of several leagues, led by the *Bonetta*, and after the *Warwick* and *Lion* had, from the shallowness of the water, been obliged to anchor, the *Aigle* ran aground, whilst her consort continued her course up the river. The *Vestal* and *Bonetta* now prepared to attack the *Aigle*, when the former grounded; but her broadside being to the enemy she opened her fire, and on the *Bonetta* anchoring within hail, the enemy struck her colours. In this manner was taken at this time the largest frigate in the French navy, with 14 24-pounders on her main deck, and a complement of 600 men, commanded by Comte de la Touche, and having onboard the Baron de Vioménil, commander-in-chief of the French army; the Duke de Lauzun, Viscount de Fleury, and other officers of distinction, who, however, were landed during the chase, which continued for two days, as well as the greater part of the treasure which was onboard, and which it appeared was considerable.

On the morning of 14 September, a cartel was sent to offer exchange of prisoners, and Lieutenant Nagle was released. The chase resumed as the French retreated up river and extended for two full days as the vessels eased their way up narrow channels and across shallow banks. This was to be the first of many demonstrations of courage and skill on the part of Keats in successfully navigating his ship through difficult waters where others feared to proceed. The senior military officers – and money – had been put ashore by ship's boat when La Touche first appreciated the seriousness of his predicament and escaped overland. Due to their light draft the *Gloire* and *Racoon* both managed to escape over a sand bank and proceed up river. The larger *Aigle* however, grounded and began to list as the tide ebbed, rendering her guns useless. Despite jettisoning some of her guns and cutting away her masts in an attempt to lighten her, she remained fast. Notwithstanding that she also grounded the *Vestal* was able to bear her guns on the enemy. The *Bonetta* of lighter draft was able to anchor in four fathoms two hundred yards off the larboard quarter and the *Sophie* and *Lion* managed to gain a raking position astern and likewise bear upon the *Aigle*, which then surrendered. Although the French had bored holes in her hull she was got off with some difficulty in the following days, and the squadron arrived off New York on 27 September. *Aigle* was taken into the navy, serving for sixteen years. The *Sophie* was also taken into the navy but was resold two years later. The whole of the crew of the recently captured *Racoon* was restored. Comte de Rochambeau, commander of the French army escaped, but the British captured several members of Marquis de Lafayette's family as well as 600 sailors and troops. Captain La Touche-Treville, reunited with his mistress (now presented as his wife), spent the remainder of this war a prisoner on parole in the town of Alresford. He served again in the Napoleonic Wars, where Keats was opposed to him in the Mediterranean many years later. This proved to be one of the last naval actions of the war.

At the conclusion of the American war, Captain Keats was employed to regulate the Hudson River communication with New-York, and afterwards in Nova Scotia, to assist a considerable settlement of royalists at Port Mouton (Map 4). Captain Keats continued on this station till January 1785, when he returned to England and was paid off, and thus found himself, for the first time during fifteen years' service, without employment, and it may be here remarked, that if during his career he had witnessed no very brilliant display of naval heroism, he had, by the most laborious service, been perfected in the duties of his noble profession. The various experiences which fell under his eye, many of them being of an important description, were the means of expanding his mind, and of calling all his faculties into action; at the same time, he enjoyed the enviable opportunity of acquiring such useful knowledge as distinguished the real seaman and a man of nautical science.

**Historical Memoirs of
Admiral Sir Richard Goodwin Keats, GCB**

Post-Captain, The Western Squadron

From this time till 1789, Captain Keats remained on shore, mostly on the Continent, but on the 4th of June of that year, at the pressing solicitation of the Duke of Clarence with the King, he was appointed to the rank of post-captain.

It was not uncommon for officers without command and hence reduced to half-pay, to live on the Continent where the cost of living was considerably lower than back home. France in particular offered active social and cultural scenes and was sufficiently close to allow a rapid return to the Admiralty if word should be received of a new posting.

The King had written to William in July 1788 expressing his pleasure at reports of his conduct and the excellent state of his ship that he had seen in a private letter from Admiral Leveson to Lord Howe. He noted that the propriety required of the captain of a ship at sea was required also of a Prince on shore and hoped he would soon equally approve of William's conduct in North America. The letter concluded with a promise to "keep Captain Keats in my eye", while noting the difficulty of making promotions in times of peace.[22] Consistent with the view Prince William had some influence in the matter, Keats was appointed post in the King's birthday promotions on 4 June 1789, aged 32.

The Admiralty Commission Book[23] records Keats being immediately posted to the command of the first rate, three decked, *Royal George* of 100 guns – an unusual appointment for a Captain of only weeks' standing. In light of the events which follow it might be assumed it was proposed that Keats accompany the Duke now in this first rate sail of the line, and that the proposal was abandoned. He does not appear to have ever sailed in her.

In September following [Keats] was appointed to command the *Southampton* of 32 guns, employed in Channel service. In 1790 the *Southampton* was paid off, and Captain Keats was appointed to the *Niger* of 32 guns. A run to Gibraltar with Prince Edward, some successful cruises against smuggling cutters in the Channel, and two cruises with squadrons of observation in the chops of the Channel [the western entrance], formed the chief variety of his employment, till the state of Holland and France produced more active and important services.

The memoirs make no mention of Keats having spent time in the fifth-rate frigate *Andromeda (32)*, under the command of Prince William Henry, but Thomas Byam Martin, at that time a midshipman onboard and who later rose to be Admiral of the Fleet, confirms it. He says Keats, although perhaps not officially posted to the ship, certainly cruised with them as the Prince's companion during the time the ship was with Admiral Leveson-Gower's squadron. That cruise was in June 1788, at a time when the memoirs indicate Keats was ashore on half-pay. A squadron of five sail of the line, led by Rear Admiral Leveson Gower in the *Edgar* and accompanied by the *Andromeda* put to sea with the stated purpose of practising sailing manoeuvres and tactics. Its real purpose was claimed to be the further naval education of the Prince – which would explain Keats's presence.[24] He was no doubt part of the crew at the request of the Prince; a request that could hardly be refused and on the contrary would have been eagerly accepted. Cruising as companion to the Prince was an excellent way to remain in the sights of the Admiralty to secure more active employment, as well as consolidating the support of a powerful friend. The squadron undertook their exercises in June in the Western Approaches and off Plymouth. Then, in July, when some distance from the Scilly Isles the *Andromeda* was ordered to replenish stores at sea from the other ships and then proceed directly to Halifax to distance the Prince from an unsuitable liaison at home. They did not return to Spithead until April 1789[25] but Keats was not onboard for the extended journey across the Atlantic.

The *Andromeda* was paid off in July 1789 after William became the Duke of Clarence and took his seat in the House of Lords. At the same time the 32 gun frigate *Southampton* was promptly and somewhat hastily re-commissioned to keep the former crew together, in readiness for the Duke assuming command. He had, on interview, passed his Lieutenant's examination in 1785 and was promptly promoted to post-captain in 1786, but lacked the knowledge and experience required for command of a war ship. At the Duke's request his naval mentor and tutor, Keats, was appointed *Southampton's* captain.[26]

The ship had been launched in 1757 (the same year as Keats's birth) and after more than thirty years' afloat was now in poor condition. As became typical of his attention to detail, Keats closely examined his new command, and on becoming acquainted with the ship, wrote to the Admiralty Secretary as to her condition. He pointed out that she had not been docked for three years, during which time she had grounded several times, causing damage, and that her bottom was extremely foul. This earned the quick rebuke that it was usual for such representations to be made through the Port Admiral.[27]

Putting to sea without any repairs having been undertaken they were initially deployed in the Channel between Portsmouth and the Downs. According to Byam Martin, Keats's heart was at the former, where his attention to a beautiful girl, Miss Crawford, sister to Mrs George Oakes, was much noticed. That these views were well-founded was, he says, well proved by Keats against all other reason demonstrating extraordinary perseverance in spending three weeks beating down the Channel from Deal to Portsmouth against an unremitting gale. Byam Martin lost count of how many times the ship was forced back, but they continued while there was "a hope of gaining an inch toward the haven of joy". On arrival they were given their orders to take Prince Edward, the Duke of Kent, to Gibraltar.[28]

King George III in the Southampton, left of centre, reviewing the Plymouth, fleet led by the Carnatic, right, 18 August 1789. William Elliot. NMM B6883 ©National Maritime Museum, Greenwich London

While the memoirs are ambiguous, other sources, including her ship's log, confirm the trip to Gibraltar was made by the *Southampton*, with Keats in command. The King effectively banished Edward to Gibraltar directly on his return from Hanover and enquired of the Admiralty as to which of his frigates were ready to sail. There were two. He selected the *Southampton*, possibly because of Keats's relationship with Edward's brother William, or because he had himself been onboard just weeks earlier reviewing the fleet at Plymouth. Detailed records show that even as a freshly appointed junior captain, Keats was well qualified to handle a sensitive voyage and conducted himself in a manner that impressed those in positions of influence.

The Commander-in-Chief at Portsmouth wrote to the Admiralty:

I am to acknowledge the receipt of your Letter by Express at ½ past 6 am with their Lordships orders to Captain Keats [who received his orders directly from the Admiralty] as follows: to receive His Royal Highness Prince Edward, His Majesty's fourth Son, with His Suite, Attendants and Baggage, onboard the Southampton, and carry him and them to Gibraltar; and having landed His Royal Highness, his Suite and Baggage at that place, and received from the Commander in Chief, or the Commanding Officer for the time being, of His Majesty's Ships there, and the Commanding Officer of the Garrison, such dispatches as they may have for England; to make the best of his way back to the Motherbank, and remain there until further orders.[29]

The above was sent together with the instruction that Keats was to ensure that he had acquired an appropriate Royal Standard from naval stores, and that it was to be hoisted in the correct places on the correct occasions.

Prince Edward arrived in Portsmouth on Friday 29 January, 1790, inspected the Fleet at Spithead, and was entertained by the Commander-in-Chief. On 31 January, his luggage went aboard *Southampton* and on the following day, after due ceremonial leave-taking, he embarked, and the frigate made sail forthwith. Keats recorded in his log for Monday 1 February 1790:

…at ½ past 3 unmoored Ship… at 5 rec'd Fresh Beef;…at 10 His Royal Highness came out of the Harbour with the Standard raised in the Barge attended by Admiral Roddam and the Captains of the Men of War and as His Royal Highness passed down the Harbour the Ships were manned and he was saluted with 21 Guns by each of the Guardships; and on his approaching Spithead we together with the other men of war at Spithead saluted him with

21 Guns. At 11 manned Ship and cheered His Royal Highness coming alongside and on his entering the Ship raised the Standard which the men of war at Spithead and in the Harbour saluted as before. Weighed and made sail.[30]

The Prince's party comprised some fourteen persons so Keats and the other officers relinquished their quarters. The midshipmen and warrant and petty officers would have had, at best, to have shared theirs with some of the royal party. Sailing time from Spithead to Gibraltar, under optimum sailing conditions and in a fast and seaworthy ship, should have been around sixteen days but this voyage was to take twenty-four. With a different captain or an unhappy ship, such a trip might have tested both the ship's supplies and relationships onboard.

The cause of the length of the voyage is set out clearly in the captain's log and confirmed in a letter from Prince Edward to the Prince of Wales, written shortly after he arrived in Gibraltar:

All went well for the first five days of the voyage, although progress down the English Channel was slow because of steady winds from the west and south-west. On 5 February the ship entered an area of unseasonable calm 136 leagues north-east of Cape Finisterre and progress across the Bay of Biscay became unusually slow, with long periods of calm, variable winds and prevalent breezes from the west.

The log's repeated references to the changing and making of sail and the use of studding-sails, top gallants, and royals, make it clear that not only were Keats and his crew having difficulty in finding much wind but also that what they did find was not always to the ship's advantage. The foul state of the old ship's bottom would not have helped. It was not until 17 February that the cliffs of Cape St. Vincent were sighted and the *Southampton* finally entered Gibraltar Bay on 24 February.

Although the voyage was longer than he might have been expecting, there is no evidence it was disagreeable. The duke wrote to the Prince of Wales on 29 February 1790:

...I arrived here on Wednesday 24th, after a passage of twenty four days, during the whole of which time we had a constant succession of calms and contrary winds. Our passage would consequently have been excessively tedious had not the continued attentions of Captain Keats and all his officers, who assisted us in spending the time as agreeably as possible, prevented us upon the whole from finding it very long. I was also lucky enough not to be sick once during the whole time, which is no small object in so long a passage.[31]

Keats recorded their arrival at Gibraltar;

> [25th February 1790] At 1pm His Royal Highness left the Ship in the Barge with the Standard flying attended by all the Captains. Hauled down the Standard and Hoisted the Pendant. Manned Ship, Cheered and saluted Him with 21 Guns. ½ past 10 the Garrison saluted Him with 21 Guns on his Landing. Employed sending His Royal Highness's luggage on shore. (ADM 51/870)

Before Keats and the *Southampton* left Gibraltar for home, the Prince presented him with a gold watch that would remain in the family for two centuries. It was manufactured by Josiah Emery, bearing the number 1143, and was inscribed: "Present from H.R.H. Prince Edward to Capt. Keates (sic) of the Navy, as a token of his Esteem". The case bore the insignia of both the Order of St. Patrick and the Order of the Garter.

The return journey was long and boisterous. As additional cargo they carried two fine horses – gifts from the Dey of Algiers to the Duke of Clarence – housed in specially built stalls under the half-deck. While running up the Channel in high seas they successfully undertook a difficult rescue of the crew and passengers of a sloop on a pleasure cruise, found dis-masted and sinking off Guernsey, before they finally arrived at Spithead in late April.

During May to November 1790 a grand fleet including some thirty-one sail of the line was assembled at Torbay under Lord Howe, ready to respond to anticipated Spanish aggression that was signalled by a dispute over Nootka Sound, an otherwise relatively inconsequential anchorage and British East India Company trading post on the west coast of Vancouver Island, within territory to which Spain laid exclusive claim. Spain demanded its sovereignty be recognised. This was unacceptable to the British and the navy was put in readiness. In what became known as the 'Spanish Armament' reports were received that an equal number of Spanish men of war had been seen leaving Cádiz, and war looked inevitable. Lord Howe put to sea in August and cruised in the Channel for a period, while the *Southampton* stayed in commission on standby at Spithead, part of a second squadron under the command of Vice Admiral Roddam. In mid-September orders were received to retire to port as the threat had dissipated. The dispute was ultimately resolved and a convention regarding access to Nootka Sound and compensation entered with Spain some weeks later, without the *Southampton* putting to sea.

Having learnt his lesson as to protocols, Keats again drew the parlous state of his ship to the attention of the port admiral who, just as promptly, copied and forwarded that letter to the Admiralty:

Sir, I herewith enclose you the Defects of His Majesty's Ship under my Command and conceive it my duty to observe that those supposed to arise from the Keel have already rendered useless one Cable and considerably damaged another. I have frequently had the Ship swept in order to ascertain the nature of the Defect and have regularly found something ragged a little before the Chesstree and a Diver who went down purposely to examine it at Gibraltar assured me that a part of the False Keel is gone there and that it is otherwise ragged about that place. In addition to this Defect, I beg to observe that the Copper on the Bottom is very foul, and the Decks are in much need of being Caulked, and cannot avoid adding, that if the Services we are to be employed upon will admit I should conceive it advisable to have her bottom examined. I have the honour to remain, Sir, your most obedient humble servant, R.G. Keats.[32]

Clearly his earlier concerns were justified. This properly channelled report was better received than his earlier correspondence and the ship was paid off shortly thereafter. Keats and his company were transferred into the *Niger* (32) in August 1790.

They were generally engaged in duty in the Channel and were otherwise on standby at Portsmouth as Britain responded once more to the territorial ambitions of other powers. In 1791 a formidable fleet including some thirty-six sail of the line and supporting frigates, including the *Niger*, was assembled at Portsmouth, awaiting Lord Hood to leave his post at the Admiralty to lead a fleet to the Baltic, while simultaneously a squadron of ten to twelve would sail to the Black Sea in a two-pronged response to Catherine the Great of Russia advancing ambitions with respect to Turkey, the Crimea and Poland. By the summer of 1791 British opposition to her schemes had subsided and, on 11 August the Peace of Galatz was signed. The Grand Fleet went out of commission from September.[33] Although at one time she formed part of an expedition to Holland transporting troops under the command of the Duke of York in support of the House of Orange, threatened by pro-French revolt, the *Niger* continued to generally be engaged in the Channel. She took several prizes, but the deployment was otherwise unremarkable.

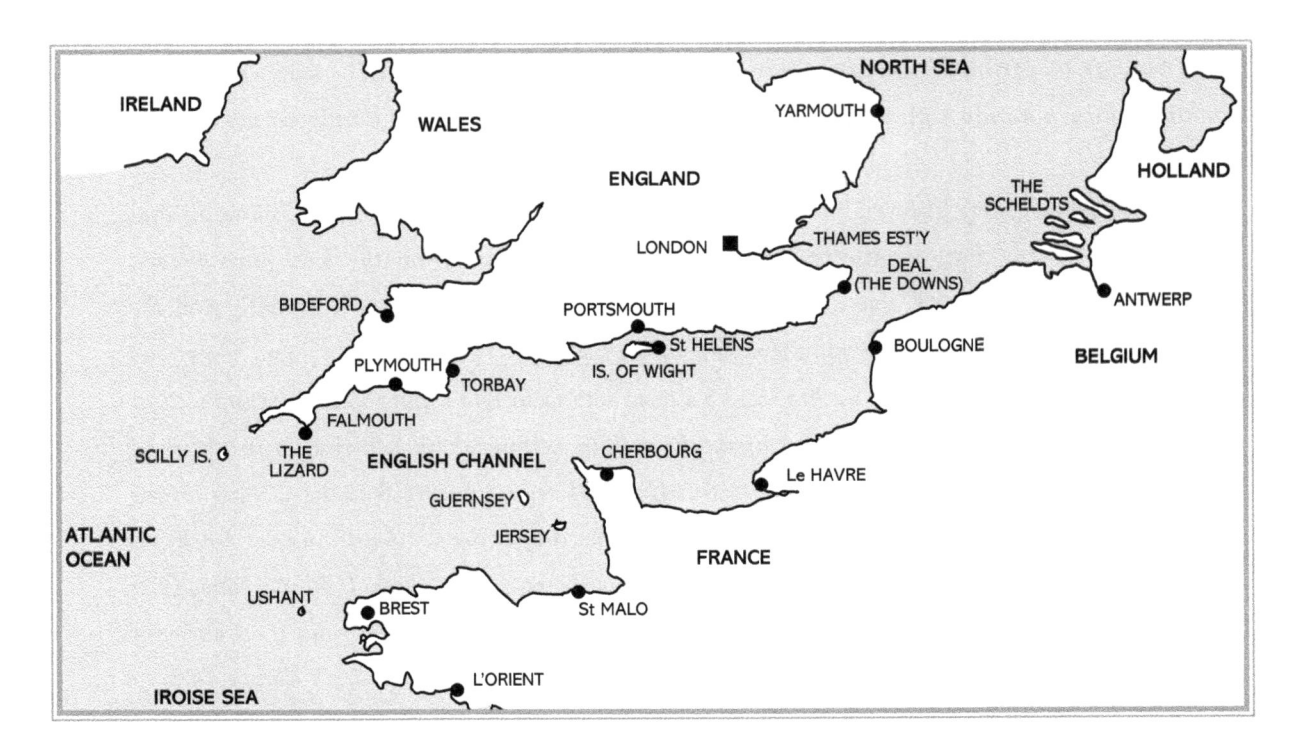

Map 1: *English Channel and ports*

During September 1792, Captain Keats, being based at Portsmouth under the orders of Lord Hood, joined others under his Lordship's presidency on the panel for the court martial of the alleged mutineers of HMS *Bounty (4)* who had taken that ship from Lieutenant Bligh in the Pacific in 1789. The events leading to and in the course of that event, and the participants' remarkable subsequent voyages in small boats, the trial, verdict, and sentences have been the subject of many detailed analyses, academic and otherwise, elsewhere.

In April 1793, Captain Keats was appointed to the *London* of 98 guns, appropriated for the reception of the flag of the Duke of Clarence, but although she was fitted for sea and joined the Channel fleet under Lord Howe, His Royal Highness, unfortunately, did not hoist his flag, and Captain Keats services in that ship were confined to one cruise.

Byam Martin describes the *London* as, "the best-manned ship, the best commanded, and the best officered we ever had, and but for politics, that bane and curse of military men, the Duke in such a ship would have been a flag officer (having been again promoted) in the battle of the first of June 1794."[34] The order with respect to the Duke was rescinded by the Prime Minister after the Duke had somewhat unwisely risen in the House to speak against both the war and the Government. Lord Howe put to sea again from St Helens for a cruise on 14 July in search of twenty-one French sail of the line and four frigates reported to be off Belle Isle in the Bay of Biscay. The initial passage out of the channel proved eventful when just four days into the cruise during a gale off the Scilly Isles the *Majestic* and *Bellerophon* collided causing the loss of the *Bellerophon's* bowsprit, foremast and main topmast. She was taken in tow to Plymouth where a number of her compliment transferred to the *London*. The Duke had still not arrived and the *London* sailed without him under Keats's captaincy to join the squadron, now at Torbay, as a replacement for the *Bellerophon*. They put to sea again on 25 July, sighting the French off Belle Isle in the afternoon of 31 July. The British stood in toward the land in line of battle in a very light breeze until dark. The next morning the French were seen to be a great distance to the north-east. After a game of cat and mouse that lasted two days in light wind which kept changing in direction they lost track of the French and the weather then becoming quite severe they quit the dangerous coast, returning to Torbay on 10 August without incident.[35] She cruised again with Lord Howe through October-December 1793. This included an unsuccessful three-day chase of a French squadron of two sail of the line and three frigates under Rear Admiral Vanstabel on its way to Virginia to escort home a convoy of ships carrying critically needed grain. The *London* was paid off the following year, without William having been aboard. We can infer that the Duke was unhappy at this whole turn of events and expressed himself freely in correspondence. Keats's papers in the Somerset Records Office include a note indicating that he had destroyed correspondence that contained reflections that might cause distress to anyone.[36]

The *London* having been paid off in March 1794, Captain Keats was appointed to the *Galatea* of 36 guns, in May following, in which he was employed with a squadron of frigates under Sir John Warren and Sir Edw. Pellew, cruising off the coast of France, or forming part of an expedition to aid royalists, and assisted at the capture or destruction of several frigates or corvettes, some privateers, and also several hundred sail of merchant vessels.

The French cruisers were generally of 40 guns, heavier and more effective than their English counterparts. Cruising in company of three or four they were proving more than a match for the less powerful English war ships that escorted convoys. Such was their impact the French had another six under construction at Le Havre. The English response was firstly, the construction of new purpose-built frigates, and secondly, conversion or 'razing' of 64-gun ships. The French had ceased building 64s some years prior. The English now cut some of theirs down to a single deck by removing the middle part of the main deck to create a 44 gun ship armed with larger 24-pounders. While it is obvious why a 64 should not take on a 74, the reason it should not take on opposing frigates is less clear. The rational argument was that it was a waste of man- and gun-power, while a smaller vessel with a smaller crew could just as certainly perform the task. Pride was also a factor: there was no honour in a powerful ship chasing and capturing a smaller one.

To counter the effect of French cruisers, frigates not assigned to convoy duty were organised into flying squadrons comprised of the best available ships, and with the best enterprising young captains in charge. They were mostly based from Falmouth (Map 1). From there, they could prey on ships entering the Channel or be off Brest in under twenty-four hours, all the while enjoying easy access to the Atlantic in the prevailing sou-westerlies that often hampered those based in Portsmouth or further up the Channel. Senior captains commanding ships of the line found themselves under the close orders of an admiral and seldom saw battle, but more junior captains in a flying squadron such as this enjoyed considerable freedom and had no need to wait for orders before seizing whatever opportunities arose.

The foremost of these squadrons was that under Captain Sir John Warren's command. It was given an open licence to protect trade between Cherbourg in the Channel (Map 1), and Cape Finisterre on the north-western point of Spain. In practice, this amounted to hunting down French war ships and preying on French merchant ships, operating largely outside of the usual fleet command. Warren has been described as "a flamboyant university-educated dandy with a gambling habit and a reputation for avarice, but adventurous and capable with it",[37] and by St. Vincent as "partisan, preferring prize money to the public good at all times, "[38] His reports to the Admiralty had a tendency to exaggerate his own role in engagements to the exclusion of others, but these are somewhat unkind summations dwelling on his weaknesses rather than his demonstrated talents as a commander and seaman. Coincidentally he attended Winchester College a few years ahead of Keats but having a greater aptitude for study went on to Oxford before joining the navy aged 21. Others have described him as a thoughtful, experienced naval captain with a strong commitment to his profession.[39] He was undoubtedly successful in his chosen career. All the captains under him came to be highly regarded: James Saumarez in the *Crescent*, Sidney Smith in the *Diamond*; Andrew Snape-Douglas in the *Phaeton*; Edmund Nagle in the *Artois*; Edward Pellew, now in the *Arethusa*; and Keats in the newly commissioned *Galatea*. A fifth-rate frigate of 800 tons; 135 feet in length, and with a crew of 260, she was constructed by George Parsons at Bursledon. She was armed with thirty-two

18-pounders. These frigates had a single gun deck, with additional guns in the quarter deck and forecastle, but no gun ports in the lower (berth) deck, allowing greater freeboard to the ports.

The captains in this squadron (other than Snape Douglas who died young as a result of war injury) rose to become flag officers; but at this time, they were known for their unity, aggression, initiative, and their outstanding seamanship. Keats and Pellew in particular came to be regarded as the two finest seamen in the navy.[40] Their leadership and their records built reputations that were in turn bolstered by attracting the best available officers and crews. There was nothing like success to build self-belief and unity in a crew. Individually they commanded formidable weapons of war. In combination as a squadron they were unequalled.[41] Possessing a touch for navigation and boat handling, experienced in joint operations, and topped with a degree of daring, Keats was ideally suited to this role. *United Services Magazine* reported; "This gallant and chivalrous division added largely to the reputation which Pellew, Nagle, Sidney Smith and Keats had already obtained; not so much by what fortune threw in their way, as from the unanimity, spirit, and perseverance of their operations."[42]

HMS Galatea (32). Thomas Whitcombe, © Alamy MWDA4T

Cruising in a flying squadron such as this was a much sought-after assignment. Only the best young officers were selected, and they were placed in some of the best available ships. They had freedom to demonstrate their capabilities, raise their profile, and enhance their claim for promotion. Additionally, these assignments could prove lucrative because of prize money claimed for cargos and war ships captured and purchased into the navy, all the more lucrative because there was no commander in chief taking a cut. A squadron comprised of ambitious captains such as these could have "explosive results-may indeed have been designed to do so."[43] In this case the result was almost unequalled and formidable success that captured the public imagination. This squadron proved unique in that these officers continued to operate effectively together in various theatres for years to come, having an instinctive understanding of each other's thinking. Keats became life-long friends with Warren[44] and Pellew. Some of the others did not stay as close. Pellew later fell out with both Smith and Saumarez.[45]

On 23 August 1794 the squadron ran the French ships *Volontaire*, *Espion*, and *Alerte* (14) on to the shore, near the Penmark Rocks.[46] The *Galatea* was present at the capture on 7 September of the French cutter, *Quartidi*, and a few days later at that of the Swedish brig, *Haesingeland*.

In October 1794, the *Arethusa, Diamond, Artois* and *Galatea* captured the newly constructed *Revolutionnaire*, of 40 guns and 370 men when cruising about ten leagues west of Ushant. She was one of the splendid new frigates, larger by 140 tons than any English frigate, and barely a week out of Le Havre on her first cruise when she was taken.[47] She was purchased into the navy, joining the squadron that had captured her. Captains (including those in sight, for their presence may have been material in the enemy's surrender) would usually receive a one-quarter share of prize money calculated on the value of a captured ship and her cargo, as well as head money for captured crew paid at the rate of £5 for each enemy sailor on board when the battle started. This particular squadron was not under the direct command of an admiral, which meant the admiral's one-eighth share was also available to the captains. The other officers generally shared in one-quarter and the crew shared in the balance.[48] Total proceeds from the captured *Revolutionnaire* exceeded £16,000.[49] By way of contrast, the annual salary for a captain of a fifth-rate ship in 1893 was around £150, and that of a third-rate 74 around £250. The return from a prize such as this was therefore equivalent to several years' ordinary pay. It acted as an incentive to engage and explains the enthusiasm and aggression for which frigate squadrons became renowned.

In February 1795, nine vessels, a convoy under protection of the schooner *Coureuse* (12) were captured off the Isle de Groix, near Lorient (Map 1). Another seven were burnt and four more scuttled. In Warren's dispatch listing the vessels, Keats was particularly thanked.[50] On 29 March, the *Galatea* shared in the capture of the *Fortitude* and then the *America, Jean Marie, Robuste, Pacific, Friendschap* and *Fantaise*. Shortly thereafter, the squadron shared in the capture of the *François Bernard*, and the *Lune*, and then in the capture of th*e Adelaide* and *Aimalie*.[51] In April, she captured the *Expedition*, of 16 guns, amongst several other vessels.[52]

An incomplete list of the captures for which the *Galatea* received prize money has been extracted from Steel's Prize List,[53] in the table below. The official prize list takes no account of various ships run ashore or otherwise destroyed, some of which are included in brackets.

Item No	Vessel Captured	Date captured (retaken/ salvaged)	Payment details
	Volontaire, Espion, and *Alerte*	Run ashore.	London Gazette, 13919, p756
78	Revolutionnaire 40, warship	Frigate 21 Oct. 1794	£10,000 Jan 29
106	Revolutionnaire, 40, warship	" "	£5,000, June 8
116	Pierre, brig Petit Jean, sloop, Gloire -lugger Deux Freres, brig, Libertie, Adelaide, Aimable Madelaine, Bot de Cayenne, Biche, brig; Coureuse (12),	Feb-March 1795	Paid Sept 22, 1795 Seven other vessels burnt and four scuttled.
117	David, Ormontaise, Phoenix,	Jan, 1795, retaken	Paid Sept 22
118	Quartidi, cutter, Haesingeland	16 Sept, 1794 retaken	Paid 22 Sept
	[*JeanAmie, François, Bernard* and *Lune*]	15, 27 Feb, 1795	London Gazette 14041, p839
	[*PetitJean, Adélaïde,* and *Aimalie*]	Feb 1795	London Gazette, 13815, p33
119	Expedition (16), Maria Francoise Fidelle	16 April 1795	Paid 22 Sept
125	Formidable, Tiere Alexander, ships of war	Battle of L'Orient, 23 June 1795	
128	Revolutionnaire (40)	21 Oct, 1794	Final payment
132	Jean Bart, corvette	15 Apr. 1795	Part proceeds £2,011
149	Revolutionnaire (40)	21 Oct, 1794	Head money, 10 Feb, 1796, £421
151	Jean Bart	21 Apr, 1795	Head money and stores, £851
162	Kent	Retaken 9 Oct, 1795	£2,260
211	Fortitude	Retaken 29 Mar 1795	
212	Illier, Don de Dieu, Paul Edward, Felicite Sultana, Nancy Marie, L'Union (22), Bonne, and a brig Harmony, Sans Fleur, Agreeable Jean Marie	20 Mar 1796 6,7, March 1796 7, 13 April 1796 11, 13 March 1796 18 April 1796	Warrens Squadron, paid onboard, 21 September Falmouth
250	Étoile (30), & four brigs Robuste, 22, corvette	20 Mar 26 Apr 1796	Paid 31 December 1796, total £8,000

347	Pacific Lodoiska Fantaise Charlotte & Veronique [Éveillé (18) brig] Andromache Providence & Marie Theresa [Divina Pastora, Sp. Brig] Jean Anne Nordzee Mary South-whaler François Bernard Lune	14 May 22 May 25 May 16 August 23 August 17 December 11 December 13 February 177 16 March Retaken, 25 April 15 February	Paid 11 September 1797, London London Gazette, 14041,p839
374	Franklin, privateer,	Ad. Colpoys, 2 Nov1796	Paid 24 Oct, 1797, onboard
1144	Sophia	6 June 1796	Paid 25 August 1800
1359	America Friendschap [Bergen] Anna Catharina, Judith	6 April 1796 25 May 1796 17 Nov.1796 11 May 1797, 2 April1797	Paid 9 April 1801, London Gazette, 15248, p 367
1734	Jonge Duisse [Andromaque (44) Frigate Liberte, Marie Anne, Catherine, Jean de Blaignal]	22 August 1796 Run ashore, destroyed Burnt at entrance to The Garonne	Paid 24 May 1801, London Gazette, 13931, p879 Warren report, State Papers

Table 1: *Details of Prize money paid to the Galatea, 38, frigate, under Captain Keats, Steel's Prize Pay lists, David Steel, London, 1805.*

In 1795 the *Galatea* preceded, fitted with royalists' chiefs and troops, the expedition to Quiberon Bay [Map 5] under the command of Sir John Warren. On 15th of June she fell in with the Brest fleet, consisting of twelve sail of the line and twelve frigates, off the coast of France, and as it was not supposed that they were in a situation for sea, the circumstance excited a good deal of surprise; and as Captain Keats was fearful of their falling in with Sir John Warren, he immediately regulated his conduct with a view to inducing the enemy to give chase to the *Galatea*, and draw them from the track of the expedition. But failing in this object, he detached a chasse-marée, which he had in tow, and an intelligent young officer of the name of Burke, off Brest, to inform Lord Bridport of the circumstance, whilst he himself went in search of Sir John Warren. By these means the expedition was saved from an attack by the enemy and Lord Bridport was enabled to come up with and defeat them off Lorient [Map 5], at which Captain Keats was fortunately present.

Bridport's instructions were to escort Warren's convoy on the final part of the journey to Quiberon Bay, having first joined with a squadron under the command of Vice Admiral Cornwallis. On 19 June the Channel fleet had parted company with Warren's expedition, and had yet to rendezvous with Cornwallis. Having been alerted by the messenger sent by Keats they found the Brest fleet on 22 June to their south east and about twenty miles closer to the land. At 6:30 the next morning in light airs the signal was made for a general chase. The British slowly made ground, being 12 miles astern by midday, until at 7:00 pm Bridport was able to order his advanced ships to attack.

This became known as the action off Isle de Groix, on 23 June 1795. By placing his fleet between the French and Warren's expeditionary force the van of Bridport's fleet overran the rearmost of the French before they could escape behind the Isle de Groix to Lorient, capturing three 74 gun ships; the *Alexandre*, *Formidable* (renamed *Belleisle*) and *Tigre*. The action was claimed a victory and the French were forced to remain sheltered in Lorient for many months. Nevertheless, it has been argued that in not renewing attack the following day Bridport missed a unique opportunity to destroy the French Atlantic fleet, and also that he ought to have done more with his Channel fleet to support Warren's expedition generally through to its conclusion. It has been suggested that had the action taken place in later years, when commanders were enthused by the relentless energy of the likes of St Vincent and Nelson (and seemingly had less respect for the capabilities and discipline of the enemy) the engagement would have been pursued to total destruction of the inferior force instead of settled for an honourable victory. Nevertheless the 'victory' cleared the way for the expedition to Quiberon to proceed unmolested by the enemy.[54]

A TREASURE TO THE SERVICE

The action off Isle de Groix: An exact representation of the capture of three Ships of the Line, and the total defeat of the French fleet, by a squadron under the command of Admiral Lord Bridport, on 23 June 1795. E Godefroy, 1795. NMM PU5494 © National Maritime Museum, Greenwich, London. The description of the outcome used in the title is a considerable exaggeration.

The expedition then proceeded to Quiberon, preceded by the *Galatea*, and Captain Keats landed some royalist chiefs.

The expedition included three sail of the line and six frigates accompanying a number of smaller vessels and fifty sail of transport carrying about 2,500 French emigrants commanded by Comte de Puisaye and assisted by Comtes d'Hervilly and Sombreuil. Barely had they anchored in the Bay of

Quiberon on 25 June when a suspicious sail was sighted and the *Galatea* sailed in chase, firing as she went. She returned a couple of hours later with three prizes: a brig, a sloop laden with wine, and a chasse-marée with dispatches for the French fleet. A number of royalist inhabitants, previously evacuated from Toulon, were landed on the coast of Brittany together with arms and ammunition. Their objective was to reinforce and invigorate a mood amongst royalists in the region that it was hoped would see the west of France rise in counter to the revolution and lead to restoration of the monarchy. Fort Penthievre was captured, but a subsequent attack on St Barbe failed, and resulted in retreat, followed by desertion. As related in the Memoir below, in what proved to be a significant blow to the royalist cause the troops were repulsed and the uprising suppressed.

Upon the arrival of the transports, he was charged with superintending the landing of the troops at Carnac, and in all the subsequent operations, whether at Quiberon, Noirmoutier, or the Isle d'Yeux [Map 5] he was particularly and actively employed. On the 21st July the fort of Penthievre fell into the hands of the enemy by an act of treachery, which was followed by a most disastrous rout, and the loss of Quiberon. On this occasion Captain Keats was employed in embarking such of the troops and royalists as could be saved from the vengeance of the enemy, and was instrumental in rescuing about 1500[55] unfortunate individuals, though attended with great personal risks, and desisted only upon receiving a message from Count Sombreuil, who was fearful it might be considered a breach of faith, and a violation of the capitulation into which he was then entering. On the succeeding day, Captain Keats was sent by Sir John Warren with a flag of truce, to claim the fulfilment, on the part of the enemy of the articles which had been entered into by the brave but unfortunate Sombreuil and the French general Le Moine. The latter was met by Captain Keats; but he denied that any terms had been entered into, and refused Captain Keats the privilege of either seeing or communicating in any way with the Count.

The terms of a ceasefire in return for evacuation of the royalists were said by various senior French officers to have been agreed but those officers departed for Lorient and the terms were unexpectedly and peremptorily denied by the remaining General Le Moine. The Count and his officers, including a Bishop, were marched to Nantes, tried by drumhead court martial, and executed. The squadron, not wishing to abandon the mission, captured the islands of Hoedic and Houat and landed troops near Lorient following which they sought to place a garrison of men on the Island of Noirmoutier, off the entrance to the River Loire (Map 5). The island was believed to be sympathetic to the royalists, but finding it well defended, the squadron was unable to land troops. They then captured the nearby Isle d'Yeux to use as a base, and over the following months were reinforced by the *Jason* (32) with transports from which they landed some four thousand troops under General Doyle and the Duke of Bourbon in support of the royalists in the Chouannerie and Vendée revolts. In time their situation became hopeless and the squadron was recalled in October, although full evacuation took until 10 December.[56]

Upon the termination of operations on the coast of France in 1796, Captain Keats cruised under the orders of Sir John Warren; and having parted company, in chase, from the *Jason*, he ran on shore on the 2nd of July, on the coast of France, the *Éveillé*, a French frigate, built gabarre, pierced for 32 guns, of about 1000 tons further valuably laden with brandy and naval stores for the enemy at Brest, and which he totally destroyed by fire.

There is some confusion between the similarly named *Éveillé* and the flûte *Étoile*. The latter was taken in the action off Point Du Raz which took place on 20 March 1796. The *Galatea* was one of four frigates cruising off the Bec du Raz (Map 5) when Keats made the signal for five sail (four frigates, *Proserpine* (40), *Unité*, *Coquille*, and *Tamise* each 36 guns, and a corvette, *Cigogne* of 20) to the south-east. They gave chase that by 8:00am led them near a convoy of about sixty under the charge of the frigates. The French escorts which included the armed store-ship *Étoile* and gun brig *Mouche*, were drawn up in line to leeward of the convoy and to windward of the British. Six[57] merchantmen were taken, but the rest escaped among the Penmark rocks. By three in the afternoon, the British had gained so much on the rear of the French squadron that her van then bore down in support. The *Galatea* being rearmost and the smallest of the British vessels bore the brunt of the action when the two squadrons briefly engaged as they passed on opposite tacks and was considerably cut up. One main-deck gun was dismounted and a midshipman (Evans) killed. By making short boards, the British got to windward during the afternoon and Keats was directed to bear down and lead the squadron through the enemy line. In the face of this assault, the French made all sail towards the Passage du Raz, a treacherous channel between Point du Raz and Isle de Sein. After some exchange of fire with the *Galatea*, the rearmost French escort, which was the *Étoile*, of 24 guns, pierced for 32, and 160 men, struck her colours at 5:30pm, her companions escaping in the night to the shelter of shore batteries.[58] She was a flûte, or armed store ship laden with brandy and goods for the supply of Brest. Prize money of £8,000 was paid.[59]

A number of sources agree with the Memoir that the *Galatea* was present also at the capture and burning of the *Éveillé*. She was not an armed store ship but a brig sloop of six guns captured by Warren's squadron some months earlier, in October 1795. Some reports her as having been burned as stated in the Memoir, but other records confirm she was taken into the navy, serving as the re-armed *Eveille* (14).

On 7 April the squadron captured part of a convoy off Camaret Point, (Point de Pen-Hir, Map 5) and on the 15th, *Robuste,* a corvette of 22 guns.[60]

On the 23rd August 1796 he was still more fortunate in the destruction of the French frigate *L'Andromaque* of 42 guns, [according to the dispatch, 44, but pierced for 48, with 300 men] and for which he received the particular approbation of the Admiralty. The squadron was cruising near the Garonne when she hove in sight, and by the skill of Captain Keats she was turned amongst the shoals at its entrance. Notwithstanding the difficulty of the navigation, and although his French pilot declared his incapacity of conducting the ship, and refused to continue his charge, Captain Keats was determined to persevere; he took upon himself the whole responsibility, chased the enemy right over the shoals of Arcachon [Map 5], on which she struck, and where she was immediately wrecked.

Keats developed a low opinion of pilots. In his experience they were often to be found wanting in courage and qualification when needed most. He had years earlier taken responsibility for his ship in chasing the enemy through shoals in the Delaware. In pursuing *L'Andromaque*, he again showed both confidence and competence in conning his ship in difficult circumstances. Throughout his career, Keats often stepped in where he considered pilots were unreliable or refused to proceed. Some years later he put his thoughts in writing to Earl St. Vincent. He in turn wrote to Thomas Grenville, First Lord of the Admiralty, forwarding that "very interesting" letter with which he confirmed he perfectly and entirely agreed, to the effect that putting blind faith in pilots had occasioned the loss of many of His Majesty's Ships.[61] St. Vincent's biographer, Brenton, adds by confirmation his own experience of having on no less than three occasions – including when in a 64-gun ship – been run on shore whilst under the charge of pilots "shamefully and alarmingly ignorant of their business".[62]

Keats felt so strongly on the matter that in giving evidence to the Parliamentary Inquiry into the Expedition to the Scheldt in 1810, he went so far as to say:

> *From the experience I have had, I think myself justified in saying, that of all classes of men in society, or at least of men attached to the navy, pilots are the least to be trusted to, and I should not have thought of taking a fleet up either of the Scheldts upon the most positive assurances of pilots without having examined the navigation, and satisfied myself; my experience of pilots makes that caution necessary.*[63]

Although he never refused pilots to his captains, he always told them 'that whoever trusts implicitly to a pilot is *sure* to lose his vessel'.[64]

In this instance Keats had crowded sail to cut off the prey, and by misleading signals induced her to anchor near the Grave Channel, at the entrance to the Gironde (Map 5). After she realised her error and cut her anchor line, he resumed the chase. Having stood into the channel between Chevrier bank and the lighthouse, he then hauled to windward of and rounded the bank in four fathoms of water before making all sail before the wind to cut off the pursued. By 8:00pm he was just two miles astern. At 9:00pm a violent squall necessitated a shortening of sail, but he continued the chase through a night of violent wind, rain, thunder, and lightning. The *Pomone* and *Anson* hauled to windward while *Galatea* continued close inshore, and regained sight of *Andromaque* around 11:00pm. The weather abating, she made all sail in pursuit until the prey ran on shore, about 5.30am, and cut away her masts. As she had shown no colours, Keats concluded she did not intend to resist and fired no more than three shots before sending his boat ashore to destroy her. Some of the crew, including her Captain, were taken off. The ebbing of the tide tempted most to walk ashore, several of whom drowned as a result. In the morning, the *Artois* and *Sylph* were hull down, and the *Anson* and *Pomone* out of sight, but about 7.00am, the *Artois* and *Sylph* came up and sent their boats ashore to assist in the destruction.[65] A raging surf made this a difficult operation. The *Sylph* anchored close inshore with a spring on her cable and fired into the bottom of the French frigate to prevent re-floating on the rising tide. At high water she returned and sent her boats ashore to complete the destruction, setting her ablaze.

Thus far the *Galatea* had acted alone, but in the morning, she was joined by the *Artois*, Captain Nagle, and the *Sylph*, Captain J C White, who assisted in setting the enemy on fire.

United Services Magazine reported that "although his Commodore's letter was miserably silent upon it, [Keats's] conduct was the admiration of the squadron."[66] Published letters, including Warren's dispatch[67] and one from an officer on the *Artois*, made more of their contribution, about which Keats wrote to Warren in protest. Warren, who was not in sight when the critical action took place, agreed, writing accordingly to the Secretary of the Admiralty, Sir Evan Nepean. He in turn apologised, blaming the oversight on editing within the admiralty office, and saw to it that Keats's own report was published.

Some say this demonstrates sensitivity to criticism of himself or his men.[68] More realistically it was sensitivity to lack of acknowledgement rather than to criticism, as there certainly was no criticism. Nevertheless, his position can be well explained by Warren's tendency to self-promotion and Keats's own desire for recognition in combination with a loyalty to the men and ship who had risked their lives and whose skill warranted due recognition for their achievements. Officers were generally quick to defend their honour and were sensitive to omissions such as this. Their status, both informally amongst colleagues and formally in terms of prospects for promotion or better commands, depended upon acknowledgement of credit for achievements at sea. If merit was to be rewarded it was important that triumphs be actively broadcast within accepted norms.

Clark, in his *Battles of England*, notes:

> *As Sir John was not even in sight during the chief transactions, it would have been an act of justice to have allowed the principal actor to have made his report, when he would no doubt have spoken honourably of those who so well seconded his exertions.*[69]

Naval historian William James echoes the sentiment, saying Keats ought to have been allowed to render his own account of the incident, not merely to do justice to himself, but to recommend for promotion his deserving subordinates. How many a lieutenant or commander, he laments, having missed a recommendation from his captain, never has a second opportunity of distinguishing himself, and has remained ever after in the background of the service, soured against a profession of which he might have been one of the brightest ornaments?[70] Promotion of the ship's successes might well be seen as part of a commander's duty, and most certainly appreciated by the crew. In any event, no offence was meant by or taken from, this exchange as the two officers remained close for the rest of their lives.

Those in the navy well knew of Keats's talents, while acknowledging they may not have been so well known in wider circles. Lord Seymour of the Admiralty Board wrote to the First Lord of the Admiralty, Lord Spencer, arguing against a particular proposal on the basis that:

> *It would be depriving Keats of an opportunity of adding to the credit he has obtained in the minds of all those who have been employed with him, though his not being the senior has prevented the world from knowing how ably he has served.*[71]

Courage and fortitude were required of a commander in all theatres of responsibility. While not necessarily apparent through twenty-first-century eyes, the courage required in intricate navigation through shallows was possibly to be more admired than that required in battle. Naval historian Cyril Parkinson says risks run in fighting, and particularly winning, were very small indeed. The real risk the sailor faced was that of being drowned. The two categories of danger both required courage, but it was evident to St. Vincent that not all commanders dealt equally with the different stresses. Writing to Lord Spencer in 1800, he observed of Saumarez, whom he initially thought one of the few suited to command the inshore squadron off Brest:

> *Sir James Saumarez does not stand the work at the advanced post with the firmness I had expected; whence it is evident that the man who bravely faces the Frenchman or Spaniard with intrepidity does not always encounter rocks or shoals with the same feeling.*[72]

Exploits such as the chase of *L'Andromaque* demonstrating his character in the face of shoal waters reinforced Keats's reputation and set him apart as being one of the few suitable to be employed in difficult coastal commands.

Shortly after that encounter, the squadron returned to Falmouth and, the threat of French invasion being of increased concern, was ordered to stay close to home. They had intended to cruise for rich prizes from vessels they hoped to intercept off the Spanish coast en route from South America, so they were not enthusiastic about the enforced change of plan. Such was the public profile they had obtained from reports of their exploits, which together with their dispatches appeared in all the newspapers ranging from the major London daily's to local papers around the country, that they had become widely known as the 'lions of the sea'. In the public perception, this squadron exemplified the romantic image of naval warfare. Old admirals seemed dull by comparison. So widespread was the expectation that this gallant and exciting squadron would continue its harassment of the enemy that the Admiralty was prompted to write a pacifying letter to Warren. It stated that it was essential Admiral Thompson have the assistance of a considerable number of frigates in support of his duties off Brest but the Admiralty was:

...intending by and by to release you from the fleet and send you cruising again on your old ground. I write this that you may not be alarmed and fancy we are going to attach you as a fixture to the great lumbersome three-deckers in the Western Squadron.[73]

The *Galatea* went on to share in the capture of the *Maria Theresa* and *Providence*, the brig *Divina Pastora*, the privateer *Franklin*, and the *Bergen*. The *Naval Chronicle* summarised the remarkable activity of Warren's squadron through 1796 as follows:[74]

23	neutrals detained
87	merchantmen captured
54	merchantmen destroyed
25	ships or vessels of war captured
12	ships or vessels of war destroyed
<u>19</u>	vessels recaptured; (14 English, 3 Spanish, 1 Dane, 1 American)
220	

Captain Keats continued to cruise under the orders of Sir John Warren till the unhappy mutiny of the fleet in 1797 deprived him of the command.[75]

At this time the whole was chaos and disorder; and though circumstances at the moment, according to superior authority, would not permit officers to justify their conduct before a court-martial, and Captain Keats was, like many others, obliged to submit quietly to indignity, we know that he now looks back (as he always has done) to the whole of the transactions of that period without one feeling of reproach; a circumstance which must be highly consolatory, after a lapse of so many years, when passion, if any, must have cooled, and reason and justice have their full sway.

It is at this point that White notes differences between this memoir and earlier drafts where it is stated to be an "event which he looks back on with the deepest concern" and another handwritten form which refers to the "horror" of the events.[76] Although few memoirs make much mention of the mutiny, even when the officer in question was intimately involved[77] it is fair to say these memoirs gloss over the episode.

The vast majority of men conducted themselves reasonably to the extent that there was little or no violence. It was generally, but not universally, more akin to a strike over pay and conditions than a mutiny, and an Admiralty in better touch with its men may have foreseen the discontent and resolved matters well before the question of mutiny even arose. St. Vincent (a noted disciplinarian) attributed blame to Bridport's slack discipline; Collingwood to Howe's inaction; and Barrow to Bridport and Parker, each having discounted the seriousness of the threat.[78] First Lord Spencer failed to read the signs until matters were out of hand. The men's grievances, which were generally with the Admiralty rather than with specific officers, were set out in a relatively respectfully worded petition and on many issues were well-founded. Basic wages had not increased since being set in 1653. They were now well below those awarded in the army, where increases had been made in 1795, and less than half those paid to merchant seamen. Pensions for retired or wounded navy personnel were similarly either non-existent or less than half those paid in the army and left aged sailors of lieutenant rank or below in poverty. Leave was hard to get. Rations were poor in both quantity and quality. For those in a frigate squadron, wages were probably not a major concern. Their thoughts were likely on prize money and transfer to more lucrative stations. Here too there were serious issues. Prize money, after first having to be proven by a prize agent in Admiralty Court, was not paid until long after the event. By then the captain may have gone to another vessel, those who had died in the interim could not benefit, and those who had been discharged were generally not informed as to where and when payment could be collected. In short, the admiralty had taken its workforce for granted for too long. Conditions in the navy had been allowed to fall well behind expectations of the day and it came to a head at a time when the country was almost completely reliant on these men to face the enemy and prevent an invasion from across the Channel.

Once the seriousness of the situation became clear to the Admiralty First Lord Spencer attended Portsmouth and met with the men at length. A substantial majority of the demands were acceded to promptly. Final negotiations dragged on while pay increases went through the process of being authorised by an Act of Parliament and a Royal Pardon was formalised for the alleged mutineers.

The Spithead (Portsmouth) mutiny took place in April and was resolved by mid-May. When word of the settlement made with the rest of the Channel Fleet reached Warren's squadron at sea sometime later, the men were indignant that they had seemingly missed an opportunity to share in the rewards and to at least rid themselves of certain officers. While the squadron was cruising off Ushant (Map 1) on 14 May, by pre-arranged signal, the crew of the *Galatea* seized her. Two days later they passed under the stern of the *Pomone*, reporting to Warren's lieutenant sent onboard that they wanted Keats, whom they had imprisoned (confined to his cabin), removed from his position on account of his being a tyrant. They nevertheless followed Warren's order to return to Plymouth.[79]

The Admiralty hierarchy feared men may take their seized ships to France and hand them over to the enemy. In the case of this frigate squadron, it would have been easy to do so, given they were cruising just off that coast and at the height of the differences on 21-23 April, the *Galatea* was almost within the Port of Brest itself, ascertaining the strength of the fleet at anchor.[80] It was never their intention to be treasonous. On the contrary, in the first instance of rebellion on the part of men facing the enemy at sea, the whole of the squadron returned to Plymouth. There was no thought of turning their ships over to the enemy. They simply wanted improvements in their conditions. And while they were at it, to remove a tough captain.

An indication of the attitude of the *Galatea's* men can be gleaned from a letter written by crew member David Crawford to his son; "On 12 May we had a full Understanding of the Sailors sticking out for more Wages. We all hands agree, both Seamen, Petty Officers and marines, & at 8 in the Morning we confined the Captain, Boatswain & Masters Mate to their Cabins….We spoke the Commodore to let him know that we was going to Plymouth, and the Rest of the Squadron followed. We arrived the 18th at Plymouth. We told the [Commodore] that we was agreeable to go out again in an Hour's Time, but we would not go with them three Officers."[81] There is some difference as to who made the decision to return to Plymouth, but in any event no disciplinary action was pursued against the men and as Crawford was writing on first June the ship was being fitted for sea now under the command of Captain George Byng, who remained with her for five years.

As a result, Brest was left unwatched for some weeks, giving rise to a fear the French may get to sea while there was no British force in a position to face them, but the opportunity was missed. On coming ashore, Keats was released by the men and took Warren's dispatches to the Admiralty. While Warren was out of his ship, his belongings were seized, and the men refused to co-operate until prize money was paid.[82] After further negotiation, order was restored to the squadron and duty resumed with little more disturbance. The thought of the remaining loyal frigates having free reign to catch all the prizes was probably as much motivation to resume duty as any resolution with the Admiralty. This train of events did not harm Keats's career or standing with the Admiralty, but he nonetheless had to reflect upon the uncomfortable fact the men of his ship had wanted him removed.

In the month of June of the same year, he was appointed to the *Boadicea*, a much finer frigate of 38 guns; but a lurking spirit of mutiny early endeavoured to deprive him of his command. This attempt, however, was checked in the bud; the seeds of sedition were crushed, the guilty were instantly punished, and the conduct of Captain Keats, after the strictest inquiry, met with the decided approbation of the Admiralty.

A TREASURE TO THE SERVICE

The *Boadicea* was one of those built in response to the new French frigates. Commissioned in 1795, her lines were based on the French 40 gun *Imperieuse* captured in 1793, but with scantlings and fastenings upgraded to English norms. She was accordingly a little longer, a little quicker, and more powerful than the *Galatea*. At 148 feet, she carried a complement of 284 men and was armed with twenty-eight 18-pounders on the gun deck, eight 9-pounders and two 32-pound carronades on the quarter deck, and two 9-pounders and two 32-pound carronades on the fo'c'sle. The carronade was a relatively new adaptation, designed by the Carron Company in Scotland. It had a short barrel and large bore like a mortar and was efficiently designed to smash timber at short range. As most battles were fought at close quarters limitation in range was more than compensated for by its light weight, heavy projectile, and increased accuracy compared to a long gun. It also had the advantage of taking less time to reload.[83] Initially experimental, carronades were not counted in the nominal number of guns; so, while rated 38, *the Boadicea* was armed with 42 guns. She was reported to be a fair sailer; capable of nine knots close-hauled to the wind and more than eleven knots with the wind on her quarter. She was described as tolerably handy tacking and wearing although she later had extra depth added to her false keel, suggesting the opportunity was taken to improve her performance to windward.

In the *Boadicea*, having usually a small squadron of frigates under his orders, he was much employed in the arduous and difficult service of watching the port of Brest, during which the vigilance and activity of his squadron were so great, and the enemy became so straitened, that they were compelled to have recourse to the difficult and expensive mode of conveying over-land, from the small ports of Quimper, Concarneau, and Abreverach, to Brest, many of the naval stores and other supplies for which they had occasion for the fleet and arsenal.

Marshall, in his *Royal Naval Biography*, commented that during this period, Keats distinguished himself as an indefatigable cruiser.[84] Many prizes were taken. On 19 September 1797 she captured the brig *Zephyr* and the *Eliza*, and the day after, the *Jenny*. In November, off Yeu Island she shared with the *Anson* in the capture of the *Railleur* of 30 guns and 160 men, quite new and only one day out of La Rochelle, purchased into the navy,[85] and also the *Henniker, Active, Fanny, Mohawk* and *Catherine*.[86]

At one time, Captain Keats then in the Iroise, standing from the Parquette rocks towards the Passage du Raz, with four frigates and a lugger, under easy sail, was apprised by the French signals of the approach of a convoy from the southward. He immediately hoisted French colours, and on the appearance of the convoy, shortened sail, and made signals for two of his frigates to tack from him, which *ruse-de-guerre* so completely threw the commodore of the enemy off his guard that he slighted all the numerous signals made from the Bec-du-Raz to Brest, to apprise him of his danger, and continued his course, till the *Boadicea, Uranie,* and a lugger were in the midst of them, when seventeen vessels, laden with naval and ordnance stores, were captured. Having obtained information from the prisoners that there were some men of war in the bay of Hodierne, which were supposed to be French frigates, Captain Keats immediately determined to run through the Passage du Raz with the *Uranie*, the only frigate then near him, but it being dark, the pilots of both ships refused to take them through.

Undismayed by difficulties of this description, and never at a loss in moments of danger, he determined to proceed, Captain Towry promising to keep his jib boom over the tafferel of the *Boadicea*. The enterprise, however, was not crowned with that success which his perseverance deserved: for though he succeeded in taking both ships safely through the passage, the ships of which he was in quest proved to be a strong Spanish squadron, making an effort to get into Brest, but which, taking alarm at the situation of the British fleet then off Ushant, returned to Basque Roads, [Rochefort] and was not visible at daylight.

The Passage du Raz, a narrow passage between Point du Raz and Isle de Seine outside Brest http://www.lordjimcroisieres.com/wp-content/uploads/2019/03/passage-du-trouziard.jpg

When Admiral Bompart left Brest in Sept. 1798, with a ship of the line [The *Hoche* (74)] and a strong squadron of frigates, filled with troops and eight frigates and a schooner, mounting a total of 392 guns, and carrying 3,000 troops, intending to support rebellion by the United Irishmen who had taken the city of Wexford [Map 4], Captain Keats was unable, from his inferiority of force, to make any attempt to arrest his flight; and though he was precluded by his instructions from leaving his station, he made such arrangements for watching the enemy, that though in order to disguise their real destination [Ireland], they made a sweep almost to the Western Islands, they were followed so closely, and in so masterly manner, by the *Ethalion*, Captain Countess, and the *Sylph*, Captain J C White, detached by Captain Keats for that purpose, that the enemy's approach to the coast of Ireland was made known to Sir John Warren, who, in consequence of the information sent by Captain Keats, had been forwarded expressly from Plymouth to look out for the enemy, and who finally succeeded in defeating the plans formed for separating that country from the British empire.[87]

It is worthy of remark and may be mentioned as a proof of his prescience, that in sending information to England of Bompart's sailing, he wrote a letter to Sir John Warren, then at Plymouth, in which he said, "My fortune sprung and watched the game, which, notwithstanding your present situation, yours will take you to the death of".

The successful manner in which Captain Keats had for so considerable a time watched the port of Brest, procured a continuation of the same arduous employment except one cruise to the westward, when he captured three large privateers and two merchant vessels, and being twice selected to open a communication with and give supplies to, the royalists in Brittany and La Vendée.[4]

Keats reported to Admiral Bridport the capture of the privateer *Invincible Générale Buonaparte* (20) and 175 men[88] in December 1798, taken into the navy as HMS *Brazen*, and shortly thereafter, the brig *Adventure* and the third privateer of the cruise, *Utile* of 16 guns and 120 men, quite new, three weeks out of Bordeaux.[89] Other prizes included *Milan (14)* with a crew of 44 and the brig *Requin* (18) and 70 men. The latter overturned in a squall en route to England, even with no sails set, and the prize crew and prisoner drowned.

---

4   He was also employed in Basque Road, under Sir G. Pole, and directed to cover an attack on a Spanish squadron under the Isle d'Aix, but the measures not being sufficient for the object in view, he was called off [see below].

In July the following year, *Boadicea* was present at the capture of the West Indiaman *Cultivator*, with cargo valued at twenty thousand pounds,[90] followed by the Spanish vessel *Union* of 22 guns and 130 men en route to Buenos Aires.[91] Ship's surgeon Benjamin Outram, who served many years with Keats recalled in his memoir "all that a frigate could do was done....Their business was constant blockade – vigilance night and day- keeping the enemy in sight and themselves clear of dangers – examining strange sail – now in pursuit of coasters and privateers – now clearing for action on the enemy showing symptoms of getting under weigh. One Western cruise only – then an object of desire with Captains of Frigates, from the prize money it was likely to afford – was given to the *Boadicea*, by Lord St Vincent. A few small captures only were the fruits. The services of Captain Keats had been deemed too valuable to the country to be permitted to be profitable to himself – a common result to active officers".[92]

The *Boadicea* was present in Rear Admiral Pole's squadron that blockaded five Spanish ships from Ferrol (Map 4). The Spanish, led by the *Real Carlos* (112), had intended joining the French fleet at Brest, but finding, or fearing, some obstruction they put in to Rochefort. On arrival of a British squadron, they retired to the roads of Aix, a fortified island about twelve miles from Rochefort, where they remained under blockade. The Admiralty ordered an attack be made on the ships anchored in the roads.

Rear Admiral Pole arrived from Cawsand Bay (Plymouth) on 1 July 1799 and anchored in Basque Roads the following day. Keats, in *Boadicea* with the frigates *San Fiorenzo (38)*, Captain Neale and *Uranie* (38), Captain Towry, and bomb vessels and cutters, proceeded unseen (due to the morning being thick and rainy) to the Isle d'Aix. Then seeing the enemy ships some four miles distant they moored in line ahead within range of a floating battery off the northern point of the Isle d'Oléron from 11:00, fitted springs to their cables, and at noon commenced firing upon the nearest ship, being that of the Admiral. The French mortars were so superior in range that whilst they easily made range, and passed overhead, the British shells all fell up to a quarter of a mile short. Keats sent the *Sylph* to relay this information to his admiral. Given the fort and floating batteries, it was not safe to move within range to cause any harm to the anchored ships, and in any event, orders had been specific: to anchor no further than the Basque Roads. Attempts over several hours to set the Spanish alight with carcasses also proved ineffectual. As the wind dropped, the Spanish sent out gun-boats armed with long 36-pounders, and Keats was directed to withdraw as the enemy ships of the line retreated to shelter up river.[93] The encounter proved harmless to both sides, but it did cause Keats to consider at length, and ultimately write a report on, a strategy to effectively attack these roads. The Spanish remained blockaded until they were enabled to escape the following September.[94]

A further expedition transported supplies and royalist reinforcements to Quiberon in November 1799. After some delays, due firstly to the unavailability of the supplies he was to be delivering and then to the weather, the *Boadicea* landed some 13,000 muskets and ammunition, together with cannon, howitzers and several tons of gun powder near Billiers and the mouth of the River Vilaine. The insurrection was by now losing impetus, and the rebels made little progress before their venture ended in surrender.

When in March 1800 the crew of the *Danaé* mutinied in the face of her captain's violent discipline, Keats chased the sloop and an accompanying French corvette into Brest but was unable to prevent her from reaching the safety of French guns. The French so detested the mutinous behaviour of the crew they marched the offenders to Dinan prison and released Captain Lord Proby (who had surrendered "to the French Nation, but not to mutineers") and his officers on parole to return to England.[95]

On Lord St. Vincent assuming the command of the Channel Fleet in 1800, Captain Keats was released from the fatigue of the inshore squadron, and was employed by his lordship in cruising, sometimes singly, and at others in the command of the frigate squadron off Ferrol and Corunna, and was fortunate enough to make several prizes.

St. Vincent brought renewed vigour to the command that included up to ninety vessels and covered the coast from Brest as far south as Ferrol. He devoted himself to positioning ships to completely close the port, an objective which was substantially achieved.

St. Vincent's confidence in Keats is demonstrated by his deployment close to the entrance to Brest, described as a "highly stressful and dangerous service".[96] Blockade was an expensive, costly business requiring many resources and skilled, attentive manpower. It required holding sail of the line at sea, ready to bring to action any escaping French man of war and placement of frigates close in, scouting and preventing all coastal trade and supply to the port. The Brittany coast is plagued by fog and strong currents running over shallow water. Having traversed the full fetch of the Atlantic, waves reaching these shallow waters stand up, making for treacherous conditions requiring constant vigilance from those deployed in the inshore squadron. Constant manoeuvring took a far greater toll on both ships and men than did a long ocean voyage.

The watching of the Port of Brest, regarded as the finest harbour in France with a roadstead capable of sheltering 500 ships of war,[97] entailed particular difficulties. The port itself is too far inland to be observed from the sea, and reefs extend fifteen miles to seaward either side of the main entrance known as the Goulet. Additional anchorages were available outside the entrance: to the north in Bertheaume Bay and to the south in Camaret Bay. Larger ships were generally kept cruising off Ushant (Map 5), for safety and sea room. Smaller frigates and sloops had to be sent close to shore to observe through narrow entrances, with the main ones being the *Passage de Four* around Point Matthew and *Passage de l'Iroise* to the north-west, and the *Bec du Raz* and the *Toulinguet* to the south-west. The task was all the more difficult in that, until 1800, there were no proper charts of this dangerous shore. The best available was the *Neptune François*, a standard French atlas published in 1693.[98] In fine weather the inshore squadron had the additional task of charting the various rocks and passages.

Vessels could easily slip out of port if frigates were forced out to sea by severe conditions threatening to drive them onto rocky shores or make their approaches through the inshore passages to be met by powerful escorts at the mouth of the Goulet, thereby forcing the British to watch without acting. Admiralty Secretary Nepean and Lord Bridport thought so strongly that these difficulties were not properly understood or appreciated by landsmen, including politicians, back home that they engaged Mr Peres – marine artist to George III and draughtsman at the Admiralty - to paint various views of the port from the sea to better explain the setting.[99]

Men were worn out by blockading, partly because of the ever-present danger of the ship sinking or grounding, and partly through lack of sleep brought about by having to change course day and night.[100] Collingwood found the responsibility of the inshore command off Brest particularly stressful reportedly sleeping fully dressed ready to personally take control at any time during the night. He described the anxious time he had of it, the tides and rocks having more danger in them than a battle once a week.[101] Statistics support the position. Throughout the war only a dozen or so ships of more than 28 guns succumbed to the enemy, whereas over eighty were lost through being wrecked, a disproportionate number of which foundered on the west coast of France.[102] Adhering to St Vincent's practice Keats ensured he was on deck whenever the signal to tack or wear was made at night. Few commanders had the skills or psychological fortitude to meet the arduous and unremitting challenges, both physical and mental, of navigation and seamanship inherent in this deployment.

St. Vincent became increasingly concerned the French would attempt to get to sea, and he required constant information as to the number of vessels in the port and their state of readiness. An insight into the process and difficulties can be gained by looking at just one week, in early May 1800. On 3 May[103] Keats reported that he entered Camaret Bay, the wind and weather being particularly favourable, and made out 45 sail of the line, all bar one rigged with their sails bent. A convoy of 30 entered the Chenal du Four. The French sent three sail of the line and three frigates out to escort them over the last distance, and three more sail of the line to drive off the British frigates. That same day, Rear Admiral Berkeley stationed off St Matthew's Light counted thirty French ships, plus the six that were sent out.[104]

Two days later, Keats reported with concern that having been as close in as possible, he could see only 37 ships and fourteen frigates but had no explanation as to the whereabouts of the remainder. The Toulinguet passage he had thought impassable due to the weather and no vessel had been seen passing St. Matthew. He was concerned that he had failed to exercise proper judgement in the task of surveillance and undertook to use greater endeavours to resolve the uncertainty.[105]

St. Vincent had full faith that nothing had escaped Keats's attention and thought it hardly possible any ships had escaped. He agreed the Toulinguet passage would have been too hazardous in the weather, and in any event any escapees would have been seen by Pellew, so it was likely there had been some change within the harbour. He nonetheless alerted the rest of the fleet as to the possibility some French ships were at large.[106]

Meanwhile, with increasing concern, Keats sent a four-oared fast rowing boat to the mouth of the Goulet under cover of darkness. Unable to fully ascertain the position, they remained until daybreak when a boat with six small cannons was found to lie between them and their cutter, forcing them to have to fight their way back out. Separately, Captain Dashwood in the *Sylph* captured some fishing boats: one from Douarnenez and one from Dinan. Independently, they confirmed St. Vincent's opinion that no ships had escaped. Rather, nine sail of the line had been taken into port to have their bottoms examined. They also divulged that the Spanish seamen had not been paid; were sickly, often deserting and quarrelling with the French; and that there were only seven sail of the line seriously intended for sea. In reporting this, Keats confirmed it was consistent with his earlier observations that several vessels had been seen riding high on their moorings, in hindsight in preparation for docking.[107]

White[108] observes these events highlight Keats's strengths as a seaman and his devotion to duty, but also a tendency to lack self-confidence. Pause for reflection ought to have given him confidence that all was as expected. Nevertheless, keeping track of the number of ships in the road and their preparedness for sea was St. Vincent's primary concern, so an unexplained variance was something that could not properly be kept from him.[109] As he expected, Keats was doing a fine job. No ships had escaped his surveillance, and the intelligence received via the frigates was considerably more accurate than that furnished by spies working for the Prince of Bouillon. By the end of June, the intelligence gathering and the close attention of the inshore squadron was such they had effectively closed the port, keeping warships blockaded and discouraging merchant convoys from attempting the final dash into the Goulet.

Shortly after having taken or destroyed several supply vessels Keats was gratified to be advised by the Admiralty on 3 February 1800 of their Lordships' "great satisfaction in finding that by the exertions of the squadron you have been enabled to interrupt so successfully the supplies sent from the Southern Ports for the supply of the fleet at Brest" such that badly needed stores had to be hauled overland in wagons greatly reducing the utility of Brest as a significant base for operations.[110]

Blockading, and particularly the close watch of the largest Atlantic port at Brest, reached a new level of dominance under St. Vincent's stewardship, with ships remaining under sail for months as they were re-supplied at sea even though only a few hours' sailing from a home port.

Whereas the daring exploits of frigate captains captured the public imagination, blockade was unglamorous by comparison. It was a case of no news is good news. The difficulty and benefits of the unremitting task were generally unappreciated back home, however, it achieved a number of strategic objectives. Preventing the enemy warships from getting to sea allowed British merchants to operate freely from the Baltic to the East Indies. Conversely, French trade was crippled, thus isolating Napoleon from the wealth of his colonies. It also prevented his navy from exercising their own seamen and gunnery so that when they did get to sea, they were at a considerable disadvantage.

In recognition of the arduous duties performed, St. Vincent handed out rewards: the opportunity to go cruising and win prize money. He wrote to Keats in July 1800:

> *Being extremely solicitous to mark my approbation of your meritorious services and those of Captain Cunningham of the Clyde, I hereby authorize you to water at Oporto in the Boadicea...and to cruise as long as your and his provisions last and you are at liberty to send any or all the three frigates under your orders, one by one, to Oporto for the same purpose and to keep them with you as long as their provisions last, giving their captains the most precise orders to return to the northward of Cape Finisterre...avoiding a trespass on the limits of Vice Admiral Lord Keith's command.*[111]

He sent the *Uranie*, followed by the *Fisgard, Beaulieu* and *Cambrian*, with the suggestion they spread out from latitude 46 degrees to Cape Finisterre to prey upon the numerous frigates and privateers known to be at sea.[112] The *Boadicea* shared in the capture of the *St Pierre, Carnac, Anna Louisa, Zeegen, Hoop, Phoenix, La Revanche* (14) *& Gironde* (16), *Joseph, Magicienne, Dicke, Rancune, El Vivo* (14), *Favourite, Jeannie,* and that of the *Venus (32)* with 200 men en route from Rochefort to Senegal[113]. She shared in the salvage of the *Edinburgh, Eliza* and the brig, *Betsy*.[114] The hard work of blockade was thus rewarded.

During this period, the Duke of Clarence, now a vice admiral, applied to be sent to sea as second-in-command to Earl St. Vincent in the Channel Fleet, with Keats as his Flag Captain. This request too was denied by the Admiralty. But Keats did not go unnoticed. St Vincent was fulsome in his praise of his squadron. Keats responded to such encouragement, saying St. Vincent's comments were not only most gratifying but softened the fatigue of the situation and inspired hope of greater success to come,[115] and indeed his diligence and success in the frigate squadrons were soon recognised by conferring a superior command.

**Historical Memoirs of
Admiral Sir Richard Goodwin Keats, GCB**

HMS Superb

In March 1801 he was appointed to command the *Superb* of 74 guns...

Keats was to be in command of the *Superb* for six years as her captain, followed by three years as a flag officer. From 1801-1805 he slept only one night out of the ship. It is little wonder the two are so closely identified.

Ordered in June 1795, laid down in August, constructed by Thomas Pitcher, and launched from Northfleet, near Gravesend, on 17 March 1798, she was a full-rigged ship of the line carrying around 22,000 square feet of canvas. Her design was based on a draught from the French prize *Pompée*, taken by French Royalists in 1793 off Toulon and delivered to England. Her gun deck measured 182 feet in length and 49 in the beam, carrying nominally 74 guns, although, as was the custom, the *Superb* was fitted with more. The gun deck had thirty 32-pounders, while the upper gun deck carried thirty 24-pounders. According to Winfield, most of her class ran 18-pounders. Her first commander, John Sutton, believing she had crank, that is abnormal heel and slow recovery, induced the Admiralty to exchange the 24-pounders for 18-pounders, but the change was reversed some time later.[116] On the quarter deck she ran four 18-pounders and ten 32-pound carronades, on the fo'c'sle two 18-pounders and two 32-pound carronades, and on the roundhouse six 18-pound carronades (a total of 84 guns). She was armed as a powerful 74, and came to be regarded as one of the finest and fastest third rates in the King's service.[117] She was crewed by a complement of 640 officers and men, including Royal Marines.

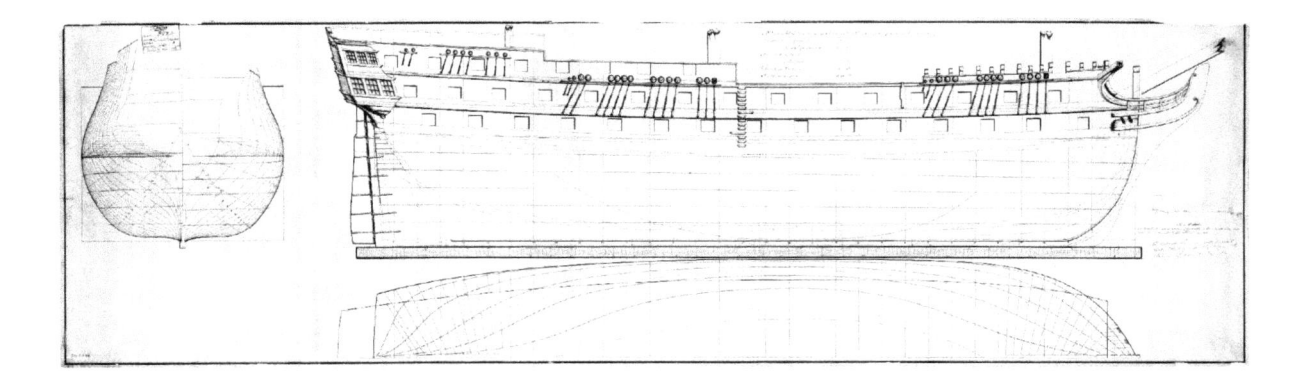

Drawings showing the body plan, sheer lines, and longitudinal half-breadth for HMS Superb (74) drafted from the captured Pompée. Made by the Navy Office. NMM J2795 ©National Maritime Museum, Greenwich, London

Keats's standing orders for the efficient running of his ship (reproduced in Appendix II[118]) was a book of 88 instructions that reflected his methods and prejudices. He was influenced by his early experience and by his time under the leadership of St. Vincent. Like the Earl, he enforced high standards of discipline and drill modelled upon his own example. His own obedience to duty and honesty were obvious to all his crew and beyond question. In these instructions he showed he was quite modern and undoubtedly effective. With a deal of St. Vincent's harshness removed the instructions recognise the benefits flowing from ensuring the crew were kept as comfortable and happy as possible, within the constraints of a ship of war.

Instruction 8 required all Officers and Petty Officers to be personally acquainted with the ship's company so that all seamen be addressed by their own name whenever there was occasion to call them aloft or elsewhere. This was more unusual and more significant than might be expected. It made clear that each sailor was to be identified and valued as an individual amongst the crew. A captain who ensured his crew was respected was more likely to gain their respect in return, and without that the ship could not reach its full potential. The lessons of the 1897 mutinies may well have been learned. The men could not simply be taken for granted. At the end of the day, no matter who the commander, the fate of the ship and quite possibly the nation were held in the hands of the ordinary seaman. Whilst he needed to be kept in order, he also needed to be provided with agreeable conditions, kept content with his lot and given some dignity if the ship was to operate smoothly. Instruction 4 required that any men who excelled in their duty be specifically distinguished and encouraged so that their merits not be disregarded, and that the undeserving be made sensible to the advantage resulting from good and respectable behaviour.

Instruction 10 reflected his brisk and practical approach to running the ship and provided that when in port, women were allowed to attend men who had behaved well, but those who had behaved poorly were denied such attention. This was formalised to the extent the Master at Arms was to keep a register. Shore leave, too, was used as an incentive, it being available in proportion to the general character, sobriety and punctuality of the men who may apply. The regime onboard a warship was firm and unrelenting. The knowledge that whenever the opportunity arose the men would be allowed the maximum possible freedoms no doubt contributed to the running of the ship being more trouble-free than might otherwise be the case.

Strangely, there was no regular system of gunnery exercise specified across the navy. Each ship had its own plan and routine, depending upon the experience of the captain and the importance he attached to it.[119] The norm amounted to up to one-and-a-half hours practice on four days in seven.[120] Drawing on the example of St Vincent, Keats clearly attached significant importance to gunnery. He understood, as few did, that good gunnery was the decisive factor in most engagements, and that it could be achieved only by practice. Practice on the *Superb* took place in accordance with his Regulation 72:

> *Two guns taking them by turns, are regularly to be exercised for an hour every Forenoon and Afternoon (except on Sunday) when at sea: at such times the Petty Officers of the Quarters to which the guns belong; are to attend, when every part of the exercise is minutely to be attended to and explained to the Men.*

This was certainly a chore, but one which paid dividends when it counted and it conveniently and productively kept otherwise idle men busy. As a result of this schedule, and the attention to detail referred to, the *Superb* was credited with a record of rapid and accurate fire second to none. Her gunnery was sharpened to a terrible intensity and, on several occasions, she demonstrated her capacity to deliver three well-aimed broadsides in five minutes that would silence even the most formidable enemy.

A warship was generally overmanned for all activities other than the firing of guns, and much nuisance was caused by idle men. It was desirable that they be kept occupied during the unremitting boredom of blockade, yet many captains reported that their men had little or no experience of gunnery before battle. Keats's regime for training addressed both issues to the benefit of the smooth running of his ship as a man of war. It is often observed the French had superior ships that could sail faster and closer to the wind, but battles were generally fought at close range when combatants were either locked together or were just a few hundred yards apart. In those circumstances the ship with the best trained and disciplined crew that could accurately discharge more broadsides in rapid succession usually emerged victorious. Time and time again crews drilled and disciplined in gunnery proved to be the winning edge. Success bred more success. There was nothing like an engagement resulting in victory to create a unity of purpose and affection amongst a crew.

Training extended to small arms and boarding. Instruction 74 provided that, when at sea, one division of small arm men and boarders, taking by turn, was to be exercised Mondays, Wednesdays and Fridays.

As illustrated by his approach to allowing women onboard, Keats was properly described as one of the more enlightened officers with regard to the granting of indulgences. On the other hand, he was of the old school when it came to discipline. The Boatswain and his Mates, "conformable to the old Custom of the Service", were permitted to carry Rattans, but they were to be used with discretion (Instruction 71).

Consistent with this approach, along with the rattan, Keats followed Gambier's practice in using the 'yoke' as a punishment for swearing. This was a wooden collar, worn by the offender until it was removed in favour of a subsequent offender. On one occasion, Keats himself fell afoul of the rule. Cruising in the company of the frigate *Revolutionnaire* (under Charles Fielding) that had been sent to reconnoitre, he flew an urgent signal reinforced by two guns, recalling that ship from harm's way. Her captain failed to see or respond to the signal, necessitating the calling of all hands on the *Superb* for a quick tack and bear away to close on the wayward frigate. In the moment, Keats let out an oath at the frigate's neglect, and the captain of the afterguard called "yoke", not realising his captain was the offender: "I heard someone swear, I did not know it was your honour". Keats apologised and at the end of the watch allowed the man to splice the main brace[121] (a saying allowing the serving of rum on account of the task of tacking the main brace being so arduous that a reward is warranted). It is not clear if this form of punishment continued thereafter. The captain of the frigate certainly received a severe dressing down from St. Vincent and from Keats.

Although described as firm, and a disciplinarian, various commentators note punishment was not applied unnecessarily, and never capriciously. Other incidents show Keats exercised discipline with understanding. White cites an example of a lieutenant and boy third class being found in bed together. The punishment if sexual intercourse were proved could be the death penalty. Instead, after discussing the matter with Nelson, Keats reported to him a little later that the lieutenant had "escaped from his confinement and absconded" while the *Superb* had been at anchor close to shore.[122]

The evidence over the years shows Keats to have been firm and demanding but thoughtful and fair. Either the claims made in the Mutinies of 1797 were exaggerated, or he had learned from that experience and matured as a leader, or both.

The majority of the instructions address more mundane – but equally vital – matters, concerning all aspects of running the ship, with particular attention to administration, cleanliness, clothing, victualling and illness. A concentration upon drying and airing between decks, and the introduction of fresh air, was no doubt prompted by the prevailing belief of the times that diseases were largely airborne. The concept of a sick bay was only introduced at St Vincent's instigation at the turn of the century. On the *Superb* those recuperating were, where practicable, to be given fresh air on the poop, and useful employment that did not require labour or "masculine effort". Other instructions went to practical aspects of sailing including the arrangement of watches and manoeuvres of tacking and wearing (gybing) the ship. Comprehensive instructions were included as to the stationing and the duties of the crew in response to fire alarms in particular. Instruction 73 required the Cook to bring a small quantity of dinner and breakfast for examination by the commanding officer or Officer of the Watch, who was required to report to the captain if at any time he found the provisions ill-cooked or inferior in quality.

These Captain's Instructions were obviously well regarded as they were adopted with little or no change in many ships of the fledgling United States Navy. They could be seen in the USS *Philadelphia* in 1803, and, for example, in the *USS President* a decade later. In the latter case, a manuscript exists showing Keats's original instructions endorsed with the handwritten alterations made by the captain of the *President*, to suit his particular application. They survived for several generations in the pre-Civil War navy.[123]

**Historical Memoirs of
Admiral Sir Richard Goodwin Keats, GCB**

Second Battle of Algeciras

In March 1801 he was appointed to command the *Superb* of 74 guns; [and] having with the *Venerable*, under the orders of Sir S. Hood, escorted a numerous convoy to 12 degrees north latitude, [They departed Portsmouth on 31 March escorting a large East India convoy past Madeira. They returned on 27 April, having captured the Spanish ship Santa Teresa and brig Virgin del Rosario in the vicinity of the Canary Islands on 17 April, as well as the Audacieux of 14 guns and fifty men captured on 5 April when they also retook the Nancy. They then escorted a further convoy as far as Cape Verde (Map 4).] both ships proceeded off Cádiz, where in the month of June, Sir J. Saumarez arrived and took the command of the whole squadron, consisting of seven sail of the line.

Rear Admiral Saumarez's orders were to use his best endeavours to prevent the enemy's ships in Cádiz from putting to sea or should they sail, to follow them and take and destroy them. He was also to keep a good look-out for any French squadron which may attempt either to join the Spanish ships at Cádiz, or pass through the Straits; and to use his best endeavours to intercept, and to take or destroy it.[124]

On the 5th July, the admiral received information that three French ships of the line, in their passage out of the Mediterranean, had anchored in the Bay of Algeciras, and immediately sailed in search of them with six sail of the line. At that moment the *Superb* was off San Lucar, eighteen miles to the north, and though the *Thames* frigate was sent to recall her, she was prevented by light airs and calms from re-joining the squadron, which had the advantage of a good breeze of wind. In the afternoon of the same day Captain Keats spoke to a neutral which had passed the English squadron and had been followed by the French ships in the Straits.

Uncertain from this information whether the enemy had cleared the Straits or not, and under no apprehensions, from the Admiral's superiority, of the issue of a battle, and confident in his own feelings and belief that the *Superb* was thrown out either for the chase or battle, Captain Keats judged it his duty, in the admiral's absence, to keep an eye on the enemy's ships in Cádiz, rather than follow him in such a state of uncertainty and therefore continued on the station.

Having been detached on the Admiral's orders to watch the entrance to the River Guadalquivir (Map 2),[125] Keats was somewhat distant from the main fleet. Saumarez intended that the *Superb* follow the squadron to the Gibraltar Straits, however, light winds saw the vessel sent with those orders delayed, and the *Superb* herself was still lying becalmed with the *Thames* frigate and *Pasley* brig several hours after she had lost sight of the rear most of the squadron. She then received inaccurate information from an American vessel recently exited from the Mediterranean that a French squadron of three sail of the line had already come out of Algeciras Bay, and was last seen standing over to the African shore with Admiral Linois, presumed to be heading east, back to Toulon. It was anticipated the squadrons would meet at a time that, given the delay and the lack of wind, would prevent the *Superb* arriving to be of use. Given that the engagement would see six British sail of the line against three French, there was no fear in Keats's mind as to the result of any contest. On the strength of that information it was thought best to remain off Cádiz to keep watch over the immeasurably superior force anchored there and by his presence dissuade them from attempting a break out.[126]

Although Saumarez outnumbered the French, the latter had not gone east but were anchored, warped inshore under the protection of shore batteries and groups of gun-boats strategically placed in Algeciras Bay opposite the fort of Gibraltar. Seeing the enemy at anchor as they rounded Cabrita point early on the morning of 7 July Saumarez launched his attack on the anchorage forthwith, signalling all ships to engage the enemy as they arrived up. A failing breeze and extensive shoals, together with some confusion regarding the plan, cruelled his chances of a coordinated assault. The *Pompée* was disabled and unable to deploy a stern anchor, drifted into a position from which she could do no damage and worse, interfered with the *Venerable's* line of fire. Having passed the enemy, the *Hannibal* (74) attempted to tack between them and the shore. Unable to manoeuvre in the fickle breeze she grounded with her bow to their broadsides, and was ultimately forced to strike her colours.[127]

Her captain, Solomon Ferris, wrote in the official narrative at his court martial (at which he was most honourably acquitted) that Saumarez signalled for a withdrawal prior to her surrender.[128] Brenton proffers a contrary view[129], but James sets out evidence taken from the logs of the flagship *Caesar* and the sloop *Calpe* that is consistent with the statement of Captain Ferris. The decision of the Court Martial seems similarly to support that interpretation.[130] In any event the remainder of the severely damaged squadron was eventually ordered to withdraw to Gibraltar after a bruising engagement that lasted some seven hours.

Reflecting on the failure of this attack, Parkinson acknowledges that Saumarez's concern was to defeat the enemy before Spanish ships he thought no longer under blockade at Cádiz could reinforce them. However, in his opinion the Spanish were unlikely to act with undignified haste, and there had been no immediate need to join battle. Saumarez could have been relying on his experience at the battle of the Nile, but in that instance, plans were well-formed and the captains were well briefed. In the absence of an urgent need to act a better course may have been to study the battlefield, plan, acquire local pilots, and wait for a steady wind, so his attack, described by Collingwood as, "A hardy measure that many men of as good judgement would not have attempted",[131] could be better planned and executed. Parkinson continues: "A day's pause for reflection would also have given him another ship, the *Superb*, commanded by an officer who was reputed to be the best seaman in the navy, better even than Sir Edward Pellew."[132] Regardless of whether the best decision was made, the outcome was regrettable, and a failure, whatever the cause, remains just that. Saumarez took six sail of the line into battle against three, admittedly well defended and supported French and emerged with only five, all severely cut up. For reasons which remain unexplained Saumarez maintained a brave face in official communication to the extent of reporting to the Consul to Tangier that he had completely succeeded in disabling the enemy ships, that would be rendered entirely useless for a considerable time.[133] That was clearly untrue and he conceded in private letters of the same date that he had "failed in an enterprise with the squadron of three French line-of-battle ships at anchor off Algeciras".[134]

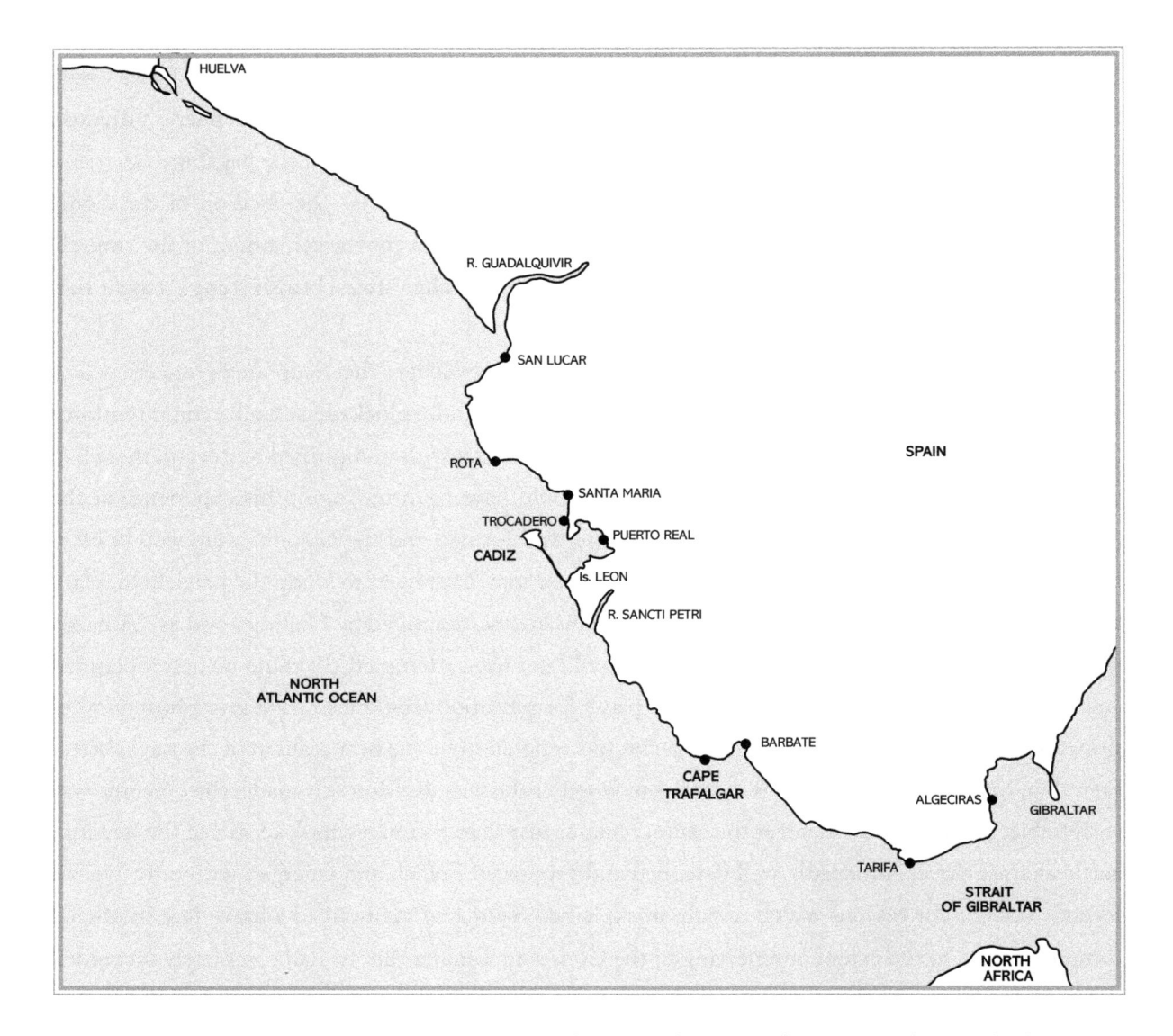

Map 2: *Algeciras: The coast of Spain – Huelva to Gibraltar*

Where Saumarez showed true merit was in his refusal to accept his initial defeat, his herculean effort to repair his badly damaged ships and in regrouping ready to resume the attack. This he did in only a matter of days, bringing on "one of the most famous scenes in naval history".[135]

As a result of the chronic difficulty Spain had in manning her ships it had been agreed between France and Spain that six Spanish sail of the line, which at the time were lying in Cádiz under the command of Rear Admiral Dumanoir Le Pelley, should be transferred to the French navy. It was initially proposed they co-operate in an attack upon British interests in Portugal, but this did not eventuate and they were then destined to join a squadron to transport as many as 32,000 troops from

Italy to repel the British from Egypt.[136] Rear Admiral Dumanoir had sailed from Brest with the intended reinforcements, including the frigates, *Libre* and *Indienne*, that had been chased into Cádiz by the *Superb* and *Venerable* on 13 June.

Admiral Linois sailed from Toulon headed to Cádiz with three sail of the line *(Formidable (80), Desaix (74)* and *Indomptable (74))* and the frigate *Muiron (36)*, to join with the six newly acquired French ships under the command of Dumanoir and an additional six Spanish ships also lying in Cádiz under the command of Vice-Admiral Don Moreno. On 3 July Linois's squadron captured the *Speedy*, a brig of fourteen guns under Commander Lord Cochrane, and learned that Cádiz was blockaded by the superior force of Saumarez. Linois therefore bore up for Algeciras, and seeing only the sloop *Calpe* (14), Commander Dundas, at Gibraltar, he anchored under the shelter of the Spanish fortifications on the other side of the bay where he was subsequently attacked by Saumarez.[137]

Following the first battle Admiral Linois had no desire to have another contest on unequal terms, but given his position it seemed impossible to avoid one, either by remaining in the harbour or by seeking to escape. Having no dockyard at Algeciras to undertake the major repairs required, he needed assistance to get his ships safely into Cádiz. Via message sent overland, he applied to French Rear-Admiral Dumanoir and Spanish Admiral Mazarredo to have the reinforcements sent immediately from Cádiz to his relief at Algeciras. Receiving no reply, he asked 'what can they be afraid of?', and wrote again seeking ships, hoping they would arrive before the British could be reinforced and mount a second attack, which he feared would be in the form of an attempt to burn his fleet in the anchorage. His request ended; "I have just received advice that the enemy intends burning us at our anchorage. It is in your power to save for the Republic three fine ships of the line and a frigate by merely ordering the Spanish squadron to come and seek us."[138] Mazarredo heeded the call and on 9 July Vice-Admiral Moreno – with five Spanish and one Franco-Spanish sail of the line, including two of their biggest ships of 112 guns, and three frigates and a lugger – repaired to the outer road of Cádiz to be ready for a start with the land breeze on the next morning.[139]

Having seen the squadron assembling, Keats kept a close watch and when at daylight they put to sea, the frigate *Thames (32)*, brig *Pasley (16)* and *Superb* preceded them to Gibraltar. Keats shortened sail for a period to ascertain the strength of the enemy, then the British came together under a crowd of canvas, signalling the approach of the pursuing enemy as they arrived off Gibraltar at 3.15pm. They had scarcely rounded Cabrita Point before the Spanish squadron (save for the *St. Antoine*, which unable to fetch out, had anchored and did not sail until later) was seen in pursuit and to then anchor in Algeciras Bay joining the French. The *St. Antoine* joined them the following day.

On the 9th the Spanish squadron put to sea and Captain Keats, thinking it would lead him to his admiral preceded its course, entered the Straits, and joined Sir James Saumarez at Gibraltar, whilst the Spanish squadron effected a junction with that of France in the Bay of Algeciras. Captain Keats had now the mortification to learn the result of the battle fought on the 6th July[5] and to know that if he had followed Sir Jas. Saumarez he might have been present.

Scholars have noted Keats's different reflections on learning he had missed the first battle. The original memoir in the first person records he "judged wrong" in remaining off Cádiz and taking upon himself the watching of the enemy's squadron in that port.[140] Saumarez records him as having been "mortified", but not wrong.[141] This memoir reflects the personal disappointment of having missed the action. It does not concede the decision was wrong. One can be confident a correct decision has been made yet still lament the missed opportunity that results.

The Log of the *Superb*, written at the time without the benefit of hindsight or the opportunity for rationalisation, accords perfectly with these memoirs. Having received a report that Linois was sailing east (when he was in fact bearing up to Algeciras), Keats rightly concluded he would never reach the action, if any, in time, and determined he could best help by continuing to watch the powerful Spanish squadron at Cádiz.[142] The presence of the *Superb* at the first battle might well have made a material difference, but there was nothing that could be done about the lack of wind. Given that Saumarez launched his attack immediately on reaching the bay and the fact the *Superb* was becalmed eighteen miles north of Cádiz it is unlikely he would have arrived in time to have been of assistance even if he had immediately followed the fleet. The conditions were out of his control and Keats played the hand he had been dealt. The circumstances support the contention that he felt keenly any conflict between orders and what he thought to be the preferred course in an unfolding series of events. It is also clear that although no blame was attached by others, he never forgot he had the misfortune to miss the battle.[143]

In the following days the British worked around the clock repairing their ships under the direction of navy commissioner Captain Sir Alexander Ball. Now considerably out-numbered Saumarez was at risk of himself being attacked at anchor. He was advised the French and Spanish ships were likely headed to Cartagena, but was also confident they would not be in a condition to sail for at least two weeks. He sent urgent messages to Lord Keith in the Eastern Mediterranean seeking

---

5   See Memoir of Sir James Saumarez (Ralfe).

reinforcements be sent to his aid.[144] However Moreno was not preparing for a long voyage to Egypt as Saumarez assumed. As became clear only a few days later, he was intent on removing his squadron in its hastily repaired state to the relative security of Cádiz without delay.

When at dawn on 12 July the French and Spanish were seen preparing their sails the British ships (other than the *Pompée*) were, as a result of the round the clock labours of sailors and the dockyards, again capable of being taken to sea. The enemy got underway at noon in a fresh easterly, making to assemble off Cabrita point to the south-west before forming up to exit the Straits for Cádiz, sailing in two lines abreast, the three French ships in the van and the powerful Spanish ships in the rear covering the retreat. The winds on the far side of the bay faded to the extent the enemy had difficulty in forming up and even had to anchor for a period to avoid the shore. The damaged *Hannibal* which was to have sailed under the protection of the van was unable to get out of the bay without a tow from the *Indienne* and returned to the anchorage, but the formation of the combined fleet otherwise remained as planned.

Reinforcements from Lord Keith 'expected hourly' had not yet materialised, but Saumarez saw and seized his opportunity.

Despite the inequality of firepower, the British nonetheless went in chase. As the *Caesar* warped out of the mole (breakwater) in the afternoon the Rear Admiral's flag was re-hoisted and the signal made for battle. Her band played *Come cheer up, my lads, 'tis to glory we steer (Heart of Oak)*, and the garrison band answered with *Britons Strike Home*. Captain Brenton proclaimed the scene as animating beyond description. Every part of the Rock, the line wall, mole head and batteries were crowded with onlookers as the British formed up off Europa Point to the south east in line astern on port tack. With the wind in this part of the bay still fresh from the east five sail of the line were heading out in pursuit of nine. At 7.00pm, they wore together and stood on starboard tack until shortly before 8.00pm, when they cleared Cabrita Point. The *Caesar* led as they bore away to stand after the retreating fleet, which now also benefited from the building east wind.

The disappointment, however, which he felt on this occasion, was fully compensated for on the 12th, when the enemy's combined squadron, consisting of ten sail of the line, including the *Hannibal*, and three frigates, got under sail from Algeciras, as did Sir Jas. Saumarez, with five sail of the line (the *Caesar, Spencer, Venerable, Superb* and *Audacious, Thames* frigate, *Calpe* sloop and *Louisa*, armed brig) from Gibraltar. About the close of the day, the enemy having sent back the *Hannibal* and cleared Cabrita point bore up with an easterly wind to run through the straits as did also Sir Jas. Saumarez; but from the obscurity of the night, or some mistake of signals, he was not immediately followed; which being observed by Captain Keats, he determined to place the *Superb* within hail of the *Caesar*, and which his advantage in sailing enabled him easily to perform.

A little before nine, being close up, he was hailed by the admiral and asked if he could see any of the enemy's ships, as they were not visible from the *Caesar*. One only was observed from the *Superb*, and Captain Keats was then ordered to make sail and attack the rear of the enemy, keeping in shore of them. The foresail and top-gallant sails were immediately ordered to be set, the *Superb* being previously under topsails only, though the *Caesar* had her fore-sail and top gallant sails. The wind soon freshened to a hard gale in the Straits and the Superb went at 11½ knots, and soon got sight of the enemy. At eleven she was drawing fast up with them; the admiral was then dimly in sight, but, from the darkness of the night, was soon lost sight of by the signal officer. At twenty minutes past eleven the *Superb* was ranging up alongside of a three-decker, the northernmost ship at that time of the enemy, and shortly afterwards Captain Keats opened his fire upon her from her larboard guns. This is supposed to have been at first returned by a ship on the larboard side of the one attacked by the *Superb*, the shot of which not only reached the *Superb*, but also the ship to which she was directly opposed.

This circumstance added to the surprise occasioned by a sudden and perhaps unexpected attack, led to mistake, and that confusion and disorder which soon manifested itself by a general cannonade throughout the enemy's squadron.

In about ten minutes the ship first opposed to the *Superb* was observed to be on fire, and as the wind blew fresh at the time, the flames spread with surprising rapidity. The disorder now increased, and in the terror and dismay which fell upon the enemy the ship on fire ran aboard another of the same class, or was herself run aboard of, and the flames communicating to the second, both were soon in flames and finally blew up. The *Superb* herself had a narrow escape from the same dreadful calamity, particularly by an explosion which took place near the after magazine. Sir J. Saumarez having arrived up, and the destruction of the ships first attacked being no longer doubtful, the foresail, but not the top gallant sails, was again set, and the *Superb* steered to close with the next nearest of the enemy, then about one point on the larboard bow, and which, on approaching, was evidently one of two decks, bearing a broad pendant, and having her starboard foremast studding-sail boom out. About twelve o'clock, the *Superb* having obtained a favourable situation abreast, brought the enemy to action with the larboard guns, when a sharp contest was maintained as close as the circumstances arising from the excessive wild steerage would allow; he then hauled his wind, and the action continued close till about half past twelve, when the enemy struck his colours, and proved to be the *St. Antoine* (formerly the *San Antonio* in the Spanish service) of 74 guns, commanded by the Chef-de-Division Le Ray, with a complement of 730 men, of whom all the Officers and 530 of the crew, were French. The wild steerage of the *St. Antoine,* and her hauling the wind, occasioned the combined squadron to get some distance to the westward by the time she was taken; in about ten minutes after which the *Caesar* and *Venerable* passed in pursuit of the enemy, the former pursuing the main body, whilst the latter chased one (the *Formidable* of 84 guns) which had hauled towards the Spanish shore, and separated from the rest of the squadron. In about half an hour after the admiral, the *Spencer* passed, and soon after the *Thames* frigate, which Captain Keats being anxious to join the admiral, hailed, and ordered her to lie by the prize, intending to spike her guns, by which the frigate would have been master of the *St. Antoine,* but which order, it appears, was not understood by her captain, and she passed on. Shortly after, the attention of those on the deck of the *Superb* was called to the cries of distress close at hand, and almost immediately afterwards a Spanish launch came alongside, filled with men nearly naked, who scrambled into the ship. Before an interpreter could be found, they had huddled aft and thrown themselves on their knees, and with uplifted hands besought protection, or in an act of devotion were returning thanks to their Creator for their deliverance. It was, however, soon ascertained that the boat belonged to the *San Carlos* [sic.] into which all that could had jumped at the time the two first rates were foul and in flames; and it so happened that an officer and seventeen men from one ship, and an officer and eighteen men from the other, were thus miraculously preserved.

An officer and a small party were at length thrown onboard the *St. Antoine*, but the weather was too unfavourable to remove the prisoners till the morning, when it having moderated, that necessary work was begun; but at the moment a cannonade was heard at a distance, and Captain Keats concluding it was a renewal of the contest, immediately recalled his boats, and made sail to join the admiral with the least possible delay, leaving the prize, in her half-secured state, to the care of the *Calpe* and *Louisa*. The haze which had existed having cleared off, the *Caesar* was discovered some leagues to leeward, which Captain Keats soon after joined, the remains of the enemy's squadron being then visible some leagues to the northward, but effected their escape.

The conduct of Captain Keats on the memorable 12th July, and the result of that contest gave conviction to the world, that, however arduous, however apparently impracticable, any proposed naval attempt may be, English seamen are not to be deterred from it by any prospect of difficulty or danger, but will exert themselves as far as men can do, and at least deserve success, when led on by those who are worthy to command them.

On going onboard the *Caesar*, Captain Keats was received by Sir James Saumarez in a manner the most gratifying to his feelings; and the admiral observed, that he could not find words to express his sense of the service the *Superb* had rendered to the country the preceding night. He was then ordered to conduct the *St. Antoine* to Gibraltar and in so doing passed through the fragments of the two Spanish ships which had blown up on the night of 12th July; a melancholy spectacle, which was viewed with feelings of commiseration, especially as the *Superb* had herself narrowly escaped the same dreadful calamity. In common with those employed, Captain Keats received the thanks of Parliament and the Lords of the Admiralty, as a farther mark of their approbation, promoted his first lieutenant Samuel Jackson, to the rank of commander.

Lieutenant Jackson was put on board the prize with one boat's crew to take command of 300 French seamen and sailors and about 500 Spanish. Some of the latter sought to resist, but were put down by the French sailors who considered they had been fairly captured in battle. The squadron returned to Gibraltar triumphant. Every point of the rock was crowded with people who had seen and heard the explosions in the night but were otherwise uninformed of the outcome and were now happy to see the fleet return largely unharmed. The Governor had the Royal Standard raised and a 21-gun salute fired as they entered the harbour – and again on the 15th – followed by a fireworks display. The officers were the toast of the town and honoured by balls and social events.[145]

The Secretary to the Admiralty wrote that the Lords Commissioners expressed their highest endorsement of the gallantry and good conduct displayed and desired it be communicated to Captains Hood and Keats in the strongest terms the sense their lordships were pleased to entertain of their meritorious services.[146] Parliament voted its thanks, which motion was proposed by First Lord of the Admiralty, Earl St. Vincent, and seconded by Lord Viscount Nelson, both pronouncing the victory as having never been surpassed in the annals of naval history. The Duke of Clarence added his support to the motion, saying he did so as a professional man, to express his concurrence with the words of St. Vincent and Nelson, stating:

Two of the Captains who had the good fortune of the day had been brother officers, Captain Keats, and Captain Hood, and he would venture to say, the Navy had not more promising Officers. He had been four years and a half in the last war Midshipman in the same watch with Captain Keats, and he knew him to be a most brave and able Officer. He was persuaded that whenever the country should be engaged in another war Captain Keats was sure to eminently distinguish himself.[147]

Keats's more fulsome account of the battle titled, Narrative of the Services of His Majesty's Ship Superb, 74, on the night of the 12 July 1801 and the two following days, by her then Captain, Sir Richard Goodwin Keats G.C.B. &c. was published thirty years later, having been found in the papers of Earl St. Vincent after his death (see Appendix III). First-hand accounts from Captain Brenton (Caesar), Captain Hood (Venerable) and the French commanders can be found in the second volume of the Memoirs of Admiral Saumarez.[148]

The Superb, Captain Richard Keats, in action off Cape Trafalgar on the night of July 12th 1801, compels the San Antonio, of 74 guns to strike her colours. Jahleel Brenton, Keats Family collection.

The enemy fleet comprised eight French ships, plus the captured *Hannibal*, that did not ultimately participate, and seven Spanish. They included two Santa Ana class three-deckers of 112 guns each (*Real Carlos* and *San Hermenegildo*), which were among the most heavily armed ships in the world. This amounted to a total of more than 970 guns against the British fleet of six ships and 434 guns, and the guns of the enemy being much heavier the weight of metal was said to favour the combined fleet by a factor of more than three to one.[149]

William James often references weight of metal and it is clearly a factor not to be disregarded. Others, such as Laughton, do not deny this, but suggest accuracy and rate of fire are two other factors which more often than not prove decisive. Two 32-pound balls that hit their mark are more effective than one 42-pound shot even if it finds its mark, although many did not.[150] This is where the crew of the *Superb* reaped the reward from the hours devoted to process under Keats's regime for gunnery practice. It is evident *Superb* managed to discharge three broadsides in rapid succession, quite nullifying the on-paper advantage of her adversaries.

The combined fleet was primarily concerned with making safe harbour at Cádiz, rather than engaging in battle. Their superiority in number and firepower reportedly led them to believe they could slip away in the moonless night unmolested and would be safe from attack by the battered British fleet and to a complacency that was to have devastating and unequalled consequences.

Whilst their conduct would support such a contention, in fairness to their commander it should be said Mareno's sailing orders of 11 July did contemplate an attack from the rear. In this event they were to abandon the formation of line abreast, which as was obvious in hindsight exposes multiple ships to the same broadside. On signal from the admiral they were, by uniform movement, to re-form in line ahead towards either the Spanish or African shore as signalled– it being of the "utmost importance that the fire from none of the ships should interfere, or be embarrassed with that of others in this squadron..."[151] The contingency had been addressed. The shortcoming was in failing to execute. The attack took them by such surprise the signal was never made. It might be thought that in any event the plan failed to appreciate that ships from two separate navies that had never before sailed in company would not be capable of the choreography required to execute the uniform movement necessary to meet an advancing enemy with the wind behind them in the conditions. The confusion that so rapidly enveloped the retreating allies demonstrates they would never have preserved, let alone reformed, any regular order.[152]

Though on counting their fleet at one time the Spanish crew reckoned the number had increased by one, the report to that effect to the captain, still dining in his cabin, was disregarded. The captain and senior officers, along with a number of the young aristocracy of Spain who had attended

Algeciras on learning the outcome of the first battle in order to be present at the fleet's triumphal return to Cádiz with the prize, remained in the cabin until fired upon. They were killed or injured in the first broadside, the arrival of which was the first and last they knew of the battle. The fleet was then left desperately short of leadership at the time of need. The plan to alter their sailing order was never enacted, and the result was exactly that which the orders had sought to avoid. The *Superb* was sailing in silence with her stern light concealed and all her other lights shaded, whereas the Spanish ships were fully lit, the officers visible in the cabin and light coming from their gun ports.

The victory was all the more remarkable because, instead of simply harassing the rear of the squadron to slow its progress so that the rest of the British ships be enabled to catch up, *Superb*, quite regardless of the fact she was alone, launched an attack on the vastly superior force and single-handedly destroyed or captured three sail of the line, suffering losses of just fifteen wounded. Lieutenant Waller lost a leg. The others were less severely wounded.

As the *Superb* came within three cables [approximately 500 yards] of the enemy undetected, Keats recalled:

> *I then said the opportunity is too advantageous to be lost. The officers had been apprised, everything was ready, and in that situation, at twenty or thirty minutes past eleven, we opened our fire. Extraordinary as it may appear, I am now convinced the enemy was not aware of his situation. This fatal security may possibly be ascribed, in part, to a habitual indolence, to confidence in their numbers, to our not having raised suspicion by making signals, or firing on our approach, and to their not suspecting an attack from a single ship.*

Keats was surprised his first broadside met with no return fire, and still more so when the *San Hermenegildo* – towards which his victim was sheering, and which probably had received some of the broadside of the *Superb* – her gunnery keener than her recognition opened fire at her compatriot, the *Real Carlos* that had first been fired into by the *Superb*. That ship, now receiving fire from both sides, in turn fired wildly on both sides. She sheered back towards the *Superb* from whom she received a second and a third broadside, bringing down her fore-topmast. Confusion amongst the Spanish was general, exacerbated by the *Superb's* first opponent being on fire before the third broadside had been completely discharged. The violence of the wind caused the flames to spread rapidly, and the fire quickly became so intense it could be seen from Gibraltar now many miles astern The *San Hermenegildo*, still believing the ship on her beam to be her enemy closed on her to send a raking broadside through her length from the unprotected stern. In doing so in the strong wind she misjudged and sheered too close with the result their rigging became entangled and very soon *San Hermenegildo* was engulfed in flame as well.

After little more than ten minutes, the destruction of the two Spanish ships became inevitable as they dispatched one another "with devastating thoroughness, falling behind the rest of the fleet, to be lost in fire and explosion".[153] Seeing no reason to remain amongst them Keats ordered the foresails on the *Superb* to be reset, it now being too windy for the top-gallants. She then closed on the next enemy ship of the line which was the *St. Antoine* sometimes given her Spanish appellation; *San Antonio*. She was near and a little on the larboard bow. She was better prepared, but after a spirited engagement by 12.30am she too was completely silenced. About the same time (depending upon which of the ships' logs is considered most reliable), the fire onboard the *Real Carlos* reached her magazine and she blew up. The *San Hermenegildo* suffered the same fate a little before 1.00am. The concussion was felt in Gibraltar and as far away as Cádiz, some 70 miles distant.

The result was described thus: "…all the damage was done by a single ship with her consorts doing no more than fire into a single wretched ship [the *St. Antoine*] which had already surrendered".[154] Allen (1842) notes that one would naturally expect that the meritorious conduct of Captain Keats would gain for him some especial mark of favour [a knighthood], or that he would at least be particularly mentioned in the public reports, however:

> *The casual reader of the Admiral's dispatch might be led to consider that the destruction of the Spanish three-deckers was achieved by the Caesar. Future generations, however, will determine upon whom the real merit should have rested, and the name of Captain Keats will, as in justice it should do, bear the most conspicuous place.*[155]

The later edition of Allen (1852) simply records, "the meritorious conduct of Captain Keats gained for him no especial mark of favour, neither was he publicly named in the letter of Sir James Saumarez".[156]

Saumarez was immediately created a Knight Companion of the Bath and nearly two years later was granted an annual pension of £1200 for life. He wrote to Sir Thomas Troubridge that he regarded his receipt of the Order of the Bath in place of a peerage as a great injustice, which mortified him more than he could express. It was an omission upon which he became somewhat fixated and about which he was still making representations in 1814.[157] But for the ignominious end to the first battle, he may well have received a peerage, and consequently Keats possibly the Bath Star.

Keats, on the other hand, was always keen to emphasise that Saumarez's contribution to the battle was modest. The *Caesar* was not within sight when the action was commenced by the *Superb* and played no part in the destruction of the Spanish three-deckers. Further, the *St. Antoine*, being the single wretched ship referred to by Allen, had quite clearly already surrendered ten minutes before Saumarez arrived on the scene. The failure on the part of Saumarez to make more of the role of the *Superb* in the official dispatch, despite the warm congratulations given in the immediate aftermath of battle caused Keats much distress. Again, there is a sensitivity regarding the allocation of credit.

In view of intermittent but ongoing undercurrents in the relationship between Saumarez and Keats – that continued even after the latter's death – these differences warrant more detailed examination. The report by Saumarez and the description provided by Edward Pelham Brenton (younger brother to Jahleel Brenton, the captain of the *Caesar*) in his *Naval History* make considerably more of the role of Saumarez and the *Caesar*, and, as James says, scant mention of the credit due to the *Superb*. Saumarez had earlier quarrelled with Nelson about the perceived lack of recognition he received for his role at the Battle of the Nile. In this instance, based on corroborated times and distances, it is submitted the version of Keats and James is to be preferred.

At 10.00pm, Keats records the *Caesar* and one other ship in sight astern. At 11.00pm, he puts the *Caesar*, "seen with difficulty", three to four miles astern, and just before commencing action, Keats is advised – and confirms for himself on going aft – that she could no longer be kept sight of. At 11.20pm, the *Superb* opened fire on the *Real Carlos*. By the time she had fired her third broadside just a few minutes later, the target was on fire. Ten minutes later, the fire had been communicated to her companion, the *San Hermenegildo*.

E.P. Brenton says the ships took fire "as the *Caesar* was rounding to, so as to open her broadside upon them".[158] For this to be so, the *Caesar* would have had to close four miles on the *Superb*, herself still under sail in a fresh gale in under twenty minutes. This would require her to sail at least five miles in one-third of an hour. Even allowing for margins of error in estimates of time and distance, she would need to be making in excess of twelve knots. This was simply not the case as the *Superb*, fresh out of port, was sailing at eleven knots and had been opening distance between herself and the hastily-repaired *Caesar*. More to the point, Ross, in his memoir of Saumarez,[159] notes, consistent with Keats's narrative, that the Spanish ships were perceived to have taken fire prior to his arrival, and the *Caesar* accordingly passed on, to close with the *St. Antoine*. It is most improbable that the *Caesar* was in any position to fire upon the Spanish at a time before their destruction by the *Superb* was already assured. The *Superb* ceased to molest them between 11.35pm and 11.40pm, resetting her foresail in pursuit of the *St. Antoine.*

Captain Brenton's reports have Saumarez seeing the magnificent Spanish ships on fire shortly after the *Superb* had opened her fire at a time when the *Caesar* was some distance off, orders having just been sent down to the officers at their quarters to fire as soon as the guns would bear:[160]

> *I was at this time standing on the poop ladder, near the Admiral, when he seized me by the shoulder, and, pointing to the flames bursting out, exclaimed, 'My God, sir, look there! The day is ours!' A more magnificent scene never presented itself, as may be easily imagined than two ships of such immense magnitude as the Spanish first-rates, on board each other, with a fresh gale, the sea running high, and their sails in the utmost confusion. The flames, ascending the rigging with the rapidity of lightning, soon communicated to the canvas, which instantly became one sheet of fire. A very general feeling of regret and sympathy seemed to be quickly experienced around us when we beheld the Spanish colours brilliantly illuminated by the dreadful conflagration instead of the French. The unfortunate Spaniards, having become at once the tools and the victims of France, were objects of our sincere commiseration.*
>
> *The Superb was now seen a little way on the starboard bow, engaged with one of the enemy's ships, while several others were in sight at a distance ahead. We kept our course, and after having fired a broadside into the Superb's opponent, (which, however, was already nearly silenced), continued the chase, followed by the Venerable...*

We know this second engagement did not commence until midnight, twenty minutes after the Spanish ships had been left to their fate. By the time Saumarez made his exclamation the *Superb* had not only singlehandedly assured the destruction of the two Spanish first-raters, but had moved on and was engaged with St. Antoine which ship was completely silenced by around 12:30am, Chef de Division Julien Le Ray having hailed his surrender at 12:25am.

The *St. Antoine* hauled down her colours, hoisted and hauled down a light frequently in token of submission and hailed repeatedly to say they had struck. As they had been steering widely in this action or were close-hauled with little headway, the *Caesar* had now (an hour after the engagement was commenced by the *Superb*) been afforded the chance to catch up, and fired into the surrendered ship. Captain Hood of the *Venerable* said he was perfectly satisfied she had struck, but fired because the *Caesar* had done so.

Keats acknowledges that the signals from the *St. Antoine* may have misled the others, as a broad pendant was flying some fathoms from the truck, the halyards having been shot away and become entangled aloft. The crew had hauled it down and intended to have it hoisted again with an English flag over it but, unable to find an English jack, they hoisted an English pendant. Despite being clearly visible to the *Superb*, the pendant was "perhaps not so visible to the *Caesar*", who the memoir records as having arrived ten minutes after the enemy struck.

The narrative records a statement from Saumarez to Keats acknowledging that at the time he "thought we were doing wrong, and said so at the time". His dispatch says only:

> *…the Caesar passed, ⟦the three deckers⟧ to close with the ship engaged by the Superb; but, by the cool and determined fire kept on her, which must ever reflect the highest credit on the discipline of that ship, she was completely silenced, and soon after hauled down her colours.*[161]

He wrote to Lord Keith, "Our friend Keats so soon silenced her that she has scarcely sustained any other damage than in her mast and yards".[162]

In confirmation of the distances above stated, Saumarez remarked to Keats the next day that he was surprised how quickly the *Superb* got away from the *Caesar* the night before. Even though he thought it dangerous to do so, given the strength of the wind, Saumarez had ordered a studding-sail prepared to avoid losing sight of the *Superb*.[163] Nevertheless, Brenton writes that the *St. Antione*, already beaten, "surrendered when the *Caesar* came abreast of her", and praises Keats only for the "gallant manner in which he arrested the flight of the enemy", with no particular mention of the destruction of the two three-deckers of 112 guns or the capture of the *St. Antoine* (74).[164] Ross, in his memoir of Saumarez, includes a footnote acknowledging the claim that the *St. Antoine* had surrendered, but says it cannot be so as she had fired at the *Caesar*.[165] This is not otherwise mentioned and is inconsistent even with Saumarez's official dispatch and the passage quoted earlier.

Order of Battle 12 July 1801

Ship	Guns	Captain	Notes
Britain			
Caesar	80	Rear Admiral James Saumarez, Jahleel Brenton	Not actively engaged
Venerable	74	Samuel Hood	Heavily engage with Formidable, badly damaged, 18 killed, 87 wounded, driven ashore, but recovered and towed to Gibraltar
Superb	74	Richard Keats	Heavily engaged, light damage, 14 wounded. Destroyed the San Hermenegildo (112), Destroyed the Real Carlos (112), Captured the St. Antoine (74)
Audacious	74	Shuldham Peard	Not actively engaged
Spencer	74	Henry Darby	Not actively engaged
Thames	32	Askew Holles	Heavily engaged with Formidable, no damage
Calpe	14	Commander George Dundas	Not actively engaged
Louisa	12	Lieutenant William Truscott	Not actively engaged
Total British guns at sea	434		
Pompée	74	Charles Sterling	Unfit to sail, remained in Gibraltar
Portugal			
Carlotta	48	Crawfurd Duncan	Portuguese, believing a peace had been made with France was prevented from engaging; not included in tally
Spain			
Real Carlos	112	Don J Esquerro	Destroyed by Superb, with the loss of most of her crew
San Hermenegildo	112	Don M Emparan	Destroyed by Superb, with the loss of most of her crew
San Fernando	96	Don J Malina	Not actively engaged
Argonauta	80	Don J Herrara Devila	Not actively engaged
San Augustin	74	Don R Jopete	Not actively engaged
Santa Sabina	36	Vice Admiral J Moreno Admiral Charles Linois	Spanish custom was for flag officers to transfer to a frigate. Linois was convinced to follow Moreno to Sabina. Lightly damaged, 1 killed, 5 wounded.
Perla/ Clara	36	Unclear	The Perla (referred to in Keats's narrative as Clara) was not part of Mareno's squadron, but nevertheless entered the engagement, was badly damaged, and later reportedly sank
Total Spanish guns at sea	546		

Ship	Guns	Captain	Notes
France			
Formidable	80	Amable-Giles Troude	Heavily damaged in engagement with Venerable and Thames, escaped, 20 killed.
Indomptable	80	Claude Touffet	Not actively engaged
Desaix	74	Christy de la Palliere	Not actively engaged
St. Antoine	74	Commodore Julien Le Ray (wounded)	Struck to Superb, suffering significant damage and heavy casualties.
La Muiron	44	J-F Martinecq	Not actively engaged
Libre	36	Guillaume Proteau	Not actively engaged
Vautour	12	Lieutenant Kemel	Not actively engaged
Indienne	42	Pierre Pouyer	Towed Hannibal back to port and did not participate.
Total French guns at sea	**442**		
Hannibal	74		French prize of the first battle, did not participate

Table 2: *The order of battle and summary of losses, second battle of Algeciras, 12 July 1801.*

Keats said that quite apart from the signals made, it should have been obvious that the *St. Antoine* had surrendered as the *Superb* had been laying peaceably alongside the prize for some time before *Caesar* fired. In this he is supported by his crew and the verbal statements of both Hood and Saumarez. The preponderance of evidence from those on the scene indicates the *St. Antoine* surrendered to the *Superb* well before the arrival of Saumarez and Brenton in the *Caesar*. For what it is worth, Commander Cochrane relies upon first-hand accounts to declare the destruction of the Spanish and the capture of the French ship as being the work of the *Superb* alone, the remainder of the squadron being witnesses only.[166]

As he had done in the past Keats goes to some lengths to press the claim of his ship saying "I am thus particular, because in my report I considered, as I felt the right to do, that the *St. Antoine* was taken by the *Superb* alone, and because I think it serves to shew in a strong point of view, the situation of the *Superb*, relatively with the *Caesar* at the time the *Superb* opened her fire on the first-rate." He records his conversation with the Admiral the next morning in confirmation: "I feel that I have said a great deal about the ship I command, but I hope you are not of the opinion I have said too much". He replied; 'That is impossible. It differs in nothing material from my own observations"[167] The *Superb*, along with the *Thames* and *Venerable* (who engaged the *Formidable*) were the only British ships to get into the action. The remainder did little more than by their presence convince the French not to turn in support of their Spanish allies, but to leave them to their fate and flea to Cádiz. There is truth to the saying that success has many fathers.

As Allen foretold, despite the omissions in the official dispatches, the daring feat of seamanship and battle craft shown by the *Superb* and her crew became legendary, renowned throughout the navy and the world at large, and it was described as "one of the most brilliant, skilful and successful attacks upon an overwhelmingly superior force, that occurred during the war".[168] It features in modern works of fiction including C. N. Parkinson's *Touch and Go*, and O'Brian's *Master and Commander*. Both these works and Parkinson's scholarly work, *Britannia Rules*, describe the *Superb* running between the two Spanish three-deckers, firing off simultaneous broadsides, passing ahead under cover of smoke and the night, and leaving the Spanish ships to fire at where she had been. *Master and Commander* being based upon Cochrane's career, it is unsurprising that he makes similar claims.[169] Captain Brenton had negotiated Cochrane's release on parole (his ship the *Speedy* having been captured on 3 July) and he was watching proceedings from the garden of the commissioner's house on Gibraltar. Though he could see the flashes of gunfire in the night, he does not profess to have had direct personal knowledge. He understands his account differs from those of various historians written from dispatches, but says his version of the affair rests upon indisputable authority.[170] Whilst it is hearsay, it is no doubt based on first-hand accounts he received in the aftermath of the battle.

Keats's narrative makes clear that he resolved to make the attack from the wing, and he emphasises the point in his narrative. He says that having been instructed to stay between the fleet and shore, he concluded – though the fleet was considerably nearer the African shore, they now being just off Cape Spartel, the north-westernmost point of Africa – that the Admiral meant him to stay between the enemy and the Spanish shore.

> *I conversed with Captain Jackson, then first-lieutenant of the Superb on the mode of attack, he observed, we could get in amongst a cluster a little on the larboard bow. I replied, but that would not be in compliance with the admiral's order; and we can, with equal advantage, and in obedience to his direction, make the attack on the wing. I determined to do so.*[171]

One would expect this to be definitive, but Cochrane invites us to dismiss the official dispatches on this point. To do so would require the judgement that Keats was so concerned to be seen to be following the order to stay inshore of the enemy that his version is a false reconstruction. The crew of the *Real Carlos* confirmed firing from both sides, which could only be so if she had a ship on each side – the *Superb* on the wing to windward and the *San Hermenegildo* to larboard. Both Keats and the crew of the *Real Carlos* confirm the latter's foremast was carried away by the *Superb*'s opening salvo.

At least some of the shot was high. As Keats states in his narrative, with two ships close to her larboard side it could be expected some shot passed through the rigging of the *Real Carlos* only two cables from the *Superb*, to hit the ship closest on her larboard side, inducing that ship to believe the *Real Carlos* to be an adversary. The matter cannot now be resolved, but it is suggested that Keats provides the more sober, detailed, and authoritative account, consistent with the evidence and, given the overwhelming success of the venture, had no reason to do otherwise. It is much more plausible that others talking around the docks, from whom Cochrane obtained his information, strayed towards hyperbole and dramatisation, given the unprecedented outcome of the engagement.

The conversation with Lieutenant Jackson as to the mode of attack nonetheless illustrates what becomes a recurring theme in Keats's career – that he prefers strict adherence to directives, even when other pathways unfold. Either way, there is no doubt the placement of his ship was advantageous, and in the events that transpired in this instance, entirely successful. Whilst the Spanish ships were mired in confusion that resulted in their mutual destruction the *Superb*, better prepared and drilled, more disciplined, and with lights covered, reset her foresails within minutes and passed further forward, concealed by the night and by smoke to engage the *St. Antoine*.

There was some talk, not alluded to in the memoirs, that the fires on the Spanish ships were due to the use of 'hot shot' by the British, rather than to a combination of freshly tarred sails, wind and misadventure onboard. This intimation caused such offence that Saumarez sent a message ashore under flag of truce to the Spanish commander, Don Joseph de Mazarredo, contradicting such claims. He received a reply that such statements were made only by the ignorant and had received no credit.

The Spanish commander acknowledged that the engagement was conducted in accordance with the rules of war and the well-known manner of combating and characteristic humanity of the British Navy. He stated that the duties of a state of war had been reconciled in a manner to alleviate miseries not connected with the great object and to secure friendship between the powers that had for a time been suspended.

This response was immediately followed by an exchange of prisoners: the crew of the *St. Antoine* in exchange for those captured from the *Hannibal* and *Speedy* days earlier, along with release from parole of Cochrane of the *Speedy* in exchange for the second captain of the *St. Antoine*.[172] The Spanish sailors taken onboard the *Superb*, by a handwritten account given to Keats, confirmed the foremast of the *Real Carlos* had been "shot away by the first broadside and in returning fire, which they did from both sides, the fore-top-sail, which was hanging down, caught fire, and occasioned the conflagration".[173] Keats's view was that it was occasioned by an explosion of powder, for he remarked at the time on a flash from port to port, followed by an unusual glare of light, whereupon he observed to Captain Jackson that he thought she was on fire.

As recorded in the narrative, Keats had assembled the first and second captains of the guns, and in addressing the coming engagement told them he had the advantage of having experienced action with the enemy at night. He predicted to them precisely what took place: the Spanish catching fire, and the most pressing danger in the conditions at night coming from fire due to carelessness of powder on one's own ship rather than the cannonade of the enemy. The *Superb* herself suffered a fire, quickly contained, but she was meticulously prepared and well-practised for such action, her crew each knowing what he needed to do and able to do it under any conditions. The great Spanish ships on the other hand had seen little, if any, action and were not so well-drilled. They had courage, but no more. In contrast, order was so good onboard the *Superb* that the narrative of events records that, having sailed on past the two three-deckers, the crew availed themselves of "the leisure which the opportunity afforded to splice and knot some of the rigging that had been shot away". Given all this was unfolding in the dark, the sun having set at 8.00pm and the new moon at 9.00pm, in a fresh gale, in the middle of a cannonade, with nearby ships ablaze, and whilst closing on the next combatant, it makes one wonder at the notion of leisure in the vocabulary of a sailor on a British warship in the Age of Sail!

The Battle off Cabrita Point, 12 July 1801, Thomas Whitcombe, 1816. © Alamy P5NGMP

Some years later M.A. Thiers's comprehensive *The History of the French Revolution* remade claims of the use of hot shot. These were immediately contradicted by Surgeon Outram from the *Superb*, whose own quick thinking in closing the door to the magazine store was credited with preventing a nearby fire leading to an explosion onboard. His response is worthy of recording:

> *In describing the action in the Straits of the Mediterranean on the eventful night of the 12th of July, 1801, M. Thiers asserts that the Spanish first-rates,* Carlos *and* Hermenegildo, *were destroyed by red-hot shot fired from the* Superb, *and heated by furnaces sent on board for the purpose. Now, Sir, at that glorious period I had the good fortune to be the Surgeon of the said noble ship, and being one of the very few survivors of her officers and crew, I solemnly pledge my word of honour that there were no means of heating balls in any of our men of war, that every spark of fire was put out early in the Superb on that memorable day, 12 July, 1801, when the two first-rate Spanish men of war, the* Carlos *and* Hermenegildo *were destroyed or blown up in an engagement with the Superb under the command of Captain Keats, who would have scorned to have employed any combustible missile or other mode of warfare than the fair old English mode of fighting, with warm hearts and cold iron.*

He continues:

> *The night was intensely dark, the wind blew strong from the east: our lanterns were all shaded, whilst the lights of the enemy's ships flashed brilliantly from portholes and cabin windows. Our decks were clear, and our brave tars at their guns. Not a sound was heard onboard Superb, until a terrific broadside was poured into the Spanish line of battle ship which was repeated over and over again before return was made by the enemy, so unexpected was the attack. At last the* Carlos *opened fire on both sides, mistaking her consort for an enemy; the sails of the* Carlos *fell over her bow guns, which set them on fire, and the whole ship was soon in a blaze. The horrors and cries of the crew were something most awful. The* Hermenegildo *got inseparably entangled with her companion, and the two crews in their dismay engaged and fought each other desperately. The fire spread to both ships and their total destruction was inevitable.... It was greatly to be wondered that the enemy squadron did not come to the assistance of those who were allies in distress, but they kept their course. Captain Keats being aware of this (notwithstanding the injuries his ship had received) gave*

> *chase and soon overtook the* St. Antonio [St. Antoine], *a French line of battleship of equal force and opened fire upon her, which after a severe fight surrendered. Soon after a large boat approached the* Superb *containing two officers and thirty-nine of the crew of the ill-fated Spanish ship the* Carlos. *Their wretched looks touched the hearts of our captain and noble hearted crew, and every care was taken of them.*[174]

The question of honour and gallantry was well raised by the *Naval Chronicle*, commenting:

> *When Captain Keats, the gallant Commander of the* Superb, *perceived that the Spanish ship with which she was engaged was on fire, he ceased to molest her, and went in pursuit of foes better able to contend with him. On the contrary, one of the Spanish ships, when it saw the other on fire, which it considered to be an English vessel, did all it could to aggravate the calamity, and deprive it of all hopes of succour in such dreadful moment. The consequence was what such unnatural cruelty deserved; it shared the fate which it so barbarously augmented; while the French, insensible of honour and humanity, meanly crowded all the sail they could, to sneak into a port of the Ally whom they had deserted.*[175]

This assessment is consistent with the reports of the rescued Spanish sailors, recorded in the narrative as saying, of the first ship on fire: "They conceived it was the English admiral; and it was said fore and aft, 'the English admiral is on fire, let us go under his stern and send 'em all to hell together', and they believed that in that effort they ran afoul of the ship on fire, and thus occasioned their own melancholy fate". Keats, on the other hand, had ceased to molest that vessel and subsequently assured those who had been rescued and sought protection that his admiral would not consider them prisoners, and they would not be treated as such on the *Superb*. The men were given spirits, and re-clothed.

Shortly after the battle, Keats sat on the panel convened on the *Pompée* inquiring as to whether Commander Cochrane had used every possible exertion to prevent his ship, the *Speedy*, from falling into Admiral Linois's hands some days before the first battle. He was honourably acquitted and not long thereafter promoted to post-captain.[176]

It should be noted for the sake of completeness that it was not only the *Superb* that became heavily engaged. After passing on from the *Superb* then standing by the defeated *St. Antoine* Captain Hood in the *Venerable* became closely engaged with the *Formidable* and was badly cut up, losing her masts, and running aground on the shoals off San Pedro, just south of Cádiz. Hood was given discretion to abandon and destroy the ship if the enemy, as appeared likely, resumed their attack, but the appearance of the *Audacious* and *Superb* deterred them. It was reported that as the *Caesar* came upon her the following morning Captain Hood was seated on a gun on the quarter deck cheerfully waiting assistance to be got off the ground. She was towed back to Gibraltar by the *Spencer*. Whilst the crew of the *Venerable* fought gallantly, and did all that could be asked, the destruction and capture of enemy ships was the product of the efforts of the *Superb* alone.

Commander George Dundas of the *Calpe* was appointed post-captain in August 1801 and ultimately sailed the *St. Antoine* back to England arriving in Portsmouth on 30 September whereupon she was purchased into the navy. Being old, and at only 1700 tons light for a 74, she was never put into commission.[177] The rules provided prize money was to be shared with those in sight, but head money, paid where a commissioned ship was taken or destroyed was generally shared more restrictively among only those who had brought about the destruction.[178] This squadron offered to include the crew of the *Pompée* and *Hannibal* (none of whom left port) in the full distribution but the Admiralty, noting the honourable sentiments, could find no precedent beyond a wider discretionary sharing of head money. Payment for the approximately 2,500 crew originally onboard the destroyed and captured ships was accordingly, in this instance, shared, as agreed, amongst the entire squadron.[179] Admiral Keith resisted Saumarez's claim to flag officer's prize money and to the latter's chagrin some years later the Court ruled that as he was under the orders of the Commander in Chief he was obliged to share with the flag officers of the Mediterranean fleet. At the same time crew of the *Superb* were able to collect their share of prize money for *Saint Olieveira, Esperanza, Tito, San Luis, Enfant de Carnival, Paxaro, Mistico* and *Santissima Trinidad* captured in the period.[180]

This victory demonstrated the British ascendency; the difference between professionals and amateurs. As Parkinson expressed it, "Trained and disciplined by St. Vincent, inspired by Nelson, led by men like Saumarez or Keats, they were on top of the world".[181] The reputation Keats had built as one of the most talented frigate captains was thus immediately enhanced by his conduct as a captain of a ship of the line. More importantly his exemplary leadership under fire allowed him by force of personality and example to stamp his authority over his ship and crew.

Following this loss, the French were unable to challenge Lord Keith's Mediterranean fleet, and critically were unable to reinforce their army in Egypt, which was taken by Britain in September 1801. Partly as a result of the heavy losses suffered off Algeciras – to that time the worst loss of life at sea in a single day – Spain began to distance herself from France, demanding Spanish forces return to home waters rather than being stationed at Brest and along the French and Portuguese Atlantic coasts. Their rocky alliance soon dissolved. This contributed to the signing of preliminary articles of peace in September, the forerunner to the treaty of Amiens between Britain, France, Spain and the Netherlands which had been under negotiation since mid-1801 and was finalised in March 1802, bringing the revolutionary war to a temporary close.

This was more a truce than a peace. Little was gained by Britain from the treaty. Ireland and Egypt were both preserved but Britain had gained nothing. France remained dominant in Europe with the majority of her territories restored, her control of the Scheldts preserved, and the revolutionaries still in power. The Italian peninsula and the Balearic Islands were under Napoleon's control and Malta was to revert to the (Catholic) Knights of St John, although this promise remained unfulfilled. Napoleon had increased his relative strength in Europe and his aspirations were not dented. On the contrary, he used the respite to rebuild his navy in preparation for a renewal of the struggle for supremacy, saying peace was necessary to restore his navy, to fill his arsenals and because only in time of peace would the drill ground for his fleet, the open sea, be available to him.

England on the other hand, welcoming the cessation of hostilities, dismantled much of her war machine. The British navy had grown exponentially since the previous peace, when it numbered just sixteen thousand men in twenty-six sail of the line and thirty-two frigates.[182] By 1800 it comprised some one hundred and thirty thousand men, including Royal Marines, manning some 127 ships of the line and 600 vessels of fewer than 56 guns. It was the largest and most complex organisation in the world at the time[183] – but not always the most efficient.

On signing this peace, the opportunity was taken to severely reduce the navy and its budget, which now ran to nearly £15million, a quarter of the national budget. As First Lord, or Minister for the Navy, St. Vincent, failing to see the fragility of the peace, applied his usual ruthless zeal as in the name of reform he introduced severe austerity measures trimming the excesses, corruption and more from the administration, the dockyards and supply lines. More than sixty thousand seamen were discharged (with little regard to their future prospects) such that the number of seamen was rapidly reduced to less than fifty thousand and sixty of her sail of the line battleships were paid off until on some accounts only thirty-two ships of the line and two hundred smaller vessels remained in commission.[184]

Fleets in the West Indies and the Mediterranean were kept on station, active and ready for action. The Government feared Egypt was still vulnerable and Malta soon became a bargaining chip. A squadron of eleven 74's, three 64's and forty-five smaller war ships under Rear Admiral Sir Richard

Bickerton was tasked with keeping watch over the French in the Mediterranean. If they put to sea he was to shadow them. Keats and the *Superb* were assigned to this squadron and remained at sea far from home in the Mediterranean for the duration of the peace. A number of prizes were taken, but it would be a mistake to think payment had become significantly more efficient as a result of reforms following the mutinies of 1797. It was some seven years after the event that *The London Gazette* advised men who had been onboard the *Superb* at the capture of the *Bolladore* in June 1801 could attend the Crown & Cushion Public House on 20 October 1808 to collect their share of head money and at the same time their share of the proceeds *Charlotte* and her cargo taken in August 1801.[185]

St. Vincent's cuts to the navy and its civil administration meant this squadron was chronically undersupplied and sustaining the health of the sailors at such a distance became a significant issue, particularly following the closure of the hospital at Malta on St. Vincent's instruction. Plentiful supplies did not arrive from England until early 1803. Just in time for a resumption of formal hostilities. The peace lasted barely a year before outbreak of the Napoleonic wars in May 1803 and the navy was once more called upon to protect Britain and her interests at sea and abroad.

Historical Memoirs of
Admiral Sir Richard Goodwin Keats, GCB

6

In The Mediterranean With Nelson

The peace of Amiens having shortly after taken place, the greater part of the squadron returned to England, but the *Superb* was employed in the Mediterranean under Sir Richard Bickerton, and upon renewal of the war in 1803, formed part of the blockading squadron before Toulon, of which Lord Nelson took the command.

This was the first time Captain Keats had served under his lordship, and consequently, his abilities were only known to him through the representation of others; but an officer of Nelson's circumstances would not be long acting in conjunction with him, without being fully convinced of his great talents and discretion and accordingly, we find that in the month of October, when writing to the Duke of Clarence, he said, "I think Captain Keats is very much better in his health; he is a most valuable officer, and does honour to your friendship. Every day increased my esteem for him, both as an officer and as a man."[186] In December, he wrote thus: "I hope to be allowed to call Keats my friend. He is very much recovered and cheerful; he is a treasure to the service."[187]

This is the first time there is mention of Keats's health. What the illness is, we are not told. From 1803 until retirement from duty at sea some eight years later illness and recuperation become a recurring theme. Keats had been at sea, without even one night on shore, for two years before Nelson's arrival in July 1803.

Nelson wrote almost immediately to the Duke of Clarence:

I joined the fleet yesterday, and it was with much sorrow that I saw your Royal Highness's friend, Captain Keats, looking so very ill; but he says he is recovering. I have such a high respect for his character, that I should be happy in doing all in my power to promote it. He is too valuable an officer for the King's service to lose.[188]

Given the talk of losing him to the service we can infer the illness was quite severe and debilitating. Days later Nelson wrote two letters to His Excellency Hugh Elliot, Britain's representative in the Kingdom of Naples, as it then was. In the official communication he wrote simply, "I send the *Superb*, 74, Captain Keats, one of the very best Officers in his Majesty's Navy". In a private letter he wrote:

Give me leave to introduce Captain Keats to your particular notice. His health has not been very good, but I hope that he will soon recover; for his loss would, I assure you, be a serious one to our Navy, and particularly to me for; I esteem his person alone as equal to one French 74, and the Superb and her Captain equal to two 74-gun ships: therefore, if it is not necessary, you will not keep him; for another ship will be on her way to Naples, at the time I guess she will be near her departure; and, although I should be glad to see the French out, even six to nine, yet these are odds which, although I should not avoid, yet ought not to be seeking.[189]

Anxious to promote his health, Nelson sent Keats to Naples again in August for two weeks' recuperation. Nelson advised the Duke of Clarence in September that he was:

Happy to inform you that Captain Keats is much recovered. I sent him to Naples for a fortnight; but having stayed nine days, he was so anxious, knowing my inferiority in numbers to the Enemy, that he came back and joined me. I need not tell your Royal Highness, that he is amongst the very best Officers in our Service. I have the highest respect and esteem for him.[190]

By December that year, he was described as very much recovered and cheerful.

Early on Nelson appointed Keats to the somewhat sensitive task of investigating the conduct of Lieutenant Layman of *Victory* as a result of his actions following the taking of the French frigate *Ambuscade* (32). Layman was put onboard the prize to deliver her to a home port. On the way he captured two more ships including the heavily laden merchant *Maria Theresa*. The agent victualler at Gibraltar accused him of embezzlement in taking some of the cargo to feed and clothe his men and taking an advance on distribution of prize money before the prize court had made a ruling. In the absence of a formal court martial Keats headed the investigation with Captain White. The difficulty was the *Ambuscade*, herself a prize of the *Victory*, had not yet been condemned by a prize court, or brought into commission as a British ship. Layman had no right to pre-empt a court decision on that issue. The contention was that notwithstanding the desirability of taking enemy vessels, *Maria Theresa* had been taken by a non-commissioned ship, and was consequently not legally a prize of either the *Victory* or of the *Ambuscade*, but was a droit of the Admiralty. This view was confirmed years later by the Lords of Appeal.[191] After considering the evidence, and the law, no doubt to Nelson's relief, Keats and White, cleared the Lieutenant of embezzlement. The proceeds had been applied to the provisioning of the ship, not to personal gain. They did find his actions 'indiscreet' and 'irregular', as the Lieutenant, both over-eager and over-confidant (as was apparently his way) had acted incorrectly having in his enthusiasm failed to pause and appreciate the subtleties of the legal position. An early demonstration of an ability to tactfully find a way through the evidence and regulations to a decision that was in Nelson's view both just and justifiable and in the common good no doubt placed the captains in good stead with their new commander in chief.

In April 1804, Nelson wrote to the Duke of Clarence: "The more I know of him the more excellent qualities I find not only as a sea officer but as a Man who knows much of the World".[192] That last phrase was quite likely informed by his handling of the Layman matter. By August he was saying:

> *Our friend Keats is quite well...in his own person he is equal in my estimation to an additional Seventy-four: his life is a valuable one to the State, and it is impossible that your Royal Highness could ever have a better choice of a Sea friend or Counsellor, if you go to the Admiralty. Keats will never give that counsel which would not be good for the Service.*[193]

The Duke was now Admiral of the Red, promoted over men who had been appointed captain many years before him. He was now more than 150 places senior to the lieutenant to whom he first reported on the *Prince George*.[194] He did go to the Admiralty some years later when in 1827 he was appointed Lord High Admiral, the first such appointment since 1709. To commemorate the occasion, a medal was struck. On one side is a profile of the Duke, and on the other, the figure Britannia walking on the sea, with the words: "Her march is o'er the mountain wave, Her home is on the deep". The newly appointed Lord High Admiral wrote to Keats acknowledging both their enduring friendship and the valuable education he had received:

> *My dear and sincere friend of nearly fifty years standing, my old shipmate and watchmate, and my first and best of instructors in the navy – To whom so properly can I give the solid metal of gold on my appointment to the office of lord high admiral, as yourself; to you, and to you only, do I owe this appointment, and accept this mark of my esteem, regard, and gratitude. God bless you...*[195]

Watching over French ports was arduous and thankless work in pursuance of St. Vincent's strategy to ensure no French fleet could leave port without the certainty of being brought to action.[196] What Napoleon had not grasped was that the only way to escape the individual blockading forces linked as they were by chains of smaller vessels was to defeat them. Evasion only ensured the presence of a British force in some other place, just as likely to hinder his plans.[197] He reflected years later that wherever there was water to float a ship, there you would find a British man-of-war. St. Vincent was reported to have declared in support of the navy's readiness to repel Napoleon's plans for England: "I don't say the French can't come: I only say they can't come by sea".[198]

The strategic significance of the constant containment of that threat was famously identified by Captain Mahan:

> *They were dull, weary, eventless months, those months of watching and waiting of the big ships before the French arsenals. Purposeless, they surely seemed to many, but they saved England. The world has never seen a more impressive demonstration of the influence of sea-power in its history. Those far-distant, storm-beaten ships, upon which the Grand Army never looked, stood between it and the dominion of the world....*[199]

When Keats had been under St. Vincent's orders off Brest, he had been enforcing a close blockade to the point of being dangerous, spending months just outside the enemy port in an unpredictable ocean with a treacherous enemy shore just to leeward. The constant wear and tear of ships, masts, yards, sail, and rigging, not to mention men, was incalculable.

By contrast, Nelson was not a supporter of close blockades. He reportedly remarked to Admiral Bertie, "I have never blockaded a port in my life: to be able to get at the enemy you must let *them* come out to *you*, if *you* cannot get at *them*."[200]

He wrote to the Duke of Clarence:

My plan is to spare the Ships & Men to be ready to follow the Enemy if they go to Madras, but never to blockade them, or prevent them putting to sea any day or hour they please. The pleasure of this fleet would be to have them out, and some happy day soon it will take place, then we may deserve the thanks of our country.[201]

While some have suggested this is indicative of substantial differences between the two admirals it ought to be remembered the strategic situations were in marked contrast. Brest was only a few hours sail from trade routes and British home ports, so St Vincent needed to keep a tight reign. In contrast Toulon was a considerable distance from the closest valuable strategic and economic assets at Sicily and Malta. Nelson was confident he would be able to chase down any escaped fleet before it could become a menace and was therefore happy if they could be enticed out of their sanctuary. He needed to be ready for a longer cruise, but did not see the need to hold station close offshore in all weather.

Accordingly, Keats's role in the Mediterranean under Nelson was a little different but challenging in other respects. The logistics of re-supply so far from home meant ships were largely and chronically unsupported and needed to remove themselves in rotation for victualling at distant ports as well as attending to other duties, and hopefully having the opportunity to capture a prize or two as reward for the long period away from home.[202] Whereas Pellew, stationed off Ferrol, was able to say at this time that the navy had never been better found or supplied, nor its men better clothed or fed, the same could not be claimed of the Mediterranean Fleet, which felt 'forgotten by the great folks at home'.[203] Weeks' sailing from home they had to make do with what they had. Unable to return for maintenance the ships were deteriorating. As early as December 1803 Nelson was complaining that some of the finest ships in the service would soon be destroyed, yet St. Vincent declared to him that he could send neither ships nor men and that with the resources of his mind Nelson would do without them very well. "Bravo, my Lord!" was Nelson's comment to Alexander Ball, whilst suggesting to others that St Vincent himself would not keep at sea in such ships.[204]

Watch was made difficult off Toulon because the land-based enemy had an advantage of height with which to see the blockaders. The French commander in Toulon was Keats's adversary from the chase up the Delaware twenty years earlier; Comte de La Touche-Treville, now a vice admiral and said to be the most competent officer in the French navy. Every day he would climb a nearby hill at Cape Sepet to observe the number and position of British ships offshore. His death in August 1804 was said, by Nelson at least, to be the result of a heart attack suffered in the process of climbing to the signal post.[205] He was replaced by Admiral Pierre-Charles Villeneuve.

Contrary to the myth of gentle summer zephyrs, the prevailing wind in this part of the Mediterranean was the strong offshore mistral which made holding position difficult and caused considerable wear and tear to men and equipment in a fleet that had no access to a home port. Years later, under Pellew's command, the fleet often sheltered in nearby Hyeres Bay which was out of reach of shore batteries and fed by a river from which they could replenish supplies. Nelson, however, unaware of this water source, withdrew his fleet almost completely, watering and victualing at Sardinia so all were ready for a long cruise, as well as relieved of the monotony of days at sea. He often left just two frigates to keep watch and report, hoping to induce the French, uncertain of his position or strength, to leave port and be brought to battle, in which he was confident of victory.

At the same time, to avoid boredom, and to provide an opportunity to cruise for prizes, variety was introduced to the calendar as various ships were sent on special duties. In just three months, the *Superb* visited Sardinia, Naples, Bay of Roses on the eastern coast of Spain and Toulon (Map 3). She went to Naples to negotiate for supplies and to allow Keats some recuperation. The nearest British territory being Malta, hundreds of miles distant, the task of supplying a floating force of more than eight thousand men off enemy shores with adequate fresh food and water was unremitting. As Nelson commented with some frustration, whenever he was forced to send a ship to Malta "I never see her under two months".[206] Naples was much more convenient but was under threat from nearby French forces. Keats found supplies could not be obtained openly, but he reported back that, if the greatest secrecy was observed, it would be possible to procure cattle and supplies to be loaded from bays remote from the city itself.[207]

On passages to and from Naples, they surveyed the Straits of Bonifacio that separate Corsica and Sardinia. On the voyage to Naples, rough conditions in the Straits restricted the survey to lookouts for shallows and rocks. On the return, in more favourable weather, by taking soundings from boats half a mile off each beam, Keats was able to reveal to Nelson that there was no doubt in his mind of there being a good and safe passage through – and sufficient room to work a ship to windward – but that the safest way was to borrow on the Maddalenas (variously spelled Magdalines), a group of islands close off the Sardinian coast. His formal record; "Report of *Superb's* Passage through the Straits of Bonifacio" was forwarded to the Admiralty to update the charts.[208] The fleet thus had an alternative route to and from the Sardinian anchorage at Agincourt Sound, La Maddalena which had been charted by Captain Ryves in the *Agincourt* a year earlier, and a more direct route to Naples. This anchorage, only a day's sail from Toulon, became a principal rendezvous point. Sardinia was part of the Kingdom of Tuscany which was a neutral state and so as well as providing useful shelter and a staging place for resupply from Malta (Map 3) the anchorage enabled resupply of fresh produce, livestock and water from the island.

The *Superb* then undertook similar work at the Bay of Roses, itself an important base for resupply until Spanish authorities became reluctant to deal with the English fleet. Finally, they undertook a reconnoitre of Toulon where Keats assessed the strength and preparedness of the French fleet, finding in September 1803 that there were a number of ships being prepared, but just three sail of the line and four frigates were currently in a state of readiness for sea.[209] A number were undergoing repair and up to five new ships were at various stages of construction. By August 1804 when La Touche ventured out of harbour, but still within protection of shore batteries, Nelson reported eight sail of the line, two frigates and a brig. The British, including five sail of the line prepared for battle, but nothing came of it.[210]

**Historical Memoirs of
Admiral Sir Richard Goodwin Keats, GCB**

Diplomacy on The Barbary[6] Shores

Nelson having this opinion of Captain Keats's judgement and general intelligence, it may be naturally supposed, that on any delicate or important circumstance requiring a detached force, Captain Keats would be instructed with it; accordingly, we find that when Mr. Falcon, the British consul at Algiers [Map 3] had been driven from his post by the reigning Dey and the merchants of Malta became loud in their complaints of the depredations committed by his highness's cruisers, Captain Keats was selected, and thrice proceeded to Algiers, to demand satisfaction for the insult offered to his Majesty.

The British consul to Algiers, Mr John Falcon, had been arrested in a dawn raid and expelled, accused of having 'received Moorish women into his house'. That is to say having Muslim women in his Christian house, which was considered a serious offence. Some commentators describe the incident as quite innocent; staff having invited the women to the house without the Consul's knowledge. Others describe it as a sex scandal that took Algiers out of diplomatic and trade commission for two years.[211]

Original directions issued in July (but received late August) required Nelson's adoption of the "most vigorous and effectual measures" in demanding satisfaction from the Dey for the insult offered to the King's Government, by requiring apology, compensation and the reinstatement of the expelled consul.[212] In responding to the order Nelson made two points. First, it would be necessary for Mr Falcon to attend in person to ascertain the validity of various claims and counter claims, and secondly, there were also issues concerning the conduct of Algerian cruisers that required resolution. Algiers

---

6   The several states of the North African shore of the Mediterranean were at the time described as the Barbary states, derived from the exonym of the Berbers or Amazigh peoples indigenous to the area and included modern day Algiers, Tripoli, Tunis and Morocco.

made her money from the sea by using a modest navy of cruisers and gun-boats to harass merchant trade, seizing passing ships and cargoes. They enslaved and ransomed crews and gave indemnity to those who paid protection money. A treaty made with the British in 1801 following the ousting of the Knights of St John by the French and their ousting as a result of the subsequent British siege of Malta, provided for immunity for Maltese merchants holding valid British passports. It was alleged a number of ships, cargoes and crews with such passports had been seized contrary to that treaty.

The Admiralty recast their earlier directions in August (received 7 October)[213] to require Nelson proceed with caution and to send a discreet captain who would not risk capture of himself or his ship, with instructions to secure the release of any Maltese vessels and crews taken contrary to the treaty and reinstatement of Mr Falcon.

Mr Falcon finally joined the fleet in January 1804 whereupon Nelson wrote to His Highness Mustafa Baba the Dey of Algiers, seeking a declaration that he would not again expel the British Consul, and as stipulated in the treaty, would deliver up all Maltese vessels and their cargoes or their values with the people taken with them. He continued, "I have sent My Right Trusty friend Richard Goodwin Keats Esq., Captain of his Majesty's Ship *Superb* to your Highness to settle this matter in the most proper manner; and whatever he shall say in my name, I beg your Highness to consider as coming from me."[214]

Nelson accordingly appointed Keats,[215] saying:

His Majesty's Ministers wishing if possible consistent with the honour of His Majesty and the British Nation to avoid a rupture with the Dey of Algiers, I therefore, placing the fullest reliance on your Zeal, Abilities and prudence, have thought you the most proper person to execute this delicate mission...[216]

He provided a copy of the relevant Treaty and documents concerning Maltese vessels, crew and passports. His subsequent orders to Keats are set out in a letter of 9 January 1804.[217] His accompanying memorandum for the guidance of the negotiation provided the Dey was not to be saluted and included the lines, "never appear satisfied with what has been granted, but demand what has not; and leave the question of Peace or War entirely open, so that it may hang over his head".[218]

When the *Superb* entered the Bay of Algiers with Mr Falcon onboard she was saluted with 21 guns, but as ordered, she did not return the compliment. Keats went ashore with his demands and was escorted past sentries armed with axes to a chamber where after a very brief period of civility he was met with a loud and violent tirade from the Dey. It became apparent that Muslim women had been in the house as alleged, but at the instigation of servants, without the consul's knowledge or consent. Keats kept his cool and explained the British position. He reported it had been impossible to fix the Dey's attention to any one point longer than two minutes amongst his violent invectives. As some concession, the Dey did offer to accept a British consul so long as it was not the expelled Falcon, and with that he stormed out. Keats returned to his ship and wrote to the Dey offering to meet at any time to progress negotiations and avoid hostilities.

Nelson's fleet had been off Cape San Sebastian when the *Superb* departed, but after obtaining provisions from the Bay of Roses they went south to the Barbary shore. In a fine example of gun-boat diplomacy the day following Keats's first interview, Nelson brought the rest of the Mediterranean fleet within sight of the town "to add weight to the mission".[219] Keats sent an urgent note saying that, in view of the dangerous emotional state of the Dey and to avoid hostilities, Nelson should keep the fleet well to sea. This he did, writing that Keats had his full confidence, although not being able to contain himself, he sent Keats four separate letters during the day as thoughts occurred to him.[220] On shore there was frantic activity as the city prepared for an expected attack. Sometime after delivery of his letter Keats went ashore again in the early afternoon, this time uninvited and thereby risking being taken captive. He was kept waiting for hours before being told the Dey had left the city, that he should return to the *Superb*, and that a boat would be sent for him the following morning. None was. Throughout a tense night, workers could be seen under lights continuing to strengthen the fortifications around the town batteries. After consultation aboard the *Victory*, and believing no more progress would be made at this time, the fleet departed to resume the blockade off Toulon.

Richard O'Brien, British pro-consul, who had been present at these meetings reported Keats had at all times maintained his dignity and conducted himself as a true representative of his country. Nelson wrote: "I beg leave to express my full and entire approbation of the whole of your conduct, which appears to have embraced every proper and conciliating measure for the purpose of accomplishing the object of your mission". To the Admiralty he commented; "I am sure the conduct of Captain Keats has been such as will merit the increased esteem of their Lordships, as it has done of, Sir, &c."[221] He sought additional instructions from the Government. Whilst expressing his personal wish to make a grand coup, he undertook to endeavour to withhold from hostilities until receiving new commands, saying "Time and opportunity will make him repent".[222] Mr Falcon was taken back to Gibraltar on the *Seahorse*.

Nelson was reluctant to make any threat that could not be realised, though he thought nothing but a flogging would bring the Dey to order.[223] One correspondent believed not only the battery but the whole town could be knocked down around the Dey's ears and the whole of his fleet destroyed in one morning by just four sail of the line judiciously placed on the flanks and out of range of the shore guns. Nelson took a different view believing all of his ten or twelve sail of the line with as many bomb vessels as could be mustered would be required.[224] However, orders were to restore diplomatic relations, not to destroy them. Furthermore, the principal strategic game for this fleet was focused on the French at Toulon, believed ready to put to sea. They had no time to be distracted at Algiers. Nor could they risk any of their limited number being crippled so far from home in the process of teaching the Dey a lesson.[225]

Cooler heads prevailed. The Government, more removed from the daily impact of Algerian pirates and slavers was keen to avoid an armed conflict over the matter. The Dey meanwhile was forced to keep his cruisers in port, not earning income, and otherwise took the opportunity to construct new batteries to better protect the city. In May 1804 new secret instructions were received from Lord Hobart, Secretary of State for War and the Colonies.[226] Confirming the King's approval of Keats's discretion and good sense to date, the instructions proposed another mission should be undertaken in the hope the means may be found for procuring satisfaction without having recourse to hostilities as it was in the view of the Government

> *without doubt of the greatest consequence at the present moment, to obviate the necessity of resorting to measures of force against the Barbary States, provided forbearance can be maintained without detriment to the dignity of his Majesty's Crown, or the security of those who are placed under the protection of his Government.*[227]

Maintaining friendly relations with the Barbary States was seen as important on account of the strategic significance of the North African coastline and the facilities to which it afforded access in support of trade and the war effort, particularly the supply of fresh produce to support the British army and navy through Malta. The use of force was now considered inexpedient and it was stated

> *that it had appeared advisable to Ministers, another communication should be made to the Dey of Algiers, in hopes that means might yet be found for procuring due satisfaction for the honour of the Country, without having recourse to measures of decided hostility.*[228]

An irritant needed to be converted into an asset. Accordingly, in May 1804 Keats sailed for Malta where the *Superb* underwent some urgent partial repairs in the Grand Harbour and he sought an 'intelligent' interpreter familiar with the language of the Dey, as that used on the first expedition was suspected of not being as faithful in his interpretation as might be desired and the Dey had purported not to understand the translations of Rev. Scott from the *Victory*. Having secured the services of the former pro-consul to Tripoli for this purpose they then once again attended Algiers with sloops-of-war in support. This mission saw some progress in negotiations over two days in June as Britain dropped her insistence that Mr Falcon be reinstated and indicated a willingness to send a different consul if the Dey expressed regret for the treatment of Mr Falcon. After lengthy discussions, firstly through Ministers and then with the Dey, Algiers formally agreed to accept a new consul and some, but not all, captured crew were freed. The Dey refused to address the question of captured Maltese ships, but it seemed to Keats he may have been correct in some of his claims concerning the application of the treaty and the fraudulent re-use of single voyage passports issued in Malta.[229] Keats provided Nelson with a detailed list of Sicilians, Neapolitans and other Italians with English passports taken by Algiers since Malta came under British protection and still in slavery at Algiers, together with a list of those taken prior to that time. Six of the eleven ships under discussion may have been taken before the commencement of the treaty. Some appeared to be Sicilian, not British. Others may have been using expired passports. Nevertheless, Algiers agreed to release all but two of the British ships.

Nelson refused to accept half success but agreed with Keats's analysis (as did Home Secretary Hawkesbury) that the Dey had made honourable amends for the treatment of Falcon. The only substantial matters left to be resolved after this second expedition were those of the vessel *Ape*, which did hold a valid British passport and her cargo and crew of fourteen and the Maltese ship *St. Antonio di Padona*, which had been sold. The Dey on the other hand was not willing to move until Britain compensated Algiers for the *El Veloce*, an Algerian vessel that had been caught shipping French goods and had been condemned in admiralty court after a full hearing.

In response to Keats's reports the Government position softened further. Lord Hobart passed on the King's gracious approval of the conduct of negotiations and noted in fresh instructions issued in October, but received 26 December 1804,[230] that the matter could be resolved if a new consul, Mr. Cartwright could be accepted, and the matter of the *Ape*, her crew and cargo could be resolved. The Government was prepared to forego compensation for the *St. Antonio di Padona*, although it would "consider it a favour" if prisoners were liberated, but would not concede on the question of the *Ape or El Veloce*.

Despite Nelson's misgivings, Keats was sent a third time with directions from the new Secretary for War, Lord Camden, and negotiating points from Nelson, who advised the mode and manner of discussions were matters entirely for Keats's superior judgement and experience. After collecting the prosed new consul – Mr Cartwright – and sloops in support from Malta, the *Superb* arrived off Algiers on 4 January 1805. Ships' Chaplains Dr. Scott of the *Victory* and Rev. Evans of *Superb*, together with Lieutenant Butler outlined their captain's position to the Dey's ministers and reported back to Keats, who then went ashore conferring directly with the Dey. Given the geopolitical significance of the Barbary coastline and the response of the ministers there was every reason to believe the Dey was under pressure from other parties not to reach any accommodation with Britain, but by patient reasoning Keats made progress. He was on shore negotiating all day on the 5th and the 6th.

The weather turned late in the afternoon, forcing the *Superb* to move offshore. The captain's boat returned to the ship but the sea state was such that it was impossible to get on board, and his party returned to shore. Arrangements were made for accommodation in the home of the American Consul, Colonel Lean, it being inopportune to open the British Consular House at this time. This was the only night Keats spent out of his ship between her sailing in 1801 and her return to home port in August 1805. Negotiations continued into the night until all was finally resolved. The British terms were fully acknowledged to be acceptable resulting in agreement to release of prisoners, payment for the *Ape* and her cargo, and withdrawal of claims concerning *El Veloce*.

At first light, Keats sent his boat with orders for the *Superb* to enter the bay and to land the new consul. There now being no wind, this was not accomplished until sunset. She was greeted by a 21-gun salute, which compliment was returned.[231] Mr Cartwright was landed the following morning and presented by Keats to the Dey, who received him in a gracious manner. Full relations were restored, and Britain returned to most favoured nation status.[232] As Keats had a final audience with the Dey the *Superb* was reprovisioned with a plentiful supply of fresh produce and final preparations were made to re-join the fleet.

Through a combination of directions from the Home Office and Nelson – and patient execution by Keats – diplomacy had avoided conflict, and British trade on the Barbary shores, including vital provisioning for the fleet with fresh produce, could continue with confidence.

Having at length, by his firm and manly deportment, obtained from the Dey the satisfaction he required, - the release of all his Majesty's Maltese subjects, and full compensation to the merchants for their losses- another consul was landed. In one of the interviews obtained on this occasion, and which, from the boisterous and unruly disposition of the Dey, was, anything but dignified, Captain Keats observed to him, that "the act of forcing the British Consul from his post was a proceeding too insulting to his sovereign to be suffered with impunity." On which the Dey, looking as surprised, said, "I insult your King! I respect and honour him! Your King is a good man, and a good King, and so far from offering him insult, it was my duty to have cut off your consul's head; but instead of so doing, I saw him myself to the water side, put him onboard, and sent him to your king; and if your king had done his duty he would have cut off his head immediately on his arrival in England." At a subsequent interview, when the Dey had fully expressed his sorrow, and had promised never to commit a similar act of intemperance, Captain Keats said, that "the King, in consequence of the Dey's promise, and expression of sorrow at his intemperate conduct, and in consideration of Mr. Falcon's indisposition, had determined to send another consul". The Dey, incapable of suppressing his feelings of joy, interrupted Captain Keats at the word indisposition and hastily vociferated, "What! Is he ill? Is Falcon ill?" And on Captain Keats replying "Mr. Falcon is unfortunately unwell", he exclaimed aloud "Spero morari, ladrone, spero morari! "--------I hope he will die, the thief, I hope he'll die!"

For his conduct throughout the whole of these proceedings, Captain Keats was gratified at receiving the approbation, not only of his commander-in-chief, but also of the British government.[233] In writing to Lord Hobart[234] Nelson said, "I have had much conversation with Captain Keats, but the whole of the conference with the Dey, if such a meeting can be called a conference, was nothing but rage and violence on the part of the Dey, and firmness on the part of Captain Keats, the stamp of whose character, if it were not so well known by his actions, is correctly marked by his sensible clear letters." And in writing to Sir Evan Nepean,[235] his lordship said, "Captain Keats has conducted himself like himself; he is one of the most valuable and best of officers I almost ever met with."[236]

A correspondent aboard the *Superb*, whose letter was published in the *Naval Chronicle* and more widely, set out details of the final series of negotiations, noting that they were tempestuous but finally had a good effect, with the Dey acceding to all requests unconditionally, and with the landing of Mr Cartwright accompanied by the usual marks of distinction. He praises Keats for his "zeal, judgement and intrepidity", which drew the respect of both sides of the negotiation, "even from the Ministers he treated with, at the very moment that they were reluctantly complying with his demands". Given the forces at play seeking to manipulate the politics of the region and dissuade the Dey from concluding any alliance and the obstacles to be contended with generally, the correspondent described the task accomplished as 'herculean'. Referring to the Battle of Algeciras, he concludes, "There we had an opportunity of maintaining the honour of the British flag, and we have now the means of hoisting it again at Algiers with increased respect and dignity".[237]

In writing to the Secretary of State for War Nelson commented on Keats's efforts:

Your Lordship will not fail to observe that the conduct of Captain Keats merits those encomiums which would fall far short of his merits, were I to attempt to express what my feelings are upon this, as upon all other occasions where the services of Captain Keats are called forth. I shall therefore, leave your Lordship to represent them to His Majesty, in the manner and language your Lordship's superior judgement shall point out as most proper to their having the fullest effect.[238]

The Secretary of State for War, in turn, described the reports as intelligent and able[239] and was well aware the diplomatic solution had avoided a conflict for which in reality the British were under-resourced given the make-up of her fleet, lack of repair facilities, and the competing demand to maintain close watch over the French. In response to Nelson's comment that Keats's handling of the very delicate mission was such as warranted being mentioned to the King, Lord Camden replied that he must feel assured that Keats's conduct in the mission and his reports of his proceedings had given great satisfaction to his Majesty, and Nelson would be pleased to signify the same to Keats.[240]

Keats had already built a reputation for daring and seamanship as a frigate captain and had successfully demonstrated his skills in a ship of the line at Algeciras. The transactions with the Dey of Algiers showed a whole new skill set. Having had a reputation for a quick temper he may have seemed to be an odd choice for the mission, but Nelson had faith. That was repaid in a manner all could see. Keats displayed qualities few had seen in him before. He had conducted himself with great dignity showing the necessary deference to the head of state and was able to remain calm and yet firm in his position in the face of tirades from the excitable Dey. He was able also to concede where justice demanded it and his intelligent reports, which found their way to ministers, the cabinet and the King, enabled the Government to make well-reasoned decisions in formulating a framework to progress negotiations. These proceedings brought Keats to the notice of a wider group of leaders outside of the navy and paved the way for subsequent appointments calling for skills beyond seamanship and command of a fleet on the open ocean.

Some months later Mr. Cartwright reported the Regency seemed happy at the reconciliation and there was every probability of the regimes remaining good friends.[241]

Keats re-joined the Toulon fleet then at the anchorage at Maddalena Bay, Sardinia for the final time early on 15 January 1805. Indicative of blockade duty not being entirely without reward it is noted that between visits to Algiers the *Superb* was entitled to a share of proceeds of a number of vessels captured during December 1804 including; *Disko, Knudsen, Masler, Virgo Potens, Maria Magdalena, St Judas Tadeo, Victoria, Agatha,* and *Il Corvo*[242].

By this time, the relationship between Nelson and Keats had developed into a deep friendship marked by frequent meals together, informality and, somewhat rarely for Keats, jocularity. Nelson was so keen to catch up with him on his return from Algiers that he certified to the Governor the cleanliness and health of the *Superb* and her crew sight unseen so Keats could avoid quarantine and dine that night on the *Victory*.[243] As Sugden put it in his work on Nelson "In this finest squadron in the world it was Keats who succeeded to such soulmates as Collingwood, Fremantle, Troubridge and Ball, and became one of the most frequent visitors to the *Victory*".[244] That this was the finest squadron in the world was well acknowledged, both at the time and with the benefit of hindsight. A century later Clowes wrote that although the ships were "much out of repair", and generally short of stores, two themes to which we will return, "all these deficiencies were counterbalanced by the fact that the fleet was the best officered and best manned that had ever served Great Britain", and as a result they succeeded in blockading and intimidating fleets who ought to have been able to crush them.[245]

Historical Memoirs of
Admiral Sir Richard Goodwin Keats, GCB

8

The Pursuit Of Villeneuve

Napoleon had for some time been planning to assemble a large fleet in the Channel. He proposed that his squadrons escape their various ports – Toulon (Villeneuve), Rochefort (Missiessy), and Brest (Ganteaume) – and cross the Atlantic independently before rendezvousing at Martinique. There they were to attack the colonies and damage British trade critical to her economy. Napoleon was confident the British would send the Channel fleet to lend naval support to the West Indies, abandoning their defensive blockades and leaving the Channel unguarded. Before the British realised what they were up to the French would then return in an overwhelming force of a size never before seen, comprising fifty to sixty sail of the line, sufficient to sweep the sea of any remaining British men of war and establish command of the Channel.[246] A superiority off the shore of Boulogne for some days (or in Napoleon's initial estimation, "for six hours only") would enable them to provide protection for an invasion force of over 130,000 troops of the Grand Armée, who had hitherto been waiting on French shores. A flotilla of some 2,000 craft of which about half were armed had been assembled, ready to transport the troops, horses and equipment across the channel.[247]

With the benefit of hindsight, it is now evident the plan failed to understand the constraints of naval warfare. It failed to sufficiently account for either the need for each squadron to first break through the blockades or to thereafter respond effectively to potential English countermeasures. It failed to appreciate the network of British fleets and scouting frigates meant it was not possible for entire squadrons to simply arrive in the Channel unheralded. The plan also drastically underestimated the logistical difficulties inherent in seeking to load and ferry such a large number of troops and equipment in a short time window, even assuming the weather would be suitable. Nevertheless, implementation of the scheme commenced in the second week of January 1805 when Missiessy taking advantage of the temporary withdrawal of Admiral Graves's blockading squadron escaped Rochefort with his squadron including five sail of the line and then Villeneuve sailed with his from Toulon.

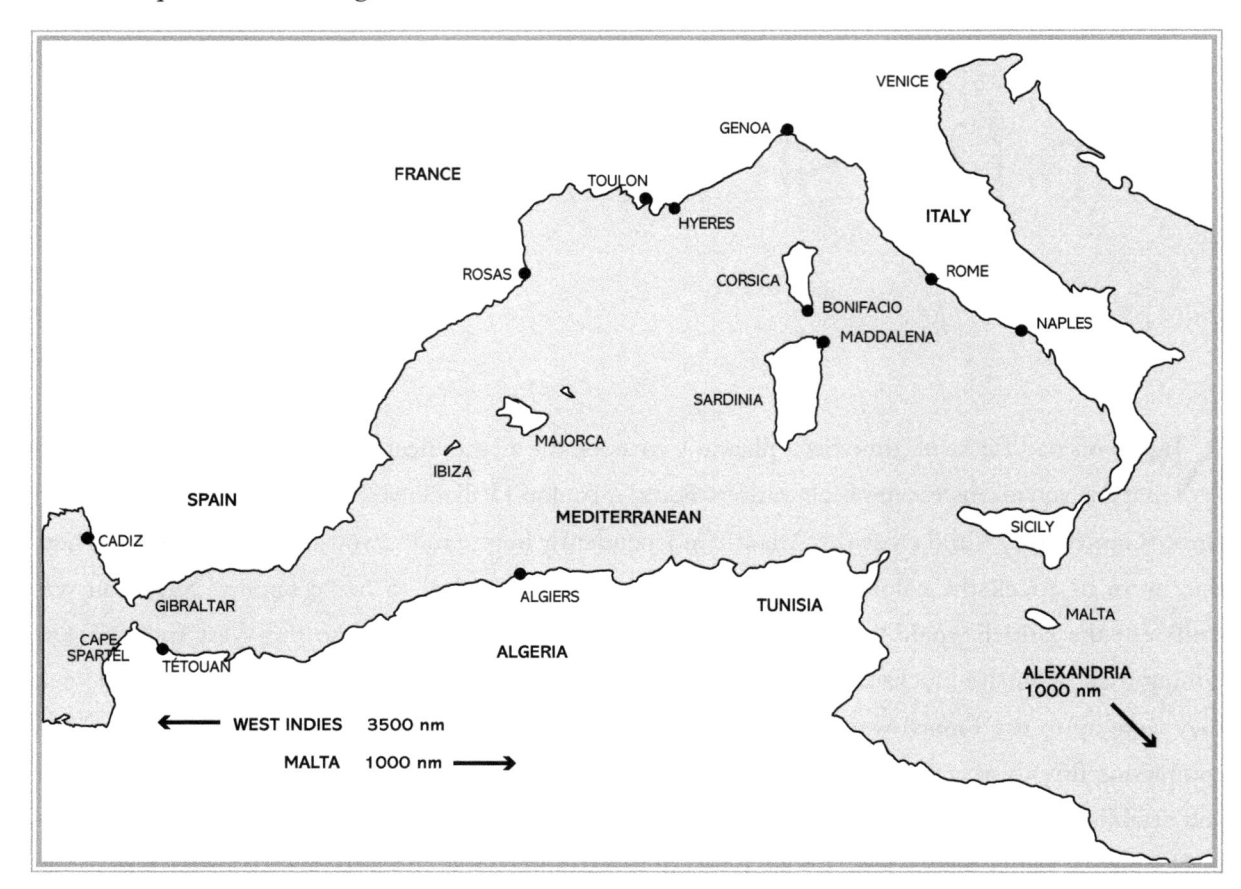

Map 3: *Western Mediterranean*

When in 1805 the French fleet escaped from Toulon, and Nelson's determination of proceeding to the West Indies was made known, Captain Keats was fearful, from the crippled state of the *Superb*, that his lordship would not think it prudent to take her on such a trip; and consequently, applied to his lordship on the subject, and requested that the *Superb* might be allowed to accompany the *Victory* wherever she went. To which he received the following reply: "I am much pleased my dear Keats, at the cheerfulness with which you are determined to share the fate of the fleet. Perhaps none of us would exactly wish for a West India trip; but the call of the country is far superior to any consideration of self. I will take care the *Superb* shall have neighbour's fare in everything."[248] Captain Keats consequently proceeded with his lordship to the West Indies in search of the enemy, but failing in their object, returned to England and it then became necessary that the *Superb* should be docked and refitted.

That final sentence covers a voyage of some months across the Atlantic and back in a ship that had been years out of port. It disguises not only the seamanship and constant attention required to the ship but also Keats's marked devotion to the cause and Nelson in particular.

It was intended that Nelson and Keats return to England, on the *Superb*, so both could recuperate and the *Superb* could be docked for much-needed maintenance. As early as September 1804 Nelson advised Lady Hamilton that; "If Captain Keats will allow me a passage with my numerous suite I wish to go home in the *Superb*, but if the Admiralty send out a senior Admiral I must be subject to his will + pleasure...."[249] By December Nelson had transferred all his things including casks and cases of wine to the *Superb* in preparation for their journey, writing:

> *I may very soon be your troublesome guest; therefore that I may not hurry your ship too much, I shall, with your leave, send some of my wine to the Superb this morning – fourteen casks, and about eleven or twelve cases; but, my dear Sir, there are so many things that I have to intrude upon your goodness for, that I hardly see how to make any amends for the trouble that I shall give.*[250]

Apart from giving an insight into the stores that accompanied a Commander-in-Chief this note shows Nelson and Keats were clearly close and on very familiar terms, their relationship extending well beyond professional sociability. Events conspired to prevent their sharing the longed for voyage home. Firstly, Keats went to Algiers for the third and final time.

Then, on 19 January, just a few days after the return of the *Superb* from Algiers, the frigates *Active* and *Seahorse*, running before a hard gale from the north-west, brought word to the rendezvous point at Agincourt Sound that the French fleet had been seen leaving Toulon the day before, heading south at ten or eleven knots. Nelson's fleet promptly unmoored and weighed. Any plan to return to England was on hold. Within three hours the fleet, including eleven sail of the line,[251] was passing single file, following one another's stern lights through the straits between Biche and Sardinia, barely a quarter of a mile wide. The wind direction prevented a more direct passage west through the Straits of Bonifacio, but within an hour they were in the open sea happy the opportunity for which they had been waiting for eighteen months now presented itself. They were fortunate to escape unscathed. The *Excellent* (74) struck on uncharted obstacles in this passage some time later, causing Keats to reflect to Captain W. H Smyth their trouble-free exit while beating under a gale was "almost miraculous".[252] On an earlier occasion, Nelson had chuckled at his escape of these waters based on a total reliance upon the charts to receive a grave reply from Keats; "Ah my Lord, you are assuredly lucky! – You must certainly have a guardian-angel on the look-out".[253] Whatever the ratio of luck to skill the fleet was now in the long-awaited urgent pursuit of the enemy.

Expecting to find the French on their weather beam south of Sardinia, they prepared for battle, cleared for action, the men sleeping at their guns, and formed in the established Order of Sailing in two columns, under storm staysails only.[254] They did not find the French in the morning, and to the contrary were to be engaged in their pursuit for the next six months.

It was part of Nelson's plan that the French be encouraged to put to sea, for it was there that he expected to realise the hopes and expectations of his country, but unfortunate that he presently had no clear idea where they were or where they were headed. He judged that his orders to watch the enemy in Toulon impliedly extended to chasing down and engaging the fleet he had hitherto been guarding. He therefore largely abandoned the blockade, leaving just a few frigates to watch any remaining enemy and protect commerce and prepared his fleet to pursue Villeneuve. But to where, he did not know.

For the previous two weeks the wind had been in the east. The French only left port after it changed to the west. They had been seen loading troops and saddles. In combination the evidence supported the conclusion that their objective lay downwind to the south-east of Toulon, most likely Egypt. After first ascertaining Sardinia and Naples were safe the fleet continued 200 miles to Sicily. Finding her safe and no sign of the French, the fleet headed east, passing through the Straits of Messina, between Sicily and the mainland and on to Greece. Still not having found the enemy, by 1 February Nelson was describing the lack of intelligence as a crisis.[255] They continued east some two thousand miles reaching Alexandria on 7 February. There was still no word of the French so they retraced their route back to Malta.

The timing of the French departure had not been in response to a favourable change in the wind direction, but due to a specific order from Napoleon; part of his coordinated plan to invade England, not Egypt. It was part of Villeneuve's tactic to depart in a strong wing, and to head initially in whatever direction provided the fastest point of sailing in order to shake off pursuers, before turning to his ultimate destination. His plan fell apart when only a few days out they had been forced by the severity of the weather, breakages and dispersal of the fleet to return to Toulon. Nelson did not learn of the French return to port until he anchored off Malta on 19 February. All this time the fleet had been sailing in a state of battle readiness, with the men at action stations. After sheltering from storms in the Gulf of Cagliari at the south of Sardinia Nelson resumed his route, but was again forced to shelter in early March, now in the Gulf of Palma on the south-west of the island, before appearing off Barcelona to give the impression the fleet was to be stationed in those waters and then resumed his former station south of Toulon on 9 March. For some weeks thereafter, the fleet resumed its prior activities of loose blockade, while the French remained in port repairing their ships which had very obviously not dealt with the severe weather as well as the British vessels had done. It was learned that the troops were still embarked, suggesting their object was still to be Egypt.

Shortly thereafter Nelson wrote to the Duke of Clarence that he hoped soon to meet the French, and for that reason had deferred his return to England, adding that for the same reason Keats wished to stay, although his ship ought long since to have been in England.[256]

With fresh orders, in which the plan was much as before but provided for a contribution from the Spanish who had now declared war on Britain,[257] Villeneuve left port again at the end of March headed to Martinique. Nelson and his fleet were some distance away off the Bay of Palma on the south-west of Sardinia, receiving the news via the frigate *Phoebe* on 4 April. As one frigate took news to Nelson another followed the enemy but through bad luck or poor seamanship lost track of them in the night, reviving the same uncertainty as to where they were headed. Twice now Nelson's tactic of a loose blockade had failed him. Success now depended upon a combination of the poor state of the enemy and the animated response of Nelson's fleet. Still fearing for Sardinia as the key stepping stone to taking Sicily, Malta or Egypt, and thinking the French likely to be taking the southern route to Egypt, he stationed his fleet between Sardinia and the African coast. When certain they were not on a southern passage to Egypt he bore up to Palermo on 7 April casting a wide net with his scouting cruisers until it was clear the French could not have gone east. It was not until 18 April that Nelson learned Villeneuve had been observed exiting the Mediterranean on the 9th. Villeneuve had initially fallen for Nelson's trap and was planning to sail south and east of Mallorca to avoid the fleet expected to be off Barcelona. However, as fortune would have it, a friendly merchant ship from Dubrovnik warned him off and he instead avoided Nelson by keeping close to the Spanish coast until seen passing through the Straits. Then, with their superior numbers the French raised the blockade of Cádiz, releasing the Spanish ships of Admiral Gravina, and with these allies, and what became a thirty-five day head start, they headed across the Atlantic. The English squadron consisted of eleven sail of the line now in search of a combined fleet believed to comprise twenty-four, including eighteen sail of the line, carrying upwards of 3,000 French and 1,500 Spanish troops.[258] The allies were shortly reinforced by two new French sail of the line and a forty-four gun frigate.[259]

On 18 April Nelson wrote that he was satisfied the French were not bound for the West Indies but were likely headed to Ferrol on their way to Ireland or Brest.[260] The pursuit commenced. He had never before been a week without an east wind, but now they deserted him causing immense frustration as the fleet struggled instead against a westerly gale. He turned to Keats for counsel and support, writing on 1 May "My dear Keats, it is an age since I have had the pleasure of seeing you. I hope you will come on board after your breakfast that I may have some conversation with you." In the event it took them, in Nelson's words, one whole month in getting down the Mediterranean, which the French had done in just nine days.[261] Tacking and wearing every two or three hours, on one day they made only fifteen miles towards their goal. Because the wind had made exiting the straits so difficult they anchored inside and the *Superb* was sent to Tétouan, Morocco, for supplies of cattle, fruit and vegetables. Such was Nelson's concern to avoid delays that as soon as a favourable wind sprang up from the east she was recalled urgently – even as the cattle and supplies were on the beach – and she consequently departed without full provisions. They got into Rosia Bay at Gibraltar on 6 May, and from there to Lagos Bay, Portugal on 10 May.

There was no word of the enemy being to the north as had been expected, so, consistent with advice from Admiral Campbell in the Portuguese service, and intelligence received from an American brig, it was finally correctly deduced they were crossing the Atlantic to the Caribbean. Now fearing for Jamaica, just as Napoleon had hoped, the fleet urgently provisioned for an extended voyage. Cognisant of having no orders to justify an Atlantic crossing,[262] Nelson sent a sloop-of-war to England to advise his course of action. Happily, Lord Barham newly installed at the Admiralty concurred, and had already predicted Nelson's strategy. On 8 May Nelson wrote to Keats "I am anxious to get off St. Vincent to meet *Amazon* from Lisbon when my route will be fixed. Will you dine here if we have little wind?"[263] He was in constant consultation with his favourite and trusted captains as to the likely whereabouts of the French and the preferred course of action. Having made his best prediction, he signalled on 9 May "provision for five months at sea". On 11 May, the fleet sailed in response to the signal "Rendezvous in Barbadoes". With the benefit of northeast trade winds, they made Madeira on 15 May and arrived in the West Indies some 3,200 miles distant just 24 days later on 4 June. The French with clean hulls, just out of port, took 34 days.

Pursuant to an advance notice sent via the *Amazon*, the fleet was joined off Carlisle Bay, Antigua, by Rear Admiral Alexander Cochrane, Commander of the Leeward Islands Station, in the *Northumberland* (74). The *Spartiate* (74) (Captain Laforey) arrived just a few hours later. They now thought themselves within days of meeting the French fleet,[264] which had arrived on 12 May.

To ensure the approach of the British would not be broadcast orders had been sent ahead preventing any merchant ships from leaving port. The first the French would know of Nelson's presence would be when he came upon them in person. Cochrane advised that Villeneuve was at Martinique, and preparations were made to bring the chase to its ultimate conclusion.

The following day plans were altered in response to advice received from General Brereton, the commandant at St. Lucia, that the enemy fleet had been seen on the night of 28 May from the windward side of Gros Islet passing in a southerly direction, their destination supposed to be Barbados or Trinidad. A note from Lieutenant General Sir William Myers, the Commander-in-Chief of the Leeward Island station said the intelligence could be relied upon, and he offered to accompany the fleet with two thousand soldiers for the relief of Trinidad or Tobago.

After embarking Lieutenant General Myers and his troops the fleet sailed south. New information suggested the French were in the Gulf of Paria, just off the Venezuelan coast. On 8 June, as the fleet sailed through the Dragon's Mouth, a narrow channel separating Trinidad from mainland Venezuela, the ships cleared for action expecting to find the French at anchor with the troops ashore. The bay was empty. The earlier information had been "very incorrect".[265] The French were still in the vicinity of Martinique, attacking a British fortification at Diamond Rock while waiting for the Brest fleet to arrive as planned. The enemy had actually been within reach of Nelson's original position, and the general had received and passed on false information. The following day dispatches were received stating that the French had been seen off Antigua, heading north. Nelson complained that he had been deceived by false intelligence and after only a few days in the Leeward Islands, with next to no time to refresh, the fleet headed back north, disembarked the troops at Antigua on 12 June and, adding the *Spartiate* to the squadron, set off in pursuit, headed back to Gibraltar. They hoped that with good fortune they could overtake Villeneuve on the journey. When nearly home, Nelson wrote to the Admiralty:

> *I have yet not a word of information of the Enemy's Fleet: it has almost broke my heart. But the name of General Brereton will never be forgot by this generation; but for him our battle would have been fought on June 6th.*[266]

And to Lady Hamilton he wrote:

> *Ah, my Emma, June 6th would have been a great day, had I not been led astray by false information...What a loss! What a relief it would have been for the last two years of cares and troubles.*

As it transpired, Keats came to have just as much, if not more, reason to lament the false information but for which Villeneuve would likely have been brought to action in the West Indies as he was putting to sea.[267]

The French frequently heard of Nelson's track. On learning the English were in the West Indies, Villeneuve headed back to Ferrol, foregoing an opportunity to further harass British trade in the region and waiting no longer for Ganteaume to make the rendezvous. To this time, it had not occurred to Nelson that the trip to the West Indies was an elaborate decoy. Nelson sent Captain Bettesworth in the fast-sailing corvette *Le Curieux* (16) to advise Lord Barham that they were now pursuing the French back across the Atlantic to the Mediterranean, still in fear for Sardinia and Egypt. Fortunately, *Le Curieux* spotted Villeneuve standing to the north, not toward the Mediterranean. This news was delivered to First Sea Lord, Lord Barham on the morning of 9 July as officials would not wake the seventy-nine year old admiral late the night before. Despite his senior roles including as Comptroller of the Navy having been largely administrative he possibly possessed the most experienced head in the navy and was then alive to the enemy strategy. He quickly sent a private letter, followed by official orders, to Admiral Cornwallis to combine with the Rochefort squadron and that of Vice Admiral Calder off Ferrol and for them to stretch out thirty to forty leagues into the Atlantic west of Cape Finisterre for six or seven days to block Villeneuve's route into the Channel.

Calder intercepted Villeneuve en route to Cádiz, resulting in an inconclusive engagement in late July in which Calder with inferior numbers in misty weather managed to capture two of the enemy. Much has been written about that encounter, or more particularly, Calder's decision not to renew the engagement in the following days. He faced a court martial for not having done his utmost to take or destroy every ship of the enemy. His defence was that he had inflicted serious damage in the course of which he had himself suffered serious damage to two ships such that any resumption of the action may well have resulted in a less positive outcome. This was found to be an error in judgement for which he was reprimanded and from which his career never recovered. Whilst not an overwhelming tactical success Calder's action marked a strategic turning point. Any chance that Villeneuve may have had to mount a challenge and force his way to the Channel was now gone. Napoleon's prime strategic objective had been thwarted, substantial credit for which should go to Lord Barham.[268]

Having chased them some ten thousand miles, Nelson had not caught sight of the French, let alone engaged or defeated them. In fact, on anchoring in the Bay of Gibraltar on 19 July, just a couple of days before Calder's action, he still had no fix on their whereabouts. Nevertheless, Napoleon's fleets had been unable to affect either the planned rendezvous in the West Indies or the joint triumphant return. Missiessy had made it from Rochefort to the West Indies, but after waiting the appointed length of time, he departed before his compatriots arrived and, on his return, succeeded in getting back into Rochefort. Ganteaume and his twenty-one strong fleet in Brest never escaped beyond the Goulet. Villeneuve's was the only squadron on the loose on the high seas and was intercepted and engaged by the strategically placed Calder. Napoleon lamented that had Villeneuve joined with Ganteaume at Brest, instead of seeking to enter Ferrol, his army could have landed and it would have been all over with England.[269] Instead, unable to join the Brest fleet and prevented from entering Ferrol (or any other French port), Villeneuve sailed for Vigo (Map 4) and then Cádiz, arriving on 20 August 1805. The French ambition to arrive unannounced in force to overwhelm the British came to nothing.

Meanwhile, the French army had been waiting on the beach at Boulogne (Map 1) until giving up hope of his navy delivering as planned, Napoleon ordered the troops away from the coast on a march to the Danube for the launch of his Austrian campaign in response to Austria and Russia joining the war.[270]

Arriving at Gibraltar and hearing nothing of the French, beyond the information that had been relayed from the *Curieux*, Nelson's fleet took on fresh provisions from the victualling yard and water from Morocco. When the levanter began to blow on 24 July they exited the Straits with the wind behind them and headed north across the Bay of Biscay before standing over towards Ireland. On 12 August, it was confirmed that the French had not been seen in those waters, and it was judged that the best course would now be to reinforce the Channel fleet, lest the enemy was headed for Brest.

They joined Admiral Cornwallis off Ushant on 15 August where they learned of Calder's action and that the combined fleet was now sheltering in Cádiz. The *Superb* - now barely able to keep the sea - and *Victory* received permission to proceed to Portsmouth for repair whilst the rest of the squadron stayed at sea with the Grand Fleet. The pair anchored off Dunnose, the Isle of Wight, on 17 August, and at 4am on 18 August sailed for Spithead, saluting the flag of Port Admiral George Montagu on the *Royal William* at 8.30am. They anchored at the Motherbank that evening. As both ships had recently visited Spain and Gibraltar, where yellow fever was prevalent, they were kept offshore in quarantine, despite Nelson's advice that "the companies of the *Victory* and *Superb* are in most perfect health, and only require some vegetables and other refreshments to remove the scurvy". Nelson's influence did not extend to the collector of customs, and apparently for the first time in his career,[271] Nelson was placed in quarantine. A cutter was stationed near the ships to enforce the isolation. Keats and Nelson accordingly dined together onboard each night until granted pratique and wound up naval affairs, including accounting for prizes, cargoes and captured specie found on various Spanish ships detained between November 1804 and January 1805 valued in excess of some £151,000.[272]

Just as the memoirs dismiss the chase across the Atlantic in a single sentence, many histories treat it as simply setting the stage for Trafalgar. The feat of seamanship and leadership is unequalled. Hugh Elliot British ambassador to Naples, put the journey in the context of the day:[273]

> *Either the distances between the different quarters of the globe are diminished, or you have extended the powers of human action. After an unremitting cruise of two long years [the Superb of course was off Toulon an additional third year under Bickerton] in the stormy Gulf of Lyons, to have proceeded without going into port to Alexandria, from Alexandria to the West Indies, from the West Indies back again to Gibraltar; to have kept your ships afloat, your rigging standing, and your crews in health and spirits, is an effort such as never was realised in former times, nor, I doubt, will ever again be repeated by any other Admiral. You have protected us for two long years, and you saved the West Indies by only a few days.*

The significance of saving the West Indies should not be underestimated. It meant saving Britain's economic well-being as a consequence. Elliot described the undertaking as "a perseverance that outdid all his former victories", and in many ways that was true. Although much of the praise is properly directed to Nelson personally, there is little doubt his captains should share in the credit and achievement. None more so than Keats and the dedicated and tenacious crew of the proud but worn out *Superb*.

And it then became necessary that the *Superb* should be docked and refitted.

Again, the memoirs show a mastery of understatement. The ship which in 1801 was clearly the fastest in the fleet had been at sea ever since and was now the slowest. In December 1803, more than a year since past, Nelson had written to St. Vincent; "The *Superb* is in a very weak state; but her Captain is so superior to any difficulties, that I hear but little from her".[274] She had large iron bolts inserted and frappings, wrapped around her hull, to keep the scarf joint in her stern together.[275] Nevertheless, St. Vincent had pronounced he could provide no more ships or men, so those on station in the blockade could not be relieved or sent to be repaired.

In May 1804, Nelson wrote again; "the *Superb* must also be sent to England before that period [winter] arrives, as her stem and the knees of her head are loose and broke - nothing but the great exertions of Captain Keats has kept her at sea this last season".[276] As they left the Mediterranean, Nelson wrote to the Duke of Clarence, "Keats had begged that his *Superb* may share our fate going to the West Indies, his ship is not quite fit for such a long voyage," and to Keats after undertaking to take care the *Superb* would have neighbours fare in everything he continued, writing "I have wrote to the admiralty that *Superb* would be sent home before the hurricane weather."[277]

It had been a serious question as to whether the *Superb* was capable of the voyage at all. If she did go it was certain she would be a drag on the fleet. But for the pressing requests of Keats not to be excluded from the glories to come, and his perceived value to Nelson, she would have been sent home. The ship was so foul and slow that in order not to retard the fleet, they proceeded under full sail with studding-sail booms permanently lashed to the yards. While the others slackened their sheets of a night to rest the *Superb* continued for long hours. The persistence and determination of the crew in facing these difficulties, crisscrossing the Atlantic under a press of sail while others slept were of sufficient note to inspire a poem, *The Old Superb*. Put to music by Sir Charles Stanford, it became the anthem adopted by all subsequent British warships carrying the name *Superb*, including the most recent, a nuclear-powered submarine:

THE OLD SUPERB

The wind was rising easterly, the morning sky was blue,
The Straits before us opened wide and free;
We looked towards the Admiral, where high the Peter flew,
And all our hearts were dancing like the sea.
'The French are gone to Martinique with four and twenty sail!
The Old _Superb_ is old and foul and slow,
But the French are gone to Martinique, and Nelson's on the trail.
And where he goes the Old _Superb_ must go!'

So Westward ho! for Trinidad, and Eastward ho! for Spain,
And 'Ship ahoy!' a hundred times a day;
Round the world if need be, and round the world again,
With a lame duck lagging all the way.

The Old _Superb_ was barnacled and green as grass below,
Her sticks were only fit for stirring grog;
The pride of all her midshipmen was silent long ago,
And long ago they ceased to heave the log.
Four year out from home she was, and ne'er a week in port,
And nothing save the guns aboard her bright;
But Captain Keats he knew the game, and swore to share the sport,
For he never yet came in too late to fight.

So Westward ho! for Trinidad, and Eastward ho! for Spain,
And 'Ship ahoy!' a hundred times a day;
Round the world if need be, and round the world again,
With a lame duck lagging all the way.

'Now up, my lads,' the Captain cried, 'for sure the case were hard
If longest out were first to fall behind;
Aloft, aloft with studding-sails, and lash them on the yard,
For night and day the Trades are driving blind!'
So, all day long and all day long behind the fleet we crept,
And how we fretted none but Nelson guessed;
But every night the Old _Superb_ she sailed when others slept,
Till we ran the French to earth with all the rest.

Oh, 'twas Westward ho! for Trinidad, and Eastward ho! for Spain,
And 'Ship ahoy!' a hundred times a day;
Round the world if need be, and round the world again,
With a lame duck lagging all the way.

    Sir Henry Newbolt.

The third verse records: "How we fretted, none but Nelson guessed". In terms of speed the *Superb*, having been at sea so long was the greatest liability, but Nelson had written with encouragement to Keats at the commencement of their Atlantic crossing in May:

> *I am fearful that you may think the Superb does not go as fast as I could wish. However, that may be, (for if we all went ten knots, I should not think it fast enough) yet I would have you assured that I know and feel that the Superb does all which is possible for a ship to accomplish; and I desire that you will not fret upon the occasion.*[278]

This was written on a day when the fleet made a paltry fifty-nine miles. The use of the word "fret" has been taken by some as evidence of constant unnecessary anxiety on the part of Keats. One can well understand some anxiety on the part of a captain and crew in a deteriorated ship concerned that they not hold back progress of a fleet whose prime object is speed in chasing an enemy believed to be just days ahead of them. Anxiety too to avoid disparaging remarks from their fellows. Others have viewed it differently.

Sir John Knox Laughton and Sir Henry Newbolt each saw the exchange in a more positive light, the latter saying it was evidence "that Captain and Admiral were worthy of each other".[279] Sailing continuously for weeks on end under full sail, in a leaking ship held together by cables wrapped around her hull, was an undertaking few crews would be willing to endure, and for few captains or admirals. Nelson's understanding letter continued with encouragement saying:

> *I hope and indeed feel confident, that very soon you will help me secure the Majestueux.*[280]
> *I think we have been from Cape St. Vincent very fortunate, and shall be in the West Indies time enough to secure Jamaica, which I think is their object...*

On receipt of this letter the crew of the *Superb* were more than ever bound to their admiral.[281] In any event, conditions improved and towards the end they were averaging closer to two hundred miles in a day. The voyage was extremely well executed. Even with the slow *Superb* it was completed in twenty-four days, compared to Villeneuve's passage of thirty-four made by a fleet of superior ships fresh out of port. That the *Superb* kept up with the fleet has been described as a "miracle".[282] The voyage was a testament to the seamanship of Keats and his crew and the husbandry of their tired ship.

A TREASURE TO THE SERVICE

The whole chase – in worn-out ships, running low on provisions, and weary from two years watching Toulon – was a triumph of leadership. Spirits were not allowed to lag as they went to Alexandria, Sardinia, across the Atlantic and back. One week into the return voyage, Nelson wrote to Keats offering some fresh meat and inviting him onboard whenever conditions were favourable to the gig making the transfer. They dined together whenever conditions allowed. On this occasion he added; "I think the *Superb* is improved in her sailing."[283] It is doubtful there had been any improvement, and more likely this was another example of Nelson's care and encouragement. On their return, Nelson's note to the Admiralty from Gibraltar specified several ships in "want" of docking. Of the *Superb* he observed; "Must be docked, and a new foremast".[284] A month later, off Ushant he advised Admiral Cornwallis she was "Greatly in need of docking and new foremast". Only five of his eleven ships were described as "Fit for Service".[285]

We may here remark a circumstance which we believe is unprecedented, that between the 19th of March 1801, and the 22nd of August 1805, a period of four years and a half wanting a month, Captain Keats slept out of the *Superb* only one night, and that night (from necessity) at Algiers.

Historical Memoirs of
Admiral Sir Richard Goodwin Keats, GCB

9

The Trafalgar Battle Plan

During his continuance in England, Captain Keats was taken by Lord Nelson to many of the ministerial conferences, where plans of operations were discussed, his lordship frequently appealing to him for the truth of his observations, and referring the ministers to him for further information.[286]

In addition to accompanying Nelson as he put his views to various ministers, particularly impressing upon them the strategic importance of various ports and territories, Keats was otherwise focused on the re-fit of his ship at Portsmouth. On 22 August 1805, as he left the ship following customs clearance, he wrote to Nelson, embracing

> *An early opportunity of informing your Lordship that the Superb is ordered to dock and refit at Portsmouth. I apprehend the fate of the Ship's Company will be determined by the State in which they find the Ship when taken into Dock. Should it be mine to take her again to Sea, I am sure no circumstance could afford me more pleasure than that of finding myself once more under your Lordship's command.*[287]

Nelson's reply:

The following letter, dated Merton, August 24 1805, particularly shows his lordship's opinion of Captain Keats: "My dear Keats, ----Many thanks for your kind letter; nothing, I do assure you, would give me greater pleasure than to have you at all times near me; for without a compliment, I believe your head is as judicious as your heart is brave, and neither I believe can be exceeded".[288]

He understood the Duke of Clarence had written concerning Keats's future commission but Nelson did not yet have orders himself. He was not presently 'appointed Commander-in-Chief' but would shortly be meeting with the Secretary of State following which he would know more and he invited Keats to pass by Merton on his way to London when he could be brought up to date.

Due to Nelson's 'unusual' domestic arrangements, setting up house at Merton with Lady Hamilton, whilst both Lady Nelson and Sir William Hamilton were very much alive and married, many in 'society' refused to visit or entertain them as a couple.[289] By the time they returned from the West India voyage Sir William had died, but the arrangement was still seen by many as scandalous. We don't have correspondence that expressly states Keats's view of the situation, but we do know of his devotion to Nelson and his practical approach to matters of this nature. After Nelson's death he went to some trouble to ensure private correspondence between the couple was returned to Nelson's brother and not become public. It can be inferred Keats was untroubled by the private arrangements of his commander and more than happy to be included in the inner circle who attended Merton.

It was there that Nelson shared with, and sought Keats's thoughts on, a plan for his next battle, which proved to be that off Trafalgar. Corbett summarises the interaction thus:

Some three weeks before, while he was still in England, he had discussed his plan with Captain Richard Keats, a close friend and trusted colleague, who served with him in the Mediterranean in the campaign of 1803-5. As the two men were walking together in the grounds of Nelson's house in Merton, a village to the south-west of London, Nelson began explaining how he proposed to fight his next battle.[290]

Years later, Keats told the story of that memorable walk to Edward Hawke Locker, a collector of naval anecdotes, and Civil Commissioner of the Greenwich Hospital, who wrote it down:

He said to me, 'No day can be long enough to arrange a couple of Fleets and fight a decisive battle according to the old system. When we meet them [for it was intended Keats be present] for meet them we shall, I'll tell you how I shall fight them. I shall form the fleet into three divisions, in three lines. One division shall be composed of twelve or fourteen of the fastest two-decked Ships, which I shall keep always to windward or in a situation of advantage and I shall put them under an officer who, I am sure, will employ them in the manner I wish, if possible. I consider it will always be in my power to throw them into battle in any part I may choose, but if circumstances prevent their being carried against the enemy where I desire, I shall feel certain he will employ them effectually, and, perhaps, in a more advantageous manner than if he could have followed my orders (He never mentioned or gave any hint by which I could understand who it was he intended for this distinguished service). He continued, 'With the remaining part of the Fleet formed in two lines I shall go at them at once, if I can about one third of their line from their leading ship'. He then said 'What do you think of it?' Such a question I felt required consideration. I paused. Seeing it he said, 'But I'll tell you what I think of it. I think it will surprise and confound the enemy. They won't know what I am about. It will bring forward a pell-mell battle, and that is what I want.'[291]

This conversation is confirmed by the sketched battle plan, discovered by Colin White when engaged on the Trafalgar 200 project, and the subject of his paper, *Nelson's 1805 Battle Plan*.[292] The sketch is described by him as 'not a finished drawing', but 'a quick doodle, drawn hurriedly by a busy man, to accompany an animated verbal description' and 'enables us to look over Nelson's shoulder and to catch a faint echo of the excitement that reduced… Captain Keats to stunned silence'. The plan is much analysed elsewhere, but it essentially departed from the usual attack which required time (in Nelson's view, time wasted) in forming up in a single column parallel to the enemy. Once achieved, forming in line with the admiral in the centre had the advantage of simplicity; hold the line and focus on the enemy ship opposite your own. It was easy to monitor those who broke out of the line, and easy to break off the engagement, but the plan lacked flexibility and often lead to an inconclusive outcome. In Nelson's view, no day is long enough to spend time in unnecessary manoeuvring before joining battle. Furthermore, he was not contemplating an honourable but inconclusive outcome. He believed his well-trained and committed crews under capable captains could bring about total destruction of the enemy if afforded the opportunity to fight ship on ship in what he described as a 'pell-mell' battle.

His plan involved approaching in two columns, (or may be three, including the support of an 'advance squadron,' if we have regard to a second sketch dated 5 September 1805[293]) near perpendicular, to cut the enemy line in two places, concentrating the attack and overwhelming that section of the line before the remainder could come to its aid. It has the advantage that a ship passing through the enemy line has, for a period, the opportunity to discharge broadsides from both sides, down the length of her opponents, causing maximum destruction at a time when the enemy ships can reply with their bow or stern guns only. The approach is more challenging. To minimise time under broadsides received bow on, the approach would be under full sail, as opposed to the usual fighting rig of topsails only. Nevertheless, even a rapid perpendicular approach with the admiral in the leading group in the face of raking fire would be audacious, which explains Keats's stunned silence.

The idea was not wholly unique. Corbett traces the headlong charge, with a reserve squadron to windward, back to 1545. He believed that what took Keats's breath away was the return to primitive methods of breaking the established order in single line, throwing the enemy into confusion. As Nelson declared to Lord Sidmouth, "Rodney broke the line in one point; I will break it in two".[294] Rodney had deployed something very similar in April 1782, defeating the Comte de Grasse in the Battle of the Saintes. He had outlined the tactic at a dinner at Storeland, using cherry stones to represent the fleets, demonstrating the confusion that would be caused in the enemy line.[295]

It may be that Nelson was referring to a less auspicious and poorly executed variant in the earlier battle between Rodney and Langara, at the battle of Martinique where he sought to break through from leeward. That plan was somewhat lacking in execution, possibly not being well understood, and certainly not well executed by his captains.[296] There is strong evidence from Captains Hardy, Berry, Durham and others that, in common with Rodney, Nelson had studied the works of John Clerk of Eldin regarding fleet tactics, and that this work is the true origin of the tactic. Nelson wanted his captains to absorb these ideas for use as appropriate when the opportunities arose, and they had been the subject of extensive discussion during the chase across the Atlantic.[297] It was Clerk's recommended form of battle that was adopted.[298]

Villeneuve largely predicted the proposed formation but failed to prepare a counter plan. His chief objective was to escape in order to reach the Mediterranean in accordance with Napoleon's orders. Regardless of the origins of the overall tactic of breaking the line, where the plan was unique, that part which has been described as 'the Nelson touch' was in recognising the difficulty of controlling the development of battle from the flagship. Rather than relying on a rigid plan Nelson gave confidence to his captains based upon provision of mutual support. If signals could not be seen, no captain could do wrong by placing his ship alongside that of an enemy or in support of a compatriot. They had licence and were given the confidence to do what they thought most advantageous without specific direction.[299] As Collingwood remarked on the day of the battle, "I do wish Nelson would stop signalling…We all know what we have to do!"[300]

Before Trafalgar, Nelson announced; "Keats is my right-hand man…'till he joins, Hardy will be first captain of the fleet."[301] The *Superb* is shown in the 10 October sailing orders in the first division of the van squadron, second in line behind *Temeraire* and directly ahead of *Victory*.[302] She was regarded as a powerful 74 under Keats's command and was thus positioned in the van amongst a concentration of larger three-deckers.

Their proven record in battle made Keats and the *Superb* much sought after by senior officers, and in this instance, in addition to being Nelson's favourite, he would have been one of the most experienced captains in the fleet. Of the twenty-seven battleship commanders now under Nelson, just eight had served with him before and only two of those had been in the Mediterranean with him since 1803. Only five of those commanding a ship of the line had previously commanded such a ship in action.[303] The squadron that assembled off Cádiz was not one of longstanding where each Captain instinctively knew how others would react or what was expected. Keats's seamanship, the disciplined and accurate fire of his crew, their experience in battle, and their close understanding of Nelson would be invaluable in undertaking the perpendicular approach under full sail, and in taking upon themselves execution of that Nelson touch.

In early September, orders were received formally putting Keats and the *Superb* under the command of Nelson:

> *You are hereby required and directed to put yourself under the command of the Rt. Hon'ble Lord Vt Nelson, K.B. Vice Admiral of the White, and follow his lordship's orders for your proceedings.*
> *Given &c 5th September 1805; [signed]: (First Sea Lord) Gambier (Vice Admiral) P. Patton, (Lord) Garlies (members of the Board of Admiralty).*[304]

Nelson left Spithead on 14 September 1805. The *Superb* was released from the dock on 25 September, but as Keats noted in his last letter to Nelson on 1 October, she had been released prematurely and was not yet ready to receive her Captain or to be supplied and crewed:

> *No time shall be lost on our parts to join your Lordship with all possible expedition. This thrusting her out of Dock before she was ready for our work answers no good purpose to any of us, and an ill one indeed to me as it had brought me unnecessarily early from my old father's*

and thereby abridged one's short comforts, which I should not have begrudged if I could have been a day sooner with your Lordship by it.[305]

Keats was at the docks, to ready his ship for sea, but still more work was required before this could be done. Two weeks later, and indeed up until the battle, Nelson was still expecting them. The sloop *Nautilus* was stationed off Cape St. Vincent in anticipation of their arrival, to pass on orders and rendezvous details.

In his discussions and correspondence with various ministers including Prime Minister Pitt, Nelson had been emphasising the strategic importance of Sardinia and the neighbouring coast. A new 74 had been launched from Genoa and made its way to Toulon joining two others and significant land forces were threatening Sardinia and Naples. If France were to possess Sardinia, which in his view, she could do at any moment she pleased, British commerce would suffer most severely. In the absence of nearby supply bases and a safe anchorage it would be impossible to maintain station or blockade off Toulon or protect trade in the Mediterranean.[306] Over coming weeks he developed an additional plan designed to both protect Sardinia, and to prevent support for the combined fleet on the Atlantic coast arriving from the Mediterranean. He outlined the plan to Sir Alexander Ball (Commissioner for Civil Affairs, Malta) on 15 October, noting it would see Keats giving up his place as Nelson's second, that is next to the *Victory* in line of battle, to command a separate squadron:

The combined Fleets are all at the Harbour's Mouth, and must either move up again, or move off, before the winter sets in. I trust we shall be able to get hold of them. I want to send ten Sail of the Line, two Frigates, and two Sloops, off Toulon, Genoa, and that Coast (Map 3) to cover our Army and to prevent any stores, provisions, &c., from moving along shore, and to save Sardinia; but as yet I have not the means; but when the Ships are released from the Expedition, and the Frigates carrying the money return, I shall have a very respectable Squadron in that part of the Mediterranean—probably under our friend Keats, if he will accept it, and give up the certainty of fighting with the Fleet, as my second.[307]

A squadron of such force and significance would generally be placed under the command of a senior flag officer. That Nelson was intending Keats be entrusted with the command says a great deal not only about the independence afforded Nelson, but the regard he had for Keats.

The *Superb* having been completely repaired, Captain Keats was ordered from Portsmouth to Plymouth, to receive the flag of Sir John Duckworth, and then re-join Lord Nelson off Cádiz; but previous to his arrival on that station, the death of Nelson, and the victory off Trafalgar had taken place, and Captain Keats was thus unfortunately deprived of the opportunity of fighting under his lordship's banner.

Vice Admiral Duckworth had been appointed to replace Rear Admiral Earl of Northesk as Nelson's third in command following the recall of Calder to face court martial. The *Royal George* was to fly his flag but she was not ready, and the *Superb* having been refitted at Portsmouth was diverted to Plymouth to receive the admiral. For reasons which have attracted much comment, they did not join Nelson's fleet until after the Battle of Trafalgar had been fought and won.

Many commentators have remarked that Duckworth unnecessarily detained the *Superb* until long after she was ready to continue her voyage, on one report until his favourite band of musicians arrived,[308] and on another until his order of Cornish mutton and potatoes had been delivered.[309] Others refer to waiting for stores, including 35 cases of wine,[310] or for his "followers" and "essential comforts" to be delivered from the *Acasta* which had not yet arrived.[311]

Duckworth has been condemned for his extraordinary self-indulgence, and several writers have concluded that the *Superb* was refitted in time to participate, but missed Trafalgar due solely to her association with him.[312] The origin of this contention lies in an account by Edward Trelawny, then a twelve-year-old boy briefly onboard *Superb* for delivery to another ship in the fleet.

At the same time as the topsail schooner *Pickle* (8) was about sixty miles from the Lizard, off the Scilly Isles (Map 1) carrying the dispatches of Vice Admiral Collingwood telling of the victory off Trafalgar and of the loss of Nelson a ship of the line under full sail was heading south-west out of the Channel. Seeing she was painted in the distinctive black and yellow chequer of Nelson's Mediterranean fleet[7] the *Pickle* signalled that she had intelligence to communicate. The *Superb*, for it was her, hove to in order to receive a boat. After delivering news of the victory and the death of

---

7 Frigates were generally painted with bright yellow sides and black upper works. 74s varied, but were usually yellow with a black streak between upper and lower deck ports. As a gesture of loyalty and solidarity Nelson's Mediterranean ships came to be painted in alternating bands of yellow and black, (one for a 74, two for a first-rater) running fore and aft, which with gun ports opened displayed as a dog tooth or chequerboard pattern. This became known as the Nelson Chequer. The black streak was not painted by the dockyards but was added by the Captain. An expensive practice, it was later criticised by the 1814 Commission of Sea Officers. Their masts were yellow and gun ports red, (see Sugden, *Sword of Albion*, p.624, and Vale, B., Pitch, Paint, Varnish and the Changing Colour Schemes of Royal Navy Warships, 1775-1815, *The Mariner's Mirror*, Vol 106:1, 2020, p18).

Nelson, the *Pickle* left the crew of *Superb* in tears before resuming her voyage to Falmouth.[313] The interaction onboard the *Superb* – as relayed by Edward Trelawny – gives an insight into the disposition of those involved:

> Young as I was, I shall never forget our falling in with the Pickle schooner after[314] Trafalgar, carrying the first dispatches of the battle and death of its hero. Her commander, burning with impatience to be the first to convey the news to England, was compelled to heave to and come on board us. Captain Keats received him on deck. Silence reigned throughout the ship: some great event was anticipated. The officers stood in groups, watching with intense anxiety the two commanders, who walked apart. 'Battle', 'Nelson', 'Ships', were the only audible words which could be gathered from their conversation. I saw the blood rush into Keats's face: he stamped the deck, walked hurriedly, and spoke with passion. I marvelled, for I had never before seen him much moved: he had appeared cool, firm, and collected on all occasions, and it struck me that some awful event had taken place or was at hand. The Admiral was still in his cabin, eager for news from the Nelson fleet. He was an irritable and violent man, and after a few minutes, swelling with wrath, he sent for Keats, who possibly heard it not, but staggered back along the deck, struck to the heart by the news, and, for the first time in his life, forgot his respect for his superior in rank: muttering as it seemed, curses on his fate that, by the Admiral's delay, he had not participated in the most glorious battle in naval history. Another messenger enforced him to descend in haste to the Admiral, who was high in rage and impatience. Keats, for I followed him, on entering the Admiral's cabin said in a subdued voice, as if he were choking, 'A great battle has been fought, two days ago, off Trafalgar. The combined fleets of France and Spain are annihilated, and Nelson is no more!' He then muttered, 'Had we not been detained we should have been there.' Duckworth answered not, conscience struck, but stalked the deck. He seemed ever to avoid the look of his captain, and turned to converse with the commander of the schooner, who replied in sulky brevity, 'Yes' or 'No'. Then dismissing him, he ordered all sail to be set, and walked the quarter deck alone. A death-like stillness pervaded the ship…[315]

If this account is accepted, as it has been by several scholars, then Duckworth's conduct caused a delay of at least three days, and the *Superb* intercepted the messenger just two days after the battle. No matter how atmospheric Trelawny's report may be, the dates are at odds with documentary evidence.

Having read Trelawny's account some years later, a correspondent to *United Services Magazine* who identifies only as M.M., a midshipman on the *Superb* at the relevant time, was prompted to put another view. He agrees that as part of Nelson's fleet, Keats was particularly keen to avoid delay in getting back to his admiral. He also agrees that on hearing the news Keats, and the whole crew were "angry and grieved". He says, however, the blame was laid only to fortune (or the lack of it), not to delay by Duckworth. He further contends that it could not be supposed that Duckworth, aware of the circumstances of the fleet in the presence of a sea-ready enemy, and knowing the high professional character of Keats, would subject the *Superb* to any additional delay.[316] This last statement is a matter of opinion to which we shall return, as it is arguably too generous an assessment, and inconsistent with comments from Duckworth's own hand.

As M.M. wrote, there is no need to rely on character or supposition. Rather the dates are unequivocal and speak for themselves. In this he would seem to be correct. Due to the re-fit, the *Superb*, he says, did not leave Portsmouth until 27 October, which is consistent with the muster records.[317] She anchored on the 28th in Cawsand Bay, off Plymouth, where Duckworth hoisted his flag at sunset on the 30th and sailed from Plymouth on 2 November.[318] On that basis, the ship was certainly delayed up to five days at Plymouth, but not at a time that it could be asserted that delay caused her to miss the battle fought on 21 October.

The log of the *Pickle* confirms Collingwood's dispatches for delivery to the Admiralty in London were received onboard on 26 October. The long delay in departure, five days after the battle, was on account of a violent storm that blew for two days, abated and then came back even stronger. During that time the priority of the battered fleet off a lee shore was its own preservation. After a well-documented journey of some days, the Pickle encountered the *Superb* on the morning of 3 November. She resumed her voyage by 10.00am, arriving at Falmouth the following morning from where Lieutenant Lapenotière continued on horseback, finally arriving at the residence of First Sea Lord Barham at 1.00 in the morning of 6 November.[319] It is not possible that the *Superb* could have encountered the *Pickle* in the last week of October, nor did she arrive off Trafalgar on 23 or 24 October as claimed by Trelawny.

Lord Barham was in lengthy correspondence with Duckworth as to his orders, but unbeknown to them at the time, the battle had already taken place. On 22 October, Barham writes that he is "anxious for your joining the fleet off Cádiz as soon as possible". Duckworth was told not to wait for the *Acasta* containing his followers and comforts, but that the *Powerful* would be diverted and he "should hold yourself in readiness to go out in her accordingly".[320] The following day, the 23rd, he was advised to go out immediately he was joined at Plymouth by the *Powerful, Superb, Eagle, Chiffonne* and *Minorca*. He was to cruise in search of the Rochefort squadron, believed to be at sea, before joining Nelson.[321]

Duckworth's reply lends credence to his waiting for his followers still onboard the *Acasta*, when he says on the one hand, "not a moment's delay shall occur on my part to fulfil your commands", but on the other:

> *...repeating the anxious solicitude I must be under for my captain, officers, and some of my essential comforts that are in the Acasta, as proceeding to hoist my flag in a ship where I am an entire stranger [the Powerful] cannot tend to promote the public service.*[322]

He had additionally written to Nelson, in mid-September stating his satisfaction at having been appointed his third in command, but complaining the Admiralty was not treating him civilly and intended he hoist his flag in a ship on which he would be a stranger, without his "Captain and officers, who, with my band, cooks &c., are in the *Acasta*, off Brest".[323] Again, by letter of 25 September, he laments to Nelson that the Admiralty

> *refuse me to have all my officers, and <u>can't promise me my band</u>, which was apparently retained for me on the Acasta, with Captain Dunn, and to which I have paid an annual income. This is increasing the injury I have already received from the Board which they well know I feel but it will not operate to gratify their hope of my declining service; and my utmost exertions shall be used to join your Lordship [emphasis in the original].*[324]

The correspondence does not reflect well on Duckworth's character or suitability for high command. One can imagine the reaction of a fighting captain – who had only recently experienced the deprivations of a double Atlantic crossing, who had just missed the French off Antigua, and who was now anxious to re-join his leader – on learning of such replies, particularly given the essential comforts referred to include a group of musicians. Admiral Page added a handwritten note to his copy of the report in the *Naval Chronicle* which suggests the episode prompted such a falling out between Captain Keats and Vice Admiral Duckworth that when they did ultimately sail for Cádiz they hardly spoke other than of necessity when on duty, and at times communicated only by writing.[325]

Lord Barham's response was more diplomatic, but certainly firm, removing any doubt as to the impropriety of Duckworth waiting for his 'comforts'. Orders were issued on 28 October:

> *...to proceed with the Superb, Powerful, and Acasta (if ready) to join Lord Nelson direct, and that your request to have your flag in the Superb has been acceded to. You will however not delay your sailing should the Acasta not be ready, as she can be ordered to follow as soon as ready.*[326]

Given that final orders for Duckworth to fly his flag in the *Superb* were not issued until 28 October, a week after the battle, it is difficult to lay the blame for missing it upon his waiting for his favourite officers or musicians. There is little explanation for the delay from then to until 2 November, but the battle having then been fought it was of little consequence.

This view is consistent with the text of the memoir, which makes nothing of the diversion to wait for Duckworth. The narrative of 1868, found in *The Shipwrecked Mariner*, similarly makes no mention of Duckworth causing unnecessary delay. It reports only that the *Superb* was ordered to refit with all possible haste and that every effort was made to do this, but still it was late in the year before she could be ready. It adds simply:

> *The Superb at last left Portsmouth, and on her way down the Channel, called at Plymouth where...Captain Keats had orders to receive the Vice-Admiral's flag, and proceed with him to his destination. Under these circumstances, the Superb sailed alone from Plymouth Sound on the 2nd November, four days before the news of the Battle of Trafalgar had arrived in London.*[327]

Almost identical language can be found in Brenton's account.[328]

The dates – and all evidence, other than that of Trelawny – confirm that any delays caused by Duckworth, no matter how idiosyncratic, unnecessary and frustrating, were ultimately immaterial, as the *Superb* was still being re-fitted at Portsmouth at the time of the battle. Trelawny's book was accepted as factual by contemporary reviewers but subsequent scholars have described it as containing generally but one-tenth truth and nine-tenths fiction, and that would seem to cover the present contentions.[329] It remains clear that Duckworth showed more interest in the arrival of his comforts than in getting to sea. One can well imagine the captain and crew of the *Superb* would have scorned such an attitude. In this light there is ample basis for the contended falling out between Duckworth and Keats.

The irony is that by his desire to stay with Nelson in the pursuit of Villeneuve and not head home for a refit a year earlier – and by delaying that refit until it could be delayed no more – Keats found himself dealt a grievous blow and out of the defining battle off Trafalgar. That realisation would not have improved the disposition of a Captain such as Keats; a close confidant of Nelson, one with whom Nelson had shared his battle plan and who was ambitious and eager both to implement the plan and for the glory of victory in a fleet battle. In all the circumstances, as one who had endured so much for so long, he now had even more reason to lament the mistaken intelligence provided by General Brereton in the West Indies, but for which he would most probably have been at Nelson's side confronting the French back in June.

On the 9th Nov. he was made a Colonel of Marines

This was one of four such Colonelcies, a largely honorary position awarded to meritorious captains yet to be appointed flag officer, and attended by a useful income of £800 per annum.

Historical Memoirs of
Admiral Sir Richard Goodwin Keats, GCB

10

Battle Of San Domingo

In the memoir of Sir John Duckworth,[330] we have described the proceedings of the *Superb* when in chase of a French squadron off Madeira, her proceeding to the West Indies, and during the battle which took place off St. Domingo, to which we have very little to add.

So far as is relevant to Captain Keats those events are now described: The *Superb* arrived off Cádiz on 15 November, three weeks after Trafalgar. Collingwood departed to refit at Gibraltar leaving Duckworth in command of those ships blockading the enemy survivors from that battle. He continued to cruise off Cádiz with his flag in the *Superb* until December.

What was thought to be one large French squadron had slipped out of Brest unseen whilst Cornwallis's fleet had to withdraw to Torbay for relief from storms. It was anticipated that the weather would keep the French pinned in their ports, but this proved not to be the case. With invasion plans temporarily halted and troops moved away from the French coast, Napoleon's tactics now evolved to having his various fleets escaping port to attack British colonies, disrupt trade and cut off the supply of goods and wealth to damage the English (that 'nation of shopkeepers') economically.

The escaped fleet actually comprised two French squadrons. The first included six sail of the line, under Rear Admiral Willaumez, who had orders to proceed to the Cape of Good Hope to disrupt the East India trade. The second included five sail of the line under the command of Rear Admiral Leissegues, whose objective was to deliver troops to reinforce San Domingo and then cruise off Jamaica, attacking the prosperous West Indies and disrupting the lucrative sugar trade; or if the British forces prevented this, to instead head north to Newfoundland, attacking the commerce of the fishery. The French fleet was in the process of parting company west of Ushant when seen on 15

December by Captain Brisbane in the *Arethusa* (38) who was escorting a convoy of merchants to the West Indies. Brisbane evaded the French and sent the *Boadicea* with word of this sighting to the fleet off Ushant and the *Wasp* with the same message to Cádiz and Rochefort. The news did not reach the Admiralty until 24 December 1805 via a cartel[331] from Gibraltar.

Two English squadrons were ordered to chase the French: one under Vice Admiral Warren from St Helens, and the second under Rear Admiral Strachan leaving from Plymouth. As news of the escape was not received until Christmas Eve, and because of delays in mobilisation combined with severe weather, these squadrons did not sail until the second half of January 1806. With the French weeks ahead of them, destinations unknown, the chases proved futile. In March 1806, Warren happened upon, engaged and defeated another squadron altogether, under the command of Rear Admiral Linois who had been at sea for some years causing annoyance in the East Indies.

Meanwhile, Captain Langford in the *Lark* (18) had been off the Salvage Islands – a cluster of rocks between Madeira and the Canary Islands (Map 4) – late in 1805, escorting six merchantmen from Goree (Senegal) when his convoy was dispersed by a French squadron of five sail of the line and frigates. The *Lark* escaped and brought news of this squadron to the *Agamemnon* off Cádiz on 26 November. Having missed Trafalgar, Duckworth was keen for a decisive sea battle and, without the knowledge or consent of Collingwood, let alone the Admiralty back home, he decided to give chase towards Madeira, taking with him the *Superb, Canopus (80), Spencer (74), Donegal (74), Powerful (74), Agamemnon (64)* and two frigates, leaving just two frigates to watch Cádiz. He was off Madeira on 5 December, to find the enemy had gone elsewhere and stood on reaching Teneriffe, Canary Islands, on the 15th.

The squadron near Madeira of which Duckworth had received word from the *Lark* was a third squadron, that of Rear Admiral Allemand. He had escaped Rochefort in July when Keats and Nelson had been traversing the Atlantic in search of Villeneuve, and Rear Admiral Stirling had raised the blockade of those roads. Allemand had instructions to join the fleet from Brest, but that fleet never escaped the blockade and his squadron had been at sea ever since. In that time, they had taken more than 40 prizes in the Atlantic, including the former East Indiaman, *Calcutta* (50), which two years earlier established the first British settlement in Port Phillip, Australia.

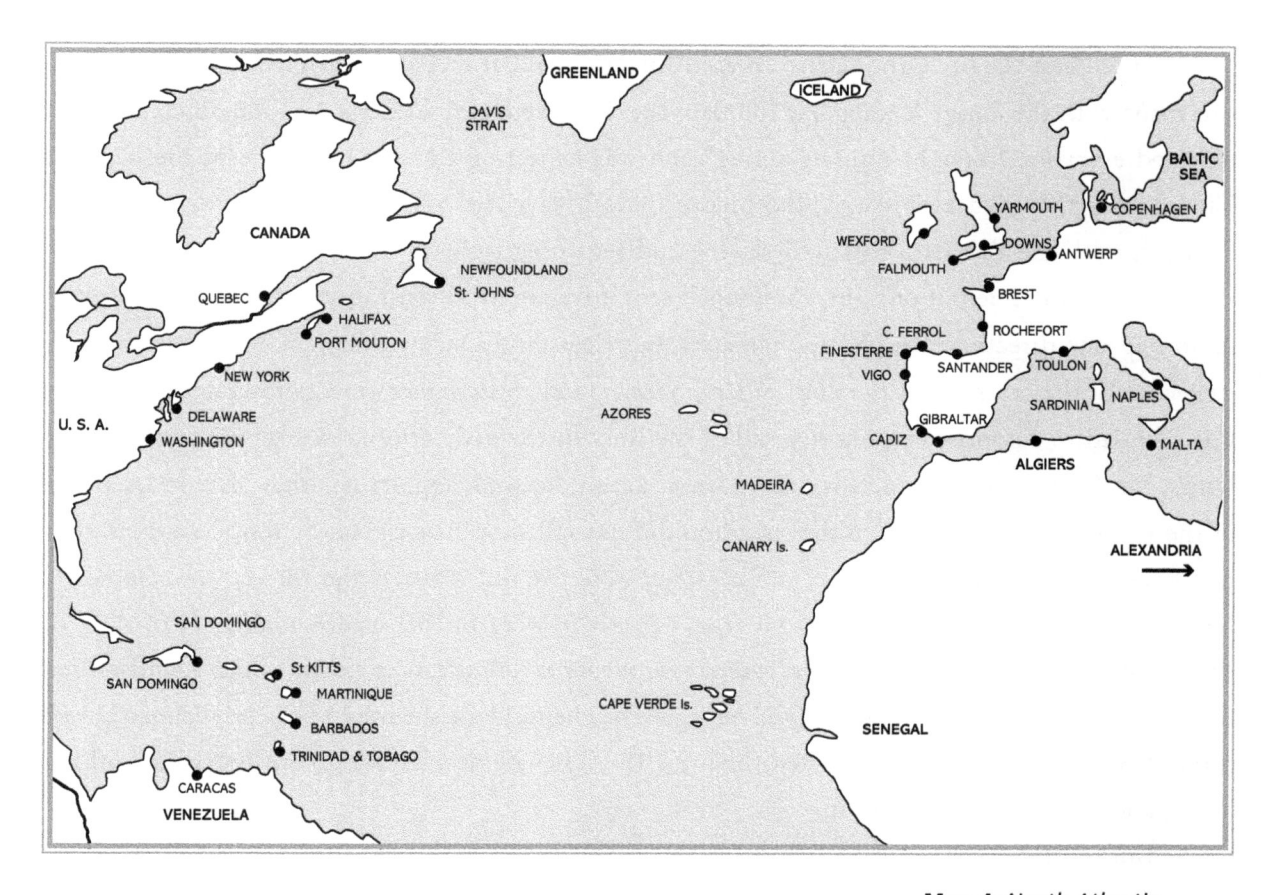

Map 4: *North Atlantic*

By the time Duckworth made it south, Allemand, for whom he was searching, well aware of the consequence of the *Lark* having escaped, was long gone. He ultimately made it safely back to France without being intercepted. Duckworth stood on as far as Cape Verde (Map 4) before giving up the search. He was between the Canaries and Madeira on his return to station at Cádiz when, on 23 December, he fell in with Brisbane and his convoy, and became aware of the presence of the further squadron.

He continued his route until, at day-break on 25 December, about 300 miles northwest of Madeira, the tips of nine sails were sighted just over the horizon, to windward and standing to the south. Given its size, he supposed this to be Allemand's squadron from Rochefort, possibly with some prizes. However, it was neither that of Leissegues nor that of Allemand. Quite by chance they had come across the squadron under the command of Rear Admiral Willaumez.

At 7:00am the squadron tacked in their direction and at 8:00am the signal for general chase was made with the *Superb* leading. At 10:00am the ships were cleared for action. An officer onboard reported everyone "thought himself a king" and was expecting the day to be one of the happiest Christmases they had ever spent. The breeze initially favoured the pursued who increased their distance, with the British occasionally losing and regaining sight of them. During the night with their ships of the line out of sight, the French sent a frigate to leeward to make misleading signals in an opposite direction to shake the pursuers, but Keats and Duckworth were awake to their *ruse de guerre*. In the morning of the 26th *Superb*, *Spencer*, and *Agamemnon* were gaining and the enemy was revealed to comprise six, not five sail of the line. In the early afternoon after a chase of thirty hours, the *Superb* was no more than seven (or according to some reports less than five) miles astern of the French. As the balance of the squadron did not sail so well as the newly refitted *Superb*, they had fallen well behind. The *Spencer* and *Amethyst* were five miles astern and the *Agamemnon* nearly hull down another five miles back. *Acasta* and *Powerful* were further astern again, out of sight of *Superb*, and the *Canopus* and *Donegal* were over twenty miles astern of them. Given his dispersed fleet Duckworth feared that if the *Superb* engaged the enemy alone she might be overwhelmed before support was on hand. Having pursued them for 150 miles he decided not to engage, called off the chase, and regrouped his squadron.

This came as a surprise and disappointment to his officers and crew. The day of expectation and dreams of glory turned to melancholy. The decision to abandon the attack is difficult to explain. James reports that "the *Superb*, with more awkwardness than she ever betrayed, before or since, shortened sail and hove to."[332] Others pointedly note that the usual tactic in these circumstances would be to harry the rearmost of the enemy, with the hope of damaging and slowing one or two, affording the other British pursuers time to come up to assist. This would test the honour and orders of the pursued commander. Does he continue to flee, leaving the stragglers to their fate, or turn his leading ships to assist, bringing on a general action?

James contrasts the action of the *Superb* here with that of July 1801 at the Battle of Algeciras. There, he notes, Keats was the first – not second – in command of her, and she attacked a significantly superior concentrated force when the balance of the British squadron was similarly out of sight some miles astern. He notes also that in the current instance, whilst the English were spread out, so too were the French, such that in his view, if the *Superb* had engaged the tail of the French, support from *Spencer* and *Agamemnon* would have been on hand in time if, as expected, the other French ships turned to assist their attacked. If a general action had resulted, he said there was every reason to be confident the issue between squadrons of roughly equal weight of metal would have been decided favourably to the English.[333] The crew of the *Superb* had not previously shown any fear of being out gunned and held similar opinions to James, backed by a strong self-belief that manifested in a unity of purpose – to get at the enemy.

Whereas Clowes says it was "surely unfortunate",[334] Woodman describes the decision not to engage Willaumez as an "inexplicable" failure that compounded Duckworth's original desertion of his station at Cádiz.[335] When Nelson had left station off Toulon, he did so in pursuit of those he was blockading. Duckworth left station in search of another squadron altogether, thereby simultaneously releasing those he had been ordered to blockade. He compounded his breach of orders by failing to keep his superiors informed. If he considered himself a second Nelson, he did so without foundation. Having pursued the enemy thus far, he did nothing. He reaped no reward and consequently lost the justification for the whole episode. At the same time, he endangered the overall strategy.[336] It was for the Admiralty to determine the grand plan and to give orders for the positioning and role of various squadrons. It was not for admirals to take it upon themselves, and certainly not without advising the Admiralty of their course of action.

There being no engagement, Keats was not required to submit a formal report, but he does make comment in a private letter to Reverend, now the Earl, William Nelson. The letter principally concerns William's elevation to titles following his brother's death and reports on arrangements Keats has made concerning various personal items that belonged to Nelson, including letters which it might be inferred they did not want to fall into public hands, as well as the welfare of their cousin, young Charles Nelson who was under Keats's tutelage serving onboard the *Superb*. It concludes that they find themselves in the West Indies, saying:

> *One of those circumstances to which we in the Navy are peculiarly subject has taken the Superb from the Mediterranean to the West Indies, and I hope will soon carry her back again....On Xmas day we had a sight of an enemy Squadron just our numbers, but they were unusually favour'd by the winds - and [as] no Action could have taken place but on very unequal terms (our squadron being much separated in the chase) none did.*[337]

He makes no comment critical of the decision not to engage, which given his supposed falling out with Duckworth is telling.

Having been allowed to continue unmolested Willaumez cruised the southern Atlantic before returning to harass trade in the West Indies and then the North Atlantic fishery. After suffering substantial damage in an Atlantic hurricane and becoming dispersed, the remnants of the squadron eventually returned to France.

Now finding himself in the mid-Atlantic with insufficient water to work back to his station at Cádiz Duckworth detached the *Amethyst* home with news of the French activity positing they were probably headed to the East Indies, and as a precaution in that regard sent the *Powerful* to India. Taking advantage of the prevailing winds, he took the remainder of the squadron to the West Indies to resupply. They arrived on 12 January and proceeded to St Kitts (Map 4) where on 19 January they were joined by Rear Admiral Alexander Cochrane with Captain George Tobin in the *Northumberland (74)* and on 21 January by Captain Pym in the *Atlas (74)*.

The sloop *Kingfisher* (18) was anchored off Tortola in the Virgin Islands, repainting and re-caulking on 31 January when approached by a merchant in a small boat who claimed to have rowed twenty miles to inform her that the French had been seen steering for San Domingo three hundred miles to the west. Her paint and tar not dry, *Kingfisher* weighed and brought the news to Duckworth who made sail forthwith. On the 5 February, the *Magicienne* (38) joined the company off Mona Passage, which separates Puerto Rico and the east end of the island of San Domingo, with confirmation from a detained Danish schooner that the French were at anchor and re-supplying off San Domingo. The British gained sight of them at 7.30 in the morning of 6 February, 1806. As it turned out this was the squadron of Leissegues who had been seen by Brisbane from the *Arethusa* some weeks earlier.

Leissegues had also been hit by the December storms. He had arrived in the West Indies on 20 January, with two of his more severely damaged ships arriving a week later. By the first week of February they had nearly completed repairing and re-caulking in preparation for the voyage home. The French squadron was led by the *Impériale (118)*, an Ocean class first rater, "without doubt the largest and finest ship in the world".[338] Launched in 1804 she was some 3,000 tons, with a crew of 1200, carrying 35,000 square feet of sail, and a broadside weight of metal of an enormous 1852 pounds, carrying in this action some 130 guns including 36-pound carronades. The British had never built such a ship. There was nothing to compare in the whole of the navy, let alone in Duckworth's squadron where the largest ship was the *Canopus* of 80 guns and a weight of metal of 1083 pounds.[339] The *Impériale* was accompanied by the *Alexandre* (80), three 74's, two frigates and a corvette.

When the British squadron hove in sight of the enemy, moored off the town of St. Domingo, they immediately weighed, and stood with all sail to the southward, pursued by the English squadron, the *Superb* leading. The advantage which the embayed situation of the enemy gave to their opponents was not lost sight of and at half-past ten the action was commenced by the *Superb*.

Despite having received word of the British presence from an American merchant the day before and the corvette *Diligente (18)* having arrived up firing her guns giving an urgent warning just after dawn that day advising the approaching squadron had been seen barely fifty miles away off Catalina the French were caught somewhat unawares. As they belatedly slipped their cables at 7:30am and sought to escape the bay, *Alexandre* leading the *Impériale* and *Diomede*, the British, formed in two lines astern. The weather line to starboard led by the *Superb* sought to cut off the escape route. Pursuant to the order, "Make all sail possible, preserving the same order", this became a pure chase, like that at Algeciras, but in daylight with both fleets well aware of what was unfolding.[340]

San Domingo sits in a shallow semi-circular bay, and the British, led by the *Superb*, being further offshore in a steadier breeze, 'strained every nerve' to block the French escape to the safety of a nearby battery. A second column led by the *Canopus*, Rear Admiral Louis with Captain Austen (brother of the as yet unpublished writer, Jane) was further astern and to sea and initially fell behind. The frigates *Acasta* and *Magicienne*, sloop *Kingfisher* (16) and brig *Epervier (14)* were to their windward. Whereas the fleets at Trafalgar approached one another at a ponderous one nautical mile per hour over five or more hours, both prepared to fight, here they were sailing at eight times that speed, making this one of the more dramatic attacks of the times.

In what has been described as a piece of theatre that may be unique, in response to a signal from Duckworth, 'This is glorious', Keats went below to retrieve a portrait of his late commander, Nelson, which he then silently fixed to the mizzen stay before addressing the crew in a manner intended to encourage enthusiasm for the cause in the coming battle. Others have described this address to be expressed "in sailors' vigorous vernacular" exhorting the crew to do their duty and fight as though the great hero was watching them.[341]

A TREASURE TO THE SERVICE

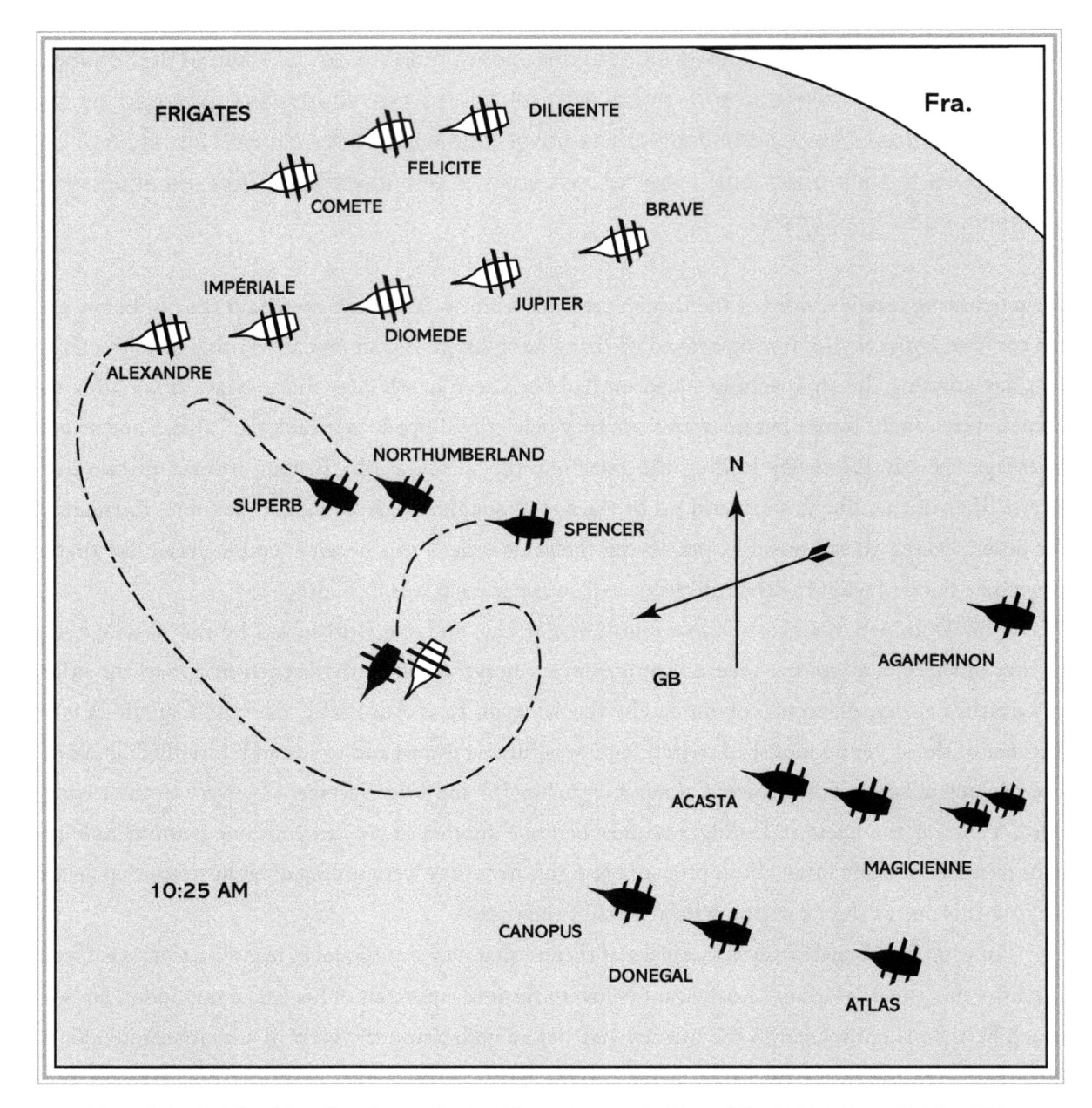

Plan of the Battle of San Domingo – Derived from James, Battles of the British Navy, Vol 2, p158

Willis argues the display of Nelson's portrait was probably motivated by spite aimed at Duckworth, whose 'faffing at Portsmouth' still riled Keats.[342] As we have seen, that faffing almost certainly had no bearing upon the *Superb* being thrown out of that battle. It is quite possible that Keats, keenly aware his ship and crew had missed the opportunity to fight alongside Nelson, was simply drawing on the memory of his good friend – who was personally well known to the crew of the *Superb* – as a means of motivating the crew. Of course, this could have been seen as a pointed contrast to the admiral presently in command. If motivation was the object it certainly succeeded. It was reported that, still recovering from the disappointment at having been forced to call off the chase of Willaumez, never was enthusiasm greater than that of the *Superb*'s crew, who went to it literally with hand and heart. The portrait remained unharmed, but it is said that during the battle both it, and Keats standing alongside, were covered in the blood and brains of the unfortunate John Brookbank, a Boatswain's mate killed in action nearby![343]

A few minutes before the action commenced, the band played *God Save the King!* then came the livelier, *Off She Goes!* and next the stirring *Nelson of the Nile!* The difference in sailing soon became apparent again, with the *Agamemnon* dropping astern, while the *Superb* gained on the enemy. At 10.10am the *Superb*, having made up all ground in a freshening breeze which had shifted to the north-east, took in her studding-sails and fired her starboard guns. Brenton says that in doing so she was boldly laid up alongside *Impériale*, whereas James and others state the *Alexandre* leading the line was the first object of her attention, which comprised three broadsides in rapid succession.[344] In a few minutes the *Northumberland*, was engaged with *Alexandre* and *Impériale*, quickly followed by the *Spencer*, Captain Hon. Robert Stopford, who made the *Diomede* her more immediate opponent, both ships running before the wind at some seven knots.

In the words of an officer onboard the *Superb*, who might be expected to be possessed of more direct knowledge than either Brenton or James, but is unfortunately un-named:

> *The enemy brought their two largest ships together, (the Alexandre the headmost, and the Impériale) seemingly with a view to quiet the fire of the English Admiral in the Superb before any of the other ships could come up; but in this they were disappointed for the second broadside from the Superb fortunately did such execution on board the enemy's headmost ship, the Alexandre, that she became quite unmanageable, and lost her station.*[345]

She suddenly luffed across the bows of the *Superb* before gallantly trying to re-join the *Impériale* but in that effort was met by raking fire from the *Spencer*. It was at this time that Keats laid the *Superb* up against the *Impériale*. She was as a consequence within pistol-shot of the *Superb*, and reserving her fire for her; but at this critical moment Admiral Cochrane, in the *Northumberland*, came up, and notwithstanding the small distance between the *Superb* and her opponent, gallantly ran in between them, and received the whole broadside of the largest, and esteemed the finest, ship in the French navy. Several of the shot passed quite through the *Northumberland* into the *Superb*.

The position of the French and English fleets, six leagues from San Domingo at 10am on 6 February 1806. The Superb (1), lower left leads Northumberland (3) and Spencer (2) seeking to close the escape route. Inshore Alexandre (D) leads the French squadron followed by Impériale (A) and Diomede (c). NMM PAF4759, © National Maritime Museum, Greenwich, London.

The conflict then became general, save that the *Agamemnon*, Captain Sir Edward Berry, was as yet unable to get up; *Canopus* also engaging *Impériale*, *Donegal* (formerly the French *Hoche* captured in the expedition to Ireland in 1798, now under the command of Captain Pulteney Malcolm), engaging the *Brave*, and *Atlas* engaging the *Jupiter*, before moving ahead in support of *Canopus*. *Donegal* then came up running onboard *Jupiter*, securing her bowsprit before boarding her whereupon she surrendered and was taken in tow. The action continued until 11.30am when the French Admiral, now under attack by several British ships was completely beaten but determined to deny the British the opportunity to capture his flagship rigged a sail on his mizzen mast and hauled directly for the land between Point Nisao and Point Catalina about twenty miles south-west of San Domingo. Some minutes later she struck the ground with such force as to cause all her remaining masts to fall. The *Superb* pursued her until the shallowness of the water forced her to haul off, to avoid the same fate on the rocky coast. Shortly thereafter the *Alexandre* severely cut up by the *Superb* and *Spencer* lost all three masts to a broadside from the *Canopus* and was forced to strike her colours. In this she was closely followed by the *Brave*, who had been raked from astern by the *Donegal*.

Titled 'Second position, at the completion of the battle', however it is clear no ships have yet been driven ashore. Superb (i) engages Impériale (B) and Diomede (D) upper left. Atlas (O) supports Donegal (M) engaging Brave (C) before moving on to engage Jupiter (E). Northumberland (K), lower left has lost her main mast. The French frigates, upper left, make good their escape. NMM PAF4760, © National Maritime Museum, Greenwich, London

The *Diomede* was by now the only enemy ship of the line in action. The *Atlas* and *Spencer* joined by *Agamemnon*, now finally in the action, soon forced her ashore just a few hundred yards from the flagship causing the loss of all her masts and the action terminated most honourably for the British. The French squadron was entirely annihilated or captured in less than two hours, with only the frigates escaping.[346] Whilst the British outnumbered the French, it was clear the disproportion between the three-decked French ship and a British 74 was significant, and the French 80, with superior scantling, calibre and manpower contributed a difference not to be overlooked.[347] Once again, however, accuracy and rapidity of fire proved decisive. As the *Shipwrecked Mariner* put it, "The English fought with skill, the effect of long practice, united in their usual valour; the French had valour, but not equal seamanship".[348]

British losses reported were 74 killed (six on the *Superb*) and 263 wounded (56 on the *Superb*, although according to her log, only 30[349]), and despite the closeness of the contest, only the *Northumberland* lost her mainmast. The French losses were believed to be more than 1,500 men and virtually an entire squadron of ships. Their captains, other than that of the *Impériale* were all captured and detained until 1814.

It was reported that the triumph of this fight "was mainly owing to the charge [Keats] personally took upon himself of conning his ship"[350] in which he was observed to have "performed particularly well, bolstering his growing reputation as one of the leading officers of his generation".[351] Duckworth's praise of his role in this action, which is recorded in the memoir below, appears genuine and well earned. It discloses no evidence of a falling out between them.

Keats no doubt manoeuvred his ship with skill and courage and the effect of her gunnery was devastating. The same could be suggested of others, and of the *Northumberland* and the *Spencer*, Captain Stopford in particular. Both ships were placed where and when needed to provide mutual support.

Duckworth was fortunate to have these captains with him, as they were used to working together instinctively. *Superb*, *Canopus*, *Spencer* and *Donegal* had all been part of the Mediterranean fleet. Consistent with the Nelson approach, they felt no need to wait for any central direction from the Admiral. This was fortunate because as it happened, no such direction was forthcoming.[352] James criticises the lack of command coming from Duckworth, lamenting the French frigates had got well to leeward during the action and hauled to the south making their escape. The British frigates *Acasta* and *Magicienne* ought, he says, to have been ordered to go in chase early in the battle, rather than standing by without orders until being called to attend to the captured ships.[353]

The battle was a graphic demonstration of the superiority of British sea power, but superiority should not be interpreted as infallibility. The smoke haze was so thick that one manoeuvre by the *Spencer* went unseen and as she emerged from the cloud of smoke both the *Northumberland* and *Superb* briefly fired into her. The *Atlas* suffered more damage from a collision with the *Canopus* than from enemy fire. Such were the risks of warfare in the Age of Sail.

Admiral Sir John Duckworth's action off San Domingo, 6 February 1806. In a fresh breeze and choppy sea: L-R: Donegal, starboard view engages Jupiter to port. Alexandre in the distance with Agamemnon & Atlas. Canopus engages Diomede partly obscured. Impériale, centre middle ground port bow view, her topmast falling, is engaged by Superb, nearly bow on. Brave is dismasted in the distance. Northumberland partly dismasted and Spencer in the distant right stern on. Nicholas Pocock, 1808, on the commission of Lord Barham. NMM BHC0571©National Maritime Museum, Greenwich London

In less than an hour and a half the *Alexandre* and *Brave*, of 80[354] guns each, and the *Jupiter* of 74 were taken; the French admiral in the *Impériale* of 120 guns, and the *Diomede* of 74 guns, running on shore were destroyed. The conduct of Captain Keats during the whole of these proceedings was such as might be expected from his reputation and long tried talents, which was acknowledged by Sir John Duckworth in his official dispatch, in the following words: "To speak individually of the conduct of any one would be injurious to all, for all were equally animated with the same zeal and ardour in support of their King and country: yet possessed of those feelings, I cannot be silent, without injustice to the firm and manly support for which I am indebted to Captain Keats, and for the effect of the system and good order which I found the *Superb* must produce; and the pre-eminence of British seamen could never be more highly conspicuous than in this contest". [8]

---

8   The first and second Lieutenants of the *Superb*, Charles Gill and ____Gooch were promoted to the rank of Commander.

Captain Keats was gratified on this occasion by receiving the thanks of Parliament and also a sword of one hundred guineas value from the Committee of the Patriotic Fund.[355]

Notwithstanding the above, there is little doubt that in place of a sword, Keats received a silver vase of equivalent value, – "for his noble and gallant efforts in the brilliant and decisive victory on 6th February -1806, off St. Domingo."[356]

Illustrative of a strong sense of propriety and the importance Keats placed on adherence to honourable rules of engagement is an incident here involving French Captain Henry of the *Diomede*. The ship had been run ashore and was beyond salvage. The crew having been rescued and removed it was ordered she be burnt. Henry, being among the rescued prisoners offered Keats his sword in formal surrender. It had been reported to Duckworth by Captain Sir Edward Berry (*Agamemnon*) that Henry had run his ship ashore *after* having surrendered, thereby destroying the ship and preventing the British from taking possession of her. On this basis, Keats indignantly refused the sword offered by Henry, believing that by his conduct Henry had breached convention. Later reports confirmed Berry, who was somewhat removed from the action, had confused the *Diomede* for the *Brave*. The *Diomede* had not surrendered earlier, but her pendant was always flying (although the ensign had been shot away) and remained flying until the mainmast fell. Consequently, Henry had honourably defended his ship and did not surrender until after the ship was on shore and beyond recovery.[357] After a fuller investigation Duckworth, to his credit, corrected the record restoring Captain Henry's honour, writing, to the Admiralty some days later: "character is much more valuable than life" and the heavy charge upon Henry should be done away in such manner as their Lordships saw fit- which as it transpired included publishing Duckworth's letter in The Times newspaper for all to see.[358]

The *Brave*, sank on her voyage to England, but the crew were saved. The *Alexandre* made it back but was so badly damaged she had to be towed part of the way and on arrival was assessed to be of no use to the navy. The *Jupiter* was purchased into the navy where she served as *Maida*.[359] Head money was paid on more than 4,000 French crew.

Order of Battle 6 February 1806

Ship	Guns	Captain	Notes
Britain			
Superb	74	Vice Admiral Sir John Duckworth Richard Keats	Lightly damaged
Canopus	80	Rear Admiral Thomas Louis Francis Austen	Lightly damaged
Northumberland	74	Rear Admiral Alexander Cochrane John Morrison	Main mast lost
Spencer	74	Robert Stopford	Significant hull damage
Agamemnon	64	Sir Edward Berry	Lightly damaged
Donegal	74	Pulteney Malcolm	Foreyard shot away
Atlas	74	Samuel Pym	Bow sprit lost in collision with Canopus
Acasta	40	Richard Dunn	Not actively engaged
Magicienne	32	Adam Mackenzie	Not actively engaged
Kingfisher	16	Commander Nathaniel Cochrane	Not actively engaged
Epervier	14	Lieutenant James Higginson	Not actively engaged
Total British guns	**616**		
France			
Impériale	118	Rear Admiral Corentin Leissegues Julien Bigot	Run ashore and destroyed
Alexandre	80	Pierre Garreau	Lost all masts. Captured, but considered beyond repair
Diomede	74	Jean-Baptiste Henry	Run ashore and destroyed
Jupiter	74	Gaspard Laignel	Captured, commissioned as HMS Maida
Brave	74*	Commodore Louis Coudé	Captured, sank the on return voyage
Comete	40	Unclear	Not actively engaged, escaped
Fèlicite	32	Unclear	Not actively engaged, escaped
Diligente	20	Unclear	Not actively engaged, escaped
Total French guns	**512**	*Not to be confused with the Brave of 80 guns captured off Cape Ortegal in 1805	

Table 3: *The order of battle and summary of losses, Battle of San Domingo, 6 February 1806*

An incident in this encounter demonstrates some of the lighter moments in what would otherwise have been a hard way of life. In the heat of battle between *Superb* and *Impériale*, a 42-lb double shot demolished a wooden structure on the poop. One compartment contained muskets, and the other was used as a chicken coop. Splinters, bayonets and shrapnel went flying and all the birds bar one were destroyed. This rooster, 'til then unknown to fame', flapped his way up to the spanker boom and started crowing defiantly. Another shot shattered the boom, behind where the rooster was perched, so he flapped again to the stump of the boom and resumed crowing. After the battle, he was found to have suffered multiple contusions and to have lost an eye to a splinter but he survived. The sailors, taking a fancy to him, decorated him with rings and ribbons and adopted him as a mascot. He was introduced to the officers with a plea he be saved from the poulterer and was thereafter given free reign of the deck, where he became accustomed to the men's attention- their 'favourite bold chanticleer'.[360]

It is widely accepted that had it not been for the victory at San Domingo, Duckworth would have faced a court martial – the fourth in his career – for both leaving his station at Cádiz to pursue the enemy, and for then failing to engage Willaumez.[361] Popham was officially reprimanded for leaving his station in South Africa to cross the Atlantic in pursuit of exploits in South America, being told that withdrawing without orders to do so the whole of any naval force from the place where it is directed to be deployed must be attended by the most serious inconvenience to the public service. Whilst it ended well, this whole series of events demonstrates the wisdom and truth of the Admiralty statement.

Having been forced to divert ships from the Mediterranean fleet to Cádiz to restore the abandoned blockade Collingwood made his disapproval of Duckworth's conduct widely known. There was a suggestion also that the decision to seek out the French at San Domingo had to be urged upon Duckworth by his subordinates.[362] One can well imagine the crew of the Superb supporting that call. The British public was now accustomed to news of victory and had come to expect a British squadron to be victorious even against a more powerful opposition and took this latest success in their stride. Admiralty Secretary Marsden was more fulsome in his assessment declaring the victory put everyone "in high spirits, and it really is a famous event".[363] The merchants[364] and insurers were delighted their trade lines in the West Indies were secure. They voted large sums of money to those involved in the action. Keats received the thanks of Parliament, a one hundred-guinea vase, and the King's Naval Gold Medal.[365] This was the last fleet action for which gold medals were awarded. Cochrane received his Bath Star, and Rear Admiral Louis a baronetcy. Perhaps equally important, Louis, Malcolm,

Stopford, and Keats had not only demonstrated their abilities in battle but had received some restitution for their disappointment at having missed Trafalgar.

In the words of Lord Barham of the Admiralty, the victory put "us out of all fear from another predatory war in the West Indies".[366] It paved the way for British possession of Curacao, Martinique, Cayenne and Guadeloupe. This was the last of the major fleet actions in the Age of Sail, largely because no fleet emerged to challenge the British. The Battle of San Domingo closed an intense period of sea warfare which defined an age characterised by seamen of courage, ability and achievement well worthy of recognition.

The end of fleet battles did not mean an end to the war. Domination of the sea thereafter meant denying the enemy access to it. It meant preventing them from building new ships, taking control of the fleets of vassal states and defending British merchant ships from attack, and in turn strangling the trade lines of the enemy. In short, overcoming Napoleon's vision for a 'Continental System'.

**Historical Memoirs of
Admiral Sir Richard Goodwin Keats, GCB**

11

Return To The Channel

The prizes having been fitted and sent to England, the *Superb* returned to her station off Cádiz,[367] and in the month of May proceeded to England. She then became a private ship,[368] and was ordered off Brest, under the command of Lord St. Vincent, by whom Captain Keats was entrusted with the command of a flying squadron, varying from five to six sail of the line, employed in the Bay of Biscay, or watching the Port of Rochefort [Map 5].

Having spent four years ashore as First Lord of the Admiralty St Vincent, now seventy-one years of age, was returned to active command flying his flag from the *Hibernia* as Commander-in-Chief of the Channel fleet. He was happy to have under him a captain of Keats's capacities to whom he could delegate command of a squadron similar in power to that Duckworth had taken to the West Indies.

On 24 July, whilst patrolling the Bay of Biscay, the *Loire*, Captain Maitland, chased a squadron of four French frigates and a corvette, under Captain La Meillerie. This squadron had sheltered in Cádiz after Trafalgar and escaped, with the loss of the *Furet*, captured by the *Hydra* in February 1806, after Duckworth's blockade was lifted. Having cruised for six months off Barbados they were now seeking to return to Rochefort. They hauled to the wind as soon as they identified their pursuer. As a result, despite pursuing them for some time, the British were not able to close to within less than eight or nine miles and abandoned the chase. The *Loire* then proceeded to rendezvous with Keats's squadron west of Belle Isle. Captain Maitland was onboard the *Superb* making his report on the 27th when the enemy was seen by the ships to windward. Chase was given instantly, but most of the squadron being far astern and it being late in the day it was the lookout ship, the *Mars* (Captain R.D. Oliver) alone who kept sight of them until shortly after dark. Having lost sight of them (as well as of her own squadron) in the night Captain Oliver calculated the enemy intentions, bore up a few points and continued the chase under a press of sail for over 150 miles through a night of rain and squalls during which a number of sails were split and replaced with alacrity. At first light they discovered the enemy precisely on the bearing predicted, although at a greater distance save for the rearmost ship on which they appeared to be gaining. They continued the pursuit throughout the day and finally captured the *Rhin*. In her desperation to escape she had too much canvas aloft and lay over in a squall allowing the two-decker to range up on her quarter. La Meillerie turned as if to support her, with the *Hortense, Thémis* and *Hermione* formed in line of battle on the larboard tack, but on seeing the *Mars* continue her approach, despite their superiority in number and weight of metal, they did not engage and at 3.00pm left the *Rhin* to her fate. The *Mars* cleared for action and fired a warning shot, which was sufficient inducement for the French to strike their colours. Two of the escapees reached the safety of Bordeaux and one Rochefort.[369] The *Rhin* (40) with 318 men, only four years old was purchased into the navy, subsequently capturing several French ships. Keats wrote to St Vincent lamenting exceedingly that the balance of the squadron had been unable to keep sight of the *Mars* through the night, but for which the encounter may have resulted in even more important success.[370]

On learning the Rochefort squadron might be broken up, and Keats redeployed, St. Vincent wrote to Thomas Grenville, First Lord of the Admiralty in the following terms: "Captain Keats has such a perfect knowledge of the coast, from Biscay to Brest inclusive, that a fitter man for the service cannot be found", and later, that while it was strategically very important, "The station before Rochefort…is very hazardous; and under the orders of any other man than Captain Keats, who possesses so much knowledge of that sea, I should judge it improper to be continued during the winter months".[371]

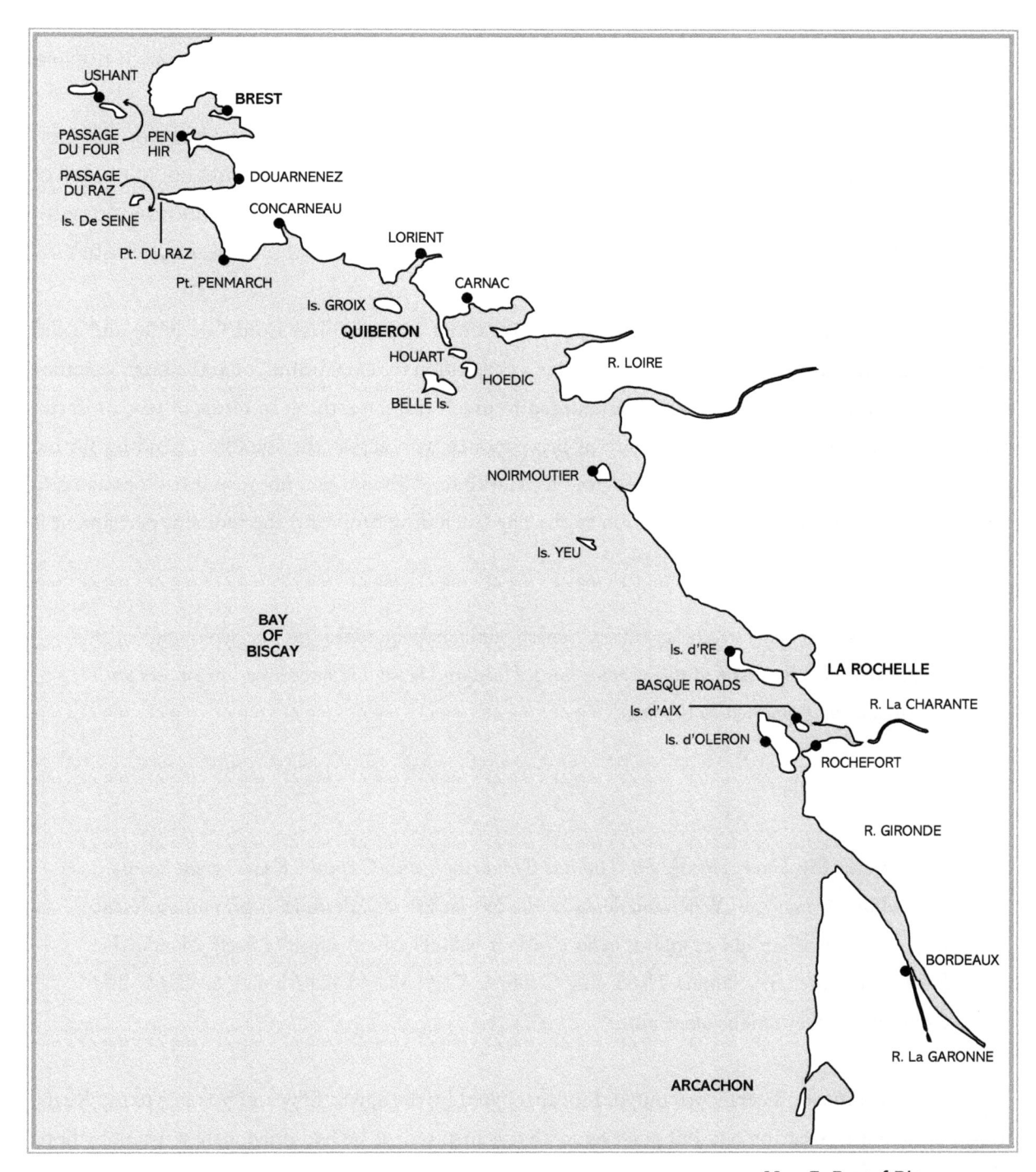

Map 5: *Bay of Biscay*

[In Rochefort,] under the Isle of Aix [Map 5], the enemy had a squadron of six sail of the line ready to put to sea.[372]

They made an attempt to affect their escape on the 28th February 1807 but were chased back again on the following day. On whatever service employed Captain Keats could not fail of giving satisfaction, and his conduct whilst in command of this detached squadron met with such approbation that he was honoured with a broad pendant, and a Captain under him.

Through 1806, Earl St. Vincent had written several times to both First Lord Grenville and Lord Markham at the Admiralty, saying Keats was due a promotion to rear admiral, or at the least "commodore with a captain under him", which amounted to much the same thing in terms of pay, uniform, and entitlement to the flag officer's share of prize money won across the squadron pending formal promotion to rear admiral.[373] In July he wrote to Markham, "Should you not give broad pennants to Hood and Keats, or make your promotion to the flag (including Stopford) the moment parliament is up?"[374] Only a few days later he wrote:

> *Captain Keats has already approved himself eminently qualified for the command of a squadron and fully justified the appointment. Hood and he should have broad pennants with captains or be promoted to the flag...*[375]

Then to Lord Grenville:

> *You have in [Sir Sam. Hood], Sir Thomas Troubridge, and Captain Keats, great seamen, abounding in resources...When one looks at the barren list of Admirals, a promotion to the Flag, including Captain Stopford, (who is also a valuable man) suggests itself. Should this [not] take place, Sir Samuel Hood and Captain Keats should have broad pendants and Captains, or they will be worn out.*[376]

Years at sea saw most officers worn out and incapacitated by the age of fifty and it is fair to say Keats, now fifty-one was 'wearing out' but persevered always inspired, as he had previously written, by hope of greater success to come.

In his biography of Saumarez, Voelcker has suggested that although brilliant as a post-captain and renowned for his fighting skills and seamanship, Keats may not have had the same self-confidence in his decision-making necessary at higher levels of authority. In support of the contention, he quotes St. Vincent's views, written to the Admiralty in November 1806, that some commanders, while brave as lions in the face of the enemy, were less suitable to high office as they displayed such a deficiency of nerves under responsibility as to sink beneath its weight.[377] St Vincent made specific reference to two officers: Lord Gardiner and Vice Admiral Thornbrough, but no reference to Keats. It is suggested he would never have intended his comment be interpreted as applying to Keats.

Other correspondence both before and after this, quite clearly shows that Keats enjoyed the complete confidence of St. Vincent. Having earlier stated that Keats had proved himself as commander of a squadron, he wrote again on 1 November, (within days of the letter relied upon by Voelcker), saying to First Sea Lord, Admiral Markham: "You really should either promote to the flag or give a captain to him and to Hood, or you will do them up before the winter is passed."[378] Acknowledging that St. Vincent had a reputation for changing his expressed views of officers, it is nonetheless difficult to believe he would be praising Keats as a proven commander and recommending promotion, while at the same time intending that he be included amongst those alleged to suffer "a deficiency of nerves under responsibility". This is affirmed by the context which described the hardship of standing off Brest, tacking or wearing at least once a night, where Keats demonstrably excelled and had St. Vincent's absolute support. St Vincent did note, possibly alluding to Keats's anxiety, that his squadron would be much relieved to know Roches Bonnes, an area of shoal waters about thirty miles off La Rochelle had been buoyed.[379]

Just a few months later, in March 1807, St. Vincent was recommending Keats for a Baronetcy having spoken to both the Duke and Lord Grenville about it – further evidence of his enduring support and confidence.[380] In the same month official notice was published confirming that St Vincent's advice had been heeded and Keats was promoted to the rank of Commodore with a captain under him.

Continuing in his old ship the *Superb,* and with a view of more effectually blockading the enemy, he took up his anchorage in Basque Roads, but the enemy did not again attempt to put to sea.

On 15 March 1807, St. Vincent wrote to Keats congratulating him most heartily on the excellent state of his squadron, after the severe trial he had experienced, which he attributed entirely to Keats's skilful and judicious management of it.[381] To the First Lord of the Admiralty, Lord Grenville, he wrote that "Under almost any other officer than Commodore Keats I should tremble for the fate of a squadron of our ships exposed to the difficulties of the navigation of that gulf…".[382] Keats continued to have the full confidence of St. Vincent.

The comments on the excellent state of the squadron after the 'severe trial' mentioned by St. Vincent are worthy of detailed examination. They refer to comments made by Captain Lord Thomas Cochrane concerning the extended period ships were kept at sea as their condition deteriorated, and specifically to the loss of two ships under Keats's command. Cochrane raised the matters in the House of Commons in July 1807, principally, it would seem, as an attack on St. Vincent in his capacity as Commander-in-Chief of the Channel fleet. The complaints were wide-ranging: from poor victualling and lack of medical supplies and surgeons to the extended period both men and ships were required to stay at sea.[383] A capable and daring captain, with a welcome concern for his men, Cochrane was an interesting and polarising character who seemed incapable of getting along with either his superiors or with many of his subordinates. He was later gaoled for stock market fraud and evicted from both the Parliament and the navy in 1814, only to be pardoned and reinstated in 1832.[384]

At this time, he claimed those on Channel duty faced unnecessary hardships, often being at sea for eight months without going ashore. Those who undertook a voyage to the East Indies spent less time at sea, and with more refreshments, than those on Channel duty who were only four hours sail from a home port. All the while, he said, St. Vincent enjoyed the comfort of his London residence, still claiming his share of prize money.

Of particular relevance to Keats was the condition of the 16-gun brig-sloop *Atalante*, claimed by Cochrane to be unfit for sea, taking 20 inches of water per hour in blowing weather. He acknowledged that Keats had ordered a survey, which reported the vessel fit to continue on station, but contended that carpenters undertaking such assessments at sea rarely reported that ships should leave station for a home port. We recall that St. Vincent refused to replenish the Mediterranean fleet to allow rotation of vessels for repair, despite the sorry state of the *Superb*, amongst others, in 1804, confirmed by no less an authority than Nelson. When Cochrane returned to port, he said to the builder of Plymouth-yard in the presence of Port Admiral Sutton, that the first news they would have from off Rochefort, if they had a gale of wind, would be the loss of the *Atalante*. Then, on 12 February 1807, she was lost.

In the House, Sir Samuel Hood declared that any blame for the loss of that ship rested with himself and Keats, rather than with St. Vincent, but that there was no blame. Her loss was not at all owing to her having been in a bad state. On the contrary, she drove ashore in a swell upon a fine day, and if she had not been sound, her crew could not have been saved.[385] Such an accident was, he observed, in no way capable of being ascribed to any neglect on the part of the senior officers, and no censure could apply to them. Admiral Markham of the Admiralty told the House he very much regretted the matter had been raised in this manner. He had spoken to Keats that very morning and he had corroborated every word stated by Hood and had declared the condition of the ship was such as he would not have hesitated to send her as far as the East Indies. As to St. Vincent remaining on shore; his squadron was so divided that he could give his orders as well while in port as if he sailed with one particular squadron.

Mr. Sheridan rose to say he had read a letter from Keats taking the whole blame for himself (thereby deflecting same from his commander-in-chief) but, he continued, there certainly was no blame.

Other reports show that the *Atalante* struck the Grande Blanche rock off the Isle de Ré, outside Rochefort. The officer of the watch ignored the command of her captain, Lieutenant Bowker, and the advice of the French pilot, M. Legall, onboard in an advisory capacity, not to take her into shallow water. The helmsman faced a court martial and was disrated.[386] As Hood declared in Parliament, a clear understanding of the case was sufficient to refute the charges:

> *And to show that neither the officers nor any other person could be fairly blamed for the fate of the Atalante, for that fate was owing to an accident against which any commander, however vigilant, might be utterly unable to guard.*[387]

Keats had requested a court martial of his own conduct, but this was refused because there were no grounds for it. Admiral Sir Charles Pole spoke of his disapproval of Cochrane's actions in raising allegations that moved the feelings of such a meritorious officer to seek a court martial. Writing to Keats, St. Vincent said, "The loss of the *Atalante* is to be lamented, although one of the accidents a people who combat the elements and watch the ports of the enemy, as we do, are liable to".[388] To the Admiralty, St. Vincent laid the blame purely on poor navigation, saying the ship had been thrown away shamefully.[389] Of Thomas Cochrane he remarked; he could not be trusted out of sight!

A good friend of Cochrane's, Captain Robert Barrie, was in command of the frigate *Pomone* (38)(1805) in Keats's squadron at the time Cochrane joined, and although he was not so keen on being subjected to the iron rule of St Vincent or on being assigned to blockade duties through the terrible winter months, he appeared to appreciate the virtues of Keats, not the least because he was given ample scope to cruise for prizes. He hoped Keats was in turn pleased with the way they watched and followed the French. In response to Cochrane's claims he records that in time the *Atalante* may well have foundered in rough weather...but as stated by Hood and others, in the mean-time, she ran aground. He was well placed to pass judgement as it was he who was tasked with destroying the wreck to prevent it falling into French hands. In appalling weather, the ship's jolly boat (for the seas were judged too violent for the larger boats) succeeded in its mission in the face of enemy fire, meeting with great praise from Keats.[390]

The *Atalante's* captain explained that the day prior French ships had been observed getting under weigh. Being alone he signalled as if to the rest of his squadron and fired guns, which deterred the French from their plans. In the night he manoeuvred his ship to better watch the anchorage, in the course of which she went aground. The loss flowed from navigational error rather than lack of seaworthiness. The enemy instead of sending boats to rescue the men, opened fire on the stranded vessel until the *Pomone* arrived up and effected the rescue.[391]

Cochrane raised also the loss of the *Felix*, a schooner of fourteen guns whose commander had represented to Keats that she ought to be sent into port for repairs, saying in private correspondence to others, "I think the chances are against us ever bringing her into an English port".[392] She was lost in January 1807. Again, it was intimated the loss was caused by the foundering of an unseaworthy ship in a gale on the open sea. However, as Hood pointed out, she had been sent into St Andero Bay, near Santander, under flag of truce, and had been there for four days, when a gale of wind blew her ashore, in circumstances where any ship, no matter her condition would have very little chance, if any, of escaping a similar fate. He continued; there was ample proof that the *Felix* was not in a bad state.[393] Hood and others stated the claims were baseless and designed only to cause mischief. Cochrane's motions to have various papers and correspondence tabled to advance his claims were denied by the House without division.[394]

In his correspondence to Keats, St. Vincent was alluding to the trials of winter in the Bay of Biscay, the loss of two ships, and the attendant criticism. The reference to the excellent state of his ships may have been self-serving, but given he put it down to skilful and judicious management on the part of Keats, it was most probably also designed to show support and lend confidence to his command in light of Cochrane's agitation, at that time known to St Vincent, but yet to reach Parliament and a public airing.

We know from Keats's own experience with the *Superb* that ships were often kept at sea when return to port for the refreshment of both ship and crew might be advisable. Despite, or because of, this experience, Keats seemed unmoved. On the other hand, there is ample evidence that the loss of these two ships did not sustain the charges made and was due to poor handling rather than poor equipment. In offering to take the blame, if any, Keats was showing himself to be a good company man demonstrating admirable loyalty to the Service, and the senior officers closed ranks in support. This no doubt enhanced his standing amongst his superiors at the Admiralty generally, as well as prompting unashamedly laudatory public support from St. Vincent.

The records are replete with ample evidence that navigation off this coast often posed more danger than enemy fire. Orders to enforce a blockade close inshore left little room for error and there was little a commanding officer could do to mitigate those risks. In January 1807 HMS *Blanche* (36) (formerly *Amfirite*) under the command of Captain Lavie of Keats's squadron blockading Rochefort intercepted the *George Washington* carrying 300 crew from a French frigate, taking the crew prisoner and sending the ship to England. Only weeks later in early March the *Blanche* was wrecked off Ushant with the loss of 45 of the 250 crew, the remainder being taken prisoner. According to the court martial at which the officers were most honourably acquitted, iron stanchions, cranks and arms under the half-deck affected the ship's compass causing her navigation to be faulty.

During the same period the gun brig *Pigmy* ran aground on the Isle de Re. Again, boats from *Pomone* were sent to destroy the wrecked hull.[395]

Keats maintained the private confidence of St. Vincent who considered him the best qualified to work the dangerous waters of the French Atlantic coast. He saw him as so superior that, when he learned Keats was to be redeployed on a special task and relieved off Rochefort by the higher-ranked Sir Richard Strachan, he proposed that when that change was implemented it would be advisable to reduce the number of the squadron.[396] Captain Barrie was similarly sorry to see Keats move on as he considered: "I stand well with Keats".[397]

The Admiralty intended that he be deployed to the Baltic, whereupon St. Vincent wrote:

> *I cannot express the regret I feel at parting with you; yet I am not so selfish as to attempt to deprive the country of your eminent services on so conspicuous an occasion; for sure I am that the allied armies will acquire a support by them which in the final event may put a stop to the career of the second Alexander. Wherever you go, you will be accompanied by the warmest wishes and regards of...St. Vincent.*[398]

In the month of April, however, he was relieved from this service by Sir Richard Strachan, and ordered to Portsmouth, for the purpose of being employed on a secret service, but which an unexpected event prevented from taking place. Captain Keats consequently embraced the opportunity of applying for leave of absence to recruit his health which was at that time very precarious. His retirement, however, was but of short duration; for a few weeks had but elapsed, when he was called upon to form part of an expedition at that time assembling.

In the interim, he used the time to prepare and deliver to the Admiralty a paper entitled *Situation of the Enemy's Squadron under Isle d'Aix (23 April 1807), with proposed mode of Attack Enclosed.*[399] He had recently been charged with blockading this port, and it will be recalled he had, whilst in the *Boadicea*, been involved in an ineffective fireship attack on these roads. The preparation of the paper illustrates Keats's continued application to the problems at hand, even during his period of leave for recuperation. Far from simply resting and waiting for his next deployment, he spent time considering tactical issues and devising modes of attack for use in the navy generally. It is also of interest as it unwittingly becomes central to one of the most controversial court martials in naval history, held some two years later. Keats was well aware that gun-boats could not get within range of vessels anchored high up in the roads. He had somewhat hastily tried to use rafts of fire on the previous occasion. The current plan was based on use of explosive vessels to lead the attack, which would deter anyone inclined to board vessels that followed. Fire ships, and rockets deployed on rafts using wind and tide would breach the protective boom across the harbour and make their way up the channel in the narrow entrance, between Isle d'Oleron and Isle d'Aix (Map 5). The approaching fire vessels would unexpectedly force the French squadron anchored in Aix Roads to cut their anchor cables. With insufficient time and no escape route, they would drift to the banks at the river mouth where they could be attacked by an inshore squadron including bomb vessels waiting in close support. In Keats's view, a considerable frigate and gun-brig force would be indispensable to the outcome of the undertaking, once the French were obliged to move.

The Admiralty considered the matter seriously. Two years later, the main French Atlantic fleet escaped from Brest but was chased into Aix Roads. Controversial Captain Lord Thomas Cochrane, a champion of innovative methods, was put under Admiral Gambier's command with specific orders to accomplish such an attack the success of which the Admiralty saw as being of the highest importance. Several bomb vessels and fire-ships were despatched along with bombs and rockets. Mr Congreve was sent to supervise deployment of his rockets. Men were given the expectation of reward in the event of success, and Gambier was told to immediately advise the Admiralty if any augmentation of resources of any description was thought necessary and it would be provided. He was instructed there should be left no means untried to destroy the enemy squadron. The orders concluded:

> *In order to give your lordship every information on this important subject, my lords have directed me to enclose to you a copy of a paper, drawn up by Sir Richard Keats, in 1807, proposing a mode of attacking an enemy's squadron under Isle d'Aix. W.W. Pole*[400]

The attack with fire vessels achieved its objective. The boom across the channel was breached and eleven of the French ships, having cut their cables, drifted onto the banks as predicted. Shortly thereafter, Cochrane signalled only two were still afloat. He signalled to Gambier to send in ships to press home the attack while the enemy ships were vulnerable, but Gambier was not one to risk all. In what was described as one of the most contemptible actions of a commander in naval history he refused, or at the very least hesitated so long displaying such "twittering ineptitude",[401] that it amounted to a refusal. The stranded French ships were one by one enabled to be got off over several hours with the aid of the incoming tide. The enemy was then able to reposition and fire on their attackers. The significant advantage was lost. Cochrane continued the offensive with the forces at his disposal, but most of the enemy escaped out of reach up the River Charente, and ultimately only four ships were captured or burnt.

The Admiralty hailed the engagement as a victory and awarded Cochrane his Bath Star, but he was so outraged by Gambier's lack of support that he used his position in the House to seek to have Parliament withhold its thanks to him: in his view, thanks for nothing. Gambier felt compelled to request a court martial. Keats's papers were relied upon in that trial in discussing the elements of the plan for the attack and the nature and sufficiency of the support required and provided. Although Gambier was acquitted, the impartiality of the tribunal was questioned, and the trial was regarded by many as a whitewash. The navy became divided into supporters and detractors of either Lord Gambier or Lord Cochrane whose career never recovered. No one questioned the efficacy of Keats's plan had it been fully adopted. Indeed, Napoleon later commented that had Gambier not hesitated, the entire French Atlantic squadron would surely have been taken out.[402]

**Historical Memoirs of
Admiral Sir Richard Goodwin Keats, GCB**

The Baltic – Second Battle Of Copenhagen

Having hoisted his broad pendant onboard the *Ganges* (74), Captain Peter Halket, he sailed with the fleet of men of war and transports under Admiral Gambier for the Baltic.

Early in July 1807 Napoleon signed the treaty of Tilsit with Tsar Alexander of Russia. Britain feared an alliance between France and Russia if unchecked would not only see Russian and Prussian ports and sea lanes closed to British trade, but the reinforcement provided via Napoleon's control of the Russian fleet would afford him the ability to secure also the fleets of Denmark and Sweden. As a result of a government registration scheme requiring seamen to serve six years in the navy if required, Denmark could call upon a pool of over 20,000 experienced seamen of whom 4,000 were already paid to be on standby at Copenhagen. This combined fleet, together with the French and Dutch already under his command in Antwerp and Flushing (Map 1), would place an additional sixty sail of the line at Napoleon's disposal in the Baltic theatre.

Denmark, theoretically neutral, came under pressure from both Russia and France, backed by an advancing army, to join a northern alliance and to pledge its fleet to Napoleon, and hence block British trade through the Baltic. Now that much of southern Europe was effectively closed to trade, the Baltic had become Britain's most important supply route for many materials, including timber, flax and hemp for shipbuilding, and the route to her most important export markets.

Denmark was regarded as the weak link in the north, unable to resist if Napoleon directed troops to Zealand (Map 6). Furthermore, Home Secretary, Lord Hawkesbury, advised the House of Lords that he had received advice that the treaty of Tilsit included secret articles to employ the navies of Denmark and Portugal against Britain. Additionally, the government received advice, incorrect as it turned out, that the Danes were fully prepared with as many as twenty sail of the line ready for sea.[403] Parliament was told it would be 'madness' to sit back waiting for an overt act of aggression before responding. To secure its position and particularly to preserve the Danish fleet before the approaching winter would curtail operations, Britain made overtures. In return for 15,000 troops to boost defence of her homeland and the protection of a British naval force, Denmark was requested to give temporary control of her fleet to Britain, for safekeeping in British waters, to be restored at the making of a general peace.

Denmark was in an unenviable position. In the absence of British support, she was unlikely to be able to repel a French invasion of Jutland that would cut off her supply of food and trade. On the other hand, agreement to the British demands would see her lose her independence and sovereign navy. The proposition was not unexpectedly refused and the armed neutrality that had hitherto preserved a precarious peace was at an end.

An expedition to the Baltic was mounted with extraordinary alacrity. By 16 July, the ink on the treaty barely dry, and even before the British proposal had been considered, Admiral Gambier was appointed commander-in-chief of 'a particular mission'. He was told Government advice was that the power and position of Denmark would shortly be made the instrument of France, excluding the British from the Baltic and depriving her of access to the means of naval equipment as well as multiplying the points from which invasion might be attempted. Britain was planning a pre-emptive strike. The resultant conflict became known as the Second Battle of Copenhagen.

Gambier was supported by Vice Admiral Stanhope in the *Pompée* (74), Commodore Hood in the *Centaur* (74), and Commodore Keats in the *Ganges*. Sir Home Popham, recently reprimanded by court martial, as alluded to above, had been appointed fleet captain, which did not go down well. The Memoir makes no mention of the matter, but in a potentially bold move Keats, Hood and Stopford wrote jointly to Gambier expressing their "extreme sorrow and concern" that as senior captains they would in any way be subject to an inferior captain.[404] Popham had been post-captain for just four years and had never commanded a ship in action, or served as captain under any admiral. By contrast having each served as post-captains for more than fifteen years the three offended officers were among the most experienced and senior in the Service. There was some suggestion the officers threatened to withdraw their services, but this was vehemently denied. Their correspondence emphasised that they were "ready to proceed on any immediate service", having been brought up to make any sacrifices the service of their country may require and would avoid any public discussion or drawing other officers into the matter. Despite his shortcomings and lack of seniority Popham did know the Baltic, and First Lord Mulgrave dismissed the complaint, unhappy at any interference in the administration of naval affairs. He refused to lay their complaint before the Admiralty Board. The remonstrating officers were unmoved by the rebuke from Mulgrave, saying they continued to be much aggrieved and humiliated at ceding rank and pressed to be relieved of their painful situations as soon as it could be done without causing any injury to the service.

Their complaint gained some notoriety. After the expedition returned a pamphlet was produced on the matter titled "Discourse on our late Proceedings in the Baltic" and reproduced without comment in the *Naval Chronicle*.[405] Naval instructions provided that a captain of the fleet be either a flag officer or one of the senior captains of the navy. It was widely understood that any particular knowledge possessed by Popham could have been procured in a manner less offensive to the senior captains. Other officers, well aware of the breach of protocol and appreciative of the significance attached to hard won experience and seniority, were less sanguine than the officers themselves, saying that:

> *Appointment of a junior officer, over the heads of men so distinguished as Hood, Keats and Stopford, was a serious administrative blunder, which might easily have become a public danger if these three officers had had a little less public and patriotic spirit.*[406]

The conflict of 1801 had shown a naval attack on its own would not likely achieve the objective. The initial squadron consisted of seventeen sail of the line, with twenty-one frigates, and vessels of other descriptions, to which others were added until the fleet that assembled at Copenhagen comprised twenty-five sail of the line and more than forty frigates and other vessels, totalling upwards of ninety pendants and three hundred and fifty transports. It carried an army of 16,000 to be joined by 10,000 men of the Kings German Legion (German troops on British pay) already in Swedish Pomerania under the command of General Lord Cathcart. Gambier sailed for Copenhagen on 26 July, just ten days after his appointment. Such was the secrecy attending preparations that the whole force was ready for sea before its extent was known to the public, and in the midst of an eight-day embargo of the British coast to preserve secrecy, it had left port before its destination was known. Gambier received his instructions directly from Foreign Secretary, Lord Canning, and apart from the First Sea Lord, not even the Admiralty Board was aware of the intended purpose. On arrival at the entrance to the Kattegat on 2 August, the Danes treated the British with courtesy, unaware of the threat they posed.

Apart from transporting the troops and equipment, the principal function of the navy was to secure the isolation of the island of Zealand: "His Majesty feels it necessary as a measure of precaution to authorise you to prevent the Danish government from sending any military reinforcements into the island of Zealand from any other part of the Danish dominions, till you receive further instructions from home, it being of the utmost consequence in the event of a rupture with that power, that the island in which the Danish naval arsenal is situated, should not be strengthened to such a degree as might place it beyond the reach of a combined (sic) attack by His Majesty's land and sea forces".[407]

The first move in the campaign was made on the evening of 1 August, the very day the fleet arrived off the Wingo beacon at the entrance to Gothenburg. A division under Keats was detached to the Great Belt, a shallow and rocky passage separating Zealand from the Danish mainland (Map 6), with instructions to allow no military force whatsoever to enter Zealand, sealing it off from Funen and the west. Keats has been described as "the perfect man for such an independent role, constantly patrolling difficult and dangerous waters with numerous shoals".[408] The squadron consisted of some seventeen ships including sail of the line, *(Ganges, Vanguard, Orion, and Nassau)*, frigates *(Sibylle, Franchise, and Nymphe)*, and several brig-sloops, to which were soon added an additional two sail of the line, along with several frigates and smaller vessels, bringing the total to twenty-nine.[409] Their objective was to isolate Copenhagen from the rest of Denmark and thus protect the British military forces from any attack from behind. The balance of the fleet entered the Sound and anchored in the road at the narrowest point between Helsingor (Elsineur) and Helsingborg. On the 5th the *Superb* (Captain Donald M'Leod) joined the fleet. As a compliment to Keats, the Admiralty sent her after Keats's squadron whereupon he transferred his broad pendant to her.

Keats's orders reflected the somewhat confused state of the mission. It was not strictly to be a blockade; commercial shipping and fishing vessels were not only to be allowed to pass but were to be given every assistance. By supplementary instruction, even smaller warships would be allowed to pass, provided they were not transporting troops to or from Zealand. The only absolute prohibition would be towards Danish sail of the line. They would be asked to return to port, failing which the utmost endeavours were to be used to capture or destroy them.[410]

Reliable charts were not available as the Danes understandably refused access and had always encouraged vessels to use an alternative route through the Sound, where they collected levies on all passing ships. The hazardous waters of the Belt therefore had to be navigated using soundings taken by Captain Jackson now commanding the sloop-brig *Mosquito (18)* and three gun-brigs, who buoyed the channels as they proceeded counter clockwise around the island. Although the waters appeared to be abundantly spacious, keeping the squadron safe against strong currents proved difficult. Currents a few fathoms down in deep channels flowed out of the Baltic at speeds up to five knots and were found to be very different from those visible on the surface. The deep-draughted sail of the line often became quite unmanageable in the undercurrents even in very commanding breezes, testing the best of navigators.[411] In what has been described as an operational masterstroke, Keats had progressed through the channels, leaving the various frigates and smaller vessels at strategic stations on the way until his blockading ships were all in position, surrounding the island, within a week, isolating 13,000 troops.[412] With these troops rendered powerless to assist, and most of the Danish army otherwise in Holstein, there remained only 5,000 regular troops to defend Copenhagen against the British forces. On 9 August a convoy of 153 vessels arrived with the troops from England.[413] With the arrival between the 7th and 12th of more ships of war and transports, including Lord Cathcart's forces from Pomerania the British commanders now had over 25,000 men available.[414] The balance was tipped strongly in favour of the British. With his sail of the line Keats addressed the southern end of the Belt to prevent any Danish ships of war from escaping their ports to attack his blockade.

Fearful that a siege could fail if it extended beyond the summer months when Keats would be driven from the Belt by weather and ice allowing reinforcements to come to the aid of the besieged city it was determined that the strategy with the best chance of success was a bombardment of the city to force an early capitulation. The offer to Denmark to deposit her fleet with Britain for the duration of the war was remade on 1 September and again rejected.

As a result of the withdrawal of the King's German Legion Stralsund soon fell to the French. Keats's squadron was then required to perform the additional task of enforcing a close blockade of the port of Rügen, on the north coast of Germany (Map 6), in order to prevent reinforcements being sent from there to Zealand.

With all forces and the chain of blockading ships then being in place the bombardment of Copenhagen commenced on the evening of 2 September, continuing until an armistice was concluded on 5 September. Terms of the Danish surrender were agreed on 7 September.

Upon their arrival in the Kattegat Commodore Keats was detached with a numerous and appropriate force to guard the eastern entrance of the sound to block the Great Belt, and to prevent any succours from being thrown, into Zealand, either from the Danish islands, or provinces. His force extended for two hundred miles; but by its judicious distribution and the activity of his officers, he was completely successful in his object.

The Danish army in Holstein was not only prevented from passing into Zealand, but not the smallest re-enforcement, or succour of any kind eluded his vigilance.[415] The City of Copenhagen was consequently left to its own resources, and the prosecution of the siege was continued without any fresh impediment.

Militarily, the ambitious operation ended in a complete and ruthless victory. Following a punishing bombardment, the Danes capitulated and the British seized nearly sixty vessels of the Danish fleet and destroyed three 74-gun ships under construction on the stocks. The terms of surrender specified the British had only six weeks to remove the ships from Copenhagen. Contrary to the claims partially relied upon to justify the expedition many of them were not in a ready state for war, some not rigged and several without guns. Due to the sensitivity of this matter a sentence to this effect in Gambier's dispatch was omitted from the report in the *London Gazette*.[416] It was a credit to the navy that in nine days they managed to repair, rig and tow fourteen ships from the harbour to the road. Those not brought away, including a large number of smaller gun-boats were destroyed. The officers on the spot set a high bar as to which ships could be reused, as they had insufficient resources to man all the captured ships. Those concerns were considerably alleviated when two thousand additional sailors became available in response to the Government advertising for seamen from the Greenland fishery, offering to pay their expenses as well as a bounty and providing immunity from impressment.[417]

Naval stores valued over £300,000 were removed, and, given the constraints on supply lines, were conceivably of more use than the captured ships themselves. Ninety-two transports measuring upwards of 20,000 tons bringing away full cargoes were deployed in removing the stores.[418] It might be thought this cargo, together with the value of vessels brought away, including the *Christian VII* and *Waldemar* of 80 guns, twelve 74s, two 64s and some fourteen frigates and nine brigs, together with smaller craft, said to be valued at over £4 million, might render the expedition a particularly lucrative operation for the officers involved, however this was the subject of some disappointment. War not having been declared the entitlement to prize money was initially rejected. A sum of £300,000 was eventually distributed.[419]

The British fleet, with prizes and transports sailed from Copenhagen on 21 October in three divisions. Keats was subsequently put in charge of the passage of those destined for Portsmouth where they arrived on 15 November and became the subject of one of J.M.W. Turner's greatest maritime paintings.[420] The return journey was not without incident as the fleet encountered two storms the first of which claimed the Danish ship *Neptunus* (80) which grounded not far from Copenhagen. The second encountered in the Kattegat claimed all but three of the small gun boats. Some fifteen captured ships of the line were taken into the navy, but only four of them (*Christian VII (84),* and the 74s *Denmark, Norge,* and *Prindsesse Carolina)* subsequently saw active service. The benefit is best understood not by what Britain gained, but by what Denmark and hence potentially Napoleon lost.

One ship – that in 1795 had been a gift from the King of England to his nephew, the Prince of Denmark – was left as a mark of respect, although on his return to Copenhagen the Crown Prince ordered it sent to Britain. The Prince himself escaped in disguise, taken by Keats's squadron. It was alleged he was instantly recognised, but those onboard affected not to know him, generously permitting him to continue his route.[421]

As a result of this expedition the shipping lanes through the Baltic, vital for trade and access to raw materials, were kept open. Unsurprisingly Denmark subsequently made an alliance with Napoleon and formally declared war on Britain in early November. However, now having no fleet, her contribution was expected to be of little consequence. The British returned to England in October but the war technically continued until a formal peace was signed in 1814.

Despite its success, there was considerable disquiet back home at the attack on a neutral power, and particularly at the circumstances in which non-military assets were targeted with mortars and howitzers, occasioning the loss of much private property and quite a number of civilians killed or wounded. The Danes claimed up to 2,000 civilian casualties and about one tenth of the city totally destroyed. The British admitted to only 700 casualties, including 200 killed, and this would seem to be now confirmed as more accurate.[422] To Gambier's regret, Danish leadership had taken insufficient advantage of offers to allow evacuation of the city, although some citizens did flea to the island of Amager. On the other side, the people of Denmark were displeased with their prince for provoking hostilities and refusing to give up a fleet that could not be defended.[423] In time it became clear the treaty of Tilsit did, as feared, allow Napoleon use of the Danish fleet (now lost to him), and as affairs in Europe developed, the necessity of the pre-emptive measures became more widely apparent and accepted although the legality of the move remained open to question.[424]

The most essential service was thus rendered to the country, and towards the completion of that object which she had dispatched her warriors to achieve, and after the capitulation of the City, the Commodore received the most gratifying testimonials from the Commander of the Troops, Lord Cathcart; and also, from Admiral Gambier.

Gambier's report included the passage:

> *I embrace the opportunity to make a particular acknowledgement of the very valuable and judicious dispositions which Rear Admiral Keats has made, from time to time, of the force*

under his command for guarding the Belt; and the vigilant attention which his whole squadron have paid to this important branch of the service.[425]

James reports that:

Although it is true, that the fleet in Copenhagen road had little else to do than to look on, the squadron under Commodore Keats in the Great Belt had an arduous duty to perform; and that it was well performed may be inferred from the fact, that the island of Zealand is 230 miles in circuit, the channel between it and Holstein, where the main Danish army was encamped, extremely narrow, and its navigation, especially to line-of-battle ships, some of which touched the ground several times, extremely difficult; and yet, during the five or six weeks that the squadron lay in the Belt, no reinforcement was enabled to get access.[426]

Whilst the rapid capitulation of Copenhagen was due to the immediate superiority of the army, this superiority was secured only by the navy asserting control of the Great Belt effectively isolating the city from any means of support.[427] The operation was an exemplary demonstration of the capability of the joint forces acting in close co-operation.

His Majesty having ordered a promotion of naval officers, Commodore Keats was made rear admiral of the Blue, and was informed by the First Lord of the Admiralty, that the promotion was extended to him as an acknowledgement of the able and judicious manner in which he had discharged the duties of his command, and the important service which he had rendered to the common cause.

The last place in a promotion often indicated that officer was one of particular interest to the Admiralty Board and drew appropriate public recognition. First Lord Mulgrave advised Gambier that there was to be a limited promotion to Rear Admiral of the Blue to recognise the role of Keats and Hood at Copenhagen. He wrote to Keats directly confirming the promotion was brought down to him and stopped at his name as a specific recognition of his contribution to the taking of Copenhagen. Hood was several places above Keats in seniority, so the promotion was extended to Keats. In providing this distinction, another seven officers, higher in the list, were also promoted.[428] Whilst this inflexibility of the system was to its detriment, it was circumvented by the Admiralty. Officers of less merit were not allocated to a fleet, Blue, White or Red, and were without a command, (informally described as the 'yellow fleet'- but the reference did not carry the implication of any lack of courage) on half pay ashore. There were generally more officers than there were ships and hence a pool of unemployed officers. Promotion was contingent upon recent sea service. Only about one-third of all commissioned officers served on active duty as any rank above lieutenant. Officers of lesser merit or who underperformed found themselves ashore and passed over.

The senior officers received the thanks of Parliament and Gambier was elevated to the peerage. Some writers have claimed Sir Richard subsequently refused a baronetcy.[429] It was certainly contemplated even before the success of this expedition, Earl St. Vincent writing that he had spoken to both the Duke of Clarence and Lord Grenville on the matter.[430] The official notices of his appointment by the Prince Regent to the Governorship and Command of Malta in 1809 and to the Command of Newfoundland in 1813, both refer to "Rear Admiral Sir Richard Keats, Bart. And K.B",[431] but these are in error.

He now hoisted his flag in the *Superb*, and having arrived in Portsmouth on the 15th November 1807 with the captured Danish Fleet, a force of twelve sail of the line was immediately put under his command, determined for some secret service; but which, owing to particular circumstances was laid aside. Admiral Keats now obtained leave of absence on account of his health, which required some relaxation from the constant fatiguing services to which he had been subject.

The newspapers[432] reported in November that following orders to immediately make themselves ready at Portsmouth twelve sail of the line under the command of Rear Admiral Keats in the *Superb* (with Captain Jackson now his flag captain) had dropped down to St Helens, Isle of Wight, ready to sail on a new expedition. The hastily prepared squadron was supplied with provisions for less than one month and having only just returned from months in the Baltic was in less than prime condition, so it was speculated its object, which had been kept secret, was both of the utmost urgency and not remote. Opinion varied. To secure the Portuguese fleet, to rescue the Royal family of Portugal for conveyance to Brazil, or to intercept the Russian squadron on their return homewards were the most plausible possibilities. In short, there was ample speculation, with little knowledge, and in the event, as stated in the memoir, the particular expedition was laid aside and Keats stayed ashore hoping to restore his health.

Having succeeded in establishing it, he hoisted his flag, in April 1808 onboard the *Mars*; and having received onboard Lieutenant General Sir John Moore, a fleet of transports containing 5,000 troops[433] was placed under his protection, with which he proceeded to Gothenburg, where he was taken under the orders of Sir Jas. Saumarez. He then shifted his flag to his old ship, the *Superb*, and was ordered into the Great Belt with an appropriate force, to keep that important channel open, and to give protection to the numerous fleets of merchant vessels against the formidable flotilla force of the enemy.

With both Russia and Denmark now lending their support to France, Britain's only ally in the Baltic was Sweden. Even she was in a precarious position. Russia declared war in February and Denmark followed suit in March so Sweden was now liable to attack from multiple fronts by French, Russian, and Danish forces. She needed support, and hence this expedition, including Sir John Moore's troops and a naval squadron under Sir James Saumarez.

On this voyage Keats was entrusted with the safe care and naval education of the young Henry FitzClarence, the second son of his old friend the Duke of Clarence and Mrs Jordan. When the boy was only twelve, the Duke wrote to Keats:

> *We must dear Keats take this world not as it ought to be but as it is. I am anxious to send Henry to sea and ultimately he shall go, but mothers must be consulted. Unfortunately, there is too much reason to believe that I have lost an unfortunate boy onboard the Blenheim,[9] which naturally enough causes great uneasiness to Mrs Jordan and makes me cautious as to my method of proceeding relative to Henry. Both as an Englishman and as a father I am truly anxious to put my second son into the navy; he will I think turn out all I can wish and particularly if under your kind care and protection…I truly hope you will shortly be employed so as to gain both honours and riches, but not too far off so that Henry may join you in the Spring. The boy himself is delighted with the idea and talks of you and the Navy with rapture.[434]*

---

9   Troubridge rashly and impetuously returned from India in a leaking ship (possibly compromised by the insertion of 'devil bolts' in her construction), in cyclone season after a dispute as to sharing command with Pellew, and the ship was lost with all hands off Mauritius in February 1807. Among the crew was William's illegitimate son from an earlier liaison, William Henry Courtney, (The Sailor King's Lost Sailor Son, *The Mariners Mirror*, Vol 82, No2, (2013) p.206).

Map 6: *Approaches to the Baltic Sea*

The boy's mother, Mrs Jordan, came to have a similarly high opinion of Keats, writing that "The attention and kindness of Admiral Keats to all the boys [in his flagship] is more like the affectionate care of a father than a master."[435] They left the Downs in the *Mars* on 20 April 1808, having acknowledged the Duke accompanying Volunteer First Class Henry FitzClarence with a 21-gun salute. Some weeks later Clarence declared, "He cannot be in better hands than yours,"[436] and wrote to Admiral Lord Collingwood, "for though I have lost one son onboard the *Blenheim*, I have just started another with my old friend and shipmate Keats".[437]

Lord Mulgrave had selected Keats for this deployment because besides his great professional merit he now had the additional advantage of being well acquainted with the Baltic. Saumarez was outwardly pleased to again have Keats in his fleet, writing to Mulgrave that he was possessed of the highest merit, and was one he would have applied for had he not already been appointed.[438] On 14 April, he wrote to Keats; "I was very happy in being informed that we were to be employed upon the same service".[439]

The brief to Saumarez was ambitious: to keep the whole of the Baltic secure for British trade. The precise role of Moore's forces had not been agreed upon between the British and Swedish governments before they arrived at Gothenburg. To some extent the British government was at a loss as to what to do regarding the support of Sweden and her unstable King, but knew they needed to do something. Saumarez arrived off Gothenburg on 7 May. On 18 May he wrote to Hood advising that Keats had anchored the previous day having been kept out of port three days due to fog, but "What is to be done with Moore's troops remains doubtful".[440]

Even Moore described his orders as inexplicit. That uncertainty soon resulted in a strong difference of opinion between the volatile King Gustav of Sweden and equally volatile, but not unstable, General Moore, which escalated to a diplomatic incident resulting in Moore's imprisonment. He escaped, according to some, disguised as a female peasant, and made his way back to the fleet, just as a ball was in progress onboard the flagship with the ladies of Gothenburg all present in their finest gowns. Moore was not willing to stray from orders to remain in Sweden, whereas Gustav sought to employ him in an attack on Zealand or against the Russians occupying Finland. The result of the impasse was the withdrawal of the British troops in early July 1808 without their having been allowed ashore, let alone put to any useful employment.[441]

Keats formed the view that, on balance, although some unpleasant circumstances had led to the precipitate withdrawal of Moore's military force, it did not appear to involve any change in political sentiment and would have no lasting negative impact on continuing harmonious relations with Sweden, at this time still allied to Britain. He remained committed to Gustav, but a British squadron in the Kattegat could have little influence on political events on shore a thousand miles to the east. Whilst offering support and hoping for no interruption to harmonious relations between the two countries, he wrote: "In these ticklish times one cannot be too suspicious perhaps,"[442] referring to the possibility Sweden may find it necessary to enter terms with Russia or Denmark, against British interests. Keats and his captains were engaged in tracing the different items of authentic intelligence, and comparing dates with the French fabrications, to gain a proper understanding of the constantly changing diplomatic positions of the various players: Austria, France, Sweden, Russia and Denmark. They were particularly concerned Austria may have been about to move on Danzig (Gdansk). Archduke Ferdinand had already overrun much of Poland.[443]

In short, the diplomatic and strategic position was complex and rapidly evolving. The role and activity of the navy were of necessity equally fluid, responding to the changing balance of power. To add to the complexity of the task, their operational area extended more than one thousand miles across the whole of the Baltic from St Petersburg in the east to the North Sea entrance in the west. An understanding was reached that the British would defend the west and south coasts against France and keep the Baltic open to trade, while the Swedes focused on Russia. In time this theatre also required the attention of the British navy. The Russian fleet looked ready to seize control of Finland. If they defeated the Swedish navy in this theatre, their combined fleet of 22 sail of the line would be more than a match for the British, who could not afford to lose safe access to the Baltic. The British could not rely upon Sweden being able to resist if left to her own resources.

The focus of Keats's activity was in the western Baltic and its approaches, particularly the difficult passages past Denmark through the Belts and the Sound. The Admiralty advised Saumarez:

> *The protection of the convoys through the Sound and clear of the island of Bornholm and Eartholm is a matter of such high moment that it is their lordships' command that you detach Rear Admiral Keats (who appears by your last disposition to be at Gothenburg) upon this particular duty, placing under his orders a force adequate to the service on which he is to be employed and giving him such instructions as you may deem necessary for his guidance; and their lordships suggest for your consideration the propriety of a line-of-battle ship or two being anchored with springs on their cables between Drago Point and Saltholm to awe and prevent the enemy's gun-boats from coming out during the passage of convoys into or out of the Baltic by the passage of the Sound, which passage, under all circumstances, their lordships are inclined to think to be least dangerous.*[444]

The Convoy Acts of 1798 and 1803 made it compulsory for almost all trading vessels other than those of the East India and Hudson Bay companies to sail in convoy with a naval escort. By way of extra incentive, Lloyds of London's terms of insurance for the 15,000 vessels on their register provided for payment for losses only when ships sailed under naval protection. The Government imposed fines upon those who did not comply, particularly if carrying Government goods. The Admiralty made arrangements with insurers and conferences of merchants for the scheduling of various voyages and their escorts. Losses under convoy amounted to less than one per cent, compared with six to seven per cent for unprotected vessels[445].

Keeping these trade routes open and free from predation was vital to the commerce of Britain – and her war effort in particular – as the vast majority of the raw materials she needed could not be produced at home. Supplies of hardwoods for ship-building had been exhausted and, along with hemp and other materials, now came from the Baltic. The best iron was sourced in Sweden, and the highest quality saltpetre giving an advantage in muzzle velocity came from India. Almost all of the trade between Europe and the rest of the world passed through British hands, and was carried on British ships. A great deal of Britain's prosperity depended upon the safe arrival and on-sale of sugar, cotton, coffee and other goods from her distant colonies in the Caribbean, and spices and luxury items from the East Indies, all of which shipments required protection if this position and her economic strength were to be maintained.[446]

So far as the public was concerned, the naval involvement in convoy duty was unremarkable. Merchant vessels came and went loading and unloading their cargoes just as expected. It became newsworthy only if something went wrong. But for the ships and crew involved, convoy duty was an arduous and exacting albeit inglorious undertaking. There were never sufficient escorts for frequent sailings, so convoys tended to be occasional and consequently, large, often comprising over three hundred vessels of various descriptions, which caused enormous logistical problems. Maintaining close formation was difficult. The captains of merchant ships were not accustomed to taking orders. The sailing capacities of their laden vessels varied enormously, often being slow and under-resourced. The superior craft, keen to reach their markets and receive better prices before their competitors arrived, were reluctant to wait for the slow, and would often be prepared to take their chances sailing ahead at their own speed. Despite provision of sailing instructions and signal books before departure, often enforced at sea by a shot across the bow, fleets easily became scattered, and then vulnerable to predation.

Convoy duty in the Baltic was becoming more onerous. In substitution for her confiscated fleet Denmark, now a staunch ally of France, had embarked on a program constructing numerous small gun-boats manned by up to 76 men and armed with one cannon of 18 or 24-pounds in the bow and another in the stern, together with several howitzers. British gun-brigs had proved no match for these craft used in numbers and capable of being rowed galley-style from concealed bays to attack their quarry. Furthermore, the gun-boats were increasing in number with more than one hundred expected to be patrolling the waters before long.[447] As it transpired by war's end up to 200 had been built in Denmark and an additional 100 in Norway such that, despite significant losses, dozens of various sizes lay in wait along Baltic shores leading to the description of the conflict from 1807-1814 as 'the gun-boat war'. The additional boats were easily manned by seamen previously employed on the confiscated ships and by fishermen put out of work by the blockade of Denmark. To counter them, it was necessary to deploy more powerful ships of the line.

The waters did not admit of manoeuvrability, and large parts of the various passages (particularly the shorter, more convenient route through the Sound) were unavoidably within three miles of enemy shore positions and inlets from which surprise attacks could be launched. Frequent sudden calms, characteristic of these waters, stole the steerage of large ships that then became easy prey for the oar-propelled gun-boats. The 64-gun *Dictator*, hampered by lack of wind and adverse currents, was nearly lost to such an attack in Kioge Bay, saved only by the appearance of a convoy whose escorts fortunately carried long-range guns. In August 1808, the gun-brig *Tigress* was overcome and taken by sixteen Danish gun-boats in the Great Belt.[448] The *Tickler* (14) and *Seagull* (16) were among a number of other ships to suffer similarly through the summer of 1808. The most significant loss was inflicted on a convoy of 70 merchantmen attacked by twenty-eight gun and mortar boats when becalmed on passage to Malmo. In what became known as the Battle of Saltholm an escorting brig, *Turbulent* (12), was taken along with twelve of the convoy, the rest escaping.

The gun-boats were not universally successful, particularly if operating in fresh conditions which allowed the larger ships to maintain way and manoeuvre or in waves which easily made the smaller craft unstable and liable to swamping. The arrival of a breeze allowed the brig sloop *Kite (18)* to escape an attack by 22 gun boats armed with a total of 44 24-pounders in a calm when off Nyborg in September 1808, but only after suffering nineteen shot holes through her hull and with her main mast supported by just two shrouds and a backstay.[449] The brig *Cruizer* (18) stationed as a beacon to mark the entrance to an anchorage came under attack from some twenty vessels on 1 November 1808 but with the advantage of the wind was able to manoeuvre to bring her 32-pounders to bear with the desired result, repelling the enemy and capturing a cutter of ten guns.[450] Although the Danish gun-boats presented a significant threat, strategic deployment of a range of British resources into positions where their characteristics could best be used to advantage mitigated the impact and ultimately reduced the gun boats to little more than an inconvenience.

A TREASURE TO THE SERVICE

Danish shallop gun-boat, an oared boat, with a crew of 76 men and armed with two cannons.
©Alamy MWT3BP

Although there was a reward of 1-2 percent for carrying treasure for the Government and for freight, which on occasion could be quite substantial[451] and the Lloyds Patriotic Fund made cash payments to those who vigorously defended their convoys, there was little or no prospect of attack and capture of enemy ships, or of gaining prize money, other than by virtue of capturing those who sought to attack any merchant ship not keeping well within naval protection. Hence convoy duty was considerably more restrictive and less appealing than the free reign offered in flying squadrons of past years. The rich bounty previously available in the Channel or to those posted in the East and West Indies was not on offer in the Baltic. Nonetheless, through the taking of many smaller warships and cargos officers could still do quite well for themselves.[452] As a subordinate flag officer Keats was entitled to a share in any prize taken by ships under his command. Although he saw this as reward for valuable service rather than incentive for doing his duty it no doubt eased the hardship of command. His was a vital task, requiring careful management of scarce resources, made all the more difficult because Britain had no base in the Baltic from which to supply or refresh her forces. Every nation along its shores bar Sweden was under French control and hostile to Britain's interests. In April 1809 Keats was complaining to Hood that he needed reinforcements if he was to face a hostile fleet, and in any event had too few ships under him to properly protect trade.

Ships heading into the Baltic would form up in the Wingo Sound off Gothenburg, while those exiting would form up off Karlskrona for escort. The magnitude of the logistical task of co-ordinating minimal resources over a wide area is illustrated by Keats's disposition of his vessels engaged in convoy protection depicted below, whereby powerful ships of the line and frigates were positioned at each end of the passages and smaller sloops and gun brigs accompanied the fleets through the narrow waterways.

Position (See Map 6)	Ship of the line	Frigates	Sloops	Gun Brigs
Cruisers – south Baltic, Livonia to Kolberg		1	2	
Between the above and rendezvous point in Sweden			3	
Off the rendezvous			1	1
Rendezvous, in port, to give instructions				1
Off Bornholm and Eartholm			2	1
Off Rugen				1
Between Moen and Falsterbo		1	1	1
To receive convoys from the belt, and to take convoys from rendezvous point to Nyborg	2	1	2	1
Total (22)	2	3	11	6

Table 4: *Plan for the protection of trade. Derived from Keats to Hood, 6 May 1809, [SRO HA 93/6/1/657] by Davey, 2009.*[453]

Whereas the coasts of France and the Mediterranean were becoming well-charted and known to the various captains, these waters were not. Shoals and currents made navigation difficult. These, in combination with headwinds blowing in confined waters, meant passage often took weeks. Keats directed all commanders as a matter of national importance to gather information: to take soundings, to note the location of rocks and shoals by reference to landmarks, and record leading marks for the channels, as well as the rise, strength and direction of tidal streams, and influences of the wind. In short, all matters that would make passage easier and safer.[454]

Ever cautious and prudent, obsessive even, he directed all ships of war be kept in a state of readiness for action, with vigilant lookouts maintained against surprise attack, particularly in light or calm winds.[455] British gun-brigs being insufficient to the task of protecting merchant ships from their Danish counterparts, more powerful ships of the line and frigates were allocated to accompany the convoys which were often directed to use the Great Belt. In Keats's opinion, the disadvantages of a passage longer by four to ten days and the number of gun-boats based from Nyborg were more than offset by the advantage the open waters provided in allowing escort by powerful warships. It provided an opportunity of advanced warning of an attack as well as avoiding the concentration of gun-boats and privateers in the Sound around Copenhagen. Having escorted a large number of convoys up and down the Sound, Rear Admiral Bertie was similarly of the view that passage through the Sound and Malmo channel should be avoided in favour of the Belt unless the wind was favourable.[456] From 1809 the Belt became Keats's preferred passage. He noted that in his opinion routes should be varied as the circumstances render necessary, so the enemy would not amass all its resources on the one waterway.[457]

Squadrons in the Channel generally remained in sight of, or at least in close contact with, their flag commander, but the Baltic operation saw single ships widely dispersed. This shuttle system required a great deal of management. Keats's allocation of resources was so effective that previously high losses to the enemy were all but eliminated after its implementation. In 1808, some one hundred and ten of the more than three thousand merchant ships that sailed in and out of the Baltic under navy protection were lost to enemy action. Many more sailed to and from Sweden with goods for delivery to British transports. In the same period more than seventy Danish merchant ships and privateers were captured while attempting to run the blockade[458] and a great number of gun boats were destroyed and their crews captured.[459] Between July and November 1809, following adoption of Keats's disposition of the increased number of escorts, fifteen convoys totalling over three thousand ships passed through the Belt, with no losses.[460] That Keats was able to respond to the Danish offensive and set up, supply and sustain an effective convoy system, continued by his successors, justified St. Vincent's confidence in his promotion to the flag and Raymond's assessment of his reputation as "a quick-thinking officer who could be trusted with independent command".[461]

Historical Memoirs of Admiral Sir Richard Goodwin Keats, GCB

13

Repatriation of Spanish Troops

At Algeciras and San Domingo Keats had demonstrated his abilities as a fighting captain in charge of a devastatingly effective ship of war. The events described as the 'repatriation of Spanish troops' presented a very different circumstance in which he was able to showcase a suite of abilities not hitherto called upon. He revealed himself as a commander and an effective and detailed planner of operations capable of addressing numerous contingencies before they arose. The manner in which this complex operation was accomplished was unprecedented. Its impact was felt across the Continent in consolidating an alliance that led eventually to the defeat of Napoleon.

When Buonaparte, elated by his conquests and flattered by his parasites, vainly hoped to add Spain to his dominion, he began his insidious and treacherous designs, by drawing from that country the bravest and most disciplined of her armies and marching them into the north of Europe; but his unprincipled invasion of that country was met by the people with becoming fortitude and those feelings of national independence which impel all men to stand up for the liberties of their country, they concluded a peace with England, rode in arms to repel the French, and the spirit of resistance extended, like an electric shock, to their brethren in the north.

For some eleven years the Spanish had been supporting – or, at the least, not opposing – Napoleon. The battle at Algeciras, the chase across the Atlantic and the Battle of Trafalgar had after all involved the combined fleets of Spain and France. Napoleon had effectively occupied Spain as an ally in October 1807 but, when in early 1808 he forced their popular royal family into exile and installed his own brother Joseph as their King, discontent grew to a patriotic uprising, which extended itself to the army. To this the British offered every encouragement and support, announcing on 4 July the end of hostilities and the lifting of blockades.

Keats had written prophetically to Captain Byam Martin of the *Implacable* that Napoleon had roused a spirit in Spain that he may find very difficult to subdue,[462] and this was soon felt in the Baltic. Following the treaty of Tilsit, and war having broken out between Britain and Denmark, a Spanish army of 12,000- 15,000 men under the Marquis de la Romana had been sent north to fight in the war of the fourth coalition and spent the winter in Swedish Pomerania. This army which included nearly 10,000 infantry and 2,500 cavalry together with artillery, formed part of a larger force under the command of Marshal Bernadotte keeping watch over the British fleet and preparing to move north to take part in a possible offensive against Sweden. Further advance was thwarted for the coming summer months by the melting of ice in the Great Belt, halting their progress and allowing British warships to resume their patrol. In march 1808 they moved north, to Jutland, Schleswig and the Danish islands.

Romana established his headquarters at Nyborg on the east coast of the Danish island of Funen, but Napoleon made sure his regiments were spread out and not able to assemble in the one place. Dutch or French troops were always kept nearby. By July 1808 there were four regiments on the Jutland peninsula including infantry, cavalry and artillery, up to one hundred miles north-west of Nyborg; two on Zealand about sixty miles to the east; one on adjacent Langeland; and four regiments plus cavalry and artillery on the island of Funen itself.[463]

The French had been intercepting communications from Spain, hoping to keep the northern army ignorant of developments in their homeland and loyal to Napoleon, but news filtered through. The Spanish soldiers became aware of both the French seizures and the Uprising and were naturally concerned at being part of the French alliance in the north when their countrymen back home seemed to be rising in opposition.

Troops in Spain had been required to swear allegiance to the new King and soon the same demand was made of the northern army. Aware of the feelings of his men Romana drafted an amended pledge that he hoped would satisfy both the men and the French commanders. This referred not to the new king, but to "that power which the whole nation would recognise and swear loyalty to". Unsurprisingly the French were not satisfied and by July orders came requiring he ensure all of his troops take an oath in a prescribed form. By way of encouragement Romana was awarded a Légion d'Honneur and, as a personal gift from Marshal Bernadotte, given a valuable pair of silver mounted flintlock presentation pistols, crafted by Nicolas-Noël Boutet of Versailles. Discontent among the men continued to grow, but the Spanish were a long way from home and surrounded by other forces loyal to Napoleon. Romana realised he would not be allowed to withdraw peaceably and was in no position to force a move by land. Britain hoped this army could be persuaded to defect and allow the British to remove them by sea.

It was naturally expected that those troops partook of the general feeling of their country, and Admiral Keats was directed to open a communication with them, as they were then mostly lying in the Danish provinces of Schleswig, Holstein and Jutland.

This was no spur-of-the-moment instruction. Both Foreign Secretary Canning and War Secretary Castlereagh (who later famously fell out, resulting in a duel between Cabinet Ministers on Putney Heath in September 1809), and various administrative arms of the Admiralty, had been working on this for some time. Successful execution of the defection was viewed as potentially strategically and politically significant to the whole of the war against France. Romana's troops could be held out as an example to all of Spain and elsewhere by rising in opposition to Napoleon. If such a defection could be orchestrated and an alliance made with Spain it would add momentum to the British war effort and give her army access to new support and new avenues for attacking the French through the Spanish peninsula.

As early as 1 April, the British envoy in Sweden, Edward Thornton, had been given instructions to aid the attempted rescue, which of necessity would need to be undertaken from the coast controlled by the British navy. British ships had been given proclamations to get ashore amongst the Spanish troops encouraging them to make their way to Sweden where they would be well received. Two secret agents, Rev. James Robertson and one McMahon, had also been sent to encourage defection. On 30 June Castlereagh had written to General Moore (presumably uninformed as to the latter's imminent departure from the Baltic) raising the possibility of his troops moving on various islands to forcibly extricate Romana's troops and indicating a confidential agent had been sent to open communications.[464] This was generally thought to have no reasonable prospect of success and in any event General Moore and his troops left the theatre shortly thereafter.[465]

On 21 July a report was received from a Swedish officer keeping watch that 9,000 troops had embarked from Stralsund on the Pomeranian coast preparing for an invasion of Sweden. Keats was directed to take the *Superb, Edgar, Brunswick* and several smaller vessels to intercept them. If that had been achieved Napoleon's designs in northern Europe would have been dealt quite a blow. The report proved to be incorrect. The troops were not at sea. Keats noted that some troops had been embarked but it must have been an exercise as the vessels were not in a position to sail. The port nonetheless required watching.[466] Following his return with this intelligence on 29 July he was sent off Langeland to protect trade through the Belt. There he had the good fortune to be joined by the fast sailing sloop *Mosquito* newly arrived from London.

On 23 July 1808, orders were crafted as secret instructions from junior Lords of the Admiralty, Bickerton, Domett and Viscount Palmerston, and sent direct to Keats as commanding officer in the Belt and Sound via the *Mosquito*. Keats was to open communications with the Spanish. The objective was to remove them to a safe place, pending arrival of transport ships to take them back to Spain. It was important, their lordships said, that no time be lost, not only because of the obstacles that might arise due to delay, but because of the important impression which was expected to result from the early arrival of these troops in Spain.[467] The mission was described by the Admiralty as being of the greatest importance, and one in which the King himself took a lively interest. There was always a risk of the French discovering these intentions, and so timing and time would be of the essence if the operation was to be successfully executed right under the nose of the enemy. Keats would be under no misapprehension as to difficulties he faced or the significant responsibility he was under.

Before leaving Yarmouth the *Mosquito* received onboard a Spanish officer, Don Lobo who was an envoy of the Spanish Junta of Seville, and had with him papers and orders for Romana; sufficient proof of the uprising in Spain and instructions regarding co-operation with a British evacuation. They sailed from Yarmouth on 25 July and anchored off Nyborg alongside the *Dictator* on 4 August. There they were informed about another Spanish officer now on the *Edgar*, who had brought valuable information confirming a widespread desire amongst the Spanish forces for British protection in the escape of the regiment based on Langeland.

Commander in Chief, Admiral Saumarez, was at this time some hundreds of miles to the east heading to Karlskrona en route to Stockholm escorting specie for Sweden. He remained in the eastern Baltic. Due to the taking of the gun-brig *Tigress* carrying dispatches, Saumarez did not receive a copy of the official instructions or news of recent developments until more than a week later when the *Mosquito* brought duplicates together with a letter from Keats setting out a progress report regarding their implementation.[468]

Just how communication between the British and Spanish was opened has long been disputed as various correspondents differ as to the precise sequence of events. In a narrative published by his nephew some fifty years later, the manuscript having been mislaid for thirty years,[469] Brother James Robertson claims the credit as a result of his approaching General Romana whilst passing as a purveyor of cigars and chocolate on a mission instigated by Sir Arthur Wellesley and endorsed by Castlereagh. Whereas he claims to be the first to inform the northern army of events back home, and to have thereby convinced Romana to join in an evacuation plan, most historians suggest it is unlikely he played such a significant role. A £200 reward for passing on news of events back in Spain had already been paid to another messenger.[470]

Robertson's instructions were to contact the Spanish general and advise him that British transports would be at his orders to convey him and his troops to any place he may choose. They were not required to fight for Britain. Nothing was to be asked in return. Romana's decision was to be communicated to a diplomat by the name of McKenzie in Heligoland, off the Atlantic coast of Denmark, for relaying to London so necessary arrangements could be made.

Robertson writes that he left London on 4 June, landed at Heligoland two days later, and proceeded to Hamburg, where he learnt the reward had already been paid to others. He claims to have ultimately contacted Romana at Nyborg and to have both informed him of events at home and convinced him to co-operate in an evacuation. Some contend he communicated this decision to the navy, relying upon a letter from Saumarez to Mulgrave as implying Robertson was onboard the *Victory* on 28 July. This is not expressly stated, and it is likely the person referred to was not Robertson at all.[471]

Robertson's narrative has him returning to Hamburg via Assens on the western shores of Funen, Kiel and Lubeck forthwith after communicating with Romana. He reports having failed in an attempt to attract the attention of a British warship from the beach to convey to the navy the result of his meeting, and then being detained by Danish guards before talking his way out of the predicament and proceeding to Hamburg.[472] He does not claim to have communicated directly with the British navy. Only once he returned safely to Hamburg some days later does he say he wrote to the British diplomat, McKenzie to report the success of his communication with Romana. By that time the evacuation was well underway. So, even if accepted, his story fails to close the loop in explaining how the British navy was able to act in concert with Romana's troops. No mention of him has been found in Keats's correspondence.[473] An extract from a biography of Romana appended to Robertson's narrative confirms communication from an ecclesiastic (Robertson), but says Romana hesitated to act until the means were found to put him in possession of dispatches from the different Juntas containing details of the insurrection of the Spanish, the capture of Cádiz and the views of the army back home.[474] There is no doubt this information was provided directly by Keats. Robertson probably did communicate with Romana at considerable risk to his own safety but his claims to have opened communications between the Spanish leader and the British navy are not credible.[475]

By this time Keats's orders had already been sent from London and the plan was in motion. Romana most probably learned of events at home indirectly from returning servicemen, newspapers, and those pieces of correspondence that escaped the censors.[476]

Lord Canning, possibly miffed that persons outside of his office had instigated Robertson's mission, had independently arranged for a Mr McMahon to undertake a similar mission, carrying letters from Canning to Romana as well as letters of introduction from members of the Junta. He likely met with Romana and claimed the reward before Robertson arrived, but there is no suggestion he managed to open communication between Romana and the navy.[477] That was the result of a happy confluence of events in the Danish islands.

The memoirs record:

Encouraged by circumstances calculated to give confidence, an officer from the Spanish army, with instructions in the general feelings of the officers and troops, voluntarily and at considerable risk made his way to the British squadron on the 4th of August, and on the following day a naval officer of rank Senor Don Lobo arrived from England.

This sequence is also incomplete but it is consistent with other records when one realises that quite serendipitously and unknown to each other, the two Spanish officers referred to were each on British ships for several days, one off Nyborg, having arrived on the *Mosquito* from England, and the other off Langeland, having been taken to the *Edgar*, and yet to communicate with one another directly.

It was actually at 4:30pm on 1 August that the *Edgar (74)* on station in the Great Belt, north of Langeland sent boats in chase of a Danish vessel as a result of which she received onboard a Spanish lieutenant by the name of Don Antonio Fabregues, from the Catalonian regiment on Langeland.[478] He had been on a mission to deliver Bernadotte's correspondence from Langeland to the commander at Zealand. Once at sea and observing the British boats chasing a small Danish vessel he drew their attention and was taken by them to the *Edgar*. This action was not instigated pursuant to any input from Romana but was undertaken without his knowledge at the prompting of Fabregues's immediate commander, Lieutenant Colonel Don Dionisio Vives in command of a regiment on Langeland, who independently sought to discover if the British were willing to evacuate his particular regiment.[479] He had no information or authority to make claims or pleas on behalf of other regiments.

One writer suggests the officer taken onboard the *Edgar* had escaped from Zealand, however there is substantial contemporaneous documentary evidence in support of his being stationed on Langeland and it is suggested this is the better view.[480]

In the meantime, Don Lobo had been transferred from the *Mosquito* to the *Superb* on 5 August and was advised that given his lack of resources, particularly the means to transport or feed ten thousand troops there was presently little Keats could do that would have any prospect of success. Don Lobo was returned to the *Mosquito* and sent in search of Commander in Chief Saumarez to plead for resources for the task.

Events were moving quickly. Fabreques had been on the *Edgar* for some days. Shortly after Don Lobo's departure, Fabreques was finally brought onboard the *Superb* and interviewed by Keats, who then had confirmation of the willingness of the Spanish to co-operate. Most importantly he now had a means of communicating with them without attracting the attention of the French. A signal was made to return Don Lobo to the *Superb*, and then the two Spanish officers finally met. As a result of those discussions, Keats decided the confluence of events was too opportune to let pass and realised that suspicion would have been aroused on account of the men from Fabregues's boat having been allowed to return to shore without him some days ago. If anything was to be done he would need to act immediately and without any input or the sanction of his commander-in-chief. He was about to embark on a bold undertaking.

Don Lobo acted as an interpreter while Fabreques provided details of the numbers and locations of the Spanish and Danish troops throughout the islands. This gave Keats the detailed information he required to prepare a plan for embarkation with the fairest prospect of success for Romana's acceptance. At this time Romana was unaware of Fabregues's activity and Keats was in turn uncertain of the willingness of the army as a whole to participate in the venture.[481]

The original intention of the Admiralty orders was to open communication, plan, communicate with London to assemble the necessary transports and supplies, which would need to be sent from England, and in due course effect an orderly evacuation. The rapid development of events meant those in charge at the scene had none of the luxuries afforded by time. Lack of shipping tonnage to deal with up to ten thousand men was a significant impediment to any plan. His means included three sail of the line, admittedly large, but not ideally suited to transport, and 'half a dozen small vessels at most'. Having no confidence in the imminent arrival of transports he took the precaution of cutting four gun-boats from a passing convoy to boost his carrying capacity. Nevertheless, he was ill equipped to either collect ten thousand men serving in dispersed locations, or to accommodate and feed them if and when collected.

Fortuitously Keats was now possessed of both information and an avenue of communication. If there was to be any prospect of achieving an evacuation he had to act forthwith with such assets he had at his immediate disposal. If a plan was to succeed it would be essential to obtain the agreement of the General and to somehow connect the movements and plans of those troops in Zealand and Jutland with those in Funen and Langeland in a manner as to not raise suspicion in the French. Fabreques was returned to the *Edgar* at 2:30am on the morning of 6 August, and put on shore to seek out his general, taking with him a letter from Keats and the documents brought by Don Lobo to satisfy Romana of the position in Spain, the wishes of the Junta, and the bona fides of the British offer to assist with whatever resources were at hand.[482]

As Keats wrote to Saumarez that same day, nothing could be determined upon until he had further communication, but using the island of Langeland as a staging point might be a viable option. Nevertheless, a decision was becoming more urgent and the risk of discovery was soon heightened by Fabreques having difficulty in keeping his excitement to himself when put back on shore, to the extent the French commander on Langeland was immediately suspicious, queried Vives about it and wrote to Bernadotte on the matter. Further communication became an urgent necessity.[483] Vives sent Fabregues in disguise to Romana taking the various documents and a letter from Keats in the following terms:

> *I have the honour to inform you, that I have received from my government the most positive instructions to endeavour to communicate with the Spanish officers commanding the troops of that nation in the vicinity of my command, and to concert with them measures to secure their retreat from any place of embarkation which they may possess, and for placing them in a state of security until transports for their reception can be provided to convey them to Spain, for which, as well as the necessary provisions measures have already been taken, and indeed of the arrival of them I am in hourly expectation. Until that period shall arrive, they are welcome to share in the accommodation and provisions of the ships under my command; but as that might not afford ample means at present, although I am in expectation of the commander-in-chief, I would suggest, under the pressure of circumstances, the removal of the troops to some of the islands in the Belt, for their perfect security. But as a measure of this magnitude to the interests of the Spanish nation would necessarily require a concerted plan, lest by attention to partial interests the general one might suffer, I request an unreserved and confidential communication either to the ships off Nyborg, that stationed off Langeland, or*

any of his Britannic Majesty's ships in the Belt; and through the bearer of this, or by any other means, I propose sending on Sunday [two days' time], unless I should earlier receive some person on board, a flag of truce, under some pretext to the Spanish post at Spodsberg; and if this should be safely received, I wish, in token of it, a small guard might parade in some conspicuous situation at noon to-morrow, near the English ship at anchor, or under sail near Spodsberg [on the east coast of Langeland].

In my present situation it is impossible, ardently as I enter into the views of my government and the Spanish nation, to attempt to lay down any fixed plan. My services, and that of every Englishman under my command, are devoted to the cause; but before measures can be adopted, we must communicate, agree upon, and combine, as far as possible, the interests of the Spanish troops in Jutland and Zealand, with those in Funen and Langeland. I shall keep a ship for some days off Spodsberg, and every ship under my command will be on the look-out to receive any boats that may approach them. [484]

Fabreques arrived at Romana's headquarters during the night of 6-7 August.[485] Earlier that day Romana had received a threatening letter from Bernadotte requiring the oath be retaken by all his troops in the prescribed form without alteration. With the knowledge of British support and time being of the essence Romana addressed his troops who enthusiastically agreed to follow him in his plan to escape the clutches of the French to fight for their homeland. The following day the *Brunswick (74)* stationed in the Belt received a Spanish officer sent directly from Romana's headquarters to consult with the British.[486]

A communication being thus opened, the situation of Spain was made known, and each man vowed to share her destinies. The rear admiral, unprovided with any additional means for this particular service, made arrangements for collecting at a short notice the ships of his squadron, and a plan prepared by him was taken back and approved by the gallant and patriotic Romana for the escape and reception onboard the British squadron of the army under his command. An unlucky discovery of the communication, before the plan in all its parts was ripe for execution, led to suspicion on the part of the emissaries of the enemy, and (in conformity with part of the plan under such an untoward circumstance) to a premature movement and a hasty execution of the terms agreed upon.

In a lengthy letter to Romana, Keats relayed his understanding of the circumstances of the various Spanish regiments based on the information received from the Spanish officers and set out his thoughts as to how the troops at disparate locations may be best assembled and collected, noting the number of ships at his disposal might prevent all being accomplished at the one time. His overwhelming difficulty continued to be a lack of transports. He was in expectation of the arrival of additional resources, but given the French were likely awake to something being afoot, waiting was not an option. Undaunted, he was now committed to the task and to overcoming all impediments. He lacked the resources to send ships all over the Baltic to simultaneously collect troops from distant and separate shores, and given French suspicions and the rapidity of communication, he lacked the time to collect them sequentially.

His letter to Romana continued; proposing that if those troops already in Langeland should be thought to be secure for now, the other troops might be embarked from their disparate locations and landed on Langeland 'at leisure' and the whole embarked from there to their final destination when transports had been procured. Keats had apprised Saumarez of this possibility by letter the day before,[487] but of course, had no prospect of a reply within time to be of reassurance.

We must be prepared, he said to Romana to "encounter even unforeseen difficulties: naval arrangements are ever dependent in some degree, on weather; but I should hope to surmount them all." He concluded that letter by raising the possibility if it were in their power or deemed preferable by the Marquis, that the Spanish seize Nyborg:

In my present uninformed state, I am not in a situation to judge how far it might be in the power of, or deemed preferable by, the Spanish commander to seize on Nyborg; it would secure the inactivity of the gun-boats in that port: but such a measure might possibly involve the safety of the troops in Zealand and Jutland, by inducing the Danes to act hostilely, when otherwise they might be disposed to wink at, or make no serious effort to impede the quiet removal of the Spanish troops. But if the principle of the plan should be approved of, and deemed feasible by those in command, I would recommend the movement to be general; that it be agreed to act upon it in all its parts on the same day, except a discovery should take place, in which event each part should act immediately without hesitation.

I acknowledge I should have little expectation of the success of any negotiation for the peaceable removal of the troops; but a declaration immediately after the movement shall have commenced, of the peaceable and unoffending object in view, accompanied with a threat of retaliation in the event of any hostile opposition on the part of the Danes or French, might perhaps be found advantageous.

In stating the naval force at present under my command, it is right to observe, that I am in expectation of more ships, and have been informed that a sufficient supply of provisions for all the Spanish troops is now on its passage to me.[488]

This plan took note of the advantages offered by the particular harbour which on advice from Envoy Thornton was not only of sufficient size to accommodate the docking of smaller naval vessels but was home to boats that could be used as ferries. It was this proposal that was agreed and adopted following discussions between Romana's aide-de-camp, Keats, and Captain McNamara of the *Edgar*.

The Marquis de la Romana immediately directed a forced march of all his troops, chiefly upon the fortified town of Nyborg [Map 6] in the Great Belt to which spot Admiral Keats was drawing the ships of his squadron, and on the 9th of August, after a march surprising for its rapidity entered and seized upon that place.

Romana cleverly used the French suspicion following the failure of various regiments to swear allegiance as an excuse to gather his troops from their dispersed stations under the guise of a military parade at which all the troops would swear unequivocal allegiance to King Joseph. It was said the presence of those troops who had already taken the oath was necessary to convince the others, and they ought to be assembled together so the senior officers could address the whole simultaneously to urge them to take the oath. The secret plan was to then advance on and seize Nyborg, signalling to the British ships when to enter the harbour.

As soon as Keats received confirmation this plan had been agreed upon orders were issued for all ships to proceed forthwith to stand off Nyborg. The *Superb* was still off Langeland, and due to the currents and lack of wind was finding it difficult to make her way to Nyborg. On the morning of 8 August, to be sure of being present where needed, Keats had himself and Don Lobo rowed in his barge from the *Superb* to the *Brunswick* to which he shifted his flag off Nyborg; an eleven-hour journey of some thirty-five miles under oar.[489] He had his ships in place awaiting a pre-determined signal from Romana when the time was right for the British to enter the harbour in conjunction with Romana's anticipated move on the town.

The congregation of troops from their distant postings was itself a masterpiece of planning and subterfuge on the part of Romana and his close aids. One regiment, that of Zamora, crossed the Little Belt from Jutland without difficulty and made a march of some thirty-five miles across Funen in twenty-one hours to ensure that the regiments would all arrive at the one time without exciting questions from the French.[490] Their colleagues in the regiment of Algarve stationed further north in Jutland had a longer march to the crossing point and were less fortunate, having been betrayed to the French by Romana's second in command and were captured attempting to cross the Little Belt to Funen.[491] Other regiments in the distant north of Jutland, thinking the sixty mile plus march to the crossing point to be too risky and adopting a suggestion in Romana's orders, seized boats from Aarhus and pressed their Danish crews to make their way by sea, escaping port at midnight on 9 August, only five hours before French troops arrived to contain them.[492] They initially headed for the base of other regiments, but found them evacuated and were met instead by cannon fire. At that time, they were met by the British gun brig *Snipe* sent to scout for them, and were escorted towards Nyborg.[493] Two other regiments took four days using small boats to cross to Langeland via the small island of Tassinge to join the Spanish regiment already stationed on that island.[494] The regiments of Asturias and Guadalajara stationed in Zealand found themselves surrounded by the Danish army and they were disarmed and unable to escape.

Despite a massive movement of troops, suspicion was not raised in Nyborg until the Spanish were present in such numbers as to make Danish opposition inopportune and the Governor effectively surrendered the town.

Having no argument with the Danes (despite the two countries being at war), Keats wrote to the local Governor from the *Brunswick*, before entering the harbour stating that as the Spanish commander had deemed it expedient to take possession of Nyborg, his duty was to co-operate with those troops, but he sought to put the Governor at ease, to the extent anyone would be at ease while within range of several hundred canons, writing:

> *To place Your Excellency as much at ease as possible respecting the line of conduct that may be adopted in the present event by the English admiral commanding in the Belt, notwithstanding the hostility of this day, I have the honour to inform you that I have given the strictest orders to all under my command, to observe towards the inhabitants of Nyborg the utmost civility and it is my wish to abstain from every hostile and offensive act, so long as no hostile and offensive measures are pursued by the troops of Denmark and France against those*

of Spain; but, if any opposition should be attempted by the Danes or French, to the peaceable and unoffending object in view, namely the quiet embarkation of the Spanish troops, I shall certainly, tho' most reluctantly, take measures which it is to be apprehended might occasion the destruction of the town of Nyborg.[495]

The Danish Governor and garrison yielded to the circumstances, but two ships of war guarding the harbour rejected the offers of security.

Its entrance by sea being defended by a corvette of 18 guns *[Fama]* and a cutter of 12 guns *[Sacorman]* moored across the harbour, the rear admiral made the commanders of those vessels an offer of neutrality, but that generosity being refused, they were attacked and taken by the boats of the squadron under the command of Captain MacNamara of the *Edgar*, the Spaniards also having fired at them from a battery in their possession.

This action, only twenty minutes or so in duration, took place between 7:30 and 8:00pm on the evening of 9 August. Leaving nothing to chance in a one-sided engagement the *Devastation*, *Kite (18)*, and *Hound (16)* together with the boats of the *Brunswick*, and *Edgar* were all involved along with those of the *Superb* that had now arrived up. Lieutenant Harvey of her company was the sole British fatality.[496] Romana, unwilling to act against the Danes with whom he had built a good relationship, had instructed his troops to take no part in the action, but a number nonetheless manned a shore battery and fired upon the Danish ships. As captured warships the *Fama* and *Sacorman* were regarded as legitimate prizes. Both were effectively taken into the navy but instead of being returned to England for survey and refit to Royal Navy standards they were employed on station as 'unregistered vessels'. They were lost in December 1808 when they each ran aground, battling ice and storms while hastily seeking to exit the Baltic after early onset of a severe winter.[497]

Later in the evening of 9 August Keats wrote again to Romana congratulating him on progress to date, and sending Captain Graves ashore with Keats's ideas and to see what use could be made of the boats in harbour saying:

I have the honour to acknowledge the receipt of your excellency's letter of this morning, and to congratulate you and the Spanish nation on the firm and manly step you have taken on this important occasion. Circumstances of weather unavoidably prevent the arrival of two ships

> *of the line now in sight. I send Captain Graves of the Brunswick, informed of my ideas, to see what uses can be made of the vessels at present in Nyborg. In my present situation I can receive nearly 1500 men onboard; and, under the circumstances, it appears to me the most advisable to convey the troops with all expedition to Langeland; and as it appears to be the opinion of your aide-de-camp, that you will be in a situation to maintain that island, and to take post there till the arrival of transports to embark the army. I shall order seamen to man twenty of the smacks at present in the ports, and more as the ships arrive. I apprehend the baggage and artillery had better be embarked in them, and moved to under our protection. Among the Spanish troops perhaps seamen may be found, and I would suggest the propriety of the immediate establishment of a marine corps on the most extensive scale possible; and I request your excellency to keep in mind, the embarkation of water and provisions with the troops in our present circumstances is of great consequence.*[498]

Keats himself went ashore shortly thereafter and in company with Romana inspected the town defences following which it was agreed that given their poor state and that the French were behaving suspiciously, it was essential the men be removed at the earliest opportunity.[499] The troops were assembled at dawn on 10 August under the guise of taking the oath. The waters of the harbour of which he now had command being too confined for a ship of the line Keats shifted his flag to the gun sloop, *Hound*, for manoeuvrability, and entered the harbour at 10:00am. From there he kept close supervision of all aspects of the operation. He wrote once more to the governor:

> *It must be evident to Your Excellency that, as my entrance into the harbour of Nyborg was hostilely opposed, I am bound by no absolute law or usage to abstain from hostilities, and to respect the property of the inhabitants. But, though neither one nor the other could be better secured than by the word of a British Officer, still it must be evident to Your Excellency that the Spanish general has occasion for several small craft in port, and that unless the masters and crews of them will lend their aid to equip and navigate the vessels, it may not be in my power to secure them from injury; but if they will, I pledge myself, after the service on which they are required (and which will be of short duration) shall have been ended, that I will not only use every means in my power to secure them from injury, but grant passports to them all to return in safety.*[500]

An offer was then made to the Danish merchants to employ the vessels then in the Port as transports, but this liberal proposition being rejected by both merchants and seamen, fifty-seven of the vessels were seized, hastily equipped and manned from the squadron with a view to the reception of the troops and military and other stores, for which the men of war were not sufficient. Although the Marquis Romana, at first, assigned a full week for the accomplishment of the embarkation, in which case the rear admiral undertook that none of the *materiel* should be left behind, yet on the following morning he was informed by the marquis, that circumstances imperiously demanded expedition. The greatest alacrity was manifested by every individual on this important occasion, and such was the exertion of the officers and seamen, that in forty-three hours after the harbour was opened by the capture of the two vessels that defended its entrance, the fifty-seven vessels were fitted out (although their sails and equipment were on shore in store and dwelling houses, and obtained only by force) and the whole of the artillery, military stores and baggage embarked and sent off.

His order book reveals extraordinary attention to detail, designed to ensure all participants were clear as to the plan and their part in it, and at the same time minimising the risk of the French learning of the venture. Once they had control of the port Keats requested the captains of the ships of the line; *Superb*, *Brunswick* and *Edgar* provide eight crews of six men each to man the captured vessels. The *Hound*, *Devastation* and *Kite* were each to provide three similar crews. Carpenters were tasked with having the boats made seaworthy and prepared in harbour while others procured and checked the rigging and fitments.

Stores, baggage and artillery were all loaded in the harbour, overnight and the following day, but the troops were still assembled some distance away and it was arranged they would be embarked from the point of Slypshavn about three miles distant where they could assemble under the protection of British men of war anchored off the island of Sproe in the Great Belt.

The Marquis de la Romana supervises the embarkation of Spanish troops to waiting British war ships - Juan Rodriguez -Jimenez, 1809, Museum of Romanticism, Madrid, CE0096, © Alamy, W3D4JN

The troops which had entered Nyborg amounting to about 6000 men were embarked at the point of Slypshavn about four miles from the town, and placed under the protection of the British squadron. The town of Nyborg, and its sea defences, the artillery of which had been spiked, but only in those situations where it could have been used detrimentally to the object in view, were then evacuated and restored to the Danish Governors. The corvette and cutter which had defended the entrance were, of course, considered by the rear admiral as lawful prizes and brought away, but the fifty-seven vessels although his proposition was not complied with, were nevertheless restored when the service for which they were required was completed. At the moment of embarkation one thousand more troops (who, in conformity with the original plan, had marched to another part of the coast, and seized upon some vessels and embarked) arrived under the protection of the *Snipe,* [gun-brig (12)] which had been detached for that purpose, to the great joy of the general and their comrades.

One regiment of cavalry, however, although it was much depended on, failed to join, and two regiments of infantry critically situated at Copenhagen owing to the rapidity of telegraphic communications, were surrounded by Danish troops, and, after some honourable effort to gain the point of embarkation, were obliged to desist and submit to their fate.

Among the Spanish troops embarked at Nyborg were two regiments of cavalry, the horses of which (besides about 200 for the saddle or draught) consisting of the finest of the Spanish breed, were black and unmutilated, with fine long manes, but which, from the shortage of time, it was found impossible to bring away, and it was determined to abandon them: at the moment of embarkation, however, they created a scene too remarkable to be omitted. The first regiment was drawn up about one hundred yards inland, and General Romana addressing himself to Admiral Keats said, "Perhaps I ought to order these fine horses to be destroyed, but there exists a sort of mutual attachment between the soldier and his horse, amounting almost to friendship, which makes me loath to give an order that might be unwillingly executed: some will go to the enemy, some to the country people, so they must take their chance". He then gave directions for their bridles to be taken off, and they were quitted with their saddles on. In a short time, they began to feel that they were without restraint, and roused perhaps by some horses and mares which had been grazing on the common (the contiguous land that had that appearance) began to move; neighing, galloping and disorder soon took place, which grew into kicking and biting, and a most furious battle ensued, which for some time interrupted the embarkation.

The second regiment at the rear admiral's desire was taken to another field of rising ground, and about half a mile farther off, when it was quitted in the same manner as the first. In a short time, disorder became manifest in this regiment also, and, attracted by the noise and sight of the distant battle, they suddenly set off at full speed, galloped over the two intermediate hedges, broke into the common, rushed amidst the raging battle, and formed a sight at once infinitely grand and astonishing. They combated with their teeth, as well as with their hind feet, but they fought principally on end, striking with their fore feet, apparently with immense force, and with a rage that approached to madness, and which surprised every beholder.

But in their utmost fury they seemed to avoid the sight of man, while their sidling movements shewed that they were desirous of preserving some military form, and which at times gave them the appearance of acting in concert. The Marquis, unprepared for this horrific scene, at length gave orders for the soldiers to endeavour to destroy with their swords such of those beautiful animals as were still living. But this was a service both dangerous and difficult, and though the common was afterwards covered with their bodies, some of them lying in groups of ten or a dozen, and in one of them the Marquis and rear admiral counted thirteen, yet more of them appeared to be killed in the battle than by the sword.

Embarkation of the troops commenced from Slypshavn on the following morning in the rain and a strong westerly wind (which same wind hampered Saumarez's return from the eastern arm of the Baltic), under the particular supervision of Captain Jackson of the *Superb* and Captain Lockyer of the *Hound*, together with the officers of the *Kite* and *Devastation*. The gun-brig *Minx (12)* with the prizes and gun-boats under the command of Captain May of the Royal Artillery provided cover. The ships of the line were loaded with 800 troops each, the *Hound* with 200, *Devastation*, and *Kite* 150 each, and the *Minx* with 100. The various boats seized in the harbour took 100 each. To say the conditions were crowded, damp and uncomfortable would be an understatement. The vessels pressed into service were far from ideal for the purpose.

In less than two days, the harbour had been secured, boats prepared, and some 7,000 troops embarked before the French had an opportunity to interfere. In the afternoon of 11 August Keats was able to strike his flag in the *Hound* having embarked 65 vessels and return to the *Superb* from where he sent a report to Saumarez that the troops were all onboard British ships.

Keats issued orders that if the convoy was approached by Danish gun-boats the British were instructed to signal a flag of truce on account of transporting the Spanish in accordance with convention in their peaceable retirement from Denmark. They were to make clear that if this was not honoured the seized vessels would all be destroyed rather than be allowed to return unharmed when no longer required.[501]

As the flotilla headed for open waters they were gratified to be joined by boats carrying the regiments that had taken boats from Aarhus and sailed directly to Nyborg under the protection of the small brig *Snipe* (12). Keats's advice to the Admiralty noted in a post-script they had received word regarding the second regiment from Jutland; "Since this letter was concluded, we entertain some hopes that part of the regiment in Jutland we thought lost, has escaped to the post at Langeland by the western channel".[502] In the event, this contingent soon joined their countrymen.

The immediate destination of the flotilla was Langeland. It was judged to be the more productive island with a plentiful supply of water, livestock, grain and vegetables capable of sustaining them for a period. Here troops would be out of immediate danger as the 1st Catalonia regiment had earlier overpowered the Danish garrison and taken control of the island. Various adjacent islands were thought to be too well defended, not secure, or incapable of sustaining 10,000 men for even a short time whilst they waited for transports to arrive from England. But no island could support an additional nine to ten thousand men or stay out of the grasp of the French forces for long.

After being held back for a time by the weather, they reached Spodsberg on the east coast of Langeland without incident on 13 August where they joined the regiments of Villaviciosa and Barcelona who had independently escaped southern Funen by sea via the island of Tassinge and the 1st Catalonia regiment already stationed on that island. They set up camp and established defensive posts to guard against advances from the west by Bernadotte's forces. To have achieved this much without having to engage with any serious opposition from Denmark or France was a remarkable achievement. There remained substantial obstacles to ultimate success.

Keats had written to both the Admiralty and via the *Ariel* (16) to Saumarez two days earlier, as the boats were heading to Langeland, detailing the various transactions and reporting the success of the mission to date. By 13 August he was able to send advice to the Admiralty via the frigate *Euryalus* (36) he had detained for that purpose that the troops had been evacuated successfully and were in the process of being landed at Langeland. [503]

Victualling an additional 10,000 men so far from a friendly port had its challenges, and Langeland turned out not to be as productive as first hoped. Some rations destined for the Baltic fleet were diverted from Gothenburg as an interim measure. As a precaution, Keats placed the men on two-thirds rations and then half rations of bread, pending the arrival of sufficient stores.

Furthermore, Langeland although secure for now, would not remain so for long. The mission was by no means complete.

The embarkation being completed, the squadron proceeded to Langeland where they arrived on the 13th, and where the Spaniards had already a body of more than 2000 men.[10] Here it became necessary to equip in a more effectual manner the Nyborg vessels to enable them to proceed with the troops to Gothenburg. They were scantily victualled from the men of war, and the whole squadron, with the transports, was watered with considerable labour and difficulty from a lake in the centre of the island, to which a road of nearly a mile was made by the Spanish troops for rolling the carts upon. On the 18th the

---

10   See Naval Chronology Vol2.2 p81

Commander-in-Chief, Sir James Saumarez arrived, and the plans and operations of the rear admiral having met with his approbation,[504] he returned to the Baltic on the 22nd.

The enemy had collected a considerable body of troops in Funen, which is separated only by a short passage from Langeland, together with a considerable flotilla force and ample means of transport, the whole under the direction of Marshal Bernadotte (the present [1926] King of Sweden) who was not idle in making demonstrations of attack, which kept the squadron continually on the alert, without being able in turn to disturb or molest them.

French emissaries were also sent amongst the Spanish troops, who, by the most insidious promises, and by attempts to create suspicion in the minds of the soldiers as to the conduct of the English, endeavoured to excite disaffection and its natural con-comitants. But the army was firm and incorruptible, not a soldier proved unfaithful; and the enemy failing in his intrigues, dared not hazard the attack he constantly menaced. On 22nd all the arrangements being completed for which the army landed in Langeland they were embarked in as comfortable a manner as circumstances would allow, onboard the ships of war and the Nyborg vessels. The arms of which the inhabitants had been deprived on landing, were then restored to them; and on the following day the squadron anchored off Romso[505] where it was fortunately met by a small convoy of victuallers for the ships of war in the Baltics, and of which the rear admiral availed himself further to supply his squadron and the transports. On the 25th the Great Belt was passed, and on the 27th Rear Admiral Keats had the gratification to anchor in Hawkes Road, Gothenburg, without any accident or the loss of a single soldier. Here, on the small island contiguous to the anchorage, and by permission of the Swedish governor, the troops were landed, to await in cantonments for the transports from England, which shortly after arrived, when the troops were again embarked and sailed with a favourable wind for Spain.

The proximity of French forces and, as Keats pointed out to the Admiralty, the rapid approach of the changing of the season dictated an acceleration and change in plan. It would be necessary to remove the troops from Langeland at a time before more substantial transports would become available. He would need to rely upon the resources currently at hand, such as they were.[506] The majority of vessels at his disposal were not capable of sailing to England, let alone Spain, and the sail of the line could not be spared from duties in the Baltic for any substantial period without compromising the security of shipping. The commander in chief in the eastern Baltic needed every available sail of the line to meet the growing threat from Russian forces. In any event, Keats had insufficient supplies to contemplate a long voyage. As Britain's sole ally in the Baltic, Swedish ports provided the only options as possible staging points. Even the voyage to Gothenburg was a considerable distance being up to a week's sailing through potentially hazardous waters. He received word that the Swedish shipowners in that port were willing to provide vessels only at an exorbitant price.

Once again Keats was required to make and implement a detailed logistical plan, using such resources as were to hand, which he commenced to do almost immediately on disembarking the troops to Langeland, advising his captains circumstances may dictate an evacuation at very short notice. All boats were to be kept ready, day and night for that purpose.[507] The various ships and smaller vessels at his disposal, including the prizes, victuallers, and any others he could get his hands on were each pressed into service. The smaller vessels, including those taken from Nyborg and those that were commandeered from Aarhus were given bow letters to identify the ships from which they were crewed and would be required to load and follow. For example, the twenty-two boats to be crewed by men from the *Superb* were marked S1, S2, S3... S22; those from the *Edgar*, E1, E2... E15 etc. etc. Each was made safe with the checking of rigging and provision of adequate ballast. The manifest reveals a convoy of 77 vessels, some quite small with a cargo of just 20-30 troops, whereas the *Superb* and *Brunswick* carried over 900 men each.[508]

Instructions were copied into the order book and the relevant officers were required to sign, indicating their particular instructions had been received and understood.[509] In this manner, similar to that adopted by Nelson, and no doubt based upon his best practice, Keats was able to maintain close supervision of the complex exercise. As a result of this operation Keats (along with Nelson and Hood), came to be regarded as one of the best planners of operations at a time when administrative detail or staff work was not seen to be as important as the swashbuckling deployment of firepower.[510]

It was apparent that Bernadotte had assembled a significant force on Jutland and was preparing to cross to Funen, from where he could launch an attack on Langeland. There was no time to waste. By 15 August arrangements were in place, and the fleet was supplied with several hundreds of tons of provisions and fourteen days' supply of water to be ready to depart at short notice if circumstances demanded it. Baggage was collected.

The lettered and numbered designations of the various boats were continued but differently allocated when the frigate *Gorgon* (44) became available. She was given the role of the mothership to the 'E squadron', the *Edgar* taking the 'B squadron' and the *Brunswick* taking the 'S squadron' from the *Superb* to leave the flagship free for overall escort, still carrying her cargo of 900 troops. Some of the Danish boats and their crew pressed into service at Aarhus were added to the flotilla designated as vessels X1-X7. For this voyage in the open sea each boat was provided with a navigator and chart and coloured pendants designating their group; *Superb*, red, *Edgar* blue etc. The leader of each group was manned by a lieutenant from a sail of the line and provided with a correspondingly coloured broad pendant. Additional convoy signals were prepared and distributed among the fleet to deal with specific contingencies, particularly in the event of encountering hostile boats.[511]

On 19 August Admiral Saumarez arrived in the *Victory*, and received General Romana on board, at which time all ships flew the flag of Spain and fired a 24-gun salute, answered by the Spanish artillery. He expressed regret at being unable to provide transports but emphasised the need for expediency, so as to free up the ships of war for possible action, and on receiving word the Russian fleet had put to sea, promptly returned to the east.

Over the following days, it became clear the enemy forces were closing in. Gun-boats were increasing their activity on the western coast of Langeland. Bernadotte had reportedly now crossed from Jutland to Funen preparing to head to its southern shores to cross to Langeland. On the morning of 23 August, there still being no word of substantial transports, and it being inopportune to wait any longer for their anticipated arrival, Keats issued orders for the embarkation of all the troops from Spodsberg. By the end of that day the convoy was on its way to Sweden.

Once troops were onboard, very specific instructions were issued governing cleaning, ventilation, fumigation, exercise, provision of water, bedding, et cetera to ensure the continued health and well-being of the large number of troops required to be housed in confined and undoubtedly uncomfortable conditions. Happily, the Victualling Board had been preparing for the success of the venture, and on the night of 23 August whilst anchored off Nyborg waiting for unfavourable winds to pass, the convoy was joined by eighteen victuallers from England allowing restoration of full rations and placing Keats quite at ease on that front. The arrival of additional ships also allowed him to appropriate vessels out of that convoy and reallocate a number of troops among them to remove some of the overcrowding. To this point, it had been standing room only on some boats and the voyage was promising to be less than pleasant for those unaccustomed to the sea.[512] Fortunately the weather for the rest of the voyage was benign.

HMS Warrior protecting a convoy passing Reefness. WA Knell. Although described as HMS Warrior, that ship was not in the Baltic other than at the Battle of 1801. Reefness (Rosnaes) is the north-western point of Zealand, in the path of a journey from Langeland to Gothenburg, and it is thought the ship is more likely another 74 gun ship of the line, most probably Superb, leading the convoy transporting Romana's troops. NMM BHC0578, ©National Maritime Museum, Greenwich London

As they passed through the Belt, and necessarily close to Danish shore batteries they were fired upon, but to no effect and they arrived at the Flemish roads, off Gothenburg on 27 August. The *Edgar* had been required by Saumarez to put her passengers ashore at Helsingborg to free her to go in search of Saumarez and the Russian fleet. Those troops then marched north to later re-join their comrades at Gothenburg.

On anchoring in the roads Keats encountered several administrative hurdles. Firstly, Baron Toll, the Governor of Scania would not allow the flotilla to land foreign troops and secondly the merchants of Gothenburg, both Swedish and British, continued to hold out demanding exorbitant rates for transport.[513] Sweden was less keen to co-operate than the Admiralty had initially supposed, some now observing that Britain was showing a much more acute interest in the war in Spain ('fishing Spaniards out of the sea') than in her own war with Russia. After some negotiation with the Governor, permission was granted for the landing of 700 invalids and the use of a building as a hospital. Troops were still not permitted on the mainland, but they were ultimately allowed ashore on various islands in the bay.

Little progress was being made regarding the cost of hiring local merchant ships for the onward journey. Given the pressing demands to escort convoys and address potential Russian aggression in the east sending sail of the line to Spain as transports was not an option. Accordingly, Keats set about preparing as many substantial vessels as he could arrange. He had several navy vessels of various descriptions already in the Baltic modified by installing platforms to provide for two tiers for the carrying of troops.[514]

On 4 September, having been sitting off Gothenburg for a week, he received welcome news from England that arrangements were well-advanced. In anticipation of a successful outcome, the Transport Board and the Victualling Board had for some time been assembling the means to feed the men and transport them to Spain, without indicating the reason for the preparations and those ships would shortly be on their way. He accordingly abandoned negotiations with the local ship owners, and focussed his attention on procuring sufficient supplies.

By early August, the Transport Board had sourced a large number of troop-ships and five store-ships from the Downs, Portsmouth, Deptford, Harwich, and Yarmouth, and had them ready for dispatch from the Nore. On receipt of favourable news from Keats, they sailed under the protection of the *Racoon* (16) and armed sloops. A convoy of more than thirty-five vessels arrived off Gothenburg on 6 September.[515]

Keats had been busy sourcing five weeks' provisions for their next voyage and the newly arrived ships were very quickly stocked so that on 9 September troops having been embarked with as much comfort as possible, the fleet sailed for La Coruna, Spain. The troops from the *Edgar* that had been disembarked at Helsingborg arrived a few days later, and followed in ships detained by Keats for that purpose. With more than an adequate supply of shipping now available the various Danish boats were released from their service in accordance with Keats's earlier undertakings.

At Keats's suggestion, Romana went to England onboard the brig *Calypso* (18) to discuss the alliance and deployment of his troops with Cabinet Ministers.[516] It was there decided the troops would be better deployed in Santander rather than La Coruna, and signals were sent to the convoy accordingly.

The convoy had to see off some Danish cutters on the way. They anchored off the Downs before proceeding to Spain. When the leading vessels were nearly within sight of La Coruna a two-day gale in the Bay of Biscay scattered the convoy, such that at one point only nine transports were in sight. This had risen to twenty-two by the time they arrived, and the remainder docked safely at Santander and Santona on the northern coast of Spain (Map 4) in the second week of October after a three-week passage with no losses. There they were re-armed by the British, strengthening the allied army by 9,000 troops just in time to assist in responding to the offensive launched by Napoleon in November.[517] General la Romana arrived in Spain in November 1808, whereupon he was appointed commandant-in-chief of the northern provinces.

Thus, by the patriotism and talents of the Marquis de la Romana, and the devotion of the troops (who submitted to many privations with patience and cheerfulness), and the zeal, activity and perseverance of the seamen of the British squadron, aided by the consummate skill, prudence and foresight of the rear admiral, which were conspicuously displayed throughout the whole of the proceedings, 9230 troops with all their artillery, military-stores, and baggage were returned from the power of Buonaparte at a most critical moment, and restored to the service of their native country.

Subsequent to their arrival in Spain, the government of that country was pleased to commemorate the patriotism and fidelity of that portion of their army by a medal which was struck on the occasion, and the inscription on which "Mi Patria es mi Norte" forms the motto of the rear admiral's arms; and for the services performed by him on this occasion, his Majesty was graciously pleased to create him a Knight of the Most Honourable Order of the Bath.

Keats's dispatches were comprehensive, showing his constant communication with London as well as the local participants, and were published at length in *The Naval Chronicle*. Lord Mulgrave passed them on to the King in full, saying they were at once so full and concise he could not summarise them without omitting some interesting and important detail of the transaction the influence of which he predicted would extend beyond its immediate effect in Britain and Spain. He wrote to Saumarez that he could not let those dispatches go from the Admiralty without first conveying his own most hearty congratulations on the important event, noting Keats had conducted himself with his customary talent, zeal, and judgement.[518] Keats's correspondence to the Marquis de la Romana (who replied verbally through his aide-de-camp and other confidential officers) and to the Governor of Nyborg (who replied in person) are set out as attachments to his report, reproduced in Ralfe's *Naval Chronology*.[519]

The Prime Minister was particularly keen to promptly reward Keats, writing to the King that the exercise had caused "such general satisfaction among all ranks of your Majesty's subjects, and the public expressions of obligation to the officer to whose conduct the measure was entrusted, are so universal that the Duke of Portland would not think himself justified in withholding from your Majesty the expectations which he finds to be entertained by persons of all descriptions, that your majesty will graciously condescend to bestow upon Admiral Keats some mark of your Majesty's royal favour".[520] The honour was recommended not simply for the execution of a complex logistical exercise, but also for Keats's part in the delicate negotiations the result of which were to have international political implications. The King concurred, and in view of the Duke having so strongly pressed for the immediate bestowal of the reward did not withhold his consent, but thought it best postponed until the end of the campaign.[521]

Lord Mulgrave was able to write to Keats's father, Rev. Keats. on 22 September[522] saying:

I feel the greatest satisfaction in acquainting you that His Majesty was graciously pleased yesterday, to confer the Military Order of the Bath on Rear Admiral Keats, in testimony of His Majesty's high approbation of the very distinguished service lately performed by that officer in the deliverance of the Spanish troops in the Baltic...an unequivocal mark of His Majesty's favour and approbation... With sentiments of cordial congratulation...Mulgrave

Notice was published in the Gazette on 15 October 1808.[523] At this time the Order was restricted to the Sovereign, Grand Master and just thirty-five knights. It was intended that a ceremony be conducted by Saumarez but he had returned to England, so the insignia was delivered to Rear Admiral Bertie with a view to his conducting the ceremony on 1 January 1809 in the great cabin of the *Superb*. Unfortunately, as Bertie arrived off Gothenburg in the *Dictator* on 31 December the ice closed in. Keats went out to greet him in the *Superb*, "but the frost was so extremely intense, that, although Admiral Bertie's barge was hoisted out, within five minutes after the two flagships had anchored, he was unable to get on board, and was ordered by Keats to make the best of his way through the ice",[524] and the ceremony was again deferred.

The London Gazette reported His Majesty, George III conducted the investiture with all ceremonial honours at Queen's Palace (Buckingham Palace) on 12 July 1809 in the presence of the HRH Duke of York, First and Principal Companion of the Order. Keats was knighted using the Sword of State and the King placed the Ribbon and Badge of the Order over his shoulder.[525] In discussion with George Nayler, genealogist to the Order, Keats selected for his arms an old family motto, '*Restituit*', together with the motto of the Order 'Tria Juncta In Uno', (three joined in one). At the request of the

King, made when Keats was dining with him, this motto was replaced by that of the Marquis de la Romana or more particularly the Spanish regiment of Zamora; *Mi Patria es mi Norte* (my homeland is my north, in the sense of pole star or guide), as featured on the commemorative medals struck by Spain. The arms can be described as: Ermine (black spots on a white background), three mountain cats argent (silver), the honourable augmentation, on a canton argent, (square upper corner), the Spanish flag over an anchor surrounded by a wreath of laurel.

The Keats crests and supporters; (left) 'Restituit', 'tria juncta in uno' as first agreed with the genealogist; (centre) the final crest incorporating 'Mi Patria es mi Norte', as requested by the King, and; (right) the simplified crest he used on his papers, silverware and the like.

Keats was at that time an extra knight. He acceded to the constituent number on the death of Sir James Craig in January 1812. His formal installation in the Order was then conducted in an imposing ceremony at Westminster Abbey on 1 June 1812, presided over by HRH Prince Frederick, the Duke of York and attended by all of the Knights of the Order processing from the Princes Chamber in the House of Lords through the Abbey Church to the King Henry the Seventh's Chapel to the accompaniment of the drums and trumpets of the King's Household. On account of his being at sea at the time, Keats could unfortunately not attend in person and was represented by his proxy, Captain Sir Christopher Cole, attended by Keats's nephew Lewis Buck, Arthur Bingham and Charles Bacon as his Esquires. He was duly installed in the Order and allocated stall 38 in the Chapel of Henry the Seventh. The stall was adorned with his crest and coat of arms and his heraldic banner hung from the ceiling above the stall during his lifetime.[526]

Acclaim was widespread. Saumarez, known to be covetous of his own honour and position (particularly it seems when it came to Keats), wrote to his sister: "Admiral Keats had been indefatigable in the management of this intricate business, which will greatly add to his well-earned fame, and I hope draw upon him some mark of Royal favour, which he so justly merits."[527] To Keats he wrote:

> *In the Important service you have rendered to the country in extricating the Spanish Troops from being any longer in the claws of the Enemy I cannot too highly applaud the Skill and judgement you have displayed, and the Perseverance and Zeal of the Captains, Officers and men under your command, and;*
>
> *The fortunate consequences resulting from [the operation] in my opinion makes it equal to having attained a Victory and I doubt not it will be regarded as such when the accounts reach England.*[528]

The removal of the northern army from the Baltic meant Sweden was safe from Napoleon for now as the troops left to Marshal Bernadotte's army were reduced to little more than a string of coastal garrisons and were insufficient for the implementation of invasion. Their redeployment to Spain brought reinforcement of troops in their home country at a critical juncture. Whilst the French had been aware of discontent amongst the Spanish army and had been sending troops to the area to quell any unrest, they were quite unprepared for such an audacious and large scale operation which was undertaken with such alacrity as gave them no opportunity to mount an adequate response. Translations of the various reports of the success of the operation were distributed through Russia and Pomerania to publicise the policies of the British Government and more importantly advertise the demonstrated capacity of its navy to effectively pursue and deliver those policies, and particularly to efficiently move and supply large bodies of troops.

E.P. Brenton wrote of the exercise:

> *The nobleness of the British character was never perhaps, more honourably displayed than in all the circumstances of this remarkable transaction. After rescuing an army from their oppressor, the Admiral declined taking away the prizes which his valour had won; and, though at war with Denmark, generously restored the whole of the fifty-seven vessels as soon as the service was performed for which they had been taken.*[529]

The operation is described by Davey as a breath-taking feat of seamanship and organisation, requiring great skill, and additional confirmation of British maritime superiority; and as an exemplary example of seamanship, organisational expertise, and diplomacy.[530] Others describe the transfer to nearby defensible islands by small boats, for collection by men of war, as an imaginative solution to the evacuation of the dispersed troops.[531]

The Duke of Clarence wrote:

The Spanish spoke in the highest terms of you...I was immediately informed of the success of your well planned expedition in favour of the gallant Spaniards... and believe me the most important service yet performed in any war is the exploit since executed by you: the advantages are incalculable and I rejoice most sincerely that it has fallen to my friend's lot to achieve this important and glorious event ...I have also seen the King, and the Queen assures me he thinks as highly of the event as I do.[532]

The Marquis de la Romana presented Keats with the cased pair of pistols that had been given to him by Bernadotte some weeks earlier when the French were flattering him, attempting to quiet any unrest. Romana is reported to have said; "I received these weapons from my greatest enemy, I now give them to my greatest and best friend".[533]

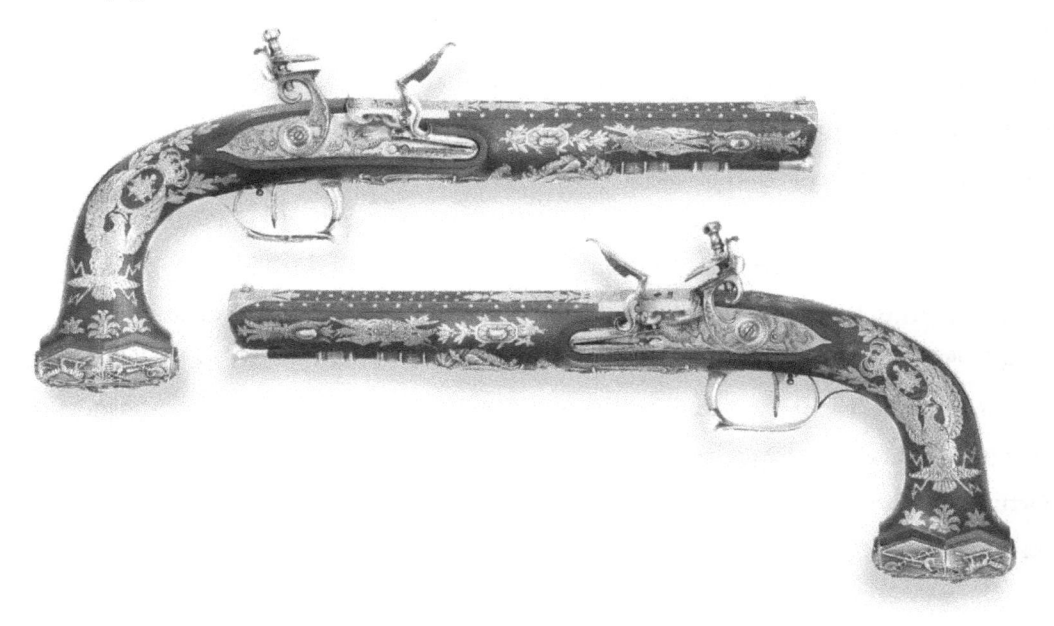

Pair of silver mounted flintlock presentation pistols as given to Keats by Romana in appreciation of his successful liberation. These rare and finely crafted pistols have a current value of around £1 million.

St. Vincent, who had earlier lamented the Admiralty removing Keats from his squadron in the Channel to take up command in the Baltic was not an easy man to please or impress, but was always a supporter of Keats. He now took the time to write congratulating him on the knighthood saying: "Long may you own the glorious career, which hitherto accompanied all your public life", and describing him as 'The Man on whom the Salvation of the Country may at some (not distant) period depend."[534]

Whilst Saumarez had described the exercise as the equal to having attained a victory and his earlier letter to his sister was quite generous, he later wrote to her with some irony:

> *I am glad to find Admiral Keats has the Red Riband. Sir Samuel Hood is created a Bart. It is a happy circumstance Sir Jas. S. sets himself above worldly Honours and is satisfied with those he has obtained – he would otherwise feel mortified at those serving and doing his Orders being thus noticed whilst he remains apparently neglected.*[535]

The documents demonstrate the honours went where they were deserved. Keats was justifiably noticed, relying upon his own initiative. In no way was he implementing orders from Saumarez.

On the contrary, instructions were sent from the Admiralty on 23 July directly to Keats, who made and supervised the complex arrangements himself and who was himself in direct communication with London regarding the details. Through numerous exchanges with the relevant parties, and then transferring his flag to the small sloop to allow manoeuvrability in the shallow and confined harbour, he maintained meticulous control of the operation to its outstanding conclusion.

As stated in his own hand, Saumarez played no part in the embarkation or arrangements leading to it. His correspondence makes clear that he received a copy of Keats's initial instructions on 9 August, and was then off Bornholm. He wrote: "Having been detained by contrary winds I received accounts from Admiral Keats, they had been withdrawn from the island of Funen and landed on Langeland".[536] He was in the Eastern Baltic and received orders to return to the Great Belt, where the sheer size of the *Victory* would have been of significant advantage in the transport operation. By 11 August, Keats was already reporting the taking of Nyborg, fitting the boats and successfully transporting 6,000 troops to Langeland, with the additional 1,000 joining from Jutland and another 1,000 arriving independently with hopes that another regiment, thought lost, would soon be joining them via the western channel.[537] On 15 August, having battled periods of calms and headwinds, Saumarez was off Darsser Ort, Stralsund [Germany], still nearly two hundred miles from Nyborg, responding to Keats's letter of 11 August and congratulating him on the successful execution of the exercise.[538] He arrived off Langeland on 18 August and departed again on 22 August.

Some have made much of the fact Saumarez allowed Keats's reports to go directly to the Admiralty rather than submitting his own as Commander-in-Chief.[539] In reality he had no choice. Saumarez was simply not present. Keats reported to the Admiralty from whom he received orders directly and to his CIC simultaneously. He had urgent need to not only report the success of the venture, but to receive transports and victuallers as a result. He had no means of knowing when Saumarez might appear and did not have the luxury of waiting for his approval.

There is an undercurrent of jealousy on the part of Saumarez, who was also known to be prone to bouts of depression, and it was noticed by others. Byam Martin recorded that:

> *On several occasions I have had reason to observe a something in Sir James's conduct that always brought to mind a belief that I was considered too much an admirer of Sir S. H. [Hood] and Sir R. K. [Keats], and too sensible of their absence from this station to be pleasing to the chief.*[540]

Keats was somewhat unlucky not to have received this honour earlier in his career. Historian Joseph Allen made pointed reference to the failure to award any special mark of royal favour following his sensational triumph off Algeciras. The impediment was not Keats's conduct, which received the glowing thanks of Parliament, but the unfortunate circumstance of his commander, Saumarez. Having been defeated just days earlier he was not awarded the peerage he sought and had to be content with the Bath Star. As captain of a ship under Saumarez's orders Keats could not properly receive equal recognition, regardless of the disparity of their respective contributions to the victory. Again, at San Domingo, the circumstances of the commander-in-chief cruelled Keats's chances of high honours. Although Duckworth thought himself due a Baronetcy, opening the way to recognition of his flag captain, the Admiralty considered him lucky to avoid a court martial for having abandoned his post at Cádiz. Whereas Saumarez and Duckworth were both vocal and persistent in seeking reparation, and each lobbied for years, there is no evidence that Keats thought himself hard done by or passed over. If he did, he kept a dignified silence. There is no doubt his colleagues and superiors well knew where the true merit lay. Awarding honorary positions as Colonel and later Major General of Marines was no doubt a public statement of the esteem in which he was held, and of course provided welcome financial compensation.

It should be added that apart from mentioning relevant officers in dispatches Keats wrote to the admiralty asking consideration be given to granting the men additional pay as recompense for the hospitality extended to the Spanish. He noted the prize money was insignificant and they were not engaged in convoy duty as such, so there was no formal avenue for financial recognition of the exemplary manner in which the arduous service was performed. Secretary Pole recommended that a liberal allowance should be made.[541]

His service being completed, the rear admiral resumed his station in the Great Belt where for the remaining part of the season he afforded the trade of his country the most effectual protection.

At the close of the season the Commander-in-chief, Sir Jas. Saumarez, returned to England, leaving the command to Sir Richard Keats with directions to keep the Great Belt and Sound open for the trade till the upper parts of the Baltic were frozen, and then afterwards to winter with five sail of the line, at Marstrand, in Sweden [Map 6], but the accomplishment of these duties was opposed by natural and political causes.

Both those channels were rendered impassable by ice from an early and severe winter, from which much distress and loss of property ensued; and the situation of Sweden was critical, menaced on the one hand by an invasion of French and Danish troops across the ice from Zealand, which the severity of the season seemed to render passable, and on the other, distracted by internal commotion, which terminated in revolution and a change of the royal dynasty.

On the advice of Lord Mulgrave at the Admiralty, the King approved the stationing of five sail of the line, (*Superb, Brunswick, Orion, Edgar,* and *Dictator*) three frigates and seventeen smaller ships at Marstrand on the west coast of Sweden, under Keats's command for the duration of the winter, whilst Saumarez and Hood returned to England. These ships were given a number of objectives centred on giving Sweden confidence in British support: to protect trade on the re-opening of the Baltic the following spring, to underpin the security of Sweden by watching the Danes and interrupting their communication with Norway, and to prevent any attempt which Russia or others might mediate against Sweden before a fleet could arrive from England in the spring.[542]

As the senior officer in the Baltic, Keats was left in a difficult position. The political situation was deteriorating. During a tempestuous meeting with the King Thornton's replacement as ambassador, Anthony Merry, had been threatened with the closure of Swedish ports to British ships on expiry of a treaty at year's end. He promptly advised Keats to avoid becoming ice bound in a Swedish harbour and to maintain a method of escape if necessary, but without showing distrust of the Swedes. The Baltic froze over for some months each winter, curtailing naval operations and adding another peril to the tasks at hand. Not only did ships become stuck in port, or worse, in the open ice flows, but enemy troops and cavalry could advance marching over what was once open sea. Both John Johnson, a Government confidential agent and Consul Fenwick at Halsingborg advised Keats such an invasion was likely if the Sound remained frozen. On Christmas day, Keats ordered his fleet to remove from Marstrand to the Hawkes Road anchorage off Gothenburg from where he expected to be confident of supplies, including an abundance of fresh water in particular. The anchorage was less likely to freeze over and was not covered by shore batteries so "in the case of a reverse I should have perhaps less difficulty to extricate myself than from Marstrand".[543] On the basis of Keats's description of the deteriorating situation Lord Mulgrave suggested he be ordered to return to Great Yarmouth. The King was 'sensible of the unpleasant and doubtful situation of [Keats's] squadron' but as a return to Yarmouth would be seen as an abandonment of Sweden and have a decidedly detrimental influence upon relations which the King was anxious to preserve, the King insisted he remain on station.[544] The winter was very severe with ice extending to areas never seen before. Lack of supplies became an issue, but the Admiralty simply replied that he would in a short time be supplied on station with what was necessary. The loss of a ship carrying a supply of winter clothing was keenly felt, and men were tasked with making shoes and clothes.[545]

Given the unstable political situation, Keats was simultaneously communicating his willingness to support and defend the King of Sweden against both internal rebels and foreign powers and also making contingency plans for the escape of his fleet.

In the event of remaining he requested a further squadron, particularly cruisers to better protect British convoys, be sent to equip him to meet his obligations in the coming summer. He contended that plans for defence should be formed based on those of attack, and proportioned to the efforts of the enemy. He advised the Admiralty that he fully expected to be facing an enemy of double the number of gun-boats in the coming summer.[546] The ships at his disposal had been barely adequate to meet the needs of the previous summer when convoys upwards of 100 sail passed with minimal protection. In consequence, he recommended that in addition to those off Helsingborg, a division of four or five ships of from 64 (of the lightest draught) to 32 guns with three or four smaller vessels should be tasked specifically with protecting the Malmo passage, from Falsterbo to Landscrona (Map 6). He recommended more cruisers be placed in the Belt to prevent privateers from interrupting merchant ships in passage from Russian and Prussian ports through to Karlskrona.

In 1808, thousands of merchant ships had passed through the Sound, half of which were going to or from Britain, and all of which required the protection of the Royal Navy for safe passage. Navy resources in this sea were stretched beyond capacity with large convoys, stretched over many miles, escorted by only minimal naval protection through passages that lent themselves to predation from hidden privateers. The Admiralty responded to these calls allocating additional, if still not sufficient, ships. In 1809 there were more British warships in the Baltic than at any other time, with total man power reaching 17,000 men.[547] Nevertheless Keats felt he had not been listened to sufficiently, writing to Hood prior to Saumarez's return for the summer that he was uninformed of both the Commander-in-Chief's arrangements and of the naval force appropriate for the tasks before him.[548] Despite his concerns there is universal acceptance that the arrangements Keats made for the safe passage of convoys were entirely appropriate and amazingly successful to the extent they were continued with little or no amendment by his successors.

Seeing the Russian army closing in, and aware of revolt in Warmeland with the rebels intending to march on Stockholm,[549] Keats became of the view (correctly) that Sweden would find it increasingly difficult to preserve her neutrality. He requested he be reinforced with a squadron sufficient to enable him to deal with the Swedish fleet if it should come to that.

As predicted, very shortly thereafter the Swedish military commanders unseated King Gustav in a coup. It was unclear for some time who would now be in control and whether Sweden would remain allied to Britain, become neutral, or possibly close her ports to British men of war.

Accordingly, whilst offering all assistance he was simultaneously urgently trying to remove all British shipping from potential harm's way, writing:

> *...the most urgent necessity in my mind is to remove with the least possible delay all British property from Sweden, for notwithstanding the assurances which the new government hold out of a desire to maintain friendly relations with England, still with a powerful Russian Army within 35 leagues of the capital, it is not to be expected it will be able even to preserve its neutrality to the period fixed for the meeting of the Diet, the 1st of next May.*[550]

Becoming therefore, convinced of the impracticality of fulfilling the latter part of his instructions, Sir Richard sent everything that could be got out of the Kattegat to England, and the *Superb* being frozen up in that sea, he had to cut his way through the ice to Hawkes Road, [using ice saws to cut out squares of ice, which with the capstan bars, handspikes and hooks were shoved under the ice on either side till they made a canal ahead of the ship enabling the crew to warp her to open water outside] and there, with the remaining part of the ships under his orders that could be got in, passed the winter. The situation of two ships of his squadron, the *Salsette* (36), Captain Bathurst, and the *Brunswick*, Captain Graves was too hazardous and extraordinary to pass unnoticed. The former, after the most commendable perseverance to get a convoy, entrusted to him, through the Sound, and after witnessing the destruction of them all by the ice, had his ship torn from her anchors, and at the entrance of that straight she was carried back into the Baltic where she floated about in a large field of ice, from which she could not be extricated for six weeks, when she was liberated, and found shelter in a Swedish port in that sea. The *Brunswick*, in like manner, was forced from her anchors, after the most persevering attention of Captain Graves to fulfil his orders in the Great Belt, forced into the Kattegat, over banks and shoals of some feet less water than she drew, though lightened of part of her artillery and whatever else could be spared. Ultimately, however, she was enabled to extricate herself from her perilous situation, to clear the Kattegat, and to reach England, after being reduced to a state of the utmost distress and destitution.

It fortunately happened that the two ships which underwent these severe trials, were, perhaps the best calculated of any in the navy to resist such extraordinary pressure: one, the *Brunswick,* being of the easiest draught of water, with the flattest floor, and strongest scantling of her class, and the *Salsette* was at that time, we believe, the only teak-built ship in the service.

As soon as the thaw commenced the small cruisers under the command of Sir Richard Keats were ordered to sea, and by their activity and diligence succeeded in intercepting several vessels with corn from the Danish provinces to Norway, which considerably embarrassed that government by distressing the inhabitants of Norway.

The moment the state of the Belt permitted, Sir Richard passed through the channel to the Baltic with a view to give the earliest protection to the British Trade. Here he was soon joined by reinforcements from England; and early in June, by the Commander-in-chief, Sir Jas. Saumarez, off Karlskrona, when Sir Richard took charge of a valuable convoy of nearly two hundred sail, which he had the address to escort through the Great Belt, and to Gothenburg, without a single accident or loss of any description, either from the numerous flotilla of the enemy, or the intimacy of the navigation, and what is still more singular, without letting go an anchor. The convoy increasing at Gothenburg to upwards of four hundred sail, Sir Richard, for its more perfect security, divided it into two parts, and proceeded with them to England, where the whole arrived in perfect safety in the month of July.

On his return with the convoy of 400 the King wrote concurring with Mulgrave's opinion that Keats had "conducted himself with his usual zeal and discretion under the late circumstances of difficulty in Sweden".[551]

On the return of his son after a fifteen month absence the Duke of Clarence wrote he was "happy to find Henry meets with your approbation and I must return you my sincere thanks for your kindness and attention to my son. I do not doubt he will require an entire refit and of course I shall be guided by you as to the manner and quantity".[552] That refit was to be brief indeed as young Henry volunteered to accompany Keats on an expedition then preparing and only ten days after his return the Duke took him back to his ship at Deal.

RICHARD GOODWIN KEATS

SIR R. G. KEATS, K.B.

Published by J. Stratford, 112, Holborn Hill, March 1st 1810.

Rear Admiral Keats, K.B, Stratford, J. Stipple engraving, 1 March 1810, NMM PU3466 ©National Maritime Museum, Greenwich London.

Historical Memoirs of
Admiral Sir Richard Goodwin Keats, GCB

14

The Walcheren Expedition

A few days afterward he was placed under the orders of Sir Richard Strachan, who was appointed to command the naval part of an expedition determined to act against Antwerp, and the enemy's force in the Scheldt.[11] Sir Richard Keats left the Downs with one division of the expedition on the 25th July [1809], and after some short delay, unavoidable from circumstances of weather, the whole assembled and anchored off Walcheren [Map 7].

Keats and Strachan were well known to each other, Strachan having been captain of the *Donegal* in Nelson's Mediterranean fleet from 1803 to early 1805.

Napoleon had his northern shipbuilding facilities and naval base in the Scheldt estuaries, at Antwerp and Flushing, respectively (Map 7), and a large number of the vessels previously assembled for the proposed invasion of England had been relocated to that anchorage. These shipyards had a great advantage over those at Brest or Toulon in that they were fed by a river and canal system which would allow the importation of shipbuilding supplies from the Baltic region to continue unhindered, regardless of a British blockade of the sea-routes. The bases could harbour up to ninety ships and were strategically worryingly close to and opposite the Thames estuary. By mid-1809 ten ships of 74 guns were ready for sea and six more of 80 guns were under construction at Flushing and four others of 74 guns were on the stocks under construction at Antwerp. It was feared a fleet based in these ports could easily attack British trade to and from the Baltic, as well as jeopardise the blockading squadrons in the Channel. As a result of the operation against Copenhagen the government was aware of the benefits of a pre-emptive strike.

---

11   see Memoir of Sir Richard Strachan

On learning that Napoleon had significantly reduced the number of troops in the area to support his war effort on other fronts Minister for War, Lord Castlereagh, moved to implement a long-held ambition to attack the facilities at Antwerp sixty miles up the estuary. Orders were issued to destroy the dockyards and stock: "To sink, burn, and destroy the whole of the enemy's ships of war afloat in the Scheldt, or building at Antwerp, Terneuse, or Flushing; and if possible, to render the Scheldt no longer navigable for ships of war".[553] The unstated objective was even more ambitious, hoping an invasion of Holland would "Give to the friends of the House of Orange, in that country, an opportunity of declaring themselves"[554][against Napoleon]. Hence, a significant military force was assembled under the Earl of Chatham. It has been asserted Chatham, who was the elder brother of recently deceased Prime Minister Pitt, owed his appointment more to connections than ability. He was appointed by Lord Canning, Secretary for Foreign Affairs rather than by Secretary for War, Lord Castlereagh. The force comprised over 39,000 men, including 3,000 cavalry, carried by some 400 transports and escorted by 245 men-of-war including 37 sail of the line, together with numerous frigates, gun-boats, brigs and small craft. It was an impressive display of power.[555] Never before had a fleet and army of such a size left the shores of Britain. Unfortunately, the project became public knowledge, allowing the French time to prepare a response.

The plan was to occupy the island of Walcheren, take the port of Flushing and then ferry the troops up-river and proceed to attack the infrastructure of Antwerp higher up the Scheldts. The entrances to the Scheldts were uncharted, riddled with obstructions and characterised by strong currents with a large rise and fall of the tide. A squadron including sixteen sail of sloops-of-war, and fifty gun-brigs and gun-boats secured its destination – in the absence of pilots – having sailed up the river at night with a foul wind, without any buoys in the river, and depending for the safe passage of the division upon personal recollection of the state of the channel. Parliament recorded that "the approbation of such an officer as Sir Richard Keats was the best proof of the manner in which that service was performed".[556] A military officer on board observed of the navigation; "You can scarcely be enabled to conceive by any description, however exact, the extreme difficulty and danger of this navigation, and the trepidation which we all felt for the safety of our ships. The manoeuvres were all executed in deep silence; and, from a sense of our common safety, the sailors and soldiers were for the moment in the most profound harmony".[557]

On [Walcheren] island near Camveere, a landing of two divisions of the army was affected on the 30th and the fortified town of Flushing immediately invested. Sir Richard was then, with the division of the army under Sir John Hope, and an appropriate naval force, ordered up the East Scheldt, when he shifted his flag first to the *Salsette*, and afterwards to the *Sabrina* sloop (18). On the 31st the important town of Zierikzee was taken possession of, on which occasion Sir Richard availed himself of the facilities which the small craft found in that port offered, for transporting troops and stores in that intricate and shoal water under navigation; which service the Hollanders appear to have performed with punctuality and fidelity. The difficulties opposed to the advancement of this part of the expedition, arising from the navigation or bad weather, being thus lessened or overcome, the troops (some 7,000) were landed on the 1st August [1809] without opposition, on the island of South Beveland, and on the 3rd the important fortress of Batz [Map 6] was taken possession of, which is situated at the southern extremity of the island, and commands in a great degree the navigation of both Scheldts. But before the artillery, which had been spiked by the enemy and otherwise damaged, could be restored to activity the enemy's squadron which prior to this event had occupied an anchorage near the entrance of the West Scheldt, passed the fort of Batz, sheltered itself under the forts of Lillo, and Liefkenshoek in the Upper Scheldt, and ultimately above Antwerp. On the succeeding morning it was followed by all the enemy's flotilla into the Upper Scheldt, with the exception of two gun-boats, which were destroyed by the English flotilla in the West Scheldt and six by the guns from Batz in the East Scheldt. This early and complete possession of South Beveland and the important fortress of Batz which ensured safe navigation of both Scheldts to the point where they merge into one, and are denominated the Upper Scheldt, seemed to presage a favourable termination of the whole object of the expedition.

But though the operations up the Scheldts were thus promising, the siege of Flushing having continued to the 15th August, occasioned great delay, and gave the enemy much time to strengthen his position, by inundations, collecting troops, and, still more, by protracting the advance of the army to the ulterior object in view [Antwerp] to a season well known in that country, and which appears to have been overlooked, or not sufficiently understood, in this, for when the fall of flushing had rendered the troops available for the most important object of the expedition, sickness had disqualified one third of the army for further operations, and threatened to incapacitate the whole.[558]

The arrival of the English at Ter Veere [Camveere on Walcheren Island] in August 1809, J Dietrich, lithograph by J Groenewoud. NMM, PAD5783, © National Maritime Museum, Greenwich, London.

Keats accepted the terms of capitulation of Zierikzee and Browershaven together with the whole of the islands of Schouwen and Duiveland.[559] Then, with his flag in the *Camilla* (20), where he was described as miserably lodged, worn and ill and heartily wishing himself on shore[560], he advanced with eighteen sloops-of-war and four divisions of gun-brigs as high as the shoals of Saestingen, cutting off the connection between East and West Scheldt, and buoyed the river to Batz.[561] Sir Home Popham's fleet arrived at about the same time. Keats informed Strachan that with his force, together with six frigates at Waerden waiting to come up, the navy were now masters of the navigation up to the battery at Lillo, although it would be in the power of the enemy, by sending a superior naval force to deprive them of use of the waters as far down as Batz. Unfortunately, earlier delays had allowed Missiessy to withdraw his fleet up-river ahead of the invaders and to a defensible position. Nevertheless, navigation of the river was now opened sufficiently high to admit the co-operation of the army, and in Keats's opinion there was nothing material that could be affected by the navy with a view to accomplishment of the ulterior object without such co-operation.[562]

It had been understood the troops would be brought up forthwith. The difficulty was that the army was still engaged in the stalled taking of Flushing, and not able to advance to provide the support required at Batz. Flushing put up determined resistance, despite days of relentless attack by mortars and Congreve rockets. Delay in prosecuting the advance – including, on one account three days lost in Walcheren just by the ceremonious laying down of arms – allowed the enemy to quickly send reinforcements. Given the change in circumstances, it was Keats's expressed view that the navy could not advance through the narrow channels to Antwerp unless the British army could first clear the river banks of the enemy army under the command of King Louis which was advancing from all quarters and now numbered 30-40,000 men.

In an approach reminiscent of the evacuation from Nyborg he arranged flat-boats for navigating the shallow water and gun-brigs in readiness for moving the army. Strachan wrote to the Earl of Chatham on 16 August in similar terms, noting the urgency of receiving instructions.

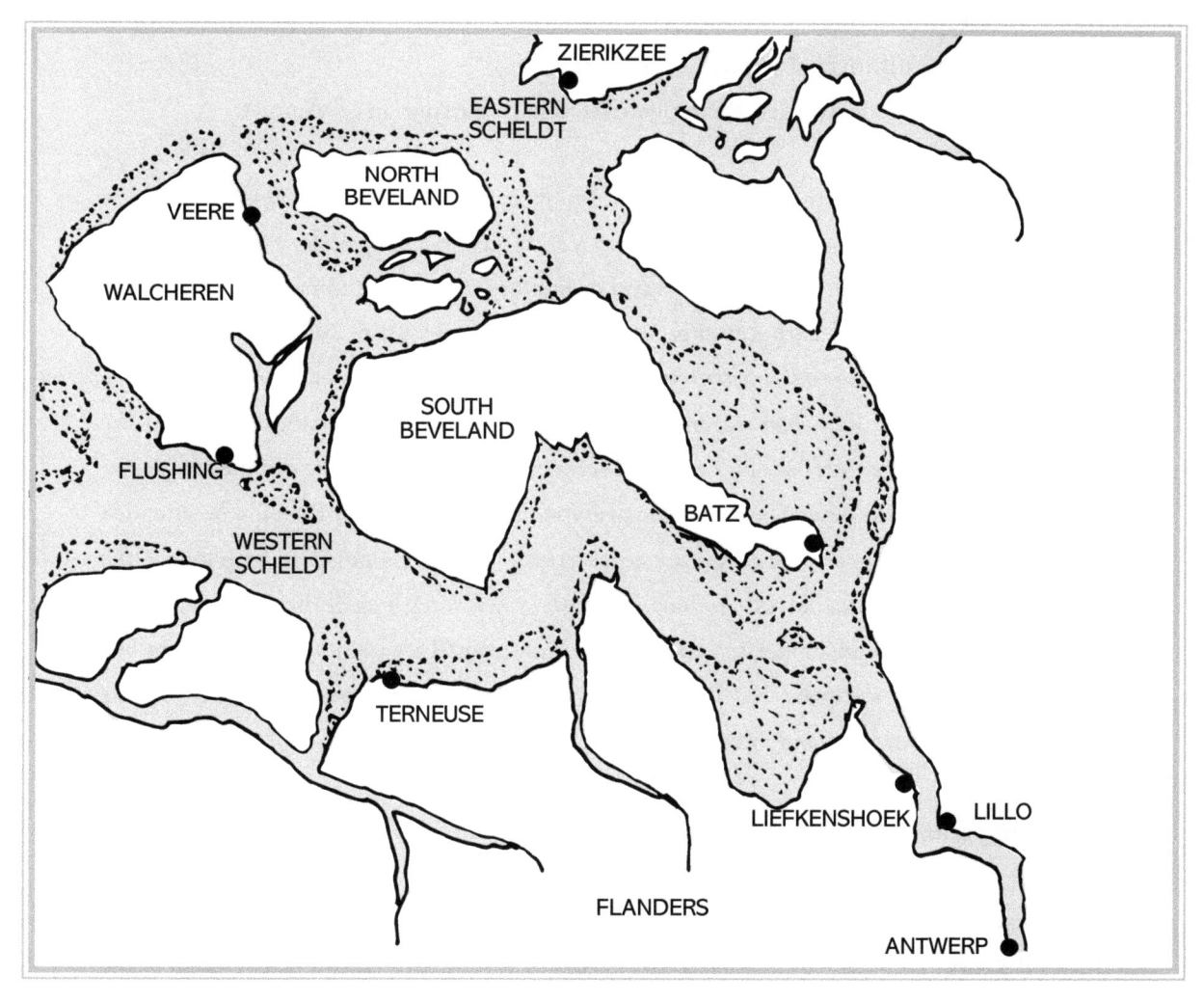

Map 7: *The Scheldt estuary; Walcheren, Flushing, Antwerp.*

Strachan gave directions to Keats to co-operate with Lieutenant General Earl of Rosslyn, commander of the army in South Beveland in using every means in his power for capturing or destroying the enemy fleet and flotilla above Lillo.[563] That same day, 17 August, Keats wrote to the General advising that he had orders to pursue the ultimate object of the expedition, namely, to advance upon Antwerp to destroy the enemy ships in that port, without delay and assuming the Earl had similar orders, that he was placing his ships and resources at the General's disposal in the prosecution of any plan they may approve. The Earl replied the same day: "I have received no instructions whatsoever on the subject of my ulterior operations", but he undertook to advise as soon as he received any.[564] It emerged in the subsequent parliamentary inquiry that there was no basis for Keats to believe Rosslyn had orders to co-operate with him, and he had seen no evidence of the army being prepared or ready to move in support of the ultimate objective at Antwerp.

Unimpressed, Keats forwarded the reply to Strachan, writing on 18 August:

> Though I now feel myself thoroughly authorised to form and act upon any plan separately or conjointly with the army it is my duty to distinctly state, (as I have before done) that it does not in my opinion, nor in that of any officer, naval or military, that I have conversed with, appear practicable to undertake, with any prospect of success, any measure except in co-operation of the army, with a view to the destruction of the enemy's men of war near Antwerp. Since the arrival of our flotilla, when the enemy retired above Lillo, my letters have professed the same opinion: our measures are and in my judgement must necessarily be confined to preparation, until it shall be determined that the army shall go forward, [as] It would be attended with extreme convenience and advantage to ascertain as early as possible the plans of the commander-in-chief of the forces, that our preparatory measures may be directed accordingly. I hope I have not been misunderstood. Left to my judgement I see nothing I can attempt but in conjunction with the army; but I am ready, and shall cheerfully undertake any enterprise you may please to recommend or command.[565]

Strachan was in perfect agreement with these sentiments, writing to the Admiralty on 22 August:

> The enemy appear in considerable force on both sides of the river.... It is the opinion of Sir Richard Keats and myself, and I believe every sea-officer, that, without the co-operation of the Army, we cannot affect the ultimate object of the expedition.[566]

E.P. Brenton wrote in similar terms; "We have good authority for saying, that the boom of Lillo would have been attempted by the ships of war, had the army advanced by land to the rear of that fort; but the offer was declined and from that moment retreat was decided on".[567] He continues, noting that although the water was sufficiently deep at half flood to float a ship of the line, the narrow and intricate channels afforded no space for working; and had one ship grounded, she would have prevented the approach of the others. Despite the difficulties Keats faced with his heavy ships he was ready to proceed, but in order to give him time to conduct his ships through the shoals it was essential that the banks of the river should be cleared of the enemy.[568]

Strachan advised he had all his vessels assembled and all necessary arrangements in place but still had not heard from Chatham in response to his letter four days earlier. In the interim the army was being depleted rapidly as men succumbed to a malaria-like disease of the swamps. At its worst fourteen thousand men, nearly one in two, were on the sick list, or worse. He expressed to the Admiralty the opinion, supported by Keats, that having regard to the advanced season of the year, the increasing number of enemy troops, and reduction due to sickness in their own numbers, the ultimate object was now unachievable.[569] He had still not heard from Chatham so he wrote again, on 26 August "to bring matters to a conclusion." Learning that Chatham had sent for the seven lieutenant generals to consult on 27 August, Strachan and Keats went on shore that day and met with the military leaders, noting the enemy fleet was by now defended by a newly constructed battery of ten guns, an immense number of small gun-boats on the boom, and behind them a crescent of sixty gun and mortar brigs. Then, the final decision being that of the army, the naval officers withdrew. The generals resolved that the siege of Antwerp was now "utterly impracticable".[570] That decision was not communicated to the Navy until the end of the day.[571]

A council of war having been called, which decided against any further proceedings, the sick were embarked and sent to England. South and North Beveland and Zierikzee being evacuated, and Sir Richard Keats having completed the portion of duty assigned to him on this occasion, left the East Scheldt on the 5th September and reached the shores of England on the 8th.

The correspondence illustrates the overall mission was characterised by delays and lack of organisation, communication and leadership. Both Keats and Strachan expressed concern that the objective could not be achieved by the navy alone, but the army seemingly had no plan beyond the day ahead and failed to provide timely indication of its intentions. Chatham was described as proceeding with prudent and methodical slowness, as though there was a point of honour in allowing the enemy all the leisure essential to outmanoeuvring him.[572]

Strachan did observe that Keats's particular operations in the East Scheldt and Beveland had met with success and that he had applied his accustomed zeal and judgement in the arduous duties he had been required to perform.[573]

The minutes of the parliamentary inquiry show that from the very outset Keats had been keen to proceed to the ultimate object at once. He had a conversation on the matter with Minister for War, Lord Castlereagh, at Deal on 14 July, before departure. Noting the weather, he observed that if the enemy fleet at Antwerp were the ultimate objective, he hoped they should not find themselves involved in the siege of Flushing or the operation in Walcheren but should proceed to the ultimate objective without delay. The Minister heard what he had to say but did not question him particularly on the subject, nor share any plan for taking Antwerp. Keats told the inquiry that the conversation was an expression of his opinion only. It was not advice, as his advice had not been sought.[574] It remained his view that this was one of those expeditions which depended very much on celerity to avoid the enemy assembling in numbers to render attainment of the ultimate objective doubtful. Parliament noted of Keats: "That gallant officer nevertheless had made a communication to Lord Castlereagh, who shewed but little disposition to consult with him".[575] As it turned out Keats had not been alone in expressing the opinion that the mission was hazardous and that destruction of ships and facilities in Antwerp depended substantially upon the speed and energy of its execution. In hindsight his analysis was perfectly correct. Admiral Sir Edward Codrington, at the time captain of the *Blake* (74), wrote home that no difficulty had occurred which had not been foretold, yet "Sir Richard Keats is, by firmness and ability, rising above difficulties which his foresight has led him to contemplate with anxiety and attention".[576]

French historians do not doubt that if instead of losing precious time at Flushing the military forces had pushed right on to Batz and Antwerp, the expedition would have succeeded. Missiessy's squadron at the entrance to the West Scheldt was incapable of defending the passage. Had the fleet pushed on from Walcheren immediately to force the Western Scheldt it would have been in a position to attack Missiessy's squadron before it could escape up-river, but due to delays on the part of the British, the squadron was enabled to escape and re-ascend to the protection of the upper Scheldt. Save for several gun-boats that grounded and were captured or destroyed the fleet managed to slip past Batz to reach the shelter of Lillo and Liefkenshoek largely undamaged[577] before the town and fort at Batz were captured by the British and its spiked cannons restored to operation. According to

Keats the French were just hours ahead as they moved up to Lillo with the same tide that brought the British up the East Scheldt to Batz.[578] Failure to proceed to the Western Scheldt and attack Missiessy's squadron whilst exposed has been described as one of the great lost opportunities of the war.[579]

When Parliament examined the whole affair, Strachan, in consequence of some reflections by Chatham on the naval part of the expedition, considered demanding a court martial to clear his name. The editors of the *Naval Chronicle* comment at this point, "It is remarkable also, that Sir Richard Keats's evidence is materially at variance with the statements of his lordship [Castlereagh]".[580] It is fair to say there was no criticism of Keats's evidence or conduct and his views as to the best strategy were endorsed. Even Napoleon agreed that Chatham had done everything possible to ensure the failure of the object of the expedition, writing as early as 9 August; "fever and inundation will render an account of the English….As long as they remain on the island of Walcheren there is nothing to fear".[581] He did note that once there had been a delay of just a few days which was sufficient to allow the French time to send reinforcements, it would have been impossible for any man to have succeeded.

The nub of the problem was well identified by a marine who saw the incompatibility of his chiefs and recorded in his journal that there was a want of co-operation between Sir Richard Strachan and Lord Chatham, there being jealousy existing between them.[582] The strained relationship between the key leaders of the respective arms of the services was a matter of considerable regret, and it highlighted the necessity of each understanding the issues faced by the other when undertaking joint operations. Although exonerated from any blame Strachan's career was effectively over. He was never called to serve at sea again.

Writing in 1825, Brenton, admittedly favourably disposed to the navy as opposed to the army, summarised the official documents that emerged in the enquiry as proving the British sea officers were in their proper places and ready to advance under any circumstances and proved their merits so as to completely exonerate them from any responsibility for the shortcomings of the expedition.[583] Lord Chatham took a less flattering view, but, nonetheless made the point in his report to the King that:

> *the navigation of the East Scheldt was found most difficult, but by the skill and perseverance of Sir R. Keats, this purpose was happily and early accomplished, though the troops were carried a great way in schuyts and boats; and this division was landed near Ter-Goes, from whence they swept all batteries in the island that could impede the progress of our ships up the West Scheldt, and possessed themselves on the 2nd August of the important post of Batz, to which it had been promised the army should at once have been brought up.*[584]

Despite the failure to meet higher objectives and attack Antwerp, the port of Flushing had been rendered useless to Napoleon, and three ships on the stocks had been destroyed. Others, including the frigate *Fidele*, and brig *Voiture*, were brought away and reused. Material prepared for construction of the *Royal Hollander* was seized and later used to build the 74-gun HMS *Chatham*. This more focused objective could have been achieved efficiently with equal reward by a much smaller force, in much less time, and at a significantly lower cost of lives.

The emergency evacuation of British troops was an operation for which Keats was well experienced, and it was undertaken with his usual attention to detail and efficiency.[585] A blockade for the rest of the war ensured the hostile ships that had escaped attack could not escape the Scheldt and be put to use.

In the following November [1809], the Superb, in which ship Sir Richard had served nearly nine years as Captain, Commodore, and Rear Admiral was put out of commission, and some relaxation from such constant succession of service becoming necessary for his health, he was indulged with some months leave of absence.

This was his first substantial period of leave in more than fifteen years of nearly constant service at sea – which of itself goes some way to explaining his fragile health. Such an extended unbroken period of active service demonstrates also the high regard his superiors had for his value as a sea officer.

On 25 October 1809 he was advanced to Rear Admiral of the White.

Young Henry FitzClarence, who had been with Keats through these expeditions, was now grown but was still the same kind of boy he ever was, and very fond of the navy.[586] When the *Superb* was paid off he was redeployed under Captain Henry Blackwood, described by the boy's mother as "the most severe not to say *tyrannical* officer in the service",[587] where life was miserable. The Duke feared some of the officers were not exactly the people he would have wished his son to have been with. On the constant solicitation of Mrs Jordan, he was transferred back to Keats in January 1811, but it was too late to restore his affection for the navy and he enrolled in military college at Marlow. The Duke wrote that he wished the boy had been allowed to stay with Keats for the duration of his service, but the less said on that matter, the better. Despite this turn, the Duke affirmed their uninterrupted friendship over more than thirty three years and his sincere interest in Keats's welfare. He and his son continued to maintain close and cordial relations with Keats, which were warmly reciprocated.[588]

The *London Gazette* of 26 December 1809 reported from the office of the Prime Minister that the King had appointed the rear admiral as "His Majesty's Commissioner for the Civil Affairs of Malta (Map 3), in the room of Rear Admiral Sir Alexander Ball," the previous commissioner, who died in October 1809.[589] Having initially accepted, Keats felt unable to pursue the appointment and resigned before taking residence. He reportedly asked the opinion of Earl St. Vincent, but the Earl could rarely if ever, see any justification for an officer to abandon his profession at sea, replying, "No, my dear Keats; Malta is not the way to the House of Peers."[590] This posting would have seen him ashore in command of the naval station, drawing upon his administrative skills overseeing the convoying of the one-thousand merchant ships that now passed through the port annually. The reason for his declining the position is never stated. In any event, in the following April, army officer Sir Hildebrand Oakes was appointed to the position, "in the room of Rear-Admiral Sir Richard Goodwin Keats, K.B. resigned".

Some have speculated Keats declined the Malta appointment on account of his illness and a desire to remain at home to recuperate. Another view is that despite his illness and taking note of St. Vincent's advice, he was not yet resigned to spending the rest of his career on shore, and was seeking more active employment. Others have said he was recalled to active service.[591] Some support for this contention can be found in a report in the *London Chronicle* of 11 June 1810 stating that "Sir Richard Keats immediately sails from Plymouth, with a squadron of frigates, to take the chief command in the East Indies".[592] The report is unlikely to have been made without some basis in fact but the foundation for it is unclear. What is clear is that if the position was offered, it too was declined. It could be he was awaiting an offer of more suitable active employment not so far from home. As a proven and valuable officer well known to the members of the Board, he had some ability to informally negotiate his deployments and was possibly willing to wait for an opportunity better suited to his circumstances.

In May 1810, whilst home visiting his father Keats was granted the Freedom of his hometown of Bideford.[593] The Mayor and Corporation assembled in their robes for an impressive ceremony in the Guildhall, where a box containing the freedom was presented to the admiral. The town arms were engraved on the box along with the following inscription: "This box, with the freedom of the Borough of Bideford, in the county of Devon, was presented by the Mayor and Corporation of Bideford, to Rear-Admiral Sir Richard Goodwin Keats, Knight of the Bath, on the 18th day of May 1810, in testimony of their high respect for his naval character, and the gallant exertions he has, on all occasions, displayed in defence of his country".[594]

On 31 July 1810 he was advanced to Rear Admiral of the Red.

**Historical Memoirs of
Admiral Sir Richard Goodwin Keats, GCB**

15

Cádiz – The Peninsula War

In the summer of 1810, though he was still suffering from indisposition his services were called for in a manner that could not be declined, and which made health a secondary consideration with him. He accordingly obeyed the summons, and in July 1810 hoisted his flag onboard the *Implacable* at Portsmouth, commanded by Captain George Cockburn, and was ordered off Cádiz, where he arrived on the 27th, which was at that time blockaded by a French army and threatened with a siege.

He was replacing Rear Admiral Pickmore who was said to have done a creditable job and, according to General Graham, was replaced without the proper "graciousness". Having served as aide-de-camp to Sir John Moore in Sweden, and under Lord Chatham at Walcheren, Graham was well-acquainted with Keats. He did not doubt his capacities, but he was concerned as to the process. The change in command was due to a reorganisation coupled with a desire on the part of the Admiralty to see a commander with an established reputation to take an independent command in what was going to be a difficult position, rather than any particular dissatisfaction with the incumbent. Keats was in good standing with the Spanish, and his management of the situation in the Baltic showed also that he would be tactful in any future dealings with the Spanish authorities.[595] The appointment was widely acclaimed in the newspapers and accompanied by the glowing endorsement of Cabinet. Secretary of State, Earl Liverpool, writing to General Graham, said; "I may say, without disparagement to any other officer, that there is no person in the profession so well qualified for this important command" and shows the confidence the Admiralty had in Keats's capacity to respond to a situation expected to be fluid, both politically and militarily.[596]

The Spanish peninsula became the theatre where England and France would decide their differences. The installation of Napoleon's brother as King of Spain, the trigger for the change in the allegiance of Romana's troops, had resulted in Spain rising against France. Napoleon now needed to allocate nearly half a million troops to keep a hold over a country that, until his miscalculated intervention, had caused him no trouble.

The Peninsular War is often regarded as that of the army alone, and Wellington's triumph with the navy relegated from global sheriff to taxi service to the army. In reality, the Navy played a critical part, landing, supporting, feeding and supplying a projected force of 48,000 troops, as well as providing firepower and intelligence. Wellington is reported to have said to Admiral Byam Martin, "If anyone wishes to know the history of this war, I will tell them that it is our maritime superiority gives me the power of maintaining my army while the enemy are unable to do so".[597]

Keats wrote to Lord Wellington advising of his appointment and readiness to pursue the common cause, receiving the reply that the chief of the army would "have much pleasure co-operating with you for the public service". Wellington's letter continued, laying out in extensive detail the whole of his plan of operations and the strengths and positions of the English, Portuguese and Spanish forces under his command (now of course including Romana's army) and that of their opponents. Given their significantly inferior numbers he confirmed the importance of detached diversionary forces attacking naval establishments along the coast thereby depriving the enemy of naval support, allowing maintenance of his own supply and tying up large numbers of enemy troops. Overall success was by no means assured, and at the time he feared he may need to remove his army from Portugal altogether. He had already applied to Admiral Pickmore to have any transports not immediately required at Cádiz to be deployed off the Tagus (Lisbon) in preparation for such an eventuality. He concluded by instructing Keats that in the event of a reverse in Wellington's fortune he was to bring the whole of the ships under his command into the Tagus to effect removal of the British army and that of Romana to a place of safety.[598] Fortunately, Keats was never called upon for this purpose and was able to concentrate upon the circumstances of Cádiz and the British forces stationed there under Lieutenant General Graham.

France had gained control of most of Spain save for the two British outposts of Gibraltar and a small fortification at Tarifa. The resistance leaders in Andalusia fell back from Seville to the city and fortifications of Cádiz which occupied the whole of a small peninsular, the Isle of Leon, connected to the mainland only by a narrow isthmus. A French squadron including five sail of the line had been blockaded in Cádiz ever since Trafalgar. In June 1808, following the general uprising, the Spanish manned shore batteries and gun-boats and opened fire on the French at anchor. Unable to escape because of the blockading British ships off shore French Admiral Rosily was forced to surrender his ships and some four thousand men and Cádiz was taken back by the Spanish. However, the city was thereafter completely blockaded by land and the French were busy supplementing the numerous coastal strong points they already held. Many of the seamen previously preparing for the invasion from Boulogne were brought into this theatre to assist in the reduction, but despite being besieged by twenty-five thousand French troops under Marshal Victor, Cádiz remained out of Napoleon's grasp, supported by an 11,000 strong army under Spanish General the Duke of Alburquerque.

The British declared support for Spain and the defence of Cádiz in particular. The isthmus had good defences and as it was accessible by sea the British navy was enabled to lend military support to the cause, ferrying ashore an additional nine thousand British and Portuguese soldiers as well as supplies to sustain the inhabitants and the forces which in combination ultimately swelled the population to 100,000.

The British squadron initially comprised the *Implacable* (74), *Tonnant* (80), and six other 74's; *Achille, Rodney., Blake, Zealous, Norge* and *Atlas*, with the *Aetna, Hound, Thunder,* and *Devastation* bomb-vessels.

Given the state of affairs in this theatre of the war it was necessary that the senior officer feel free to act as he saw best without having to wait for the sanction of a Commander-in-Chief situated many miles distant off Toulon and so the command at Cádiz was now made distinct from that under Admiral Sir Charles Cotton in the Mediterranean. Keats was thus able to take measures independently as and when required with promptitude.

He immediately took upon himself the command of the squadron which consisted of eight sail of the line; and as a flotilla of gun-boats was found absolutely necessary for the service he requested a company of shipwrights from England.

The Admiralty permitted him to take thirty men from each ship of the line sailing to the Mediterranean, and sent gun-boats from Gibraltar. The original gun- and mortar-boats armed with a single eight-inch mortar useful in close combat at sea were found to be inadequate. More powerful weapons of a longer range were required where the prospective targets were shore-based fortifications.[599] Keats had at least one replaced by a 68-pound carronade, with twice the range. The ten new vessels constructed under his supervision were armed with 10- and 13-inch mortars similar to the armaments on the bomb vessel *Devastation* (8). Her capacities were well known to Keats as she had served with him in the Baltic, at Walcheren, and now at Cádiz. At 104 feet, she was fitted with one each of 10- and 13-inch mortars, two 24-pound carronades and six 9-pound guns. Although generally armed with a small number of canons for defence, the prime purpose of a bomb vessel was not to fire solid shot at a low trajectory, but instead explosive shells (bombs or mortars) were discharged from deck mounted guns set in clear space between each pair of masts and fired at a high trajectory – needing both a strengthened structure to absorb the recoil and clear space above the deck to avoid hitting her own rigging. They were not so effective in a battle at sea, but as had been proven at Copenhagen and Walcheren, were particularly useful when anchored and deployed against a fixed position on land. He also requested small cruisers around fifty feet in length, armed with 24-pound carronades to keep privateers in check. Rear Admiral Pickmore, had similarly requested more gun-boats for the same objective, but his plea had fallen on deaf ears. Now the Admiralty immediately promised Keats frigates and small warships, demonstrating both the importance of the objective and the high regard they held for his opinions.[600]

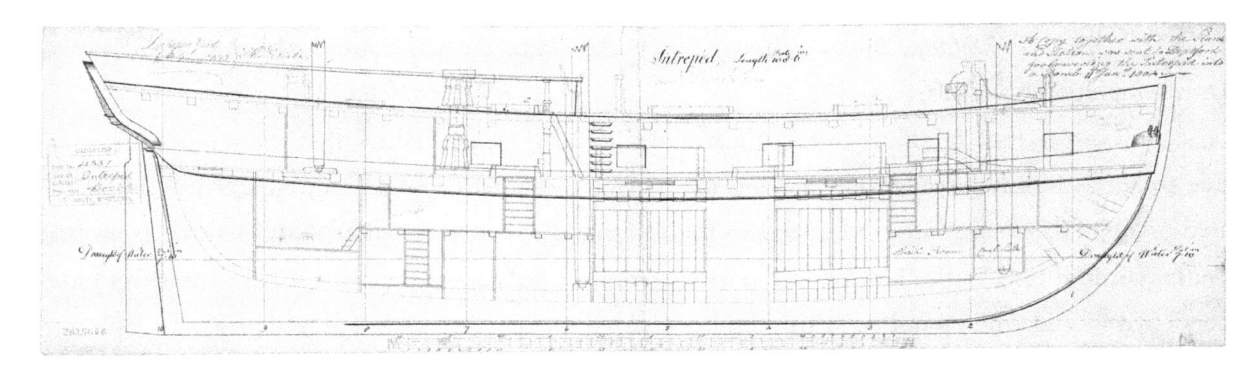

Plans of HMS Devastation, (and sister-ship Intrepid) bomb vessel. Constructed as an 8-gun bomb vessel at Deptford yard in 1803, re-armed with 10- and 13-inch mortars, two 24-pound carronades and six 9-pound guns, she served under Keats in the Baltic, at Walcheren, and at Cádiz. Henry Peake, Deptford Yard, NMM J0033 ©National Maritime Museum, Greenwich London

A small yard was established at Cádiz, and undertaking it with his accustomed zeal, several vessels of that description were constructed under his direction, and having procured some others from Gibraltar, a strong body was collected, to act separately or jointly with the Spanish gun-boats in defence of the town, and its dependencies. As there were many ships belonging to the Spanish navy, some of them totally inefficient, and others not required for the defence of the place, they were fitted out and removed to Cartagena, or sent to the Havana, as well as to disembarrass the garrison, as to prevent them, in the event of a reverse, from falling into the power of the enemy.

In Keats's view the harbour was overcrowded with ships that would be of little use to him and were at risk. Eleven or twelve sail of the line were anchored as close to shore as the water depth would allow and some 300 merchant vessels were crowded in between them and the city. To clear the harbour and prevent their falling into the hands of the enemy who appeared to be advancing, they were equipped as well as the circumstances would allow and removed to other ports, such as Minorca and Cuba. That it took thirty-eight days for the convoy of leaky and decayed vessels to reach Minorca gives an indication of the poor state they were in – their bottoms so foul they could not gain to windward even in fine breezes.[601] On 2 September Keats shifted his flag to the *Milford* (Captain Kittoe) as the *Implacable* was sent in escort of the two Spanish three-deckers to Cuba after which she was to collect treasure to the value of two million dollars from Vera Cruz in Mexico to help fund the war. Having remained longer than intended in Mexico in order to remove sickness from the crew she did not re-join the fleet off Cádiz until 18 February 1811, with a load of indigo and cochineal,[12] the supply of dollars having been depleted.

Keats did not hold out much hope that if put under pressure from the French he would be able to rely upon the Spanish navy for salvation, writing to the Admiralty:

> *The more I see and reflect on the Naval Means of Arrangements of our Ally, the more I am inclined to believe in the Event of the Siege being vigorously pushed, it will be prudent to trust to our own resources. Not that I am suspicious of any favourable disposition on the part of the Seamen towards the Enemy, but from an habitual Inactivity, a seeming Want of Authority or energy to command their Services and a Conduct in many of their Naval Officers disproportionate to the Zeal of ours creates a Want of unbounded Confidence.*[602]

Years earlier Keats had attributed the Spanish failure to perceive or react to the danger they were in when pursued by him off Algeciras to habitual indolence on their part and it would seem his views had not changed since. He was not alone in his assessment. Both General Cockburn (not to be confused with the Captain of the *Implacable*) and General Graham commented on both the poor state of the Spanish ships – foul beneath the water, often leaking from decay and neglect and cultural differences in the approach and capacities of the Spanish seamen as had Lord Wellington.[603] That these views were well founded is illustrated by the deplorable state of the 74-gun *El Vencedor*. When called upon to transport troops in October 1810 she was incapable of going to sea and required

---

12 Cochineal; a red dye made from an insect found in Mexico and highly valued for its brilliant colour

A TREASURE TO THE SERVICE

several day's maintenance in the yards just to be fit to be towed by the *Rodney*. She sank not long thereafter. Given Keats's well-known position on discipline, training and attention to detail it is little wonder a contrast was discernible. Whether 'indolence' was the problem is a question for elsewhere. There were certainly distinct differences in culture, structure, and training regimes. In comparison to Britain, Spain was lacking in supplies and finance. The difference in means available and applied to their respective navies was significant. Suffice to say Keats believed he would need to rely upon his own resources in supporting the besieged. Nevertheless, where he provided officers and men to help crew the Spanish vessels he issued an order that 'As the ships are in every respect Spanish and will have on board each a captain and other officers &c &c, it is strongly recommended to observe the greatest delicacy of behaviour towards them.'[604]

Stern gallery, HMS Implacable, reconstructed and on display in the entry hall to the National Maritime Museum, Greenwich. Originally the French Duguay-Trouin, she survived Trafalgar to be captured shortly after in Strachan's action at Cape Ortegal and remained in service for many years until scuttled in the Channel on 2 December 1949.

Although the garrison which was composed of British, Spaniards [sic], and Portuguese troops, was not found sufficient to attempt to raise the siege by a direct attack in front of the enemy, it was still sufficient for purposes of annoyance, and, considerable enough to admit of offensive operations by detachments conveyed by water. Expeditions were in consequence formed to act on different parts of the coast, one of which, consisting of a considerable body of Spanish troops, commanded by General Lascy, and a naval force under the orders of Captain Geo. Cockburn, left Cádiz on the night of 22nd August 1810, and the Spaniards landed on the following [night] to the eastward of Huelva [Map 2].

The General immediately commenced his march for Moguer, a distance of 22 miles which he reached about eleven o'clock the following morning. Notwithstanding the fatigue which the troops had undergone, the enemy, consisting of 1100 French troops was immediately attacked and driven from the town. Several desperate attempts were made during the day to regain possession of the place, but all proved ineffectual, and the enemy was obliged to retreat to Seville. General Lascy, having fully accomplished his object, returned to Cádiz by the same route he had advanced. This expedition, and others of a subsequent date, were proved by intercepted letters to have given the most serious annoyance to the enemy. In one of these letters it was stated, that "when the annoyance we receive from these expeditions, the boats, and flotilla is considered, it may be said that we are the besieged, rather than the besiegers".

This harassment continued for months, the British constantly mounting attacks on various forts along the coast whenever the weather permitted. On 12 September the bomb vessels were in action with the French batteries near Mantagorda. They harassed the installations on the east of the bay on the 15th, Santa Catalina on the 17th, and on the 19th silenced a battery in the Bay of Bulls.[605] On 2 October a night attack by bombs, gun vessels and armed launches was mounted on Santa-Catalina once more, causing severe damage. Three days later the Forts of Napoleon and Luis were attacked. On the 18th they engaged a French privateer under the fortifications at Rota and on 1 November a French gun vessel lying at the entrance to the Guadalquivir was destroyed.[606]

On 22 September the French privateer *Le Bon Francois* captured a merchant ship carrying a load of timber destined for the Gibraltar ship yard. The *Rambler* (14) accompanied by gun boats was sent in pursuit finding the culprit entering the Barbate River. Captain Hall with thirty sailors and marines marched five miles up-river, surprised the French crew and drove them from their camp, swam to the ship, took charge and sailed their prize out the river mouth.

Not all the operations were confined to Cádiz or as successful. In October 1810 the frigate *Topaze (38)* and gun brig *Sparrowhawk (18)* together with a number of smaller vessels, transported a detachment of troops under the command of Lieutenant Colonel Lord Blayney to mount a feint attack on the fort of Fuengirola, with a view to drawing the French garrison out of Malaga to its relief, whereupon the troops would re-embark and sail for the undefended city, the inhabitants of which were thought to be disaffected with their French rulers. The *Rodney* (74) and Spanish ship *El Vencedor (74)* were to bring a regiment of the 82nd foot as well as their own considerable fire power, but were delayed as *El Vencedor* was incapable of making the journey under her own sail and required to be towed.

The walls of the Castle of Sohail from which the defenders were firing were particularly sturdy and the armaments of the gun brigs and small ships were insufficient to the task of breaking through. Whereas bomb vessels with 68-pound carronades may well have succeeded, none were on hand. Blaney declined to wait for the arrival of additional troops and the large guns of the sail of the line. During the ensuing action a gun-boat was sunk, and the crew rescued. The execution of the attack on the part of the army, which outnumbered the French defenders by a factor of two to one, was marked by a series of errors. As the diversion become the main focus all hope of taking Malaga dissipated. Late on the 14th the *Rodney* arrived, disembarked the reinforcements and renewed the attack. Just as momentum was beginning to change Blayney made his most costly error misidentifying approaching enemy reinforcements as allies leading to his being taken prisoner along with a significant number of his men. Ultimately the remaining troops were taken off by the ships' boats and returned to Cádiz and Gibraltar "in disgrace".[607]

In November, Keats resolved to attempt to destroy the enemy vessels in Cádiz in their ports. After recognisance expeditions towards San Pedro led by Captain Hall ascertained the water depths and tested the range of shore batteries, it was concluded that at high tide gun-boats could be placed at Santa María (Map 8), such that enemy ships could not be removed sufficiently upriver to be out of their range. On the 23rd two divisions of gun boats under the direction of Commander Fellowes and Lieutenant Carroll supported by *Devastation*, *Thunder*, and *Aetna* swept west of Santa Catalina, and Keats in his gig headed the rocket and howitzer boats to Santa María under the direction of Captain Hall. In engagements that continued nearly eight hours, well into the night, the majority of the enemy flotilla was destroyed, along with a substantial portion of the region's store of sherry.

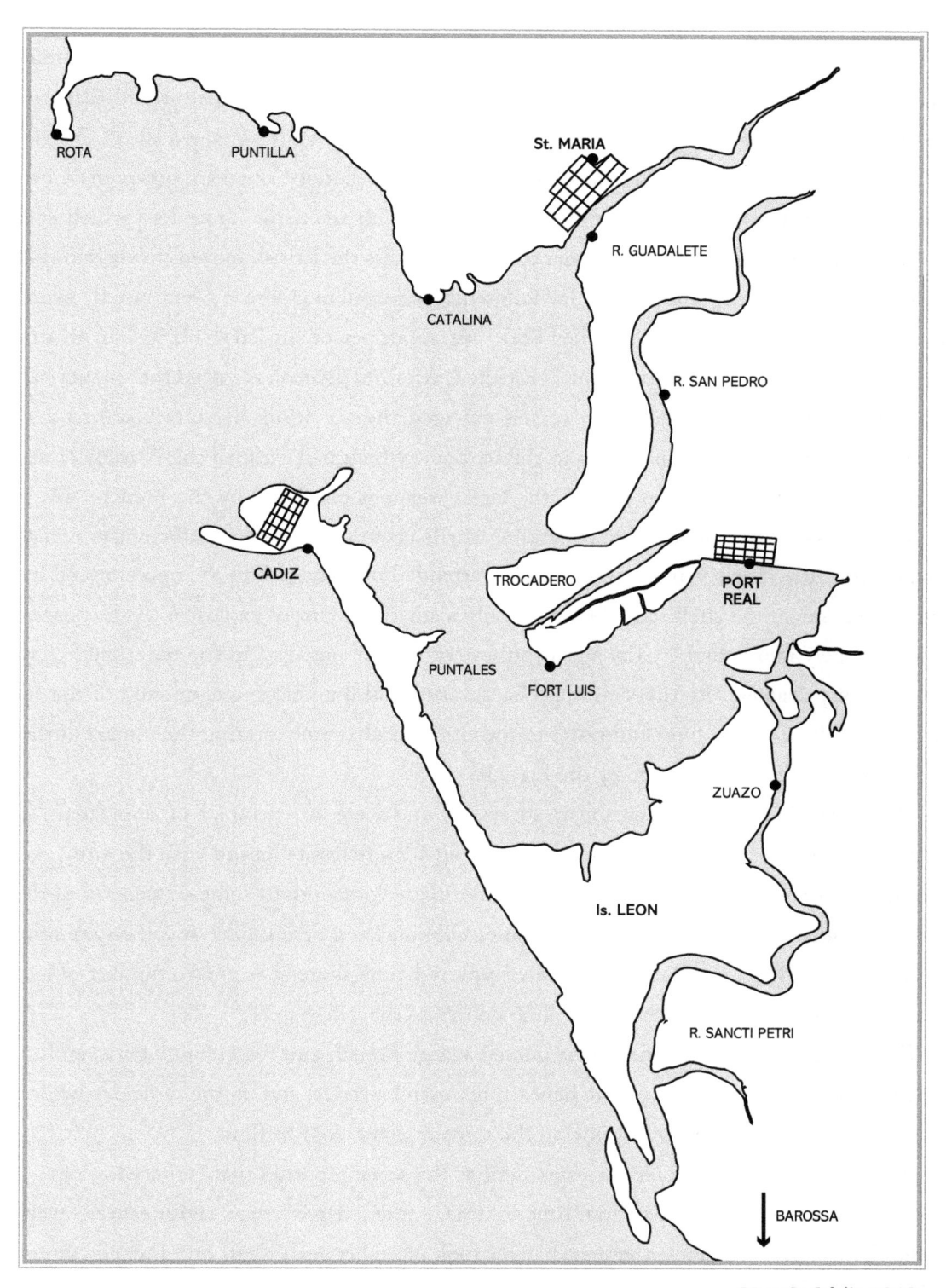

Map 8: *Cádiz 1810*

The French attempted to move their gun-boats overland, mooring some in the marshes and removing others to boost the San Lucar fleet and thought as a consequence that there would then be some respite, but Keats was determined to continue his harassment whilst any remained afloat. On the night of 22 December 1810, the ships' boats attacked a three-gun battery and took prisoners. Christmas Day was spent in preparation for a more significant assault upon the Trocadero which sheltered a large number of French gun-boats. Under cover of darkness the British moved slowly into the inner harbour. At high water, at 1.00pm the day following, the combined forces swept rapidly over to the Trocadero side where the Spanish attacked Fort Luis. Keats personally led the British in an attack on the northern batteries and the vessels they protected. Another division engaged the smaller batteries in the outer harbour, while the bomb vessels engaged the attention of Santa Catalina and Fort Luis. All seventeen French gun vessels in the harbour, which had escaped the November assaults, were destroyed.[608] They failed to destroy the latest weapons employed by the French: two howitzers specially cast at Seville, capable of sending shells up to 6200 yards – sufficient to menace the occupants of Cádiz. Their firing was fortunately attended by some risk to the operator and in order to achieve the range the shells could contain only a small amount of explosive. As a consequence, they were largely ineffectual.[609] The squadron was otherwise engaged in the occasional chase and destruction of privateers. By this continual harassment and maintaining command of the sea, the British were able to supply food and water to the city of Cádiz, ameliorating the impact of the siege and effectively stalled any advance by the French .

These exercises were conspicuously successful and were an exemplar of how small, mobile naval units mounting hit-and-run attacks, carried out with first-rate liaison with the army, could be used to tie down much larger land forces.[610] The flotilla now comprised some sixteen sail of the line, and three squadrons of gun-boats, from England, Gibraltar and Spain. Such was their attention and flexibility, constantly on the alert and actively employed alongshore at as great a number of locations as circumstances demanded, that they became known as the 'fire-eaters'.[611]

Early in the new year the fire eaters chased a large French gun vessel found between Rota and Fort Santa-Catalina driving her ashore beneath her own batteries, and on the same day while under heavy fire disposed of another gun vessel in the same manner close to Rota.

A *United Services Magazine* correspondent at the scene reported that "otherwise, affairs went sluggish enough", so much so that from time to time, under a flag of truce, civilities were exchanged with the French. On occasions, these exchanges took place between Keats and French commander, Marshal Victor. More commonly, French men were allowed to sea, but only on the flagship *Milford*.

British boats were permitted to land but only on the outer beach of Santa María. Boats went ashore almost daily at Zuazo, where the parties were only a pistol shot from each other. They stayed for a set period, returned to their compatriots, and then hostilities resumed.[612] That the courtesies of life continued between men at war seems remarkable through modern eyes.

During this period, Keats had been applying his usual energy and attention to detail to intelligence gathering, sending reports to General Graham at the British garrison in Cádiz. Huw Davies writes that he:

> *Spent a large quantity of time collecting the intelligence he received, comparing various accounts to ensure he sent Graham the most accurate intelligence possible. If he received a certain piece of intelligence, he would use all possible means to establish its veracity, frequently by sending out frigates and sloops to perform reconnaissance...*[613]

He also dispatched officers on intelligence gathering sorties on shore or up the various rivers between Huelva and Cádiz. No doubt he had learned lessons from his reconnoitres off Brest years earlier.

His previous experience in covertly arranging the repatriation of Romana's troops stood him in good stead, both with the Spanish and in arranging operations under the nose of the enemy. He was by now "an accomplished intelligence director".[614] The permanence of his operation meant he was able to build a widespread network of informants. He had a signals officer by the name of Robert Simpson stationed in the cupola of a church on the summit of a hill overlooking the Trocadero from whom he received details of every movement of the enemy.[615] Other information was derived more forcibly, by interrogation, as occurred on 22 December 1810, when the Marines from the *Milford* were put ashore between San Pedro and Santa María, taking a battery by assault, and returning with prisoners.[616] Unlike some others, he provided only verifiable information derived from a variety of sources that would advance the cause, not that which he wanted to find or which might most please the recipient.

In January 1811 Victor, was ordered to send a third of his troops on a mission to assist the assault on Badajoz. Seeing an opportunity Graham and Keats formulated bold plans for a siege-ending assault in co-operation with the Spanish, made possible only by the British command of the seas, although the weather nonetheless forced a reassessment.

Another expedition of a more formidable description under the command of General Graham was landed at Algeciras, and by acting in the rear of the enemy's line produced the battle of Barrosa, the 5th March 1811, a battle glorious to the British general and the troops he commanded.

It was, however, expected that the ships under Sir Richard Keats would have co-operated in a more effective and decisive manner on this occasion than they did; but the failure of dispatches from either the English or Spanish generals, announcing, as was intended, the approach of the enemy, but of which the first notice received was the distant sound of the cannonade, and the suspected fidelity of the Spanish pilots, who refused to take the ships to the stations assigned them at the moment the signal was made for that purpose rendered abortive a connected and prepared diversion on the part of the navy.

His orders were to co-operate cordially and confidentially with the general [617] and his official statement records that Keats had been determined to give the General his personal assistance, together with that of a considerable portion of the troops under his command. He felt it his duty, (after stating the risks involved in mounting an operation to attack the enemy from behind their lines at this season) to lend the expedition all aid and assistance under his command. The combined army to be delivered behind enemy lines comprised some 4,340 British troops and a Portuguese regiment, transported onboard the *Stately* (64), *Druid* (32), *Comus* (22) and numerous coasting craft under his command together with available Spanish craft. Due to a strong Levanter springing up the sea on the exposed coast at Tarifa was too rough to allow landing (or just as critically, re-embarkation if necessary). The flotilla headed east to the next British enclave, Gibraltar, where General Graham's troops were landed behind the shelter of the Rock at Algeciras and from there marched the thirty miles back to Tarifa. The roads were not capable of taking gun carriages so, notwithstanding the sea conditions, through the extraordinary exertions of their crew the ships' boats transported the artillery and stores to the same place. At Tariffa they were joined on 27 February by some seven thousand Spanish troops and together they moved west toward the Barbate, attended by such naval means as the circumstances would permit. They then pushed across the Sancti-Petri behind the enemy.

The victory at Barrosa, which is about three to four miles from the mouth of the Sancti-Petri, was achieved by a handful of British over two divisions of the French army, commanded by Marshal Victor in person. Graham had ceded overall command to the Spanish General La Peña who, contrary to the plan, and displaying contemptible feebleness, remained in plain view offering no assistance, failing it is declared, to fire a single shot. After a fierce battle Graham held his ground and Victor withdrew toward Seville, which allowed Graham to march back into Cádiz. The French were left bloodied and bruised, but still surrounded the City. As a result, a tactical victory that could have ended in the complete defeat of the French, their exit from Andalusia and the raising of the siege was rendered strategically inconclusive in terms of the overall liberation of Cádiz.[618]

As recorded in the memoirs, Keats had intended a diversion in favour of Graham. His aim was defeated by a lack of timely information. The officer charged with the task of delivering news of the launch of the attack on shore had thought it proper to go in chase of a suspect ship and failed to promptly deliver the news. The first Keats knew of the commencement of hostilities was the sound of cannon and musket fire. In order to provide the planned diversion, the *Implacable* and *Standard* (64) weighed anchor to engage Catalina but were thwarted on account of adverse weather causing dangerously high surf such that their pilots refused to take them to their appointed stations.[619] Under these circumstances, Keats reported that their measures on that day were necessarily confined to feints, save that Captain Cockburn, who had now returned from Havana, was able to deploy boats to secure the prisoners and bring off the wounded.[620]

But embarrassing and mortifying as this circumstance must have been at such a moment, it fortunately could have had no influential effect on the field of Barrosa, and though we should not reason from events not contemplated by the projector, had the squadron proceeded according to the original plan and intention, Sir Richard would in all probability have been prevented from forwarding to the army that evening the succours he was immediately called upon to supply, and which were forwarded under the care of Captain Cockburn.

Understanding, however, that the Spanish troops had not arrived within the lines, Sir Richard put the flotilla force in motion, and nearly the same disposition was made as he had proposed on the preceding day, provided he had received timely notice of the advance of the army. One detachment, composed of seamen and marines, was landed under the command of Captain Kittoe of the *Milford* near Rota (Map 8) which entered the town, threw the guns into the sea, destroyed the platforms, and communication, and dismantled all the defences between that town and Catalina. Another commanded by Captain Spranger, of the *Warrior* (74) , and which Sir Richard accompanied in person, was landed between Catalina and St. Mary's, took the fort of Pontilla by assault, also a sea battery commanding the north entrance of the Guadalete, summoned Catalina and entered the town of St. Mary. During these operations the division of gun-boats under Lieutenant Carroll battered

Catalina, and Captain Fellowes [made post on 5 March] with another division battered and finally took by assault, a redoubt on the south side of the Guadalete.

These proceedings having had the effect of inducing the enemy to detach about two thousand men towards that part of his line, and thereby fully answering the object for which the diversion was made, Sir Richard gave orders for the re-embarkation of the detachments and they quitted the coast almost at the same moment that the advance of the enemy reached the place of embarkation. On this service 5 seamen were killed, 1 officer and 12 men wounded, and Lieutenant Carroll's gun-boat sunk.[621]

The enemy's loss, however, was much more considerable in killed and wounded. Although the enemy contrived, from the Trocadero and Catalina to cross his fire of shells on their anchorage of the squadron for a considerable time, and by means of mortars newly invented, and cast at Seville on purpose, to throw shells into Cádiz at the extraordinary range of upwards of five thousand yards, yet no material injury was sustained, nor any sensible impression thereby made on the minds of the inhabitants, and expeditions continued to be sent from the garrison, which under the protection of the navy were brought to act on parts of the coast, and in situations best calculated to annoy the enemy.

Taking advantage of a calmer sea, the following day Keats launched two diversionary landings: between Rota and Catalina, and between there and Santa María with 280 men. At the same time, Catalina was bombarded by the *Hound* and *Thunder*. A redoubt of four guns at Santa María was taken by the marines of the *Milford* together with a second to the south of the Guadalete and the small fort of Puntilla, near Rota. In this exercise, Keats's men dismantled every fort from Rota to Santa María, spiking the guns as they left, and took possession of Santa María, causing such alarm in the French camp to cause them to retreat behind San Pedro. Preparations were made to take the tête-de-pont and bridge of St Marias, but 2,000 infantry and cavalry were seen advancing from Port Real. Knowing that General Graham had now re-entered the Isla de León, the men were re-embarked.[622]

Hearty cooperation between the Duke of Wellington, General Graham, Keats and the Duke of Alburquerque did significant good for the common cause and ensured the French never captured Cádiz. As a consequence, Cádiz became the birthplace of the new Spanish constitution and a vital foothold contributing to the ultimate defeat of Napoleon.[623] Eventually the British and Spanish prevailed, and by the end of 1811, Napoleon had withdrawn some forty thousand troops from Spain to join the Russian campaign. The siege formally ended in the aftermath of the British victory in the Battle of Salamanca in 1812. Marshal Victor and his demoralised army retreated from the region to join the remainder of Joseph's army in the north.

The fleet was greatly exposed to the waves thrown up by the west winds, but as demonstrated by the disruption to plans for deploying troops at Tarifa the hardest gales came from the east. The merging of contrasting weather systems in the Mediterranean can trigger the levanter which blows out of the straits for two days or more with a great intensity. Such an event on 27 March 1811 was so severe fifty-three merchant ships at Cádiz were wrecked, four gun boats sank and a couple of gun brigs were blown out to sea. Captain Smyth writes that the barge of the *Milford* of which he 'was accidentally in charge' was nearly blown away, saved only by the crew getting hold of hawsers streamed from the stern of the frigate *Undaunted* on Keats's orders as he saw the situation unfold from on the *Milford*.[624]

As circumstances at Cádiz were partly the basis for a claim that Keats lacked the self-confidence in his decisions necessary in high office,[625] it is opportune to examine those events in some detail: Due to the decayed state of the Spanish Navy, British warships had been made available from time to time to escort Spanish vessels bringing treasure back from South America, to fund the war. The *Implacable* had been sent on such a mission and in September the *San Pedro d'Alcantera* had arrived with specie valued at several million dollars. At the end of January 1811, the Spanish Foreign Minister, Bardaxi, requested of Henry Wellesley, Britain's Special Envoy to Spain, that Captain Fleeming specifically – he being well-respected by the Spanish – and the *Bulwark* (74) be sent on such a duty to Lima, where a large amount of money, public and private, was awaiting collection. The Admiralty had ordered Keats to send the *Bulwark* home.

This put him in a difficult position. He understood the vital need for the funds and that the value of treasure to be consigned in this particular voyage was estimated at $5 million (£1 million). He knew of both the custom of sending a warship as an escort, and that the business community of Peru would not consign the funds unless confident of a powerful guardian. His position was made more difficult when he received a new directive on 27 February specifically reiterating the order for the *Bulwark's* return, and stating that a warship of her size should not be tied up on such a mission. In the view of the Admiralty, a vessel of 64 guns or a frigate would be quite sufficient. Keats had two diametrically opposed requests, one of which was a clear direction from the Admiralty.

This prompted his lament to the Secretary of the Admiralty:

Nothing Sir, can be more unpleasant to me than the situation in which at this moment I find myself. Feeling that by a Departure from their Lordship's Instructions, I subject myself to their Disapprobation and by a rigid adherence to them, to an Imperfect and unsatisfactory accomplishment of the Service in Question.[626]

After some weeks of correspondence, he solved the problem by sending the respected Fleeming to Lima, not in the *Bulwark*, but in the *Alfred*, a 74-gun ship short of her full complement and less of a loss to the forces during her months of absence. Ultimately, the Admiralty approved the decision, excusing its original stance on the grounds that it was unaware of the value of the treasure to be shipped, now estimated between $9.5 and $10 million (£2 million).[627] These events show a clear discomfort at departing from orders, and that he did delay in making a decision. They also demonstrate he was ultimately prepared to find a way to compromise even very specific orders where necessary to secure the best outcome. Moreover, they demonstrate that the Admiralty were similarly prepared to back his judgement, whilst saving face all around.

An un-named correspondent to the United Service Magazine reflects of the same period that Keats was "resolved to worry (the French), and to do it in his own way: he knew himself to be strictly responsible, and therefore acted to the best of his judgement, thinking, with Wellington, that a person 'without defined duties, except to give flying opinions, from which he may depart at pleasure, must be a nuisance in moments of decision'. So, he cared as little about the apathy of the Regency divan[13] as did General Graham…".[628] If seems that when it came to operational matters, and in the absence of conflicting orders from above, he was quite prepared to take timely and independent decisions. Other commentators say of Keats at a similar period of his career that he had not only distinguished himself in multiple single ship engagements and squadron actions but that he had secured for himself a reputation as an agile thinker capable of managing complex operations independently.[629] Brenton recalled that "Wherever you saw Keats, whether as a captain of a frigate, or of a ship of the line, or commanding a squadron, he was sure to distinguish himself."[630] There is no suggestion of indecision, but there is a constant backdrop of anxiety.

---

13 'Divan' is used in the archaic sense of council

We have already observed, that at the time Sir Richard left England his health had been very much declined; his indispositions so increased as to render him at times incapable of that activity and exertion which was requisite to his own comfort and feelings; he, however, continues to bear up against it 'till that service which more particularly required his presence at Cádiz was fully accomplished, when a choice was given him of either continuing the command at Cádiz, or joining the fleet in the Mediterranean.

**Historical Memoirs of
Admiral Sir Richard Goodwin Keats, GCB**

16

In The Mediterranean With Pellew

He preferred the latter, was succeeded in his command by Rear Admiral Legge and joined the fleet off Toulon, as second in command under his friend Sir Edward Pellew, with whom he continued to serve 'till September 1812 when his health continuing to decline, he obtained permission to return to England in the *Centaur*.

In the absence of a written record we can only rationalise as to why he chose to leave the post commanding at Cádiz in favour of a position as second in command. Was he now of an age and physical condition that ambition for superior commands was less of a priority than a more comfortable life? Was there a self-awareness of the characteristics some writers have identified, namely an excessive anxiety and feeling the burden of high command which resulted in him being happy to work beneath another with whom he enjoyed mutual friendship and respect? From this distance we can only speculate.

During the second half of June the *Milford* together with three other sail of the line cruised at the entrance to the Mediterranean, where they fell in with Sir Edward Pellew on his way to take command of the Mediterranean fleet. Keats returned to Cádiz, accompanied by his replacement, Rear Admiral Legge. The *Milford* then proceeded from Cádiz visiting the British fortress at Ceuta and then to Gibraltar, Cartagena, and the Catalonian coast after which she joined the fleet off Toulon. On 31 July, Keats shifted his flag to the *Hibernia*, Captain Kittoe, described as a beautiful first rate of 110 guns, and which remained flag-ship in the Mediterranean and Malta for decades to follow.

On 1 August 1811 he was promoted to Vice-Admiral of the Blue. For the second time in his career the promotion was 'extended to' him – that is to say it was Keats in particular whom the Admiralty wished to recognise, in this instance following his exemplary service at Cádiz.

Pellew's letter to his brother in December 1811 indicates the services they were performing and their anticipation of a battle:

> *It is possible we may attempt to lay in Hyeres Bay, should we find the ground good for winter gales, of which at present we are not quite assured. We lay there a month in full expectation it would force the enemy to give us battle, and it will probably at last compel them to do so next spring. They are actively fortifying the islands and bay all around, in order to guard against attack, and have at least ten thousand men at work: they suspect our army will move this way. As far as we can judge from appearances, I have never yet seen a French fleet in half the order the Toulon one is. They have, I am sorry to say, adopted too many of our arrangements.... The ships are magnificent; four of 120 guns, larger than the Caledonia, and twelve fine two deckers, are all ready and manned. Two of 120, and two of 80 are building, and may launch by March or April; so that I think we shall have twenty to fight, without any from Genoa, Naples or Venice, and I trust a glorious day we shall have. Keats is a host of strength to me; and we are all well together, eager for the day, which I trust will help to put an end to the miseries of war, and the irksome eighteen years' confinement between wooden walls we have all experienced.*[631]

Pellew's biographer says he was blessed with his deputy in Keats whom he had known for twenty years, since serving together in the western frigate squadron. With Keats he found a friend and able confidante. As Keats put it, "Lord Nelson had the luckiest knack of hitting us off". Their relationship has been described as to the credit of each of them and testament to the navy at its best; that as rival frigate captains they could become and remain the closest of friends and colleagues. They were two of the most highly regarded officers of their time. The Duke of Clarence, visiting Lady Bentinck, whose husband Lord William Bentinck was commander of the military operations in the Mediterranean, observed of Pellew, "You may tell him from me that I regard him the best Officer in the Service after Sir R. Keats".[632] As one of Pellew's biographers put it:

If ever Pellew found a kindred spirit it was in the warm-hearted warrior soul of Keats; and if ever he yielded to another in seamanship, it was the same man. They made an odd pair: Pellew - big, gregarious; Keats - short, urbane, but they were as one in purpose. 'With such a man you have everything to expect and nothing to fear', Pellew wrote.

Keats in his own generous way encouraged his new Commander-in-Chief, writing "the greater the Command the greater the exercise of your patience... Your judgement and self-command will do much and your Champagne complete the business".[633] He was reassuring Pellew that with patience in time he would get the battle of which they had been in expectation and would then complete the business, vanquishing the French Mediterranean fleet.

Not long after they arrived their hopes of a battle were raised. Two French ships from Genoa were seen running the blockade. The English ships inshore sought to cut them off, which drew out thirteen sail of the line under the command of Vice Admiral Emeriau. It may have been expected by some that the English ships would sacrifice themselves in engaging with the superior force long enough to enable the main fleet to come in from their cruising ground off Cape Sicie but they thought better of it. By the time reinforcements arrived up, the French were heading back to port and the protection of shore batteries. A few distant broadsides were fired, but no engagement resulted. Pellew and Keats did not get the battle they expected and hoped for that day, in the spring, or at all. Apart from the occasional testing of the blockade, or smaller vessels escaping or making it to port along the shore, the French did not come out sufficiently far or for long enough and went back to port before they could be brought to action. Unlike Nelson, this pair gave them no encouragement and little opportunity to do so.

Occasional minor engagements resulted if an English ship strayed too close on recognisance or was trapped by adverse winds. A number of prizes were taken. Of passing interest because of familial connections is the otherwise unremarkable sinking off Sardinia of the privateer *Aventurier* by the frigate *Franchise* (36) captained by Keats's nephew Captain Richard Buck in February 1812, but on the whole the deployment was uneventful and the opportunity for glorious victory for which they no doubt longed did not present itself.

Captain W H Smyth, who had been on the *Milford*, and seen action off Cádiz in the gun boat raids reports Keats entertaining the Duchess of Orleans, Loise Marie Adelaide de Bourbon, mother to the future King Louis Philippe I, and at the time said to be the wealthiest heiress in Europe, from time to time when the *Hibernia* was off Mallorca.[634] The two maintained an irregular correspondence in years to follow.[635]

Continuing to be plagued by ongoing health concerns, Keats retired from duty at sea arriving home in the *Centaur* in July 1812, a month before the death of his father, Rev. Richard Keats. In Sir Sidney Smith replacing him, Parkinson says, "Pellew lost a very able advisor and received in exchange one who might be called the maritime aspect of the Gothic revival."[636] Not all admirals were equal, either to one another or to the tasks required. Despite his reputation – enhanced by daring raids, one of which led to his capture and two years in Temple Prison, from which he escaped – Smith had never fought a single ship action as a frigate captain. He was regarded by many senior officers as all style, vanity and self-interest and no substance – quite a contrast to the precise and taciturn manner of Keats.

Long years of warfare at sea had seen most senior officers worn out, generally suffering from rheumatism, which they would suffer for life, and Keats was no exception. The nature of other health issues, which had dogged him for years, besides a number of wounds, is never made clear. Quite apart from forcing him to leave the front line at a time when he was otherwise at his peak in terms of experience and regard, illness had caused him to seek leave for recuperation several times through his career. There is no doubt he had the sympathy and understanding of his superiors, who could not afford to lose such a talented officer. Nevertheless, one suspects his career was curtailed at various points as a result of his inability to accept prestigious assignments. As the war progressed an increasing number of flag officers, indeed a substantial majority, found themselves ashore and unemployed. In serving over twelve years at sea continuously on one command closely followed by the next as he was promoted Captain, Commodore, Rear Admiral and finally Vice Admiral, Keats was one of very few exceptions to the rule. He sailed home from Toulon in agony, then aged fifty-five. He and Pellew remained friends for life. Pellew was a regular correspondent and, whenever in London, a visitor to Keats's residence at Greenwich in their later years.[637]

With the transformation of the war since Trafalgar and San Domingo to an economic struggle, day-to-day naval operations were characterised by many minor excellencies, rather than by glorious victory in fleet engagements. During this time Gambier, Saumarez, Hood, Pellew and Keats participated in the whole diversity of activities necessary to prosecute national policy and the reframed war against Napoleon. Each demonstrated their talent, determination and courage in making their individual contribution to the final triumph.[638]

Keats returned to Devonshire to recuperate. Earl St. Vincent encouraged him to take advantage of the medical benefits of the spa waters at nearby Cheltenham, a facility frequented by his wife, amongst others, writing; "Considering you as I do, and that you are Public Property; the preservation of your health is most important and I trust that it will be perfectly restored by the Effects of Cheltenham Water."[639] Taking the waters had become very fashionable since King George III took up the habit some years earlier. His health did improve somewhat. Whether this was a result of the mineral springs, one could not say.

Although home for recuperation the Admiralty did not leave him entirely to his own devices. Officers ashore were expected to sit on court martials and attend to various tasks on behalf of the Admiralty. In December 1812 Keats was asked to witness an ordnance demonstration in Sussex but declined on account of his health. Couched as requests, these were in reality orders, and the Admiralty found his refusal 'not quite satisfactory' given the task would involve little time or trouble and no fatigue. Always quick to defend his reputation, and taking offence to their position, Keats launched his own broadside in the direction of his superiors advising their 'severe reproof' was unmerited. His word ought to have been sufficient for the Admiralty, he said, and for that reason felt justified in remonstrating with their superior authority, particularly given he had been forced to retire early from a dinner at the home of Admiralty Secretary Croker only days earlier. On that basis, he had not provided details of his indisposition. Nevertheless, he now provided those details, quoting the opinion of his eminent physician. Their Lordships now accepted his position, and excused him from attendance, but said he ought to have provided those details in his earlier letter.[640]

Such bumps in the road were by now probably known to be part of dealing with Keats; capable and valuable but as some put it 'sensitive at times'. His strong reputation had seen him at sea on a variety of challenging assignments almost continuously for twenty years, the last five as a flag officer during a period where competition for active postings was intense and prestigious commands closely held. It may be that everyone was more content when he was on the quarter deck. Within only a few months the Admiralty found him a prestigious posting, he found acceptable, pending re-establishment of his health.

**Historical Memoirs of
Admiral Sir Richard Goodwin Keats, GCB**

17

Governor Of Newfoundland

Time, relaxation, and his native air having somewhat improved his health, he was appointed in the most gratifying manner in February 1813 to the government and command at Newfoundland, with an assurance that if his health should be restored, more active employment would be assigned to him.

On 4 June 1814, he was advanced to Vice-Admiral of the White.

On 2 January 1815 on the expansion of the Order, he was appointed Knight Grand Cross of the Order of the Bath in recognition of his conspicuous services to his country.[641]
   The rapid succession of great and glorious events in Europe, terminating eventually in the memorable and decisive battle of Waterloo, having broken the spell and power of Buonaparte, given peace to Europe, and restored it once more to itself, Sir Richard, at the termination of his command in 1816, returned to England, without any circumstance having occurred in the limits of his station that deserve particular notice (although a war with the United States prevailed during the period of his command), beyond the protection afforded to the fisheries, and the attention paid to the commerce of England.

The memoir, which focuses principally upon naval engagements, covers three years' service, including during a war with America, in one sentence. It is apparent from other sources that Keats gave the command his full energy and attention. While no events of national military significance took place during his tenure the command was certainly an active one. His friend Admiral Warren was appointed commander-in-chief of the North American station and had primary responsibility for protecting British interests but his purview excluded Newfoundland and the surrounding territories and seas. These became strategically important due to the economic significance of the fisheries and the island's position in the shipping lanes to North America. Newfoundland had generally supported only a modest naval squadron. However, it became more active after 1812, when war again broke out between America and Britain. Unhappy with Britain's continuing impressment of American sailors and her blockade of U.S. trade with Europe and seeing her focused on the war with France, America took the opportunity to attempt to expand by seizing Canadian and Indian territories. A minor command for a convalescing Admiral soon became more significant.

His journey to the new post was onboard the *Bellerophon* (74), Captain Hawker (the ship upon which Napoleon ultimately surrendered in 1815). She had just completed a partial re-fit including gun replacement at Portsmouth, and on 7 April 1813 the flag was flown for the convoy to North America to assemble. Keats hoisted his flag as Vice Admiral on the 22 April. He is described by the historian of the *Bellerophon* as "A well-known figure in the Navy and one very popular with the men".[642] No sooner was he onboard than the signal was made to get underway. After picking up a smaller convoy from Torbay, the fleet comprised eighty-four vessels, escorted by the *Bellerophon*, frigates, *Niobe* (38) and *Loire* (44), gun-brig, *Contest* (12), and the gun sloop, *Comet* (18).

A journey to Newfoundland involved passing areas of potential icebergs, and several were sighted. Due to intermittent fog, a sharp lookout was required.

> *In fog there was not only the danger of colliding with icebergs, but also with each other, as well as the possibility of American privateers sneaking in under its cover and making a quick capture. Signal guns were ordered to be sounded at regular intervals as the ships groped their way through the cold mists towards the coast of Newfoundland.* [643]

The convoy finally sighted St John's, Newfoundland, on 31 May 1813 (Map 4). The wind dropped and they had to be warped into harbour. The next day, accompanied by all the escorting captains as the men manned the yards and fired a seventeen gun salute in recognition of his status as governor, Keats went ashore and was shortly thereafter sworn in as Governor.

The command encompassed Newfoundland and the islands adjacent, including St Pierre and Miquelon, and all the coast of Labrador from the river St John in the south to Hudson Strait in the north, and the Island of Anticosti and other adjacent islands except Madelaine.

His role included heading both the civil government and command of a naval station. The Governor resided in Fort Townshend, above the town of St John's. The harbour which was capable of sheltering up to 200 ships was accessed through the Narrows, a passage barely 100 yards wide, with high cliffs on either side, well-fortified with the added security of a chain that could be deployed to prevent access by hostile fleets. Depending on the conditions and wind direction ships often had to be warped through the entrance. The Governor's residence was of dubious quality and unsuited for winter use. Technically, his flag flew from the *Bellerophon* and, from March 1815, from the newly commissioned *Salisbury* (50). Before the construction of the residence, earlier Governors had operated solely from their flagship. The area had hitherto been treated as a seasonal fishery. In line with past practice, Keats governed by way of a summer and autumn visitor for three seasons, returning to England for the winter months, during which time command passed to the Lieutenant Governor who oversaw the hardy souls who wintered on the island.

As might be expected of him the first thing he did on assessing the position was to complain to the Admiralty that he had insufficient resources to do justice to the task. To cover the vast area, he initially had only the *Bellerophon*, two frigates and an assortment of smaller craft, although numbers were boosted as new convoys arrived under the protection of the *Crescent* (38) and others. As a matter of course, so as not to keep any of his scarce resources idle in the harbour for the purpose, the Admiral's flag routinely flew not from a battle ship or frigate but from whichever was the most senior ship in the harbour no matter how modest the vessel, often while she was undergoing a refit. Also high on his list of things to be done was a detailed hydrological survey of the harbour. He continued to require he be the best informed as could be regarding all the circumstances of his command.

The *Bellerophon* escorted convoys on to the Americas, capturing several American ships including *Le Genie*, a privateer of 16 guns,[644] and assisted in blockading the eastern coast of the United States. The number of war ships grew until some twenty-one frigates and up to forty brigs, sloops and smaller ships of war came under the direction of the commander-in-chief. England was again at war with America, and her shipping and trade were again at risk. The privateers doing the most damage were schooners carrying two to six guns, rigged fore and aft and able to out sail many of the larger square rigged war ships. Often all the war ships could do was chase them off. Captures were less frequent. The *Crescent* for example had many encounters with the privateer *Amelia*. Through the vigilance of Captain Quilliam she was inevitably chased away from her prey without causing harm, but never captured. Furthermore, when he first arrived Keats had no authority to purchase captured prizes and commission them into the navy to combat the threat with vessels of comparable

A TREASURE TO THE SERVICE

performance. By way of example, when in July 1813 the brig sloop *Electra* (16) captured the schooner *Growler* (5) she could not be purchased into the navy for use against her former compatriots.

He took particular delight when his ships were successful in capture of privateers such as the *True American* and the brand new *Elbridge Gerry* (14) with 66 men, taken by the *Crescent* off Cape Race. She was said to be remarkably fast and with much potential to disrupt trade.[645] As Commander-in-Chief Keats continued to collect a flag officer's share of prize money, which since 1808 had been reduced to one twelfth, now being calculated as one third of the captain's two eighths share.[646]

As the *Bellerophon* was still in need of further re-fit, she accompanied Keats on his return to England in the autumn with a convoy of 32 vessels, accompanied also by the *Rosamond* (20) and schooner *Adonis* (10), arriving safely, but not without incident, at Spithead on 19 December.[647] The twenty-eight-day passage was stormy, and *Adonis* became separated from the fleet as they reached the Channel. Then, off the Scilly Isles, she encountered a superior French squadron that she escaped only by jettisoning her guns.

HMS Bellerophon off the coast, William Frederick Mitchell, 1818 © Alamy PDCYXH

Keats struck his flag on 22 December to begin his leave ashore. First, of course he wrote to the Admiralty noting the severe wear and tear of sails and rigging resulting from the constant activity required of ships under his command in consequence of the American War.[648] During his time back home he met with Nelson's brother, now Earl William Nelson, who presented him with the Order of the Bath Star of his departed friend and commander as a mark of the esteem and mutual friendship that had subsisted between them.[649] It was also quite possibly bestowed in appreciation of Keats having taken the Nelsons' cousin, young Charles Nelson under his care on the *Superb* from her sailing in 1805. It had been intended Charles join Nelson's fleet off Cádiz, but as we know the *Superb* arrived too late and then diverted to the West Indies. As a consequence, Charles Nelson served with Keats at San Domingo, in the Baltic and again for a time off Cádiz, when passing his lieutenant's exam. The medal is inscribed on the reverse:

> *The star of Vice Admiral Lord Viscount Nelson, Duke of Bronte K B &c &c Who fell in his last glorious victory off Cape Trafalgar the 21 October 1805. Presented to Vice Admiral Sir Richard Goodwin Keats by Earl Nelson 24 March 1814.*

Late in 1813 First Lord Melville contemplated posting Keats to the command at Halifax to succeed Admiral Sir Herbert Sawyer,[650] but he returned to St Johns in April 1814, again in the *Bellerophon*. Official reports could be interpreted as though all the Admiral had to do was step aboard and the fleet would set sail for an Atlantic crossing. If we have learnt anything of Keats it is that he was a detailed planner. Some would say bordering on obsessive, driven by anxiety. Illustrative of his approach it emerges from other sources that far from simply stepping aboard he spent weeks in preparation. On receiving his renewed commission on 10 February, he conferred with various merchant representatives, with the Secretary of the Colonial Department and planned the crossing and management of the convoy he would have under his protection before finally departing on 22 April.[651] The *Bellerophon* was supported by escorts including *Medina* (20), *Perseus* (32), *Pike* (14) and *Wolverine* (14). After picking up more vessels at Torbay, the convoy comprised seventy-eight ships. Those destined for St Johns arrived in company of the *Bellerophon* on 4 June, while others were escorted on to Halifax and Quebec.

As might be expected having regard to his known approach to the operation of a ship of war the crew were rarely idle. One of a number of passengers picked up at Torbay was a Thomas Bulley whose family ran a substantial fishing operation known as Bulley & Job from Newfoundland. His diary gives an insight into Keats's management of the ship and convoy. The crews were put through their small arms drills and the great guns of the war ships were regularly exercised, which to a landsman was awe inspiring to experience close hand. The smaller vessels went in chase of potential predators or towed the slower merchants when required. They provided medical attention and assisted in undertaking repairs, some quite major. One ship lost a bowsprit when it collided with an iceberg at night, others lost topmasts rolling in the swell.

The escort *Medina* was a brand new sixth rate ship of 450 tons armed with twenty 32-pound carronades and two bow chasers with a crew of 135 men. Keats was keen to put her through her paces and arranged 'match races' between her, the seventy-four gun flag ship, and the captured American schooner *Pike (14)* of just 250 tons. Before the wind they were found to be of roughly equal speed, but beating to windward the ship of the line proved significantly superior.[652] The *Bellerophon* was considered a bad 'roller', once rolling her masts away in near calm, and a sluggish sailer at best, but under Captain Hawker and Keats she was so well trimmed and much improved in her weatherly qualities the problems were cured. According to Edward Belcher onboard there was not a frigate that could compete with her. He reports her chasing and equalling the fastest American privateers including the *Amelia* (said to have escaped due only to disappearing in the fog). At times the guns were hauled in on the lee side and run out on the weather side to allow the royal studding sails and sky sails to be set without excessive heal, getting her up to 11 ½ knots.[653]

These activities, typical of Keats's attention to detail and constant need to be active kept the crews similarly busy and Mr Bulley and his fellow passengers entertained and impressed by naval operations.[654]

Keats was more circumspect. Following his Baltic experience, he was certainly not new to convoy management. Nonetheless it is apparent he was more comfortable and suited to operating with a purely naval fleet where orders were given and followed and ships maintained position. His natural anxiety was exacerbated by the merchants' inattention to signals or inability to execute instructions. A universal complaint of those tasked with their protection, it was made worse by the dangers posed by ice and the impediment of constant thick and wet fog formed over the Grand Banks when warm waters of the gulf stream meet the icy Labrador current.

The fog at St Johns was so thick they had anchored in the harbour before those on shore knew what vessels had arrived.[655] From there warships continued to cruise, or in some instances were sent north towards Davis Straits and Greenland, protecting British commerce, whalers and fishers, and capturing enemy vessels.

Dispatches were relatively dry documents, recording the minimum facts such as vessels engaged, captured or destroyed together with men wounded or killed and specific mention of those men warranting particular approbation. It was in the ships' logs that details of weather, progress and sails carried were recorded, but even these were kept to the minimum. So, we know the *Superb* ran at 11 ½ knots in the chase at Algeciras, that Nelson's fleet sailed down the east coast of Sardinia in a gale under storm sails only. It is left to the knowledgeable reader to imagine what the conditions must have been to result in these records. Keats's return on the Bellerophon in 1814 lends some atmosphere. Midshipman Belcher recalled the waves were so high the ship was 'becalmed' in their lee. He wrote: "At 6 am, one of these boiling 'heaped-up' seas becalmed the ship, scudding at the rate of 12 knots under close-reefed main topsail and foresail, broke over the stern, some 50 feet (height of taffrail), cut away the port quarter galleries, and swept the main deck fore and aft – clean! At 8 o'clock, when all were at breakfast, another sea boiled upon the starboard beam, at right angles to the direction of the wind and the course of the ship, broke high up the mainmast, about 100 feet, overwhelming the ship, staving boats on the booms, cutting away iron stations as smoothly as by cold chisel, and giving 6 feet of water in the hold!"[656] We gain an insight into the conditions that accompany the succinct entry: "reefed the main, ship under close reefed topsail and foresail".

Returning to the situation of Newfoundland: trade with New England being closed, supplies were difficult to obtain and became very costly, to the extent that during the previous winter the residents had been in fear of famine. On Keats's urgent representation to the Secretary of State, large quantities of stores were sent from Britain, replenishing stocks for both the military and civilian population, bringing down prices and removing the apprehension of shortages for the following seasons.[657] His prompt and decisive action met with the thanks of the merchants who welcomed the plentiful supply of provisions in the market.[658] During the period of Keats's governorship nearly three thousand merchant and transport vessels were escorted across the North Atlantic.

One of those serving at Newfoundland was Edward Chappell. He had been on the *Kingfisher* sloop at the Battle off San Domingo in 1806 and commander of a gun-boat at the siege of Cádiz in 1811, on which deployment he was severely wounded in the thigh. He was now lieutenant on the *Rosamond* (20) and had a high regard for his commander-in-chief. The *Rosamond* was engaged to escort a spring convoy from England to Newfoundland in 1813, and thereafter to undertake expeditions, both cruising and in exploration. Lieutenant Chappell took the opportunity to record a detailed narrative of his North American adventures for the benefit of readers back home. He wrote of Keats that:

> *Sir Richard suffered no person under his command to suppose that he held a sinecure situation. The utmost activity pervaded every branch of the public departments. Ships of war were continually anchoring and sailing from the harbour; and the coasts of Newfoundland scoured from North to South by the most vigilant cruisers. The only sure way to the Admiral's favour was by evincing the same indefatigable exertion, which he manifested himself upon every occasion.*[659]

Keats had no hours; he was always on duty.[660] He required to be kept informed of shipping movements, particularly in respect of British convoys on their way to Newfoundland and the sighting of any enemy ships or privateers. Of the latter, he required to be informed immediately, without regard to the hour. Lieutenant Chappell continues:

> *In the execution of his duty the author had occasion to wait on Sir Richard Keats with intelligence of this description. The Admiral had retired to bed; but in five minutes he entered the audience-chamber, wrapped in a flannel dressing-gown. With the most patient scrutiny, he made himself acquainted with every minute particular; and in less than half an hour afterwards, a frigate sailed out of the harbour, in pursuit of the supposed American corsair.*[661]

He stated; "Wherever the head of a department is known to be so exceedingly vigilant, the inferior officers are ever attentive and diligent in the execution of their respective duties", and on the Newfoundland Station such was the acute observation and inquiry of Sir Richard that every officer under his command "exerted himself to the utmost, to obtain the approbation of so distinguished and able a chief".

He continues:

> *Never was the protection of this valuable colony confided during a critical period, to more indefatigable or able hands. The bravery, abilities and brilliant achievements of Sir Richard Keats are known throughout Europe; but his patient assiduity, excellent precautions, and unremitting vigilance, can only be manifest to those who were witnesses of the able disposition of his naval force, whereby the shores of Newfoundland might be navigated in security during the most violent period of the latest contest with America.*[662]

Under Keats, whether by capture or constant patrol, the coast was cleared of American privateers that had hitherto done much to disrupt trade. The destruction of American commerce and capture of privateers was said to have exceeded by ten to one the gains on the republican side.[663] As Chappell recorded, a lack of ships caused Keats to ensure those his did have at his disposal were never idle. Ships were continually anchoring and sailing. Captain Quilliam of the frigate *Crescent* (38) records returning to St Johns with the prize *Jane Whitehaven* and sailing again just seven hours later to resume patrol. On another occasion she escorted a convoy on the latter portion of their voyage from Quebec and didn't even get warped through the Narrows and into the harbour, but hove to briefly at the entrance before continuing at sea.[664]

Keats expected his officers to meet his own high standards and was not particularly understanding of those who did not. This, and the difficulty faced by the navy escorts on convoy duty, are illustrated by a disagreement with Captain Dillon. They had served together in the *Niger* many years before, and again off Cádiz, and Dillon often refers to Keats with warmth and respect. Dillon, in the *Horatio* (38), was tasked with escorting a convoy from England to Quebec before heading on to Newfoundland. It comprised 116 ships and was one of the most valuable convoys of its kind that ever crossed the North Atlantic, with cargo in just four of the ships valued at nearly £1,000,000. According to Dillon, the convoy gradually scattered till, after a gale more like a hurricane, he had only two sail in sight. After standing in various directions to try and find the convoy when the weather permitted, he failed. He concluded they had reached Newfoundland. Having obtained a fix on his position as being not far from Cape Race on the south-eastern tip of Newfoundland and the *Horatio* herself having suffered damage in the rudder and stern he thought himself justified in heading to nearby St Johns instead of proceeding up the Gulf of St Lawrence to Quebec as ordered.

Keats had sent for and read both the Admiralty orders and the ship's log, as the ship was still being warped into the harbour, and was well prepared before interviewing Dillon. He informed the captain in no uncertain terms that he took a different view regarding his unauthorised change in destination.

The cause of his upset is not clear. He possibly thought the log showed the *Horatio* deserting the convoy and making for port at eight or nine knots while the lame ducks were labouring at three. This would have been out of character with the Dillon well known to him. More probably, he took the view that the damage to the *Horatio* did not justify a departure from Admiralty orders in heading directly to St Johns, rather than continuing into the St Lawrence. He told Dillon he had no business being in St Johns and threatened court martial, but for the absence of sufficient officers to hear the matter. Most of the convoy eventually made it safely to various ports. Nevertheless, Keats ordered Dillon to return to his ship, resupply through the night, and weigh anchor the following morning to proceed forthwith up the St Lawrence to Anticosti in accordance with his original orders. Once again, we see that in his mind orders are paramount, whereas Dillon was being more pragmatic and arguably dismissive of strict adherence to orders which seemed to him to have outlived their intention.

On Dillon's return to St Johns, Keats's displeasure had quieted and he dismissed the earlier matter saying that he had written to the Admiralty with explanations that would see Dillon all right there, and invited him to dinner. Relations between the two were strained for some time until a thaw was brokered by Captain Hawker. He insisted that Dillon accept Keats's invitation to dinner on the eve of the latter's departure for the winter and resume his usual countenance, telling amusing anecdotes and merry stories, to remove any unfavourable impression. Dillon reported this final dinner passed "In a very sociable and friendly manner. Thus, we were all right again". Editing Dillon's narrative, Lewis questions his account, noting that with Dillon two sides of a story were rarely recognised, and he had a somewhat prickly personality. He says that Keats's outburst – if it was correctly reported – was quite out of character for the Keats well-known through the navy, but he does note that at this time his disposition was impacted by illness and pain. Others have noted that Keats, too, could be prickly. It is no surprise that relationships between the two did not always stay on an even keel. In any event, all was well shortly thereafter. The next day Keats proceeded to the *Bellerophon* for return to England, "the crews of the various ships-of-war cheering him as he passed".[665]

Newfoundland was experiencing considerable growth. Over the previous ten years the population had doubled to 70,000. If not a colony by law, it was becoming one in fact. The rapid growth brought with it a desire for a popular say in government, which was not a cause that found favour with the Admiral. He also noted the significant increase in the number of Irish (Catholics) settling in the colony. According to his sources, more than 6,000 arrived in the summer of 1815, attracted by high wages in the fishery and adding to what he described as that "already-volatile component of the population". Keats was sad to report that in the face of increasing numbers of Roman Catholic priests, there was insufficient provision made by the Church of England to meet the religious wants of the settlement, three only such missionaries residing in Newfoundland. Concerned at one time that Irish immigrants were bringing with them longstanding political differences from their home counties and in order to avoid infiltration by those who might be inclined to promote such disorder on the island, Keats sought to have potential new priests preapproved by the Catholic 'Bishop' at St Johns, Patrick Lambert. Keats had a high opinion of Lambert and through him ensured the Government maintained good relations with the Catholic element of Newfoundland society.[666]

As a seasonal fishery, the question of settlement, land ownership, and permanent agriculture had not previously been adequately addressed. For many decades the vast majority of fishermen arrived from England in the spring, fished over the summer months and returned to England in the autumn with their salted catch, leaving only a few hundred permanent residents. There had been little need to formally address land management or permanent settlement. At the time of Keats's governorship, the rapidly growing settlement still relied almost entirely upon the importation of food and supplies. With the outbreak of a new war, there were, in addition to the fishermen, many hundreds of men associated with the ships of war requiring to be supplied and fed. The fear of famine greatly stimulated interest in local agriculture.

Keats was given the authority to issue the first leases to industrious individuals for activities beyond fishery, and particularly for cultivation. He found that proclamations issued by his predecessors forbidding enclosure had been largely ignored. Significant areas of land had already been claimed, without authority and where grants had been made they had often been exceeded. Nonetheless, in response to advertising for applicants, by autumn 1813 he had granted 110 leases for settlement and cultivation of small plots, taking care to charge an annual rent, nominal or real, depending upon the circumstances of the lessee. On his recommendation, recognising the colony could not sustain itself on fishing alone, and accepting the settlement already in place, the Colonial Office agreed to allow formalising of leases of existing unauthorised enclosures on similar terms to those granted to new leaseholders. This reversal of government policy did much to encourage permanent settlement and support food security.

Construction of buildings for purposes other than fishery still required the Governor's consent, and this caused some dispute. One Sweeney of Belle Island, Conception Bay, enclosed 40 to 50 acres, as opposed to the usual few acres, and constructed unauthorised improvements despite warnings not to do so. On the Sheriff's orders, the crops were confiscated and buildings demolished, and he was required to relinquish the land.[667] By the end of his term, Keats had recommended constraints on the building of houses and enclosures be lifted within certain settlement boundaries, and more than 1000 acres were under cultivation.

View of the Entrance of St Johns Harbour from Fort Townshend. Miss M. le Geyt 1823. P C Le Geyt was secretary to Governor Keats at Newfoundland, and later his secretary and Clerk of the Check at the Royal Hospital Greenwich, and finally an executor of his estate. Although affording protection from the enemy, the harbour entrance, defined by steep cliffs, is so narrow that in certain winds it was impossible to navigate under sail, resulting in the need to warp ships into harbour using anchor points in the cliffs. NMM PAD2012, ©National Maritime Museum, Greenwich London.

The indigenous peoples of the region were the Beothuk, a small branch of the Algonkian people. When first encountered by Europeans in the 16th and 17th centuries they numbered around 2,000 hunters and fishers who depended upon the caribou in the interior during winter and fish and marine mammals during the summer thaw. By proclamation of 10 August 1813, regarding relations with the Beothuk population, Keats called upon settlers to "cultivate and improve a friendly and familiar intercourse with this interesting people", and provided for a £100 reward to those who succeeded "in establishing on a firm and settled footing an intercourse so much to be desired". Those who forgot themselves so as to "exercise any cruelty or be guilty of any ill-treatment towards this inoffensive people" could expect to be punished with the utmost rigour of the law.[668] The reward went unclaimed.

In 1810, Lieutenant Buchan had taken the schooner *Adonis* (10) to the River of Exploits and marched some 130 miles inland to open discourse with the inhabitants, but this regrettably ended in an altercation that resulted in the killing of two of his crew. Keats reasoned that this altercation had left a bad impression not easily forgotten and that this explained the lack of progress in establishing cordial relations. He then concluded that the most effective way of securing the confidence of the indigenous peoples was to establish a post in their country and to display kindness and engage in an equitable exchange for several seasons. Such thoughts were several years too late, as by this time the Beothuk were virtually refugees in the remote interior of their own country, largely deprived of access to their traditional maritime food sources, and the last known survivor died in 1829.[669]

Having for many years had the responsibility for manning his own ships, Keats was well aware of the issues surrounding impressment and was alive to these issues in Newfoundland where many newly arrived vessels would lose men to desertion and resort to impressment to replenish their number. The old theory upon which the preservation of the island as a fishing station was based was that the fishery acted as a nursery for the navy, providing qualified seamen for recruitment. A licence to fish these lucrative seas was granted on the condition that boats would take on three men who had never been to sea for each one regular seaman, thus training every year many hundreds of men to be qualified for service in the navy. It will be recalled that some two thousand fishers answered the call to man the captured Danish fleet on its delivery to England, but as a general rule if the theory was ever true of Newfoundland, it was no longer so. More chose to desert than sign on. Captains would seek to make up numbers from other ships, and if still short, would send a shore party to impress more. This caused such discontent that in 1794 the leader of one such shore party was murdered.

Frustrated by desertion Captain Cumby of the frigate *Hyperion (32)*, told Governor Keats that he had followed the port orders, but had still failed to replenish the ship's numbers by pressing from incoming vessels. He had then sought without success to impress men on shore – there being up to 10,000 eligible men who would be compelled to the navy should they return home after the fishing season. Cumby had lashed out at Thomas Coote, the Chief Magistrate in St John's, demanding the magistracy assist him in pressing on land. Coote politely informed the captain that although he would willingly assist the navy, particularly in rounding up deserters, he could by no means sanction the landing of parties from the King's Ships for the intention of effecting impressment on shore, well knowing, that such a measure would inevitably lead to the most serious and dangerous consequences. Cumby appealed to Governor Keats, expecting the Admiral to support the navy, but Keats backed his Magistrate whom he regarded as a man of integrity, and as one who well understood the feelings of the inhabitants. Newfoundlanders thereafter considered themselves immune from impressment, a "universal practice in every other part of His Majesty's Dominions".[670] Some claimed that contrary to promoting Newfoundland as a nursery to the navy this resulted in the territory becoming a refuge for those weary of the service and worse, for those who were unwilling to serve their nation.

On a lighter note, Keats made it illegal to kill seagulls in Newfoundland on the basis that they acted as good foghorns, making a noise as ships approached otherwise unheralded through the fog.[671]

The settlement was prosperous. From 1813 to 1815 some 60,000 tonnes of salted cod was exported annually, mostly to newly opened markets in Spain, Portugal and the Mediterranean, where they enjoyed an effective monopoly and sold their produce at record prices. Keats recognised that this was due in significant part to the wartime exclusion of French and American fishers from British waters. The western approaches to Newfoundland were free of ice earlier than the eastern, giving American fishers early access to the salmon fishery, but Keats and his fleet were alert and effective in enforcing exclusivity. During this period as a result of the exertions of the navy the Newfoundland fishermen enjoyed exclusive access to a bountiful ocean for several favourable seasons. The fishery was stated to be worth more than £7,500,000 annually, with as many as 2,300 boats of a range of tonnages involved. The economy was almost wholly based on the fishery, including whaling and sealing, which had been enjoying an unsurpassed, albeit artificial, prosperity. Substantial fortunes were made, but relatively little was spent on improving island infrastructure.

All this was up for negotiation at the war's end. As an American newspaper put it, where patriotism may have failed, self-interest was uniting the citizens of Newfoundland against the reopening of the fishery. The instructions to the American peace negotiators at Ghent were to in no event surrender the fisheries, seen as one of the glorious trophies of the War of the Revolution;[672] *'No peace without the fisheries'* said the British residents. A memorial presented to Keats on behalf of the merchants and principal resident inhabitants arising out of a town hall meeting in October 1813 claimed Britain's existence as a great and independent nation depended chiefly on preserving her sovereignty of the seas and drew on the colony's claim to be the nursery for the navy in arguing strongly for complete exclusion of "foreigners from sharing again in the advantages of a fishery from which a large proportion of our best national defence will be derived."[673] Despite these representations and an elaborate plea from Governor Keats himself, which was described as a very able paper,[674] the treaties with France in 1814 and 1815, and with America in 1814, re-opened the area to competition. Secretary of State for War and the Colonies, Lord Bathurst, wrote to Keats in June 1815 advising that the rights that existed in 1783 were reinstated and he was "to abstain most carefully from any interference with the fishery in which the subjects of the United States may be engaged, either on the Grand Bank of Newfoundland, the Gulf of St Lawrence, or other places…".[675]

France was allowed to repossess her previously held colonies, fisheries, factories, and establishments of every kind that were possessed by her in 1792, including St Pierre's and Miquelon. In the Treaty of Paris made after the seven years' war France had ceded much of north eastern America to Britain but retained fishing rights, and these were now preserved. The United States was reinstated to the position concerning fisheries, that had been enjoyed since the peace of 1793. In the words of Dillon, "We gave away abundantly". These terms of peace had a significant impact on the English fishing fleet and processors based in Newfoundland. The peace that brought joy to Europe triggered a series of events that had significant impacts on the prosperity of Newfoundland for which she was ill-prepared. By late 1815, the settlement faced financial difficulties as the price of fish fell almost immediately by half, and continued to slide thereafter.[676]

Keats's three-year term expired in 1816. The wars now over there was little prospect of returning to active service even if his health allowed it.

Having struck his flag, Sir Richard retired to the north of Devon, where he possessed some property.

This was the estate *Porthill* in Northam, a double storey square stucco house built around 1760, together with several surrounding fields of approximately 2,700 acres which he had purchased from the family of Augustus Saltren-Willett for £5,000 in 1814.[677] The elevated position just up river from Bideford afforded a view of the estuary and of ships entering the Port of Bideford, at this time the major shipbuilding and trading port in the region. It is said he arranged flag poles at strategic points to communicate with neighbours and read naval signals from down the Torridge River and along the coast. His sister Martha and her second husband, Lt Colonel John Kirkman, occupied part of the property described as *Merrifield*.

He had previously purchased *Irishcombe*, in a detached part of the parish near East Worlington, in 1801. He also acquired the estates described as *Blagrove* and *Heath*, and the *Parkham* Estate near Bideford.[678] In 1810, he purchased *Durrant House*, adjacent to Porthill and affording views over the Torridge estuary. He undertook considerable improvements to both the house and grounds before selling to a Mr Ley several years later.[679] Today, a substantially modified Durrant House stands as a 125-room hotel.[680] Other property in his ownership, recorded for land tax purposes in 1815 included *Lenwood House*, another substantial house, situated to the south-west of Porthill. All three homes survive and are listed on the Historic England Register. Despite not having spent any significant time ashore during his long career Keats became a substantial landholder in the Bideford district.

It was at Durrant House that Sir Edward Pellew visited Keats before his expedition to Algiers. Knowing Keats had spent some time in that bay when negotiating with the Dey, years prior, he sought his knowledge. As was his habit when in new waters, Keats had ordered soundings be taken throughout the bay, and with this information and Keats's knowledge that the battery was constructed in a way that would allow battleships to anchor safely close in on its flank, Pellew now suspected there was water of sufficient depth to allow him to place his ships close inshore, out of the line of fire of the shore-based cannons. The frigate *Banterer* (Captain Warde) was sent to take more detailed soundings. Together with the record they made of all the gun emplacements this confirmed Pellew's thoughts and the tactic that led to the successful bombardment of Algiers in August 1816 that brought an end to the enslavement of Christians in that state.[681] Before sailing, Pellew entrusted to Keats a letter addressed to his son, Pownoll, to be delivered in the event of his death. It was agreed that if needs be, Keats would be the one to break the news to Lady Pellew.

Pellew indeed came close to death in that battle, being struck in three places. A cannon shot tore away the skirts of his coat, a button from which was later found in the signal locker. The shot also broke a pair of glasses in his pocket, bulging the frame. As an indication of the bond between them, Pellew gave these glasses to Keats – who caused their history to be engraved on them – and left instructions that on his death they should be restored to Pellew's family.[682]

On one occasion when Pellew was visiting Keats in Devon, the two Admirals were invited to dinner at Annery House, the estate of shipowner and builder, William Tardrew. Annery was a carriage ride from Durrant House, crossing Littleham stream, which had no bridge. The roads being steep and rough their host volunteered to be coachman, for safety's sake. The dinner, apparently quite convivial, did not conclude until well after midnight, during which time there had been a severe thunderstorm and heavy rain, turning the stream to a torrent. On the way home, the two horses and carriage were overturned in the stream – with the admirals inside. They were both rescued through the exertions of the driver and his servant. They then walked three miles home, very wet. So, two of the most experienced seamen of the day – with a combined 80 years on the high seas and each with thousands of miles under their keel, having survived countless encounters under enemy fire – came close to drowning together in a stream in North Devon![683]

**Historical Memoirs of
Admiral Sir Richard Goodwin Keats, GCB**

1818

Board Of Longitude

Following its restructuring in 1818, Keats was appointed one of the Commissioners of the Board of Longitude,[684] fully described as the *Commissioners for the Discovery of Longitude at Sea*. The board had first been established in 1714 following a dreadful loss of life when, due to inaccurate fixing of its position, a whole squadron ran onto the Scilly Isles. The board's mandate was to evaluate proposals and award prizes of up to £20,000 to those who could demonstrate a reliable method of calculation of longitude, which had long been an impediment to accurate positioning and navigation on the open sea.

The formation of the board encouraged a great deal of activity, particularly during the mid-1700s when John Harrison was developing and presenting his portable clocks, H1-H4, that ultimately proved capable of keeping accurate time onboard a ship at sea, and hence calculation of position. Every 15 degrees of longitude was represented by a one-hour time difference from the point of origin. A clock that was transportable – and continued to work in the harsh environment of a sailing ship keeping accurate time from (say) Greenwich – could be read at noon in the present position, noon being easily determined as when the sun reached its azimuth. The difference between noon and the reading of the Greenwich time clock could be used to calculate degrees of distance east or west from Greenwich. It must be observed that by 1818, the problem of determining longitude had been substantially solved, in theory at least. In practice, despite being considerably reduced in price from twenty years earlier, chronometers were still prohibitively expensive for many. Captains often had to purchase their own when the navy had insufficient, and lack of reliability meant it was wise to have more than one onboard.

Other proponents were still refining the use of complex mathematical computations of lunar distances based on sextant observations and the use of pre-computed tables contained in nautical almanacs. As a complete set of tables could be purchased for just £20, the lunar distances method was much more affordable than a clock, and so remained in wide use. The publication of these almanacs continued to be an important function of the board.

Before its reconstruction, the board had comprised twenty-two members and had not performed creditably. The commissioners, including Royal Astronomer of some forty-six years, Maskelyne, failed to properly acknowledge, let alone encourage, Harrison's efforts, placing unreasonable hurdles in its evaluations and only reluctantly paying incomplete amounts of the prize over an extended period. Ultimately, King George III himself concluded that Harrison had been treated unfairly.

Restructure was seen as a way to repair the standing and operation of the board and to redirect its attention to matters of wider scientific interest, particularly under the influence of Joseph Banks of the Royal Society and his supporters. The new board included three commissioners resident in London, the Lord High Admiral, Judge of the Admiralty Court, three fellows of the Royal Society, including Banks and Society president the esteemed chemist Sir Humphry Davy, and the professors of astronomy and mathematics from Oxford and Cambridge Universities.

From this time on it was mostly concerned with the improvement and testing of chronometers and with the refinement of other instruments of navigation, such as the sextant with an artificial horizon. Attention moved away from a determination of longitude specifically to a more general concern with navigation, meteorology, improvement of charts, consistent measurement of ships' tonnage, and support of voyages of discovery, including to the southern oceans. The new act provided specifically for the payment of prizes for the discovery of a northwest passage to the North Pole and the Pacific. To support navigation in the Southern Hemisphere, the board established an observatory at Cape Town on the Cape of Good Hope in 1820. The Board became, in effect, the scientific department of the Admiralty and throughout its existence "One of the most important and interesting bodies in the development of science and technology of the period".[685] Keats held this office until 1828 when the board was replaced by an advisory panel of three scientists.

In 1818 Sir Richard was appointed the Major-General of Marines.[14]

The most senior officers in His Majesty's Royal Marines were: A General, at this time Admiral Earl St. Vincent; a Lieutenant General, Admiral Sir Richard Bickerton, who had replaced Admiral Lord

---

14   In the room of Sir Geo. Hope, who was appointed to that office in January of the same year, and who is the Officer alluded to in the memoir of Sir Jas. Saumarez. [He had been Saumarez's flag Captain in the Victory in the Baltic.]

Collingwood; a Major General, now Keats, and four colonels. These positions were esteemed honorary titles accompanied by a stipend of more than £1,000 a year which provided a welcome supplement to the half-pay of an admiral. The position was described in Parliament as reserved for those officers foremost in the catalogue of those who had rendered brilliant and glorious public service, and who had most perilously served their country under the hottest fire.[686] Of Keats's appointment the newspapers commented; "Among the numerous officers whose talents and services entitle them to the gratitude of their country, we are satisfied that there are none who stand higher in the opinion of the navy and the country than Sir Richard Keats and that this appointment will be highly satisfactory to both".[687]

On 12 August 1819, Keats was advanced to Vice Admiral of the Red.[688]

Believing his days at sea were behind him, Keats threw himself into life in Devon. Although often reported as taking time ashore to rest and recover it is quite evident that rest did not come easily to Keats, who was a man used to constant activity. In just three weeks newspaper reports see him become Chairman of the Great Torrington Agricultural Society,[689] an area in which it might be thought enthusiasm and stature might outweigh experience; supporting the society for the raising of funds for relief of the residents of the Scilly Islands off the Cornish coast;[690] and as a steward for the annual meeting and dinner of the Wykehamists,[691] despite his relatively short tenure at the school. No doubt his farm managers and tenants were the object of his constant activity and would have found his full-time presence ashore exhausting.

**Historical Memoirs of
Admiral Sir Richard Goodwin Keats, GCB**

Governor Of The Royal Hospital Greenwich

He was called [from his retreat in Devon] on the death of Admiral Colpoys in 1821 to the government of the Royal Hospital at Greenwich; an appointment which was the more acceptable and agreeable as it was unsought for on his part, but which was most graciously bestowed by his Majesty at the recommendation of Lord Melville, the first lord of the Admiralty, as a remuneration for his long years of toil and warfare in defence and support of the interests of Great Britain.

It is likely the Duke of Clarence had a hand in the appointment.[692] As alluded to in the memoirs, it was a lucrative position, being attended by a handsome stipend of £1,000 for life (although as a consequence the position of Major General of Marines was relinquished) together with allowances and even more handsome apartments known as the 'Admiral's House' on the Thames riverfront. The appointment proved to be a wise one and it proved to be much to the benefit of the Hospital and pensioners to have an active and influential Governor of Keats's energy and capacity.

The Royal Hospital at Greenwich is to this day one of London's most famous landmarks. Once the site of the Royal Palace and birthplace of Henry VIII, Mary and Elizabeth, it was granted by William III by Royal Warrant as the site for the Royal Hospital for Seaman in accordance with the wishes of his late wife, Queen Mary II. Designed by Sir Christopher Wren, work began in 1696 on the four major courts to accommodate veterans of the Royal Navy. The finished work is one of considerable grandeur and the finest example of baroque architecture. The wealth of the country and the power and might of her navy is on permanent display for all to see as they approach London by water.

The Governor's apartments were located on the river frontage to the King Charles Court, to the right of the Water Gate when arriving by boat. They were furnished in grand style thanks to a gift from Mrs Fish in 1815, of a Regency-style suite which, after the closure of the hospital sixty years later, remained in use in Admiralty House, Whitehall, for a century. When the position of First Lord was abolished it went on loan to the Royal Pavilion at Brighton. The Governor's premises included the spacious apartment, a coach house and stables and an associated garden, greenhouse, and gardener's house.

The Royal Hospital Greenwich. Inscribed: 'To Admiral Sir Richard Goodwin Keats G.C.B. this view of the Royal Hospital for Seamen, at Greenwich is dedicated". Keats's flag as an Admiral of the Blue flies above the Governor's apartments. The dome to the left sits over the chapel and that to the right over the painted Hall. W.P. Kay NMM PAI7100 ©National Maritime Museum, Greenwich London.

At the time of Keats's governorship – following the end of the major sea wars of unexampled duration that had seen the navy expand to over 140,000 men – the Hospital was at its maximum capacity, nearing 3,000 pensioners. Those who had joined the navy in their prime, having given long service, were now worn out by age and wounds, many becoming applicants for asylum in the Hospital. The term 'Hospital' was used in the historical sense of a hospice, although by 1831 Keats was moved to write that the "pensioners are now generally so much wounded that the Hospital is more like an infirmary". As a hospice it provided accommodation and food for retired and injured sailors – both officers and enlisted men – in a variety of wards, as well as financial support for out-pensioners, and for the widows of seamen slain or disabled in the sea service and unable to provide for themselves. Between 1814 and 1820, 21,000 men applied for support as outpensioners of the Hospital. The criteria for acceptance was not always clear, particularly in the face of intense demand after the wars, but applicants were required to have served at least some time in the Royal Navy. Merchant sailors in distress could, after 1821, make application to the Seamen's Hospital Society which operated from the hulk *Grampus* in the Thames, not far from Greenwich.

Pensioners enjoyed conditions in their retirement at Greenwich that far exceeded their lot on a ship of war. They were clothed in a uniform of sorts; a tri-corn hat, jacket, and trousers, and were provided with accommodation, and an allowance. Food was provided in quantities and of a quality they had only dreamed of at sea and consumed, at least on special occasions, in in the Painted Hall, one of the grandest and most finely decorated rooms in all England all as just reward for the years of going without comfort so their countrymen might continue to enjoy theirs.

The Royal Hospital also included upper and lower schools for educating the children of sailors who died in the service, both boys and girls, who entered the school, aged eleven. With the assistance of the Lloyds Patriotic Fund the Royal Naval Asylum acquired the Queen's House, Greenwich in 1807, added two wings connected by a colonnade and from there educated up to 1,000 students. In 1821 this facility was placed under the management of the Hospital Board and in 1825 became the Lower School of the Royal Hospital. The Upper School for 200 boys was the original Hospital school under a new name.

Girls were taught reading, writing, sewing and skills necessary for servants. Boys were taught arithmetic in addition to the other two Rs. Boys showing the most potential in such matters went on to the Upper School. From 1821 the Master of the Upper School was much published and acclaimed mathematician and astronomer Edward Riddle. Often described as the Nautical School, boys in the Upper School were taught quite advanced mathematics and the fundamentals of nautical astronomy, navigation and other skills, such as surveying and charting, necessary for seamen in particular but also related trades, including those required for work in the dock yards. Entry was conditional on every boy agreeing to go to sea on completion of his education if a situation could be found for him and so the school was seen as the cradle of the navy. It continued as such for another one hundred years.

At the direction of the Duke of Clarence, when Lord High Admiral, the Upper School was extended to allow admission of a further 200 children being those of officers unable to otherwise provide for their education. Despite the worthy intention, this was contrary to the Hospital Charter, and when the Duke left the Admiralty the number was reduced to 100. This prompted a meeting of a group of officers to form the Royal Naval School Society. With the support of Keats, the Hospital and the patronage of King William they resolved to raise funds by voluntary donation and subscription for shares for the establishment of a school for the children of serving officers unable to meet the cost of their education.[693] Through the efforts of Commander Dickson in particular, supported by a great many officers including Keats and substantial financial contributions from several benefactors, a Royal Navy School for the children of distressed officers was established in Camberwell in 1833. It was subsequently formally constituted by an Act of Parliament in 1840.

The Royal Hospital derived income from a diverse range of sources, including, for example, the effects of the pirate Kid, from 1705 and the forfeited wages of men who deserted. A significant portion came from its northern estates of some 37,000 acres which became Crown possessions following the execution of their former owner the Earl of Derwentwater for taking part in the rebellion of 1715. These estates included lead and coal mines and agricultural holdings around Keswick and Berwick and on the coast at Scremerston in particular. Their Alston lead mines were claimed to be the richest in the world.[694] The enterprises required close management by the Hospital receivers and construction of significant infrastructure under the supervision of the Hospital board. They were among the first to build roads using Macadam's new method. Macadam himself was retained to oversee construction of more than one hundred miles of roadway. Other income was derived from a share of the freight of treasure conveyed by Royal Navy ships and a share of prize money – which even for the Hospital was notoriously difficult to collect, but provided an income of up to £100,000 a year[695]– and from the management of the Chatham Chest. Created in the sixteenth century this latter fund which arose from a levy upon the wages of sailors now had a capital of some £1,000,000 which, by Act of Parliament, was transferred to the Hospital in 1803. Not only a fund, it was an actual chest, now in the collection of the National Maritime Museum, Greenwich, into which funds were deposited. The value of the Hospital's cash investments was over four and a half million pounds (close to one billion pounds in current terms).[696]

There was much for a governor to do. On his appointment, Keats set to work to bring about what he called "A more liberal system which will contribute greatly to the Welfare & real comfort of the pensioners".[697] His experience in administrative matters, his capacity for work and his eye for detail made him an ideal candidate for the governorship at this time. He was blessed to have with him, firstly as Secretary to the Hospital and later as Civil Commissioner, Edward Hawke Locker. His father had been Lieutenant Governor of the Hospital and he had himself been Civil

Secretary to Pellew in the Mediterranean. They each had considerable energy. Together they made a formidable team.

Far from treating this appointment as a sinecure of retirement, Keats was active in the management of the Hospital. He was surprised as to how backward conditions had become and set to work improving circumstances for the pensioners for whom he showed considerable empathy. The most significant improvements he made in that regard were in the regulations governing an improved system of diet and activities for the residents.

His open letter of 1 July 1831 to Sir James Graham, then First Lord of the Admiralty, that argued forcefully for financial support of the institution as a means to encourage enlistment and to ensure delivery of the statutory obligation to provide support for those maimed, wounded, or worn out in the King's naval service, was published with editorial acclamation by *The Times*. The editors commented that Keats's statement appeared incontrovertible and they were sure that Sir James Graham, yet in his noviciate as an administrator of the naval establishments, would, with his characteristic candour and modesty, apply the most respectful attention to the suggestions of the highly distinguished and most experienced officer who had addressed him on a subject of such great professional, or rather national, interest.[698]

There was discussion in Parliament regarding the abolition of a 6d-per-month levy on the wages of merchant seamen which for many decades had been collected by the Government and applied to support the Hospital. The hospital facility was available as a sanctuary only for those who had served in the Royal Navy, so why should merchant seamen be subjected to such a levy? Keats's letter, described as containing a "clear and able lesson" and "Good advice to the Cabinet", argued for the retention of the levy on the basis that society generally and the merchants in particular, had benefited from the achievements and resources of the navy and the work and sacrifice of its sailors; yet no improvement had occurred at the hospital for pensioners.

It was, Keats argued, important to preserve the hospital facility, and every other encouragement, to enable the country to man her fleets in time of war by volunteers (as opposed to the evil of impressment). It was entirely equitable that the men of commerce, whose trade had been protected, should bear some of the cost. The wages in the merchant navy were considerably higher than those in the navy, and the conditions more suitable to family life, with merchant seamen returning home after every voyage. By contrast, Keats well knew many navy men who had been away from home for stretches of five years.

Some noted that this was undoubtedly true, but the direct benefit to the merchant seamen, as opposed to their employers, was more difficult to see. It was argued the more equitable course would be to expand the hospital to accommodate merchant seamen, even acknowledging it was struggling to provide for all the applicants from within the navy.[699]

In the Commons, Sir James Graham noted that it was not fair to represent the merchant seamen as deriving no benefit from the Hospital as it had been "Ascertained by Sir Richard Keats (than whom a higher authority does not exist) that at least one half of the whole number of merchant seamen have passed through the Kings Service; that is to say, 75,000 out of the 130,000",[700] and so could claim refuge at Greenwich if needed. Hospital records confirmed that in accordance with the Charter all pensioners had served in the Navy – an average of 13 years. Over 1,000 of those resident in 1831 had also served a time in the Merchant Service. Ultimately, the payment was abolished in 1834 but Parliament voted a sum of £20,000 annually to maintain equivalent funding noting:

> *It being highly becoming the honour and character of the British nation that those seamen and marines who have been, or shall hereafter be, maimed, wounded, disabled or worn out in its service onboard any of the ships of war of His Majesty, or in the naval service of the country, should be supported according to the original design of the foundation of the said Hospital.*[701]

A hiccup in the financial management discovered in 1828 led to an overhaul of the hospital accounting functions. Receivers managed the various enterprises and collected the rents, while the accounting was handled by the deputy treasurer. Although under the authority of a treasurer the latter appointment was largely a sinecure, and at times filled by a senior officer still on active duty at sea. Admiral Colpoys when treasurer had appointed Thomas Austin his deputy around 1803. It was a well-known custom that Hospital debts were paid on terms of six to eight weeks. Austin was alleged to have devised a scheme whereby in return for a 5% discount, certain accounts would be paid more promptly. All well and good, except that he recorded the full invoiced amount in the books and apparently pocketed the 5% to himself. The Hospital did not suffer significant financial loss from this particular scheme, and in any event was in the custom of holding twenty thousand pounds surety against the Treasurer – but Austin unjustifiably enriched himself.[702]

Despite audits, this went undetected for some time, as the books, bank account and supplier invoices presented to the treasurer and board meetings were all in proper alignment. Admiral

Colpoys's successor, Admiral Sir Boulden Thompson kept Austin on in the position as his deputy and as Chief Clerk of the Treasury. It was only on Thompson's death and replacement by Sir Alexander Hope that inconsistencies came to light. Hope intended to be a hands-on Treasurer. He appointed a deputy of his own selection. In undertaking an accounting and balance of the books for the handover discrepancies were revealed. Some small amounts were explained and others repaid. It was then further alleged that Hospital securities had been sold without fully accounting for the proceeds. Explanation became more difficult, and Mr Austin absconded.[703] He was located, arrested, charged, and committed for trial on several of counts of embezzlement from the Hospital and as his clerk, from the Treasurer. He faced at least two trials but was ultimately acquitted of all charges due to what might properly be described as technicalities. The Solicitor General had, for some reason, pursued charges of 'embezzlement' instead of 'misappropriation'.[704]

Hundreds of thousands of pounds would pass through the deputy treasurer's hands each year and he had almost unfettered access to a floating fund at the Bank of England up to £100,000 from which invoices were paid. He had significant autonomy and authority, and as it appeared was subject to little surveillance. There was no indication of wrongdoing on the part of any of the treasurers in office from time to time, but clearly the system as dictated by the current constitution was not sufficiently robust to withstand temptations such as those belatedly uncovered.

A review recommended the Governor and military officers should concentrate on providing for the pensioners, widows and children including the Schools and the running of the various hospital enterprises including the Northern Estates. It was proposed the civil department be reorganised under the authority of five Commissioners responsible for the collection of prize monies and payment of out pensions and other administrative functions. The accounting role was to be transferred to the office of the Treasurer of the Navy under the authority of the Lords Commissioners of the Admiralty.[705] Following St. Vincent's review of naval administration and a commission of enquiry in 1802 which resulted in an impeachment trial of then treasurer Henry Dundas the Treasurer of the Navy was now subject to rigorous checks and balances. The Secretary to the Commissioners suggested Keats agreed to this reorganisation, but he did not, and remonstrated to the Admiralty against the plan. He noted the problem could be as well solved by requiring a counter signatory to cheques without removing from the board the counsel and expertise of the military officers. He pointed out the impracticality of the Governor taking responsibility and making arrangements for the pensioners, but having no place at the board table with the Commissioners where budgets were framed and decisions made for the benefit of those same pensioners.

However, the die was cast. Legislative changes were made in 1829 separating the administration into Military and Civil functions. The Commissioners included Lord Auckland and Edward Locker. It appears that under their administration with Keats as Governor the extent of the division of governance responsibilities was not substantially altered and in practice through hearty cooperation between the particular individuals all worked well. In July 1830 Keats was re-appointed 'Master of the Hospital and also one of the Commissioners or Governors'.[706] He was described by the First Lord of the Admiralty as demonstrating "constant and anxious endeavours" in his role and displaying "exemplary zeal to uphold the character and sustain the honour of (the) institution which is the pride of our naval history".[707] Years later new enquiries and reports recommended the Governor and Lieutenant Governor also be Commissioners, reversing the 1829 restructure, which was described as having been detrimental to the general interests and harmony of the Hospital, having resulted in unnecessary trouble and correspondence and as having done more harm than good.[708]

Greenwich itself was a town of some 24,000 people. The Hospital was certainly the landmark but relations with the parish were often strained. No doubt many staff and contractors came from the town, and pensioners spent their pocket money with local traders, but it was also felt the Hospital was a financial drain on the parish which on many occasions was left supporting impoverished relatives of deceased pensioners from its own resources on account of the obligations of support imposed by Elizabethan Poor Law which also prevented such persons being forced to return to their original homes for others to support. To avoid significant loss the parish had for some years required, and the Hospital had from 1807 agreed to pay, above legal rate for its residents. Keats caused an upset when in 1829 he argued these claims were much exaggerated and the Hospital terminated the arrangement. Relations on this score remained tense. The Parish Churchwardens took legal proceedings against Keats seeking to levy rates on his Governor's apartments and those of other officers which had hitherto been regarded as exempt and provided tax free. Keats argued that as the apartments were occupied by officers of the Hospital in direct succession from the Royal Palace and being used in conjunction with charitable purposes in accordance with royal direction they should be exempt. The Consistory Court ruled against him, giving the parish a minor win. The court noted the Governor, as guardian of public property devoted to most useful and charitable purposes, had acted very properly in resisting the payment till the opinion of a competent jurisdiction had been ascertained upon the point.[709] The argument concerning the annual surcharge of £2 per pensioner being based on equity rather than law, continued until well after Keats's death five years later.[710]

Residency at Greenwich brought Keats back into the centre of naval affairs. It was during his term that Edward Locker successfully realised his father's vision in establishing the Naval Gallery in the Painted Hall.[711] The collection was enthusiastically and generously supported by King George IV, who provided works from Windsor and St James's Palaces and Hampton Court. Keats personally funded acquisition of Richard Paton's depiction of *The Battle of Barfleur, 1692*, the aftermath of which battle was the catalyst for the establishment of the Hospital soon thereafter.[712] This gallery was an instant success. Even before the steamboat service and railway improved access to Greenwich, the painted hall was attracting 50,000 visitors a year,[713] many no doubt drawn to see the extensive collection of Nelson memorabilia. The gallery became a significant collection of maritime art, later to form the foundation for the Royal Museum's Greenwich collection.

Keats drew praise from the liberal members of society for establishing a library at the Hospital for the amusement, information and moral improvement of the inhabitants. *The Log Book* declared with its usual enthusiasm that he was thus shown to be as liberally minded as he was brave, generous, and humane.[714] How many pensioners made use of the library is less certain.

Evidence given to a parliamentary inquiry into drunkenness revealed that when Keats was first appointed to the governorship, he found great need for reformation in the area of alcohol consumption, as well as diet more generally. Intemperance was "At such a pitch that the pensioners were in the habit of selling their rations of food to obtain spirits."[715] Under his patronage a temperance society was formed with upwards of 500 to 600 pensioners joining. The greater part of them kept steady, with the Lieutenant Governor keeping a memorandum of their conduct. No doubt years of rations of alcohol at sea and the drinking habits of the period created difficulties. Keats took the temperance movement to heart, becoming one of the Vice Presidents of the British and Foreign Temperance Society at its founding under the patronage of the Lord Bishop of London in July 1831. It should be understood that while the fundamental principles of these societies required subscribers to abstain absolutely from the use of distilled spirits, there was no prohibition on the moderate use of other liquors.[716]

A sincere and practising Christian, Keats stated that his long experience at sea allowed him to observe that in his opinion "those seamen did their duty best who were best acquainted with their religious duties."[717] He was well aware that men at sea had little time or opportunity to join a congregation and often believed they had no right, thought themselves unwelcome or in any event were unwilling to introduce themselves to a congregation on shore. At a meeting in the City of London Tavern on 20 July 1825, along with the Lord Mayor of London and others, he became a Vice President on the foundation of the Episcopal Floating Church Society. Edward Locker joined the Committee. The objective of the society was to provide religious education to seamen. Due to their feeling out of place and possibly unwelcome at congregations on shore it was proposed to establish floating chapels in various ports. The Society commenced by providing a chaplain who would visit ships afloat in port. By 1829 they had at their disposal HMS *Brazen* (not that captured by Keats in 1798, but a sloop formerly of 28 guns launched in 1808), which could accommodate 500 men and was used for this purpose until 1845. King George IV became a patron making an annual financial contribution, and this was continued by his successor, King William.

Keats also instigated the construction of a new church of St Mary in the Hospital grounds in 1823 overseeing the laying of the foundation stone by the Bishop of Oxford and HRH Princess Sophia Matilda.[718] Demolished in 1935 a memorial to King William now stands in its place. Not long thereafter Keats was one of the subscribers to the publication of a book; *Plain Sermons on Important Subjects Chiefly for the Use of Seamen.*[719]

During his governorship, the authorities planned to reroute the road to Woolwich, thereby allowing the Hospital to purchase additional land and demolish slum properties, to put it in an improved setting. This involved moving the market to the centre of town and creating new streets being; Nelson, Clarence, and an extension of King William Street to the Thames. The Hospital acquired the Ship Tavern and constructed both a new pier to be serviced by a paddle steamer from London and a railway. The new market commenced operation in 1831. The steam paddle boat serviced the new pier from 1835, and the railway from London finally reached Greenwich in 1836.[720]

There was a great deal to be done, and a substantial part of the work was administrative, but there was no shortage of ceremonial occasions. Royal visitors were not uncommon. In 1822, King George IV attended Greenwich before commencing a royal tour of Scotland, (the first such tour by a monarch in two hundred years) departing from the Greenwich wharf in the *Royal George Yacht*. Having refreshed at the Governor's house following the carriage ride from London, the King was escorted by Keats, arm in arm, to the waiting barge to take him to his yacht.[721] Such events were major attractions and members of the public attended by the thousand, both on land and in whatever vessels could be secured for the purpose.

Onboard the royal yacht, before it departed for Scotland, Earl St. Vincent, then 87 years of age, and Admiral of the Fleet, was presented with a baton honouring his long and distinguished services. He had stayed the previous night with Keats, having accepted "With inexpressible pleasure your obliging offer of a bed in your hospital mansion",[722] and enjoyed chatting with former captains early in the morning. Those who had served with him well knew his habit of rising before dawn, and independently they assembled outside the Governor's house at an early hour to catch the opportunity presented.[723] This was to be the Earl's last time afloat.

The embarkation of His Majesty George IV, on board the Royal George Yacht off Greenwich to visit his Scottish Dominions, 10 August 1822. John Serres. @Alamy PO2AMR. The barge is shown rowing towards the Royal Yacht. The Royal Standard still flies over the Admiral's House.

The Hospital was often the venue for the official welcome of dignitaries visiting London and coordination of these events fell to Keats. In June 1827 the Queen of Wurttemberg (Charlotte, Princess Royal, the first daughter of George III) was greeted on the steps of Greenwich by her brother the Duke of Clarence, an assortment of Duchesses, and Keats supported by the Royal Marines, Grenadier Guards and pensioners. The royal party frequently retired to the governor's apartments for refreshments awaiting the Queen's long-delayed arrival.[724] Prince Don Miguel of Portugal, who soon became King Miguel I, received a similar welcome in the following year.[725]

King William IV was a frequent visitor to his old shipmate arriving by royal barge for afternoon tea or lunch. It was well known he always liked meeting seagoing men on easy terms and these visits to his old friend were one of his sincere pleasures. On more formal occasions, particularly when visiting as Lord High Admiral, he came in the uniform of an Admiral, inspected the marines and pensioners, and visited the painted hall and chapel as well, as the wards.[726] By way of example; in August 1830 the visiting Royal party headed by the King and Queen included the Duke of Sussex, Prince Leopold, Prince Frederick of Prussia and other dignitaries who arrived by royal barge, accompanied by the Lords of the Admiralty in the Admiralty barge. The King, after changing from the uniform of a Field Marshal assumed that of an admiral, inspected the facilities, and lunched with Sir Richard and Lady Keats while the band of the Royal Marines played outside the entrance hall until at five o'clock the party departed for London in a suite of carriages.

The Royal visit in May 1832 caused much excitement as the party, including the King and Queen together with the Duke and Duchess of Cumberland, the Duke of Gloucester and the Princes of Cambridge and Cumberland and several noblemen travelled in a suite of seven carriages accompanied by the royal household and preceded by troops of the 9th Lancers to inspect the Woolwich yards. They then headed back along the Thames to Greenwich in a flotilla of oared barges which made their way through a throng of vessels so numerous as to nearly obscure the river. They were received by Keats at the Greenwich landing, and together with some one hundred dignitaries and officers retired to the Governor's residence for a splendid 'dejeuné à la fourchette' whilst the band of the Royal Marines played tunes on the lawns. At the conclusion of luncheon, the party emerged to inspect the Hospital, commencing with the Painted Hall. They reviewed the 2,700 occupant pensioners assembled around the great square, the King stopping to chat with those former companions in arms whom he recognised and inspected some 1,000 pupils of the Hospital schools who all gave an enthusiastic and warm welcome to the royal party.[727]

Just a few days prior, while arranging the protocols and ceremony for the royal visit Keats himself was at Woolwich yard, with First Lord Graham and Sir Thomas Hardy to witness (in incessant rain) the launching of the new frigate *Vernon*. She was the first of a new breed of frigates of 2,000 tons to be fitted with 50 thirty-two-pound guns, and together with the miniature frigate *Royal Louise* intended as a gift to the king of Prussia, the prime object of the King's forthcoming inspection.[728]

Although there is ample evidence of Keats requiring due process be met and that exterior marks of respect be given at all times, there is little evidence throughout a long career of his standing on ceremony beyond proper formalities simply for the sake of it. Hospital Governorship gave him a taste of the pomp and ceremony that accompanied events on shore and the trappings of the governorship offered comforts only dreamed about when confined to the wooden walls at sea. During his term the Hospital commissioned the construction of a new Hospital Governor's Barge. At thirty-seven feet, manned by twelve crew and boatswains it was an ornate and somewhat extravagant mode of transport reserved for ceremonial occasions.

Keats's old friend, Edward Pellew, visited whenever in London, providing lists of men in need of sanctuary in the Hospital, and they corresponded to the end, sharing news on shipmates' passing and their common suffering of rheumatism.[729] Admiral Sir John Warren was also a regular visitor, until on his final visit in 1822, he passed away in Keats's apartment.

At the time of the passing of George IV during Keats's governorship, it was remarked the Hospital "Was richer than ever before and full to capacity with a well-loved Governor. It was high in the affections of the Navy".[730]

The Hospital constitution had some difficulties but it generally worked well when Earl Auckland was Senior Commissioner and Admiral Keats the Governor. Some difficulties arose in later years when Rear Admiral Hardy, and after him, Admiral Fleeming – both distinguished officers of the utmost integrity – were said to be men not as suited to the administrative requirements of the governorship. Keats had the advantage of the able support of both Earl Auckland and Edward Locker.[731] As an administrative team they oversaw significant reform and improvements to the pensioners' conditions in terms of diet as well as activities and facilities and maintained the institution on a sound financial footing. There is little doubt, too, that Keats had the ear of those in power when needed. His old friend, the Duke of Clarence, took a keen interest in all naval affairs, whether as chair of the Board of Longitude, Lord High Admiral or ultimately as the King. He continued to pay high regard to Keats's opinion and was sure to see to it that any concern Keats might raise received attention.

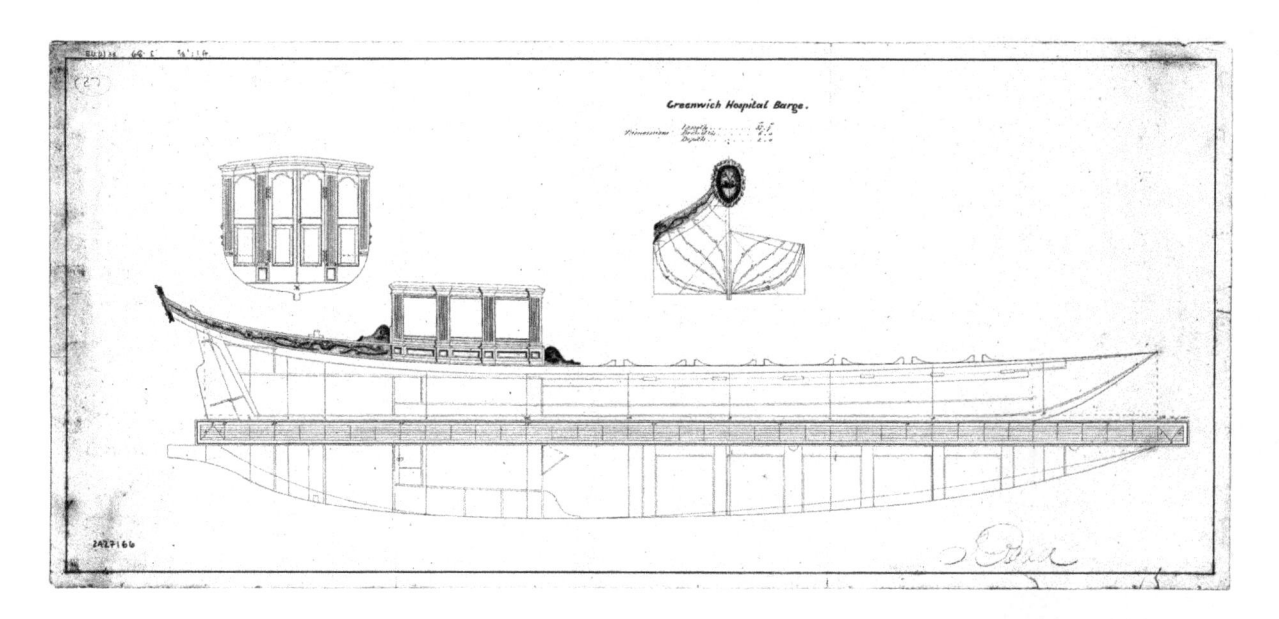

Plans for the 12-oared 37ft Greenwich Hospital barge, showing body plan with full crest on the sternboard, front section of the cabin, longitudinal and half breadth. NMM J0862, ©National Maritime Museum, Greenwich, London

Historical Memoirs of
Admiral Sir Richard Goodwin Keats, GCB

20

A Diversity of Interests

Described as one of the most influential survivors of the Napoleonic Wars, (having outlived virtually all his wartime contemporaries) Keats was called upon to act as patron to many young officers of promise, particularly given their reduced prospects after the war. By the mid-1820's, the war years receding into history, many officers and men were out of work or on half-pay, the size of the navy having been much reduced and its budget cut to half what it had been twenty years earlier.[732]

Early on in his governorship he secured the prestigious position of Hospital surgeon for William Beatty over more senior men. He had been surgeon on the *Spencer* off Toulon before moving to the *Victory* for some years including during the pursuit of Villeneuve, and at Trafalgar. He served at the Hospital for seventeen years from 1822. Keats no doubt played a role in Beatty's appointment as surgeon to George IV in Scotland and from 1827 as 'physician in extraordinary' to the Duke of Clarence.[733]

Another person of interest to benefit from Keats's interest and patronage was Midshipman John Roe, who had served on the frigate *Horatio* under Captain Dillon on the Newfoundland station when Keats was Governor. When he was put forward by Captain Dillon based on his having shown a talent for navigation and cartography Keats provided a letter of introduction to the Hydrographic Office. On the basis of this support the Admiralty posted him to the Surveying Service of New South Wales and he secured a position with Captain King on the four Australian expeditions of the *Mermaid* & *Bathurst* designed to complete the work of Flinders in surveying the Australian coast, particularly the north and west. Roe rewarded his patron to "shew that I am not unmindful of his good offices" by securing his name to Port Keats and nearby Mount Goodwin on the Australian northwest coast.[734]

Roe settled in Australia, becoming Surveyor-General of Western Australia. An additional indication of his esteem for Keats can be found in his naming his son, born 1852, Augustus Sandford Keats Roe.

Port Keats is now better known by its indigenous name *Wadeye* and, having been an Aboriginal mission for some time, is now under the control of its indigenous owners. Nearby Mount Goodwin was home to 39 Radar Station of the RAAF during the Second World War, participating in the defence of northern Australia, but the area is otherwise largely undeveloped.[735]

Hydrographer George Richards, in surveying Canada from 1857-62 in the sloop *Plumper*, named the islands in Howe Sound off Vancouver after officers in Nelson's navy, including Keats Island.

John Franklin, encouraged by the Board of Longitude to explore the Arctic sea for a northwest passage, named Point Keats, on the storm ravaged shores of the Northwest Territories of Canada, for the Governor of Greenwich Hospital. He did this while surrounded by sea ice and observing piles of sea drift timbers some twelve feet vertically higher than the shoreline.[736]

On his second visit to the Torres Straits, in 1792, with HMS *Providence (10)* in which Matthew Flinders was a midshipman, Captain Bligh claimed possession of all the islands seen in the Strait. He described them as Clarence's Archipelago and named one Keats Island.[737] It is reasonable to think this was due to Keats's involvement in the *Bounty* court martial. That was taking place almost to the day that Bligh was passing through Torres Strait, so he could not have known of the composition of the tribunal at the time. The answer may lie in the group of islands being designated simply 'M' at the time and being given their names; Marsden, Yorke and Keats sometime later.[738]

Even in his final years Keats remained engaged in promoting exploration. When the expedition of Captain John Ross – which left on the steamer, *Victory*, in 1828 to explore the Arctic – had still not returned by 1832, Keats was instrumental in sending rescue. Together with Saumarez, Viscount Goderich, and publishers Pinnock and Maunder, he raised £3,000 by private donation with another £2,000 from the government for 'research' and launched a two-year expedition to the Arctic. Ross finally returned onboard a whaler in October 1833 after spending four winters trapped in the ice. With his nephew and second-in-command, James Ross, he had become the first European to discover the North Magnetic Pole.

Keats was in comprehensive correspondence with Captain Charles Phillips, his former flag-lieutenant in the Walcheren expedition and at Cádiz, assisting him with various endeavours and promotion of his inventions. Captain Phillips had designed and patented a capstan, which by use of epicyclic gearing was far more powerful than those previously in use, and which was ultimately installed on all navy ships. He also devised a system for the suspension of a compass so that it was only minimally affected by the concussion of gunfire.[739]

Keats played a minor but pivotal role in fostering a significant invention of the brothers John and Charles Deane, who had both graduated from the Greenwich Hospital School. John went to sea on an East Indiaman, the *Warren Hastings*, and Charles took on employment at Deptford Yard with a Mr Edward Barnard, the builder of the *Warren Hastings*. They had conceived a diving helmet, for which a patent was sought, whereby fresh air was pumped by hose from the surface to a diver below wearing an India rubber suit and a metal helmet with glass viewing panes. After several private trials in the Thames they were attempting to put the invention in front of the Admiralty for use in salvage and the effecting of repairs underwater, thereby obviating the expense and inconvenience of taking a ship into dry dock. The Admiralty was notoriously reluctant to investigate such matters often giving a convoluted rejection; "their Lordships will give him no trouble on the subject". The patronage of someone in Keats's position was invaluable in opening the door to a hearing. On 30 December 1831 Charles Deane was able to write that following an interview with Admiral Keats the day prior he would be proud to make a decent in the presence of their Lordships now having a convenient vessel lying off the steps of the Royal Hospital Greenwich near the Admiral's residence, which vessel with the Governor's consent would be allowed to remain to await their Lordships pleasure.[740]

The Admiralty had little option but to attend. Following this formal presentation, public demonstrations were advertised to take place on 3 January 1832 and the following days in the Thames "directly off the Royal Hospital, Greenwich; from where Spectators may have a good view", (and if so inclined contribute funds to the project).[741] The fact these exhibitions were facilitated by Keats and by association, the Hospital, made them difficult to ignore. The demonstrations themselves were a success. The Admiralty was in the process of being convinced, lending support to demonstrations at the Sheerness yard in the following weeks. A patent was granted shortly thereafter. Soon the Deanes were full-time divers.[742] They went on to be instrumental in not just salvage and repairs but in deploying underwater explosions in the Crimea, and of course the invention became widely used in a range of diving applications beyond the military, particularly in diving for pearls.

Speaking in Parliament some years after Keats's death Sir Francis Burdett said Keats "was attached to the naval system of this country, and was strongly prejudiced against innovation, but he possessed a candid mind."[743] He was promulgating a common misconception of Keats. He was most certainly attached to the naval system and a strong believer in following the expected way of doing things, but it is apparent from the foregoing that he was not at all prejudiced against innovation properly investigated and approved within the system. A reputation for being 'old school' when it came to discipline and order should not be extrapolated to conclude he had a closed mind. It was ironic but, as a result even more persuasive, that an aged admiral with a reputation for being attached to the system should be the one lending his support to the inventions of the young and was the one putting these before the Admiralty. He was able to do so in a manner they could not ignore, gently prodding the establishment to accept innovation. It demonstrates that an enquiring mind can happily exist in the absence of a significant formal education, that enthusiasm for innovation need not be blunted by age or physical impairment and that lengthy service does not imply acceptance of the status quo. As his report as to a method of attacking the Aix roads demonstrated, Keats was always looking for a better way of doing things albeit within the constraints of the system.

One gets the impression that after forty years of life at sea, navy officers had difficulty in understanding why others might go sailing for recreation. That was certainly the view expressed at the time of the *Southampton's* rescuing the crew of the dismasted sloop when returning from delivering Prince Edward to Gibraltar years earlier. Byam Martin had described the crew of the distressed vessel as 'persisting' in describing their voyage as a party of pleasure. "How strange it is that people will call their yachts pleasure boats!" he exclaimed.[744] All these years later cruising and competitive yachting emerged as a leisure activity as sporting pursuits took hold in England in the respite that followed the conclusion of the wars. Sailing for pleasure as opposed to necessity was still seen as unusual and the participants bordering on the eccentric. It was probably for this reason that association with the navy was seen as desirable and adding respectability to their endeavours which might otherwise be portrayed as frivolous. Keats became quite involved with several yacht clubs.

For some time, he served as a director of the Royal Sailing Society.[745] One object of the society was to promote the 'amusing and agreeable recreation of sailing', to which end members competed in races against other yacht clubs on the Thames. The society was keen to make known, however, that drawing upon its naval members its principal objective was a higher purpose: to foster improvements in naval architecture and those inventions by which life might be preserved in the appalling dangers which so frequently happen at sea.[746] It may be this aim that principally motivated Keats's involvement. On acceding to the throne, King William agreed to be Patron of the Society, and at a meeting in Oliver's

Coffee House, Westminster, in the absence of club rooms, the traditional venue for club meetings, Sir James Graham, Lord Saumarez and Sir Richard Keats each accepted honorary membership.[747] One year later the Society match on the Thames was a splendid affair conducted in front of a large crowd, advertised as the first time such an event had taken place in the presence of their Majesties.[748]

The Duke of Clarence was also involved with the Coronation Sailing Society. It had initially formed as the Cumberland Fleet under the Patronage of Prince Henry Frederick, Duke of Cumberland, the younger brother of George III. He had first presented a cup for the winner of a yacht race as early as July 1775.

At a dinner convened to present the cups following a regatta in 1823 to celebrate the coronation of George IV it was decided to change the name of the society to the 'Coronation Sailing Society', comprising new subscribers and members of the Old Cumberland Fleet.[749] The very first match under the new name conducted on 30 July 1823 ended in controversy concerning the helming of the winning yacht. Following dissatisfaction at the outcome of subsequent protests a breakaway group met at the White Horse Tavern in August and reformed the Cumberland fleet under the name of the 'Thames Yacht Club', appointing William Harrison its commodore. This new club gained the patronage of the Duke of Clarence in 1827[750] and on his accession to the throne in 1830 he confirmed his continued patronage granting the Royal Warrant to what as a result became the 'Royal Thames Yacht Club'.

The Coronation fleet continued for some time. Keats accepted appointment as a director of this society when it was reconstituted after a brief hiatus under the patronage of the succeeding Duke of Cumberland, William's younger brother, Prince Ernest Augustus.[751] Consistent with the higher objectives referred to above it held out "as an encouragement to genius, offers of reward to such person or persons who may discover and bring to bear any improvement in the art of building, rigging, or sailing a vessel; combining, therefore, with its amusements a desire to prove of service to the country by bettering her navy."[752] Following the death of George IV a meeting of members held in the British Coffee House in January 1831 resolved the club be dissolved.[753] The members of the former society who had not earlier seceded, including Commodore Lord Cholmondeley, were then largely absorbed into the Royal Thames Yacht Club.[754] The club continues to use the description, 'The Cumberland fleet', and thereby maintains a claim to be the world's oldest continually functioning yacht club.

Yachts of the Cumberland Fleet (the precursor to the Royal Thames Yacht Club, of which Keats became Vice-Patron) racing on the Thames, William Havell, 1815. NMM BHC1196. ©National Maritime Museum, Greenwich, London.

Quite possibly at the King's instigation, Keats accepted appointment to the newly created office of Vice-Patron of the Royal Thames Yacht Club.[755] It subsequently became a custom to invite the Governor of Greenwich Hospital to become vice patron, and the minutes record that Rear Admiral Hardy was accorded that honour on Keats's death in 1834, and later, the appointment of Admiral Stopford to the position.[756]

Several regattas or 'matches' were held for different classes of yacht each year; 'above the bridge' for smaller craft and 'below the bridge' for larger craft, the latter often using the Greenwich Hospital as a start or finish point. The records reveal particulars of entered yachts, their tonnages and owners, the winners, and post-race celebrations, but do not reveal whether any participants included the vice patron amongst their crew. One suspects his involvement was due to a combination of his association with the Duke, his obvious interest in the promotion of innovations of utility to the navy, and the fact he was by then a well-connected and influential officer whose involvement lent credibility and substance to the professed higher objects of these clubs. Given his age at this time, his participation was most probably otherwise limited to that of a social member, although it was customary for the Commodore and officers of the club to attend on Greenwich with the prize cups for the inspection of the Vice Patron.

Again, following the lead of the Duke of Clarence, at the time of his being Lord High Admiral, it would seem Keats became one of twenty-one vice presidents, said to be men of high position and influence, who were equivalent to honorary members on formation of the Port of Plymouth Royal Clarence Regatta Club. Formed in 1827 the club merged in 1833 to become the Royal Western Yacht Club.[757]

In June 1815 a group of gentlemen meeting in the Thatched House Tavern, St. James formed the 'Yacht Club' for those interested in sailing in saltwater. In 1817 they welcomed the Prince Regent as a member. On becoming King, he consented to give the club the royal title; the 'Royal Yacht Club'. Membership came to include also, the Duke of Clarence, Duke of Gloucester, Commodore Earl of Yarborough (whose yacht was a formidable 351 Tons) and Vice Commodore Earl of Belfast. Again, keen to show the usefulness and patriotic nature of their endeavours it was claimed the spirit of innovation inherent in their matches produced sailing craft of such celerity in sailing and beauty of construction as to be of utility to the Royal Navy. The club fleet included the Admiralty Yacht (Viscount Melville) and the Navy Board Yacht (Vice Admiral Byam Martin) amongst its register and conducted events from Plymouth, Southampton and Cowes. Racing became a principal focus of the Cowes Regatta from 1826 and was soon pronounced to be the principal summer amusement of most young men of fortune.[758] The castle of Cowes became, and is to this day, the Club headquarters. From shortly after inception it was a practice that naval officers could apply for honorary membership and at a meeting before the 1829 season Admiral Keats along with ten other gentlemen was elected an honorary member.[759] In 1833 King William requested the club be styled the 'Royal Yacht Squadron', of which he considered himself the head.

It was claimed that the racing activities of the various clubs provided a national good by employing seamen, boat builders, and sailmakers otherwise out of work at war's end, and thereby kept up their skills in the event they may be required to serve again. Additionally it was claimed that the trialling and introduction of new designs and machinery, combined with the professional knowledge and experience of the naval members which made itself felt among the various building operations, advanced the science of naval architecture, to the benefit of the navy.

There is little doubt senior naval men like Keats were recruited as honorary members or patrons to lend gravitas to club activities, which might otherwise have been regarded as frivolous. It was said that during the wars it had been British men, not ships, which brought victory and it was important that the science of ship design and construction be advanced.[760] There is some evidence that the claims of these clubs to be of utility to the navy were not all idle puffery. Attention can be directed to the frigate *Vernon (50)*, whose launch at Woolwich was attended by Keats. She was the largest of several warships including the brigs *Snake (16)* and *Serpent (16)* commissioned by the navy to new designs by Captain Symonds, who first proved himself in producing fast cutters for racing, and in particular for Lord Vernon. Under the patronage of the Duke of Clarence he was later appointed designer to the Lord High Admiral.

The vessels of various club members, particularly those of the Duke of Portland and Earl Belfast participated in trial cruises with the navy and proved superior, in speed at least, leading to direct purchase or new commissions of improved cutters and gun-brigs with an enhanced beam but finer bow. The *Pantaloon* (10) cruised with the Navy and was purchased as the model for an improved ten-gun brig. Other purchases included the *Columbine* (18), *Rover* (18), *Vestal* (26), and *Vernon*,[761] and finally the Joseph White built *Waterwitch* (10). The latter underwent trials in a squadron commanded by Sir Pulteney Malcolm proving superior in speed on all point of sailing and under all conditions, and the equal of vessels larger by one hundred tons. Navy men were of course vitally interested in both the speed and seaworthiness of their vessels. The idea of sea trials was not new. Keats had conducted his own such trials on many occasions, including testing the new *Medina* (20) on the voyage to Newfoundland. The involvement of senior officers such as Keats, Hardy, Graham, Saumarez and Popham in the activities of these clubs combined with the competitive instincts of the members did lead to advances in naval architecture and lend substance to the higher objectives. Any impact was soon overwhelmed by the innovation of the marine engine.

In 1825 he was made Admiral of the Blue.

On 22 July 1830, he was promoted to Admiral of the White.[762]

**Historical Memoirs of
Admiral Sir Richard Goodwin Keats, GCB**

Captain Warner's Inventions

A Samuel Warner claimed to have invented two weapons that would forever alter naval warfare and offered that in exchange for £200,000 (millions in today's currency), he would share the specifics with the government. Better known as a smuggler he returned from serving King Dom Pedro IV in Portugal, styled a captain, claiming to have developed these weapons when serving on covert operations during the French wars. No record was found of the ship in which he claimed to have served, or of the ships he claimed to have sunk using his inventions.

One invention was an 'invisible shell', better understood as an underwater mine. It was claimed:

The many ways in which it can be applied leave no doubt...it is impossible for any ship whatever to avoid coming in contact with it. For the defence of harbours, riverways, or roadsteads it would be of the greatest service to this country, as they could all be defended at a trifling expense, and in a very short space of time.[763]

The other invention was described as a 'spike shell', to be projected ten feet under the surface with such precision as to sink an adversary at the first discharge. It may have been fired underwater, like a torpedo, but the details were not divulged. The inventions were brought to the attention of King William who, seeing the potential for such weapons if they could perform as claimed wanted to know more. As a first step, he appointed Keats to investigate.

There was much correspondence between Keats and Warner arranging meetings over a period of eighteen months, which of itself would have been a long time if the matter were straightforward. The King and Keats called in Sir Thomas Hardy and they investigated together for some time.

The matter dragged on, long past the death of the two admirals, through various parliamentary committees and the like, until a widely promoted large-scale public demonstration took place off Brighton beach on 17 July 1844. The ship *John O'Gaunt* was moored just offshore and duly blown up in full view of spectators who had arrived by the hundred from London. Through all his demonstrations, including this grand show, Warner consistently refused inspection of the target before the test, or to provide a satisfactory explanation as to how the invention operated.

To prosecute his case Warner relied strongly on the claimed approval of King William IV, Keats, and Hardy. He particularly proffered a report supposedly written by the admirals recording their conviction as to the efficacy of the inventions; a report he claimed was shared only with the King and Prime Minister, Lord Melbourne. The report now produced by Warner still failed to include any description of the mechanism or means of delivery and lacked the detailed particulars generally conspicuous in a report by Keats.[764]

Warner claimed to have had the handwriting in the report verified as that of Keats. No other copies were found, and first-hand evidence was not available given all this took place long after Keats and Hardy had died. The matter was addressed in Parliament several times, where it was stated by various Members that they did not doubt the integrity of the two admirals, but pointedly noted: "It is singular that they should die, and that no report should be found: it is notorious that they were men of business, and were not very likely to have lost their papers."[765] Not a single copy of the report, its antecedents or proposed next steps was found in the papers of Keats, Hardy, King William, or Prime Minister Lord Melbourne. Even acknowledging the security implications of such a report this seemed extraordinary in an era when the most mundane correspondence was copied and filed. The persons involved were known to be meticulous.

All the evidence is that Warner was a charlatan and fraudster. Did he hoodwink Keats and Hardy in support of his cause? There is no doubt that, as requested by the King, they conducted extensive investigations over a considerable period. That is as it should be, having regard to the express request from the King and to the implications of the claims made by the inventor which, if true, would afford the navy a considerable advantage in war. However, the facts that the report did not have the characteristics of one prepared by Keats or Hardy, that the claims regarding the Admirals' support for the inventions and the existence of the alleged written report emerged only long after their death, and that no trace of it has been found in their papers all indicate strongly that the report Warner was touting was a complete and fraudulent fabrication, and the support he claimed was never given.

This uncertainty together with the lack of disclosure by Warner meant the various parliamentary committees reached no resolution over many years. The supposed inventions were displayed in the West End gallery of the Great Exhibition of 1851, still claiming the support of Keats and Hardy and quoting from the alleged report, but any further development effectively died with Warner in 1853.

Historical Memoirs of
Admiral Sir Richard Goodwin Keats, GCB

22

The Man

Such have been the important services rendered to the country by Sir Richard Keats; and though flattery may rightly be considered a most sordid act, yet praise truly due can never be displaced, and to withhold it is unjust and improper.

"It is" says Dr. Barrow, "an imperfect charity which doth not respect one's neighbour according to his utmost merit and worth, which doth not heartily desire his good, which doth not earnestly promote his advantage in every kind according to one's ability and opportunity".

He also thinks it laudable to bestow praise: "By it", he continues, "both parties are pleased, the one whilst he receives the recompense of his worth, the other in performing an act of justice." And he further says- "That man is most happy in his act, who, like a skilful painter, retains the features and complexion, but still softens them into the most agreeable likeness." We have always endeavoured to do so; and though we are not, at all times, enabled to draw the likeness from a personal knowledge of the original, but often from rough and imperfect sketches, the touches we have ventured to add have never been hazarded without receiving what we considered good authority for so doing.

Although we might rely with confidence on the foregoing narrative and the opinion of Nelson, for conveying a just idea of the talents and services of Sir Richard Keats, we may be permitted to state the substance of the sentiments of all those whom we have ever conversed on the subject, and by which we are led to believe, that one of the peculiar qualities possessed by Sir Richard is modesty. By modesty, however, must be understood that degree of reservedness which prevents him from boasting or talking of that conduct which has gained him so much reputation; that is neither assuming, nor arrogant, nor vain; but that his whole demeanour is correlative with his countenance, both being marked by mildness and placidity, but at the same time accompanied by an expression of firmness and decision, which is indicative of a strong mind. Dr. Johnson, we believe, says, that, "boastfulness without merit is awkward, and merit without modesty is insolent; but modest merit has a double claim to attention." So that by this test and by this authority, we are warranted in using the utmost care in collecting the particulars of and regard which others entertain for, his character and conduct.

As an officer, we are informed that Sir Richard belongs to the high discipline school, but that his natural disposition has kept his actions from being marked by any cruel or arbitrary proceedings. That upon all occasions of sudden emergency, his genius and ability were proved by the ready expedients which appeared ever at his command; that he possessed solidity of judgement, united with dignity of deportment, but blended with so much genuine spirit, and so much of "the skill and fire of professional genius" that all his operations have been conducted with and distinguished by, foresight and dispatch. "He never met difficulties halfway, nor suffered his courage to be quelled by danger, nor the edge of his resolution to be blunted by opposition", but on the contrary, difficulties rather appeared to add a stimulus to his exertions and to increase his natural vigour, before which all opposition gave way.

Thomas Byam Martin says:

> *There was no man in the service for whom I had higher respect than Keats: he was once my Captain, and always my friend. His opinion was often taken upon professional matters, and relied upon with just confidence in the soundness of his judgement.*[766]

And:

> *Keats was not only my captain in the Southampton, but from that time to the present moment he has been my intimate and sincere friend.*[767]

This is just one example of Keats establishing firm friendships based upon mutual trust and respect with colleagues of all ranks that lasted a lifetime. According to the correspondent at *United Services Magazine*:

> *Sir Richard was a sincere Christian in his belief and practice, and both were characterised by an enlarged benevolence. He was a personable, smart, and strict officer; but, at the same time, a kind, intelligent, moral and generous man, with a shrewd and penetrating discrimination.*[768]

Many felt that penetrating discrimination. Keats was well experienced, ever attentive to what was happening on his ship and not easy to fob off nor easily fooled.

Others described him as:

> *One of the bravest, most correct and most skilful Admirals that ever graced the lists of our Navy. Sir Richard Keats possessed all the attributes of the polished gentleman; at the same time that greatness of mind, and the most unflinching integrity and honour, marked his every step through life.*[769]

He was "By no means ostentatious in the performance of his public duties, yet strictly maintained the dignity of his office",[770] exemplified by his polite yet firm stand in the face of tirades from the Dey of Algiers.

United Services Magazine questioned:

> *Whether the great nautical talents he possessed were ever called into full play; for ⟦they⟧ had no scruple in placing him at the very head of our naval phalanx, having proved himself second to none in gallantry, genius or talent.*[771]

As several writers point out, there would have been a greater opportunity for these abundant talents to be brought to bear had illness not intervened to restrict some of the assignments available to him or to call him home for rest. Those who speak of him off Cádiz, Toulon and in Newfoundland note that he lived with considerable pain, which on the one hand explains the curtailment of his activities and on the other, makes his perseverance and achievements all the more remarkable.

As commented in the opening paragraphs, Keats was at his peak at a time of intense and unmatched conflict at sea that epitomised the great Age of Sail. The British Navy grew from 16,000 men in 1792 to around 135,000 in some 600 ships by 1811.[772] It was populated by men of valour whose service and record warrant the highest possible recognition. That Keats stood out as among the best of those men in so many ways is a significant testament to the man. He proved himself as one of the few officers able to withstand the physical and psychological demands of command at sea and consequently one of the few upon whom the country came to rely to do so much.

In private life, it is said, that he is both generous and just; and though at first, he appears somewhat reserved, it becomes less apparent by degrees, and disappears on acquaintance, settling in a composed and uniform frame of mind, with an inoffensive but intelligent conversation.

Michael Lewis, editing Dillon's narrative says, "His habitual courtesy, urbanity, understanding and equability made him beloved among all his contemporaries."[773] This is despite Dillon disagreeing with the Admiral regarding the 'lost' convoy to Newfoundland. Dillon himself describes Keats as intelligent, and one from whom at all times, other than that disagreement, he had experienced kindness. Keats was no doubt an imposing figure to a young man on his first ship, in Dillon's case the 32-gun frigate, *Niger*, in the Channel fleet. He describes one of his first personal encounters thus:

The Captain desired me one day to attend him in his boat. This was a marked compliment; but whilst on our way to shore he asked me innumerable questions upon Navigation, Seamanship, and, last of all, upon my schooling in France. I was at my wits end to reply, fearing I should commit some blunder. But luckily, I escaped clear. On our return journey to the ship he desired me to dine with him. I felt the attention he conferred upon me. After dinner he renewed his enquiries; then, taking up a map, desired me to inform him of the situation of the place where I had been at school in France, whether to the northward or southward of Paris. This last question was to me a regular puzzle, and I hesitated: but he pressed me for an answer. I gave him one and, very fortunately it was correct. The captain was much pleased at all that passed between us; then, telling me I might retire, observed that I should make my way. 'You will get on. Goodbye.'[774]

Such an encounter was no doubt daunting for a young boy and led to the description of Keats as one who commanded awe and respect rather than affection.[775] Being the subject of affection as opposed to respect was probably not a requisite characteristic of a successful commander. Running a ship of war was not a popularity contest. A commander needed to have the confidence of his crew, and Keats most certainly had that. His crew would follow him to the end of the earth. Respect was the key – the crew's respect for their captain and equally important, the Captain's respect for his men.[776] Keats's eighty-eight instructions for the running of his ship required his men be shown respect and consideration – that they are called by name, that they are made comfortable, that when in the harbour they are granted as many liberties as possible. Various exchanges reported from onboard, including consulting his lieutenant and trusted seamen at critical times, show the value he placed on the opinions of good men.

Whilst he no doubt awed the young Dillon that relationship was characterised by mutual respect and the two got along fine. As Dillon left the ship, he reported:

> *Although Captain Keats was of a retiring disposition and rather serious, he expressed himself during this interview in a familiar and friendly term, which I acknowledge made a most gratifying impression upon my feelings, to be thus noticed by an officer who already stood well in his profession. I had, not long after my joining the Niger, formed a very high opinion of his character, and frequently mentioned to my messmates that our captain would one day rise to marked distinction in the navy. By the result I proved a true prophet, as at this day [1820] no one stands higher in reputation as a naval officer than he.*[777]

The writer of the memoirs and Dillon concur that Keats was reserved, and hence initially seemed to be lacking jocularity or warmth, but that this disappeared on acquaintance. Dillon's biographer went so far as to describe Keats as "lively and near great".[778] At the same time, it is clear he set high standards for himself and expected no less of others. He was stern and calm. He did not use the hyperbole of the more emotional Nelson. However, his praise when given, though not effervescent, carried weight, and was both well-meant and well received.

Keats's reservedness was never more apparent than when dining at St James's Palace at a function hosted by King George for Knights Grand Cross. The King honoured Keats with a toast. Obliged to reply to the great compliment, without notice, Keats was perplexed as to what to say in such company, never having been called upon to make a speech in like surrounds: "Every thought ran out of my mind, and I said to myself, 'What the devil can I do; at last a thought struck me – I will do what I have always done – my best'". He acknowledged His Majesty and the company assembled but "for the life of me I could not now relate a single word I said on the occasion". He nonetheless received hearty congratulations from many of those present, including the Duke of Wellington.[779]

The contributor to *The Shipwrecked Mariner* described Keats as:

Firm and decided, he was yet mild and placid. As an officer he was a high disciplinarian, without being cruel or arbitrary, solid in judgement, quick in perception, and dignified in deportment; he was both generous and just, and, in public as well as private life, was held in high estimation for his many great and noble qualities.

In Parliament he was described thus; "as great an officer, admiral, or seaman, as this country ever produced."[780]

We recall that Mrs Jordan agreed to commit her son, Henry FitzClarence, to a naval education under the care of Keats, even after the Duke had already lost one son at sea. While the taciturn Keats was held in awe by his young crew, he was more than capable of adjusting his practice and demeanour to the circumstances. Mrs Jordan wrote that his attention to the young crew in his flagship was more akin to the affectionate care of a father than a master. She offered far less flattering views of other officers. Her views are corroborated by the circumstances of Nelson similarly committing his young cousin, Charles Nelson, to Keats's care. His father had died when he was four, and Nelson himself died only a few months after Charles commenced in the *Superb*. Serving alongside Keats's nephew, William who commenced at the same time, he saw action at San Domingo, Copenhagen and the repatriation of Spanish troops. Keats remained his mentor for several years, until he passed his lieutenant's exams at which time, as Earl William Nelson commented, it was appropriate that he should then properly find his own way.[781]

Consistent with Mrs Jordan's observations, we see Keats encouraging the advancement of the boys on the voyage to Newfoundland. They attended school in the Admiral's cabin on the *Bellerophon*. Keats entered the class one day to say that the boy achieving the highest score in his exams would be granted a midshipman's rating. That boy was one Henderson who received a promising start to his naval career, becoming a Captain and later naval architect and ship builder.[782]

Though rigid in exacting from all a strict fulfilment of their duties, in doing so he expected no more than his own example be followed. As was recognised by Lieutenant Chappell, this was an example that tended greatly to encourage and expand the energies and application of those under his command.

As a leader he was said to be 'just and temperate in the use of punishment'. His approach to the discipline of offenders showed understanding and respect and an ability to apply a lightness of touch where required. He specifically required that those of good behaviour be identified and publicly applauded. As a result, it was his happy knack to have his ship an example to all others, by means of well-considered method. His stance in seeking recognition for his ship assisted in forming a respectful and productive attachment between his officers and the ship's company. He took these values with him to Newfoundland and Greenwich and achieved much as a result.

One might conclude from numerous reports and circumstances recorded later in his career that either the claims made in the Mutinies of 1797 were overstated or, with experience, Keats learned valuable lessons from those events, matured and mellowed as a leader. Both may be so. Perhaps resulting from his relatively humble beginnings, or as a result of his growth as a leader he became over time a thoughtful and generally understanding commander demonstrating an awareness of the needs and aspirations of his crew, and subsequently of the pensioners at Greenwich whose contribution he honoured.

On Keats replacing Admiral Pickmore off Cádiz in 1810, General Graham wrote he was:

...sure everything will be done here that skill and judgement in his profession can do with the means at his command – but I have my doubts of his being able to bear with the Spaniards tho I believe time has taken off something of the great natural warmth of his temper.[783]

Again, we see confidence in his capacities and a reference to shortness or irritability, but also that with experience he had mellowed over time. As Graham foresaw, he continued to hold a low regard for the extent to which he would be able to rely upon the training and resources of his Spanish allies.

Various commentators have described Keats as prickly, and there is no doubt he could be difficult when he thought his ship was not receiving its due. In March 1805, as the fleet prepared for its chase of Villeneuve, Keats required new hammocks for the men. Rear Admiral Murray, Captain of the Fleet, with limited supplies at his disposal, was not in Keats's view responding satisfactorily to his requests that the *Superb* be fully supplied. Murray took offence to Keats's persistent requests, so much so that Nelson had to intervene, writing a letter headed *Most Private*.[784]

That letter is instructive, both as to Keats's pursuit of necessary equipment for his men to the point of offending the Captain of the Fleet, and as to Nelson's leadership. He noted he felt most exceedingly at finding Keats's friend hurt at some conversation that had passed between them, about hammocks. He privately and gently asked Keats to reflect on his conversation and relieve Admiral Murray of the uneasiness the conversation had given him.

He went on to assure Keats that far from withholding supplies, Murray would stretch to any length which Keats could desire to provide for the wants and wishes of the *Superb*, well knowing that of the scanty supplies Keats would take no more than was absolutely necessary for present use. Whether on account of the value of her captain as an officer or the importance of preserving the Ship's company the *Superb*, he said ought to have every comfort the service would allow, well knowing Keats would husband the supplies in a most exemplary manner. Nelson was gently chiding on the one hand and flattering on the other. Supplies were deficient and no ship could be fully provided for. True to the value placed on their relationship Nelson intervened, sending across funds and arranging for the purchase of the additional hammocks requested to meet the needs of the *Superb*.

This exchange supports the various claims that Keats was not always an easy companion, but it is also clear that his continued undiplomatic prosecution of the request was motivated not by self-interest, but by the interests, comfort and well-being of his men. His attitude no doubt saw him in good stead there, as they were the clear beneficiaries of his persistence. It was possibly to the advantage of the unity of the ship's company that her captain is seen to occasionally stand up to the administrators. In this regard age did little to mellow him. As Governor of Newfoundland many years later he advised the Admiralty that the conflict with America necessitated his keeping ships at sea for long periods in bad weather protecting the fishing grounds and other trade. He hoped that the Admiralty would ensure the men were adequately provided for and ships "encouraged" to take their allotted extra woollen slops (woollen clothing mass produced under contract to the Navy) as in his experience "it has scarcely happened during my command that any ship has taken with her to Newfoundland this extra Provision of Slop Clothing from which a frequent necessity has arisen of purchasing at a loss and disadvantage to the seamen".[785] Empathy for the ordinary seaman, at war or indeed as a resident of the Royal Hospital is a continuing theme and goes a considerable way to explaining why he was held in high regard by such a wide cross-section of those with whom he dealt. The General Biographical Dictionary provided a succinct assessment saying he was "exemplary in all the relations of life".[786]

Despite being regarded as old school Keats also displayed a keen interest in innovation in a variety of areas. These ranged from tactics and strategy to inventions that would improve the safety or operation of a ship. When his body was no longer up to the rigours of months at sea he became engaged in fostering young officers such as Captain Phillips, the Deane brothers and others in the promotion of their inventions. We can speculate as to the various sailing clubs' balance of priorities between sailing for pleasure and fostering innovation for the improvement of the navy, but Keats's acceptance of positions as director, honorary member and vice patron of these organisations no doubt added weight and substance to the latter. Through the Board for Longitude and otherwise he displayed a keen interest in fostering improvements in navigation and exploration. In the case of Captain Ross's failure to return from his expedition in search of the northwest passage, his commitment extended to subscribing his own funds towards the rescue mission.

His enthusiasm for the temperance movement might mislead the casual observer to conclude he was against alcohol at all times, however, that was most certainly not the case. In his view there was a time and place for everything in moderation. An anecdote from a 'Captain Wetherall', published in the *Naval Chronicle*[787] provides an insight: Weatherall and the Admiral were seated in the cabin of a steam-packet, the Admiral telling a yarn on nautical affairs when two demur gentlemen came down and ordered two tumblers and plenty of water. They proceeded to dissolve some powders in the two tumblers before combining the solutions making a 'whishing' sound.

'What do you call that?', said the admiral. 'Soda-water, sir'. 'Soda-water!' exclaimed he: 'Were you tipsy last night?' 'Oh, sir' said the younger of the two, 'we never take spirits;' and, lengthening out a very sallow visage, 'total abstinence, sir; and this soda-water is also an excellent remedy for sea-sickness.' 'Sea-sickness, my man!' retorted the veteran admiral. 'Good heavens! How your wants are multiplied. A glass of cold brandy and water is certainly a much better remedy in my opinion.' 'We maintain,' said the elder gent, 'that ardent spirits are an abomination anywhere, in any circumstances.' 'Indeed!' replied Sir Richard. 'Hark'ee, my fine fellow! I have been surrounded by many ardent spirits in my time, and an abomination they were to the enemies of their country: but if we had mixed a tub of soda-water on each hatchway while taking the ships into action, you would have been drinking your trash perhaps in slavery, or, at best, under some other sovereignty. Temperance is necessary; and in his Majesty's Service was rigidly enforced, while sobriety and good conduct was promoted to honour; but total abstinence is perfect humbug. It would soon destroy our national energies. Sailors are neither monks nor hermits. It's all humbug! All humbug!'

As the writer continues, Keats saw no reason why the hard life of a seaman should not be occasionally relieved by cheerful, social, and rational enjoyment, or by those little luxuries which landsmen, "with all their sanctimonious talk", seek for themselves.

It is apparent Keats involved himself in a significant number and variety of causes he deemed worthy, whether through bodies such as the temperance society, the promotion of a school for the children of distressed officers, sailing clubs pursuing innovation in design, or promotion of the causes of young innovators or officers worthy of advancement. *The Times* reported, consistent with his reserved character and tendency to simply get things done with a minimum of fuss, that

his beneficence was extensive, and of that character which is rather felt than seen.[788]

One minor illustration of this and of his sense of a wider obligation to society was his subscription to the variety of charitable bodies already noted, such as the local agricultural society, that for the support of residents of the Scilly Isles, the establishment of the Royal Navy School, temperance societies, the floating episcopal church and others. He was for example an early subscriber and vice-president of the London Vaccine Institution established under the patronage of the City of London in 1806, funded wholly by subscription, with the object of providing small pox vaccinations, which had only recently been developed, free of charge throughout London.[789] Some years later he is to be found as one of the presidents (for which might be read 'subscribers') of the Royal Naval Annuitant Society, of which the Duke of Clarence was Patron. Its purpose was to raise sufficient capital to pay annuities to the widows and children of deceased members.[790] In a similar vein we see him as a Vice-President of the Royal Naval Charities Society under the presidency of Lord Gambier.

Whilst he was certainly "the seaman's seaman",[791] to describe him simply as a retired fighting captain would be to significantly underestimate the complexity of his character and scope of his interests, abilities, and contribution throughout, to again quote *The Times*; "a career of active usefulness both in public and private life."[792]

Civil and naval leaders such as the Duke of Clarence, Lord Nelson, Viscount Pellew, and Earl St. Vincent each had no shortage of candidates for friends, confidants or advisors. Yet, whatever his flaws, all put Keats at the forefront amongst their closest and most steady life-long companions, as one for whose character they had the highest regard, and whose counsel was most valued on account of the clear cut and good sense advice he provided on matters both private and professional.[793] Nelson was renowned for using hyperbole in praise of his favourite subordinates. St. Vincent was notoriously more difficult to impress. The two did not always agree, but on the question of the ability and qualities of Keats they were as one.

He was sometimes described as a protégé of the Duke, but in reality, their relationship was more complex. Initially it was Keats who was the more experienced and who took the young Duke 'under his wing' in terms of his naval education. The Duke thenceforth maintained a keen interest in Keats, transforming from an admiring subordinate at the relief of Gibraltar and the chase up the Delaware to a powerful patron in maturity, during which time he was able to use his influence to repay that early mentoring. If patronage is the correct description it is beyond doubt the relationship was founded upon a gratitude, respect, and warm and sustained mutual friendship of half a century. The Duke was often regarded as eccentric but as Blackwood's Edinburgh Magazine recorded "it will always be recalled to his credit how warmly he admired and helped Nelson, how he valued the merit of Keats, and how he encouraged the young Victoria".[794]

Although particularly active in the Governorship of Greenwich, being involved in all aspects of its administration as well as the establishment of the Naval Gallery, a library and the temperance society, Keats still found time for activities outside the Hospital, including the Board of Longitude, The Royal Sailing Society, Royal Thames Yacht Club, and the foundation of the British and Foreign Temperance Society. He was conditioned to be engaged and involved, and despite his illness, he continued that momentum in many aspects of life in London. Amongst other engagements he was a regular attendee at court levees and at dinners for the Knights Grand Cross of the Order of the Bath.

In stature Sir Richard is of the middle size, but stout and rather portly. He was married in 1820 to the eldest daughter of the late Francis Hurt Esq. of Alderwasley in Derbyshire, a very ancient and respectable family.

The Hurt family can be traced back to the early 1500's and for some two hundred years occupied Alderwasley Hall in the County of Derbyshire. Keats married Mary, daughter of Francis Hurt and Elizabeth Arkwright. Her brother, also Francis, had the good fortune to marry the daughter of a man said to be the wealthiest commoner in the country.

Noting that Keats was over sixty years of age at the time of his marriage on 27 June (at St Werburgh's church, in Derbyshire), we can speculate that he agreed with the sentiments of St. Vincent on the subject of marriage: "Sir you want to go on shore to get married, and then you won't be worth your salt."[795] On the other hand the Admiralty kept him so fully engaged on a variety of commissions away from home over so many years, he was barely at home long enough for the question of marriage to arise before his retirement. There were no children of this marriage.

Seemingly making up for lost time after forty years at sea, social life on shore was busy and varied. The couple enjoyed the full offerings of London circles, being frequent guests at the various society balls. *The Court Journal* reported on a Royal Artillery Ball at Woolwich:

> *The dresses of the Ladies were elegant in the extreme, and the display of jewellery superb. At one o'clock the supper rooms were thrown open, and displayed a profusion of every delicacy in season. The dancing was afterwards resumed and continued with great spirit till nearly six o'clock on the following morning. Amongst the ladies who shone the most conspicuously in the glittering throng were Lady Keats...*[796]

Lady Keats chaired the Ladies Benevolent Society whose object was to relieve distress among pensioners' wives in Greenwich and was otherwise involved in the various ceremonial occasions. She survived her husband by many years having moved to a substantial home on Brunswick Terrace, King's Road on the beach-front at Brighton from where she devoted considerable time to painting. She maintained some links to the navy and to the Hospital, at least to the extent of continuing for many years as a Patron of the Queen Adelaide Memorial Fund for relief of the orphan daughters of officers of the Royal Navy and Marines. The Greenwich Hospital continued to be made available for the fund's annual Grand Fancy Bazaar.

Keats's health declined severely late in 1833, to the extent newspapers were reporting the King had sent messengers by carriage expressly to Greenwich several times to know the exact state of his health, which the paper regretted to add was "still very seriously indisposed".[797] On 23 September 1833 he suffered what we now know to be a stroke which deprived him of the use of the right arm and right side, to the extent that when amending his will in December 1833 the Hospital surgeons Sir William Beatty and Sir Richard Dobson attended his bedside, took instructions, wrote them down and read them back to him for his attestation. He was unable to sign in his own hand and the codicil was duly attested to by the witnesses and in time probate granted accordingly.[798]

Historical Memoirs of
Admiral Sir Richard Goodwin Keats, GCB

Funeral

Sir Richard died of a paralytic stroke on 5 April 1834, aged 77, and was buried at Greenwich Hospital with full military honours on Saturday 12 April. It had been Lady Keats's wish that the funeral be a strictly private ceremony, but the King had other plans and wished his esteem and debt of gratitude be demonstrated by the accompaniment of the pomp and dignity of full naval and military ceremonial observance to be attended by members of the King's household and Lords of the Admiralty in full uniform. As a consequence, the event was scheduled for the following Saturday and from early in the morning the Greenwich township was "much thronged" as thousands of spectators descended on the town anxious to witness the imposing ceremony.[799]

His funeral was attended by the Lords of the Admiralty including the First Lord, Lord Auckland, and his predecessor, Sir James Graham together with First Secretary of the Board, Captain Elliot. Senior officers of the service included the Vice-Admiral of the United Kingdom, Sir George Martin; Rear Admiral of the United Kingdom, The Hon. Sir Robert Stopford, and the senior officer or professional head of the Royal Marines, Deputy Adjutant-General Colonel Sir John Savage.

In conformance with the King's wishes naval officers of the King's Household in attendance included: Principal Aide-de-Camp, Admiral Lord Beauclerk, and Aides-de-Camp; the Lords of the Bed Chamber: Captain Lord Adolphus FitzClarence (William's third son and Captain of the Royal Yacht), Rear Admiral James O'Brien (who had served as a midshipman on the *Andromeda* with Keats) and Captain Lord Byron and the Grooms of the Bed Chamber. Master of the Robes, Admiral Sir George Seymour (who had been on the *Donegal* in the Mediterranean and the *Northumberland* at San Domingo) and third Naval Lord Admiral Sir Charles Rowley were in attendance together with Admiral Lord Radstock, a former Governor of Newfoundland. All officers were in full dress uniform displaying the crosses of their orders and medals. On some reports the King himself was present,[800] however that would have been contrary to protocol and those reports are mistaken. There is no such mention in more contemporaneous reports,[801] or on an annotated copy of the Order of Procession preserved in the papers of Admiral Seymour.[802]

The coffin was borne by pensioners who had served with Keats in the *Superb*, and the pall by six admirals: Sir William Hotham, Sir Francis Laforey, Hon Sir Robert Stopford, Frank Sotheron, Sir Charles Hamilton and Sir George Martin, making for what Admiral Hotham described as a very solemn and imposing ceremony. Some seventeen admirals were in attendance. Together with two bands, a battalion of Royal Marines, the Governor's Guard all accompanied by cannon fire echoing from the summit of One Tree Hill, they made for an impressive display of naval pageantry.

Having by letter of 9 April confirmed to Admiral Byam Martin his attendance and availability to carry the pall, Admiral Saumarez was conspicuously absent, being sworn in as an Elder at Trinity House. The writers in the *London Observer* pointedly noted Sir James Graham had found himself able to attend both events.[803] Saumarez's absence earned him a public admonition from the King at his next appearance at Court on 7 May, when the King mentioned how much he owed to Keats above all others, including Saumarez, such as to reduce Saumarez, always somewhat sensitive regarding Keats, to tears.[804]

The funeral procession was led by boys of the Hospital School and 100 pensioners, followed by twelve crew of the Governor's Barge, sixteen boatswains, and the Admiral's colours between regulating boatswains. They preceded the drum and fife band; warders, wardens, two and two; and the men who sailed with him in the *Superb*, two and two. Then followed the Admiral's flag and the Governor's Guard with halberts covered. They were followed by the Band of the Royal Marines, Inspecting Boatswains, visitors, the heads of the Hospital Schools, Hospital surgeon, Sir William Beatty and fleet physician, Sir Richard Dobson, junior officers, Commissioners of the Hospital, flag officers, the Lieutenant Governor, Rear Admiral Sir Jahleel Brenton (from the *Caesar*), senior flag officers, King's Aide-de-Camp, and the Lords of the Admiralty.

The coffin was followed by the chief mourners, the Admiral's nephews, Captain William Keats and Reverend Richard Keats, recently presented by King William to the living at Northfleet, Gravesend, and other mourners including of course his widow, Lady Mary. They were followed by the Civil Officers of the Hospital, visitors, boatswains and men who sailed with Keats in the *Milford, Boadicea, Galatea* and *Niger*. The procession concluded with another 100 pensioners and boys from the Hospital School. The course of the procession was marked by a battalion of 400 marines in single file, with arms reversed. The whole of the great square was lined by pensioners and the upper quadrangle, in addition to lines of pensioners, was skirted by 100 nurses and 200 girls. Other officers in attendance who had served with Keats included Captains Dillon, Fellowes, and Dundas, now comptroller of the Navy, Rear Admiral J. C. White, as well as Keats's successor as Governor, Rear-Admiral Sir Thomas Hardy.

A little before three o'clock, the procession headed by the band of the Royal Marines formed in the main quadrangle, opposite the Governor's House, and on a signal being hoisted from the top of the house, a party of artillery with field pieces stationed on One Tree Hill (site of the Observatory) raised a flag to half-mast and commenced proceedings firing minute guns which echoed across Greenwich and the Thames. The firing paused as the body entered the chapel and resumed on the reforming of the procession continuing until they reached the mausoleum of the Hospital.[805] Owing to an unwillingness to distress the feelings of Lady Keats more than was unavoidable the ceremony dispensed with the usual discharge of guns over the grave.

The King commissioned a bust by Sir Francis Chantry to the value of some £500 which to this day sits to the left inside the entrance to the Chapel. It was the King's custom to attended divine service in the Chapel Royal at Greenwich if the anniversary of a significant battle should fall on a Sunday. Accordingly, the anniversary of Admiral Duncan's victory off Camperdown falling on Sunday 11 October 1835 the King in full naval uniform accompanied by Queen Adelaide and Prince George of Cambridge attended Greenwich, to inspect and converse with the pensioners, to attend divine service in the Chapel and oversee the first public exhibition of the completed bust of Keats in the chapel.[806]

Busts of Thomas Hardy by Behnes on the left of picture and of Richard Keats, by Chantry, commissioned by King William on the right, sitting inside the entry to the Royal Chapel, Greenwich Hospital.

A TREASURE TO THE SERVICE

The inscription reads:

> THIS MARBLE IS ERECTED BY
> KING WILLIAM THE FOURTH
> TO THE MEMORY OF
> ADMIRAL SIR RICHARD GOODWIN KEATS, G.C.B.
> GOVERNOR OF THIS HOSPITAL
> WHO WAS HIS MAJESTY'S SHIPMATE AND WATCHMATE
> ON BOARD THE PRINCE GEORGE OF 110 GUNS[15]
> IN WHICH THE ADMIRAL SERVED AS LIEUTENANT,
> AND THE KING AS MIDSHIPMAN,
> FROM JUNE, 1779, TO NOVEMBER 1781.
> IN COMMEMORATING
> THIS EARLY PERIOD OF THEIR RESPECTIVE CAREERS
> THE KING DESIRES ALSO TO RECORD HIS ESTEEM
> FOR THE EXEMPLARY CHARACTER OF A FRIEND,
> AND HIS GRATEFUL SENSE
> OF THE VALUABLE SERVICES RENDERED TO HIS COUNTRY
> BY A HIGHLY DISTINGUISHED AND GALLANT OFFICER
> DIED APRIL 5, 1834, AGED 77 YEARS.

The chapel itself is a neo-classical masterpiece, featuring rich plasterwork and decoration representing one of the finest eighteenth-century interiors still in existence.

The pensioners had already commissioned another bust of the Admiral from the sculptor Behnes, in acknowledgement of Keats's role in improving conditions and the comfort of the pensioners, and particularly the introduction of regulations to improve the system of diet.

The 1842 *Guide Book to the Naval Gallery*[807] describes this as being in the anteroom to the Council Room, which adjoins the Governor's apartment (item 137), and more accurately as having been presented by his officers. Hatchway's 1838 description differs saying, "At the upper end of the West dining hall is a cast from a correctly executed marble bust of the late governor, Admiral Sir

---

15 The Prince George was constructed with 90 guns, later increased to 98 with the addition of 8 x 12-pounders on the quarter deck.

Richard Keats, by Behnes". This work describes the improvements to the Hospital implemented by the Admiral.[808]

Newell's history of the Hospital says this bust was placed in the senior officers' mess room as a "Heartfelt acknowledgement by the officers of the Hospital of his introduction of an improved system of victualling for the Pensioners".[809] Its present whereabouts is unclear.

It was inscribed:

Admiral
Sir Richard Goodwin Keats, G.C.B.
Governor of Greenwich Hospital
A.D. M,DCC,XXXII.[810]

A Testimonial of personal respect,
from the Military and Civil Officers
of the Hospital,
and
in commemoration
of the benevolence that devised,
and zeal that accomplished,
the improved system of victualling
the Pensioners
Mi Patria es mi Norte

Keats was buried in the Hospital Mausoleum, Maze Hill, which is to the left of the hospital buildings when viewed from the Thames. Seamen were generally buried in the Hospital burial ground in Romney Road. Due to the construction of the London and Greenwich railway, those buried there were disinterred and reburied at East Greenwich Pleasurance in Chevening Road, Greenwich. A memorial erected by the Lords Commissioners of the Admiralty in 1892 marks the former Devonport burial ground in Romney Road, to the right of the current museum. The Governors, including Keats, are specifically named on the memorial.

A further memorial can be found on the Spanish Mediterranean island of Mallorca. The Marquis de la Romana was from that island. On his death in 1811 his body was returned to

Mallorca, and the Cortes voted a monument which can be found on the east wall of one of the northern side chapels in the Cathedral. The figure of the marquis rests on a tomb, all in white marble. Above is Wellington, and below is a bas-relief depicting both Romana and Keats superintending the embarkation of Spanish troops and baggage at Nyborg, in the island of Funen.[811]

Keats's estate was substantial. After making cash investment bequests, along with his plate and other possessions to his widow, Lady Mary, he provided smaller bequests to his sisters Martha, Mary, Ann, and Silvester along with some close friends including his long-time secretary Philip Le Geyt, his brother-in-law Francis Hurt, and friend Captain of the Royal Marines, Zachary Bayly. Servants who had been in his employ for an extended period were not forgotten. The properties were divided among his nephews. Captain William Keats was bequeathed the Porthill estate and Rev. Richard Keats the properties Irishcombe, Blagrove, Heath and Parkham.

Monument erected at the former burial ground, Royal Hospital, Greenwich. Stephen C Dickson Creative Commons CCO Licence.

**Historical Memoirs of
Admiral Sir Richard Goodwin Keats, GCB**

Conclusion

A career in the navy was the perfect choice for Keats. His achievements provide a clear illustration that advancement could come by demonstrating merit at sea without having to rely upon money or influence on shore for promotion, as was so much the case in the army. Such connections as he did acquire were done so by the strictest attention to his duty. It was, of course, a happy circumstance that one of the first he should impress was the young Prince William. He deservedly earned his friendship and respect which opened up opportunities throughout his career, but more particularly following his retirement from service at sea.

His early experience on small craft and in joint operations provided an excellent circumstance for the development of fine ship-handling and navigational skills, as well as the planning, coordination and execution of operations involving various arms of the services which were to become the hallmark of his achievements as a captain and flag officer in years to come as the wars evolved to emphasise amphibious operations in place of purely maritime undertakings.

His rise in rank and reputation was the reward and effect of his talent and application, by which he became a master of his profession, with an attention to detail, devotion to duty and an eagerness to co-operate in pursuit of the common good.

Keats was highly regarded by those who came to know him well: William, St. Vincent, Nelson, Pellew, Dillon, Strachan, Martin.... The list goes on. Given his natural reservedness, the key was to know him well. Earl St. Vincent had a dim view of some of his senior officers but saw in Keats a great seaman, bounding in resources. His biographer noted that wherever you saw Keats, whether as a captain of a frigate, or of a ship of the line, or commanding a squadron, he was sure to distinguish himself.[812] Pellew, summed up their relationship thus: "with such a man you have everything to expect and nothing to fear".[813]

His single-handed attack upon the combined fleet at Algeciras deservedly became legendary. As demonstrated then and again in laying the *Superb* up against the largest warship afloat in leading the fleet at San Domingo he exhibited an acute understanding of strategy, and he had the seamanship and fortitude to react accordingly, confident of the support of a well-trained and disciplined crew.

The chases of the enemy up the Delaware, through the Passage Du Raz, onto the shoals of Arcachon, and through the Baltic and the Scheldts are each striking examples of confidence and skill in both himself and his ship's company, which justifiably led to his being recognised as one of, if not the, finest seamen of his time.[814] Where St. Vincent had identified a distinction between courage in the face of the enemy and the courage to face rocks and shoals, there is no doubt Keats was conspicuously possessed of both.

In no small part, this confidence was borne out of training. His eighty-eight paragraphs of standing orders indicate he ran a tight ship. He was one of the few to require regular and specific gunnery practice. The accuracy and intensity of the *Superb's* gunnery, capable of accurately discharging three broadsides within five minutes, combined with the skills of her captain, saw them devastatingly effective in combat with minimal loss and without the need to risk boarding parties in hand-to-hand combat. He is consistently reported to be energetic. He was also an exceptional administrator with an attention to detail and staff-work rarely seen at the time. All these talents became well known and respected throughout the navy.

Without doubting his obvious talent, courage, and devotion to duty, and acknowledging that difficulties seemed only to increase his exertions and determination to achieve an objective the question remains as to whether as a result of an inherent anxiety he tended to question his own actions to an unnecessary degree and whether he felt excessively the burden of responsibility in the absence of a clear objective from a higher authority.[815]

Keats lived up to his own Ship's Instruction No. 5: keeping constant and steady attention to whatever is carrying on and would not suffer the most trifling thing to be done with indifference. Every task was taken seriously. He would not stand for things to be done carelessly or casually. This may have led to a view that he was stern, lacking in humour, and not always easy to get on with. On the other hand, everyone knew where they stood and what was expected and this constancy earned respect, and at times of need, no doubt saved lives. There are numerous examples of his conduct, significant and insignificant, earning him the respect of his crew, contemporaries, and the public. Whether it be giving full attention to the report of a junior officer in the Governor's residence in the middle of the night, still in his dressing-gown; transferring his flag to a small sloop to ensure close supervision of all the necessary details at Nyborg; personally leading a gun-boat assault at Cádiz; or leading his ship in the destruction of vastly superior forces, he was most certainly due and accorded respect.

In character, the *United Services Magazine* described Keats as a smart and strict officer, but at the same time a kind, intelligent, moral and generous man, having a shrewd and penetrating discrimination.[816] A ship's boy described him as cool, firm and collected. From afar, this may well have been tinged with awe rather than affection, but there is no shortage of evidence of affection from those who overcame that initial reservedness.

Dillon's biographer says, "that of all the great naval names of the period, none stand higher than that of Keats", who was "beloved among all his contemporaries."[817] His long term Lieutenant and later Captain of the *Superb*, Samuel Jackson, named his first child Charles Keats Jackson, indicating both respect and affection from the subordinate who knew him best.[818] There are multiple reports of his barge being cheered by the men of any ship in port as he passed, which indicates he was well known, respected and, at the very least, warmly regarded, even if as a senior officer.

It became obvious that his talents were not limited to warfare. At various times he was called upon to act as a diplomat, albeit with the backing of a warship, and invariably acquitted himself with distinction finding a suitable balance between strength and prudence, standing firm where called for and allowing concessions where appropriate. When Nelson sent him and the *Superb* to negotiate with the Dey of Algiers, his conduct received the decided approval of his superiors. Years later, his arrangements for the repatriation of a whole division of Spanish troops simultaneously ruined Bernadotte's army and invigorated the fight for independence on the peninsular, earning him his Order of the Bath. He displayed great diplomatic skills in liaising with Sweden and both of these examples held him in good stead when later appointed to support the British and Spanish armies at the siege of Cádiz. He could be described as the complete officer.

The exercise of command in the Baltic and off Cádiz, in particular, showed that Keats justifiably earned a reputation as one who could adapt readily to changing circumstances.[819] Various episodes do, however, show that the *Naval and Military Remembrancer* was quite perceptive in describing him as being 'most correct'. He was at all times determined to follow the expected process and to stay within the bounds of his orders without going on any frolic of his own.

Early in his career, when in the Channel Fleet under Bridport in August 1799 and tasked with watching Brest, he was on one occasion faced with an escaping enemy and insufficient force of his own to arrest their progress. He remained watching the port in the *Boadicea*, tasked *Uranie* with shadowing the squadron, and sent the cutter, *Lurcher*, to advise his admiral, saying: "In so doing I trust I have acted, if not to the letter, to the spirit of my orders and to the satisfaction of your lordship."[820] His express orders had been to stay on station keeping watch. On the other hand, it was vital to understand the whereabouts of a departed squadron. He could not do both satisfactorily because the *Diamond*, *Clyde*, *Fowey* and *Mondovi*, which had been promised to him, had been removed by Lord Keith. He shows anxiety to be seen to be faithfully following his specific orders, at the same time acutely aware of the greater objective. He need not have worried. Bridport was fulsomely supportive, writing to the Admiralty that he was sorry to find that Lord Keith had removed some of the vessels specifically placed under Keats's command, for had he not done so it was probable Keats could have been in a position to prevent the French squadron from putting to sea.[821]

Keats retained this element of correctness his whole career and was intolerant of those who did otherwise. His desire to precisely follow orders was quite proper and soundly based. It was, after all, vital that captains could be relied upon to follow orders and place their ships where their commanders expect them to be. Placing and moving its fleets on the world's chessboard was a matter for the Admiralty. It emerged later in his career that benefits might flow if senior officers of Keats's experience and capability felt a little less restricted while remaining within acceptable boundaries.

Keats could have been well advised to pay more regard to his instincts on occasion. His continuing anxiety in this regard is illustrated from his own hand when faced with the conflict between Admiralty orders to send the *Bulwark* home or send her to Peru as requested by his allies. He could have had more confidence in the Admiralty to support his exercise of discretion in departing from orders which, if followed to the letter, would result in an unsatisfactory outcome. On that occasion, he did compromise his orders, and the Admiralty subsequently gave its approval to his decision. In the event, he had little to fear.

In what has been described as "the fluid world of orders, expectation, honour and duty",[822] Keats felt more constrained to adhere to a strict interpretation of orders, where others, such as Nelson, felt less so. Most officers who strayed from orders were, at best, recipients of the Admiralty's disapproval, and, at worst, found themselves explaining their actions to a court martial. Nelson was the exception to the rule. Whereas he did the unexpected, it might be said of Keats that he did the expected, but did it exceptionally well.

Keats excelled when given clear instructions as to an objective and was fearless in its execution when working with a commander-in-chief whom he knew well and trusted. In turn, commanders-in-chief such as Nelson and Pellew provided leadership based on fellowship and trust that brought out the best in Keats. He responded equally well to the less consultative command and obey model of St. Vincent's leadership. The common elements were a no-nonsense approach and mutual respect and trust.

He did not suffer fools. He required his own high standards and work ethic to be met by those serving under him. As one of his officers put it, the only sure way to his favour was to demonstrate the same enthusiastic exertion which he manifested himself upon every occasion. [823]

He was, in the words of Captain Dillon, 'rarely jocose'.[824] Nevertheless, being part of a well-drilled crew, producing what was described as 'cool and determined fire,'[825] capable of silencing any enemy under an exceptionally capable seaman, sharing in prizes, and coming through engagements unscathed was an attractive proposition. There was no shortage of men and officers alike keen to serve with him.

Despite the formality alluded to, he was one of the more enlightened officers when it came to the granting of privileges, such as shore leave and the attention of women in port. Both were used by him in accordance with the ships instructions as an incentive for good performance. Whilst regarded as old-school on the question of discipline, it also becomes clear he had a deal of empathy for his men and exercised compassion and understanding when required.

He showed great loyalty to his men and ship, and that was reciprocated. This has led some analysts to claim he was sensitive to any lack of appreciation of the role of his ship. It can equally be contended that he was advocating for the men who had put their lives at risk in the encounters and, as their leader, required that they (and he) receive appropriate acknowledgement. Advancement was dependent upon such recognition. Writing to the Admiralty expressing sorrow and concern at being placed beneath a junior appointed captain of the fleet was a bold move illustrating that he was sensitive to any lack of recognition and departure from the proper order. The fact that letter was co-signed by two other eminent senior captains, Hood and Stopford, and the support offered by others, suggests this sensitivity was neither unusual nor out of place.

Sailing home from the Mediterranean in agony, unable to recover from his recurring ailments and unable to continue at sea, was an unsatisfactory and inappropriate end to a glittering career of active service. It was a stark contrast to his return to port on other occasions, most notably to Gibraltar after the battle of Algeciras. His ailment may explain his occasional irritability and simultaneously draw admiration for his perseverance and sense of duty. He had considerable sympathy in the navy at a personal level, as well as a realisation they were to lose one of their most experienced and valuable officers. It was hoped he might recover and return to sea. The Governorship of Newfoundland was bestowed and accepted on that basis. But it was not to be. In the circumstances, it is little wonder the *United Services Magazine* questioned whether, as a result of this premature curtailment, the great nautical talents he possessed were ever called into full play.

The memoirs pay little regard to his postings following his return to shore. Other material makes clear that whilst these postings were bestowed, in part at least, due to the patronage of the Duke of Clarence, and as rewards for exemplary service to the country, Keats did not treat these offices as a sinecure of retirement. He was energetic in the governance of Newfoundland. During the War of 1812 it was noted his patient assiduity, excellent precautions, and unremitting vigilance in the disposition of his naval force ensured that the shores of Newfoundland were protected and could be navigated in security.[826]

On commencing at the Royal Hospital at Greenwich Keats applied his customary energy to raising standards for the pensioners. He brought the full weight of his reputation and service – he then being one of the most influential survivors of the French Wars – to representing their cause to the Admiralty, Parliament, and the public at large. The raising of funds by the pensioners for the erection of a bust in his honour in the Hospital dining hall in recognition of the improvements effected for their benefit during his term says as much, or more, about his character – and the regard in which he was held by those who served – than does the funding by the King of a similar bust by Chantry, which stands in the Hospital Chapel to this day.

He had few equals as an officer and undertook his tasks with the most unflinching integrity and honour. He showed an unmatched exertion and attention to detail, in whatever duty was assigned, and he expected to see the same in those around him.

When his body was no longer able to take the punishment of months at sea, his mind was still agile and his areas of interest expanded. He made significant contributions across a wide compass in pursuit of improvements to the benefit of the navy, those who had served, and those continuing to do so.

The memoirs record many episodes in support of the opinion that he was the finest seaman of his time, and that he made a significant contribution to the prosecution of the sea wars and defeat of Napoleon's continental system. That he is not more widely recognised probably stems from a confluence of factors. The traditional concentration upon Nelson, which pushes even his closest associates into his shadow is no doubt one. The *Naval Chronicle* was lamenting this focus to the detriment of others of equal abilities and gallantry even before his heroic triumph and death at Trafalgar further elevated his status.[827] The curtailment of Keats's career by illness is another factor together with the assessment that his career was built up consistently by countless minor excellencies, rather than by any one achievement of transcendent brilliance.[828]

Richard Goodwin Keats was
"A Treasure to the Service".

Appendix 1

Career by rank, promotions and honours

Month	Year	Event	Ship (s)	Theatre / Events
16 January	1757	Born		Chalton in Hampshire
October	1770	Enlisted	Bellona, Yarmouth, Cambridge	Portsea, Plymouth
	1771		Captain, Halifax	North American Station
May	1773	Midshipman	Kingfisher, Mercury,	
December	1776		Romney	
February	1777	Lieutenant	Ramillies,	The Downs
	1778		Prince George	Battle of Ushant
January	1780			Moonlight Battle
	1781		Lion	North American Station
January	1782	Commander	Rhinoceros, Bonetta	Capture of Aigle
	1785-88		Ashore, France	
June	1788		Andromeda; (Companion to Prince William)	
June	1789	Post-Captain	Royal George	
September	1789		Southampton	The Channel, Gibraltar
August	1791		Niger	
September	1792			Bounty Court Martial
April	1793		London	Channel Fleet
March	1794		Galatea	Western Frigate Squadron
				Capture of Revolutionnaire
June	1795			Action off Isle de Groix
March	1796			Action off Point Du Raz
August	1796			Destruction of Andromaque
June	1797		Boadicea	Blockade of Brest,

July	1799			Action off Aix Roads
March	1801-09		Superb	Cádiz; Second Battle of Algeciras
	1803-04			Mediterranean Fleet
				Negotiations with Algiers
	1805			Pursuit of Villeneuve
November	1805	Colonel of Marines		Cádiz
February	1806			Battle of San Domingo
				Bay of Biscay
March	1807	Commodore	Ganges, Superb	Expedition to Copenhagen
				Second Battle of Copenhagen
October	1807	Rear Admiral	Superb	The Baltic
April	1808		Mars	The Baltic
August/October	1808	Knight Companion of the Most Honourable Order of the Bath	Superb	Repatriation of Spanish troops
October	1809	Rear Admiral, White	Superb (Salsette, Sabrina)	Expedition to the Scheldts
July	1810	Rear Admiral, Red	Implacable, Milford	Relief of Cádiz
				Battle of Barrosa
August	1811	Vice Admiral, Blue	Hibernia	Mediterranean
February	1813	Governor of Newfoundland	Bellerophon	CIC Newfoundland
January	1815	Knight Grand Cross of the Most Honourable Military Order of the Bath		
March	1815		Salisbury	
June	1815	Vice Admiral, White		
	1816			At home, Devon
May	1818	Major General of Marines		
May	1818	Commissioner Board of Longitude		
August	1819	Vice Admiral, Red		
October	1821	Governor of the Royal Hospital Greenwich		Royal Hospital Greenwich
May	1825	Admiral of the Blue		
July	1830	Admiral of the White		
7 April	1834	Died		Royal Hospital Greenwich

HMS Keats, Captain Class Frigate K482, 1943, constructed in the United States and provided to Great Britain under the 'lend-lease' programme, Second World War.

Appendix II

Captains Orders for HMS Superb

CAPTAIN'S ORDERS FOR H.M.S. *SUPERB*, 1803-4

ADDITIONAL ORDERS and REGULATIONS
FOR THE GOVERNMENT
OF HIS MAJESTY'S SHIP *SUPERB*
R. G. KEATS, Esq., CAPTAIN

GENERAL ORDERS

1. The Officers, Warrant and Petty Officers of His Majesty's Ship under my Command are required to conform to the established Rules of the Navy relative to appearing in Uniform. Round Hats, Blue Jackets with Blue, White or nankeen Trousers or Pantaloons are allowed to be worn at Sea and occasionally in Harbour, and those Petty Officers who walk the Quarter Deck are reminded that the most acceptable Dresses they can appear in are blue with white Waistcoats and breeches or jackets and Trousers as above specified.
2. Officers are required to exact upon all occasions of Duty from the Warrant and Petty Officers, and they also from their Inferiors, the most ready unequivocal and respectful compliance with their Orders; and it is expected of all Inferiors that they do not neglect any exterior Mark of respect whenever they address or are addressed by a superior upon Duty.
3. Officers of every Denomination are expected when the duty requires them at Quarters or their different Stations, to be particularly attentive to preserve silence amongst the Men, and see that the orders issued from the Quarter Deck are executed with celerity and without any noise and Confusion.

4. It is my particular request that Officers will upon all occasions, encourage and pointedly distinguish those men that are particularly cleanly, alert, and obedient, from those of different Characters in order the deserving may see their Merits are not disregarded, as well as the undeserving be made sensible of the Vigilance of the Officers and the advantage resulting from good and respectable Conduct.
5. Discipline (as it respects Alertness) can only be preserved by a constant and steady attention to whatever is carrying on. It is requested the Officers of the Ship will not suffer the most trifling thing under them to be executed with Indifference.
6. Blasphemy, Profaneness and all species of obscenity or immorality are peremptorily forbid; and it is hoped the officers of every denomination will upon all occasions Discountenance and Discourage such disorderly and despicable practices amongst the Men.
7. The Commanding Officer is directed to avoid as much as possible the calling of all Hands, but when the service to be performed cannot be executed by the Watch and Idlers, they are required to be very particular that no men remain, of their department below.
8. The Officers and Petty officers are required to make themselves personally acquainted with the Ships Company in order to their being able to address them by their own names whenever they have occasion to call them aloft or elsewhere.
9. As permission to go on shore will be occasionally granted by the Captain or Commanding Officer, it is to be understood that those indulgences are to be proportioned to the general Character, Sobriety, and punctuality of the men who may apply.
10. In Port, women will be permitted to come onboard, but this indulgence is to be granted (as indeed are all others) in proportion to the merits of the Men who require them, and upon their being accountable for the conduct of the Women with them.
11. The commanding Officer in Port will therefore permit such men to have Women onboard as he may choose; and he will direct the Master at Arms to keep a list agreeable to the following form; which he will carry to the Commanding officer every morning for his Inspection.

Women's Names	With Whom	Married Or single	When rec'd Onboard	Conduct

12. Every Seaman belonging to the Ship is expected to supply himself with the following Lists of Clothes; viz:

Jackets	Waistcoat	Trousers	Trousers	Shirts	Pair	Hats	Pair	Pair
	Inside Jacket	Blue	White		Stockings	Cap	Shoes	Drawers
3	2	2	2	4	3	1 Hat or1 Hat & 1 Cap	2	2

In addition to the List of Clothes above named, the Ships Company are expected to supply themselves with a white outside Jacket and Waistcoat to be worn occasionally in Summer or a warm climate with long white Trousers.

13. Whenever all Hands are called no person is to go below from his station upon pretence of the work being finished before the People are piped down.
14. The Captains of the Forecastle, Tops, Afterguard, and Waist having command over the Men at those stations, are expected to keep them clear & clean, the Ropes &c neatly coiled, the Captains of the Starboard Watches are considered as particularly responsible for the Starb'd side in Harbour. The Captains of the Larboard Watches for the Larboard side and the Captains of the Third Watches or auxiliary Captains are to be responsible in the absence or illness of either of the others for their stations.
15. Three Lieutenants only can be absent from the Ship on leave, but not the first and second at the same time.
16. At sea and in Harbour a Commissioned Officer is to have charge of the Watch.
17. The first lieutenant is not to keep Watch. The Junior Lieutenants are to be at four Watches.
18. The Mates and Midshipmen are to be at Three Watches at sea and in Port. One third of which may be absent on leave at a time.
19. In a Road, leave is not to be understood to extend to the night unless particularly required, and whether in a Port or a Road, no leave (unless particularly specified) is to authorise absence from the Muster on Sunday.
20. The Keys of the Magazine &c. warrant Officers store rooms are to be kept in the possession of the first Lieutenant. The former is never to be opened without the Captain's leave, nor the storerooms without the knowledge of the first Lieutenant and Officer of the Watch, when a Midshipman is to attend at the storeroom and return the Keys.
21. The Keys of the Steward room are also to be kept by the First or senior Lieutenant, they may be delivered to the Purser from 7 to 10 in the morning, and from 4 to 7 in the afternoon for the purpose of obtaining Provisions.
22. The Keys of the after Hold, Spirit, & Fish room are to be kept in the Master's care, but are not to be opened without the first Lieutenant's permission; & at all such times the Master is to take care that one of his Mates attend who is to be the last Person in the Hold or Room, in order that no accidents may arise from Lights, and that they may be carefully lock'd afterwards.
23. Between the setting and relieving of the Watch in Port and at least twice a Watch at Sea a Mate or careful Midshipman, besides the Master at Arms and Corporals, are to visit the between

Decks, After and Fore Cockpits, and cable Tiers, and to report to the Officer of the Watch if any lights have been discovered, or Men seen out of their Beds, and in improper places. After setting of the Watch great attention is expected from Officers of all ranks not to disturb the tranquillity of the Ship.

24. The Decks are to be washed in the morning Watch, when the Gun Carriages, Port Cells, Quick work, Head, and Head Rails, Chains, sides &c. &c. are to be washed and great care taken that the Waterways are dried. In Port the necessary Boats are to be hoisted either before or after the washing of Decks as circumstances of Weather and Duty may make requisite; Yards neatly squared, Ropes hauled taut, and Hammocks stowed to admit of piping to Breakfast precisely at 8 o'clock.

25. In like manner great care is to be had that the Duty of the Service be either completed or suspended at 7 bells, in order that the Decks may be swept and nothing prevent piping to dinner at 12 o'clock.

26. The first Lieutenant or commanding Officer whether at Sea or in Harbour is to visit the Ship throughout every Forenoon to see that the Tiers, Cockpits, Wings, Storerooms, passages, &c &c are cleaned, Clear and in proper condition and report is to be made to the Captain when ready for his Visitation.

27. The between Decks are to be cleaned every Forenoon, to be washed once a week, and fires shall be made over which Sentinels are to be placed and the People not permitted below until the decks are dry. The Cockpit is to be cleaned whenever the Between Decks is, as are all Ladders, Gratings, Port Cells, Coamings, Hatchways, store Rooms, and Magazine Passages, and Wings &c.

28. The Officers are requested to see that the Men do not work in their best Clothes and when Employed washing Decks they are desired to make them pull off their shoes & stockings and tuck their trousers up.

29. Every Day after Dinner and just before the Hammocks are piped down in the Afternoon the Decks are to be swept.

30. The Cockpit and Cable Tiers are to be visited occasionally by the Master at Arms & Corporals during Day, and once, at least, each Watch by a Midshipman who are to report any deviation from the general Orders and if any Lights are discovered out of Lanthorns or improper Persons found there.

31. Warrant and Petty Officers Lights to be put out at 9 o'clock at sea – and at 10 in Port.

32. No lights on any Account whether at Sea or in Harbour, are to be allowed to remain unattended in any Berth or Cabin, and none but in Lanthorns are to be allowed in the Tiers.
33. No Smoking Tobacco is allowed but in the established place under the Forecastle.
34. The Commanding Officer and Officer of the watch will remember that spirits are always directed to be drawn off upon Deck and never by Candle Light.
35. The Main Deck is constantly to be kept as clear as possible, and no Chests, Empty Casks, or Lumber of any kind suffered to remain on it.
36. Great attention both at Sea and in Port is necessary to be paid to the Lower Deck, Ports and Scuttles; the great object being the Health and Comfort of the Men. Dry air should be admitted, especially in summer or warm climates, but rain and the wash of the Sea should be avoided and air that is damp admitted with great caution. A thorough draft of air in the Channel is not necessary for any length of time, and should be introduced in Preference, at such times as the men are employed on Deck.
37. The Ventilator is to be constantly worked by Day in Winter and by Night and day in summer or a warm climate. The Windsails should be used at all times in summer when the air is dry, and at times in the Winter when the Weather is fine.
38. In Port the Commanding Officer is required to have all Parties sent on Duty elsewhere onboard within 12 o'clock, No Boats (except on very particular service) are to be absent during Meal times nor in Roadstead after Sunset, or in Port after Gunfire.
39. No alteration is ever to be made in the Ships Company's Provisions, or allowance but by the Captain's order.
40. The Men are to Mess in Messes of 6 each, the Boatswains Mates & Petty Officers by themselves or with some other Petty Officers.
41. The Boatswains, Gunners and Carpenters, Mates, Quarter Masters, Captains of the Forecastle, Tops, and Mast, Armourer, Serjeants, and Corporals of Marines are allowed to have Chests- and one to each Mess.
42. The Men of the different Messes are every Sunday to appoint one of their Messmates to keep the Berth and Mess utensils clean, and in proper order for the following Week. Such Men are to be responsible to the Officers for any Neglect they may discover and none but Men belonging to Boats when in Harbour are to be exempted from this Duty.
43. Any person finding himself Ill is to make his complaint without loss of time to the Surgeon's Mates as no excuse for neglect of Duty on the score of illness will be received but through the Surgeon.

44. Washing days will be appointed as the Weather and Duty of the Ship will admit and their things are to be dried on lines stretched from shroud to shroud forward or in such places the commanding Officer shall appoint.

45. Mates and Midshipmen being acquainted with the Established Orders and Regulations are expected zealously to enforce them and to report any slackness or deviation they may observe in particular Persons.

46. The Mates and Midshipmen are ordered to sleep in Hammocks which are to be brought upon Deck and taken down same time as the Ships company's.

47. Mates and Midshipmen are to keep Log Books, a Public Order Book, Clothes List of their sub-Divisions, Watch, Quarter, and station Bills clean and well written, all of which are to be brought to the Captain the last Sunday in every Month for his Inspection.

48. Twelve Minutes and no longer will be allowed from the time of piping Hammocks up 'till they are completely stowed. The same time will be allowed to take them down and hang them up.

49. The Hammocks belonging to People absent on Duty are to be lashed and taken up by the man berth'd next him, but if an outside Man should be absent the Man next within him is to perform that service.

50. The Clothing and Bedding of all run Men or men suspected to be run is to be ordered by the Commanding officer into the Boatswains store room a List of which is to be taken by the Petty Officer of the Division to which he belongs.

51. Foremast men going out of the Ship upon leave are to leave their Clothes and Bedding with one of their Messmates, the Petty officer of the Division to which such Men belong is to satisfy himself that every thing they do not wear is left behind and that the Messmate considers himself responsible for its safety and forth coming.

52. When the Weather is so bad that the Hammocks cannot be stowed in the Nettings, they are to be taken down and piled up in such places as the Commanding Officer shall appoint.

53. Officers answering signals are to carry the Public Order Book with them, and all officers of every denomination going out of the Ship on Duty are expected to be dressed in their Uniforms with Swords.

54. No Seaman or Marine will be suffered to go out of the Ship on leave who shall not upon examination of his Divisional Officer to be found clean & decently dressed.

55. No body is allowed to lounge in the Ports, and it is strictly forbidden to throw bones, Dirt or dirty water out of them, but dirt of all sorts is to be taken to the Head and lowered well down before it is started.

56. It is forbid to enter the Ship or get into Boats through the Ports or down the sides or any other way than the Gangway steps, or stern Ladders.
57. No men are to be allowed to lounge in the Chains, or in the Boats, or on the Booms, n'or are Clothes of any sort ever to be spread or hung below the Hammock nettings, or in other than the established places, n'or are wet or damp clothes ever to be hung in the Lower or on the Upper Deck.
58. Upon the loss of any Money, Clothes, Bedding or other Articles, the loser is immediately to make it known to the Officer of the Watch or Commanding Officer, who will take such measures as appear requisite to discover the Thief. No Man is permitted to appropriate to himself any Clothes or other Articles that he may at any time find about the Ship, and if he cannot find the owner he is commanded to take it to the Officer on the Quarter Deck.
59. The Officers of the different Divisions will order the Petty Officers under their Command occasionally to examine into the state of the Peoples Mess utensils of their Divisions to see that they have a sufficiency of those articles, and that they are kept wholesome and clean.
60. Boats Crews are commanded to obey with as much alacrity, and punctuality the orders of their Coxswains as those of any other Officer onboard. No excuse therefore will be received for a Boat being left on shore or for anything lost or damaged belonging to a Boat, unless previously reported to the Commanding Officer.
61. Coxswains are strictly forbid taking anything whatever into their Boats to carry on shore without permission from the Quarter Deck.
62. Boats are not to be left at any time without Boat Keepers, they are not allowed to lay at the gangway, n'or indeed ever alongside when they can lay astern.
63. One Mate is to be nominated to the Launch, and one to the Barge & a Midshipman to each of the other Boats, who are to consider these Boats and their Crews as particularly under their Inspection: to keep Lists of them, have attention to their Masts, Sails, Carronades, Swivels, Magazines, Furniture &c. &c. to take care that the Boats and everything appertaining to them are kept neat, and in proper state for service.
64. In Port a Boat is to be sent on shore every Evening to bring off whoever may be on leave which Boat is to be put off at Sunset.
65. The Ships Company are to be mustered every Evening at Sunset at Quarter, or Divisions. All absentees or men found in Liquor to be reported, and a proper notice to be taken at such times of men that are dirty or slovenly. No long untied hair to be allowed & Clothes however old should not be ragged.

66. The People are all expected to be clean shaved and dress'd by 10 o'clock every Sunday Morning, when they will be mustered in Divisions by the different Officers commanding them and the last Sunday and Thursday of every Month is appointed a Day of general Review, or muster of Clothes when the Officers are expected to examine very particularly into the Peoples Clothing and Bedding, and are to report to the Captain any Deficiency that may appear.

67. On Thursdays as well as Sundays the Ships Company is expected to be shaved and to put on clean shirts and to shift their trousers.

68. No man is to be confined by Night or Day when I am onboard without representation having been made to me of his Crime or Offence, and my Orders having been given to that purpose.

69. The Master at Arms is to keep a List of the boys and their Clothes and to have an especial eye to their Conduct, cleanliness, and Behaviour. Every morning at 7 o'clock he is to take care that they are assembled on the Quarter Deck, attended by himself or one of his Corporals, & after having been examined, reported to the Officer of the Watch whose orders he is to receive to dismiss them.

70. The Commissioned, Warrant and Petty Officers, having Boys attending upon them as servants are expected to take care that they are properly clothed, and kept cleanly and neat.

71. The Boatswain and his Mates conformable to the old Custom of the Service are to carry Rattans, but they are to be used with discretion.

72. Two Guns taking them by turns, are regularly to be exercised for an hour every Forenoon and Afternoon (except Sundays) when at sea. At such times the Petty Officers of the Quarters to which the Guns belong, are to attend, when every part of the exercise is minutely to be attended to and explained to the Men.

73. Whenever the Ships Cook reports the Dinner or Breakfast ready he is to bring aft a small quantity of the Provisions, whether Beef, Pork Oatmeal, Pease or substitutes of any kind for the examination of the Commanding Officer or Officer of the Watch, who is required to make his report to the Captain if he shall at any time find the Provisions ill Cook'd or inferior to what they ought to be in Quality.

74. When at sea one Division of small arm Men and Boarders taking by turn, are to be exercised in the Forenoon on Mondays, Wednesdays, and Fridays.

75. The different Warrant Officers are to report every morning before 8 o'clock, and every Evening at Sunset the state of their several departments to the Officer of the Watch in the Morning, and to the Captain or Commanding officer at Quarters in the Evening.

76. Bills of Lading to prevent improper practices being directed to be delivered to the Warrant officers with the stores as they receive them from the Dock Yards. The Commanding officer is required to take care they are delivered to Him by the Warrant officers on their arrival with their stores onboard, and to be particularly careful that the stores so brought correspond with the Articles mentioned in the bills of Lading; and any omission, irregularity or deficiency is desired to be reported by him to the Captain.

77. Upon an alarm of Fire, the Boarders, Engine, and Fire men with their respective Officers are to repair to the Quarter Deck, the Boarders are to be ranged on the starboard and the Firemen with their Buckets on the Larb'd side. The Marines with the Marine Officers are to appear under Arms on the Poop. The First and Third Lieutenants are to repair immediately to the Place from whence the alarm has arose. The Boatswain, Gunner, and Carpenter to the Magazine, and their store rooms. The Surgeon and his Mates and Purser to their store rooms and slop rooms and to examine those places and to report with all Haste to the Quarter deck. The Day Mate, the Master at Arms and his Corporals are to proceed to examine and report the Tiers. The Pumpers with their Officers are immediately to rig and fetch the Pumps, and fix and fill the long Hoses, and water (by the Carpenters stationed in the wings in Action) is immediately to be let into the Cistern and well. The other Carpenters with their axes and Mauls are to assemble on the Larboard Gangway. The remaining Officers and Men are to repair to their different stations as watched (unless the Drum should beat to Divisions) and wait for orders from the Quarter Deck.

78. Upon the return of Men to the Ship that may have been absent any time and upon receipt of Men whether as part of the Crew, Supernumeraries, or Prisoners, they are to be mustered and examined by the Surgeon or his Mates, and any found ailing to be reported immediately -their Clothes and Bedding are also to be aired (and smok'd if at all necessary) before they are allowed to mix with the Ship's Company; and frequent Musters and examinations to be observed for a Week after their receipt, or until the Surgeon shall be satisfied that no Injury can accrue to the Health of the Ships Company from their mixing with them.

79. No Midshipman is allowed to quit the Deck at the expiration of the Watch under pretence that there is no one to relieve him, without having made such representation to the Officer of the Watch and obtained his permission for so doing.

80. Complaints of whatever sort that may be made by any of the Ships Company of the quality or quantity of Provisions are to be reported to the Captain, and no alteration or deviation from the established allowance of Provisions is ever to be made without the Captain's immediate direction.

81. It is my direction that at all times when the Weather is fine and at others when bleak or rainy, that the Convalescent sick, and such others in the Surgeons List as it may be serviceable to, are assembled on the Poop or under the Half Deck, according as the weather may be at 10 A.M. and at 2 P.M. and that they be kept in such situations for at least an hour and a half, and are employed in picking Oakum knotting Yarns, or other gentle and useful employment which may serve to amuse without requiring labour or masculine effort. The Surgeon is to note in the sick List, such as air and gentle Employment of this nature may be useful to; and the surgeons Mate to muster and report them to the Officer of the Watch, who is required to take care that this Order is properly complied with.

82. [13 October 1803] When in action or at Exercise on both sides it shall be found that any of the Guns are so weakly mann'd that some additional strength is requisite to run them properly out (which it should be remembered is the only part of the management of a Gun in which increased strength can be requisite, as all other parts of it can be well performed, by Four Men only, at the largest Guns) such further aid is to be borrowed from, and lent in turn to the Gun next to it on the same side, taking care that the captain and one loader of the gun borrowed from is never taken from it, and in order to avoid confusion It is to be understood that the 1st Gun is to borrow of and lend to the second. The third to the Fourth and the fourth to the third in like manner, and so on throughout the Deck.

83. [1 October 1804] It is my direction that no service or work done by any of the Ships Company in future for Officers of any denomination onboard is paid for in wine or spirits.

84. [14 October 1804] No Officer or Petty Officer, of H.M. Ship under my Command that may be ordered to any vessel met with at Sea or arriving in Port is to go alongside before he has informed himself from whence the Vessel is and on no account to board her if it from Gibraltar, Cádiz, Malaga, Alicante, Cartagena, or any Places where the contagious fever is or has been, and on going alongside the Victory or any other ship, the Superb not excepted after having boarded any Vessel whatever, he is not to attempt to go up the side before he has made known particulars, and has permission so to do.

85. It is my direction that the Officers or Petty officers commanding as it may happen, on the Fore-Castle, in the Waist, Poop, Tops, or other parts of the Ship do use their endeavours to preserve silence and keep at all times an attentive eye towards the Quarter Deck, and answer sufficiently loud to be heard in reply whenever his part may be hailed by the Captain or Officers carrying on the Duty on the Quarter Deck.

86. Frequent complaints having been made by the Officers and Petty Officers that the Seamen and others do not readily answer or obey their Orders unless particularised by Name, especially by night, I therefore desire & hereby Command that when in future any of the Officers or Petty Officers shall observe any remissness or any negligence in obeying their Commands, that they do instantly seize upon and report (no matter whether called by Name or not) any one or more that may shew any tardiness in executing their orders after they have been distinctly given.
87. When the signal to Tack or Wear is made at or about the expiration of the Watch and before it is relieved; The officers & Men whose Watch is expired are not to go off the Deck before the evolution is completed and the Watch called.
88. In Tacking Ship it is my Direction that the Bowlines are particularly attended to – for which purpose One third is to be considered the proportion of men for the Tack and two thirds for the Bowlines until the Yards are effectually Swung, and the Bowlines stopped – then the Bowlines on the Weather side of the Waist may be quitted for the Tacks & on the leeside of the sheets.

R. G. KEATS

Appendix III

Narrative of the Services of HMS Superb, 74, on the night of 12 July 1801 and the two following days.

The original autograph copy of the narrative prepared by Keats was found by Jedidiah Tucker in the papers of his father, Benjamin Tucker, who had been the Secretary to Earl St. Vincent whilst he was commander of the Channel Fleet, and then at the Admiralty when St. Vincent was First Sea Lord. It was published by him in the public interest in 1838. Longman, Orme, Brown, Green, & Longmans, London 1838. See also Somerset records office, DD/CPL/30.

He also published a memoir of the life of St. Vincent based upon his father's papers collected for that purpose.

NARRATIVE
OF THE
SERVICES
OF

HIS MAJESTY'S SHIP *SUPERB*, 74

ON THE NIGHT OF THE 12 JULY, 1801
AND TWO FOLLOWING DAYS
BY HER THEN CAPTAIN

SIR RICHARD GOODWIN KEATS, G.C.B.

NARRATIVE

On the 12 July, 1801, at 3 p.m., the wind easterly, Sir James Saumarez weighed from Gibraltar with his squadron, consisting of five sail of the line, one frigate, the Calpe sloop, the Louisa armed brig.[16] The combined squadron of the enemy, which, the Hannibal included, consisted of ten sail of the line and five frigates, had been for some time under sail, endeavouring to work out of the bay. But the wind, which towards Algeciras and the middle of the bay was very light, with us towards Gibraltar was steady. In denoting our stations, according to the method prescribed in page 12 of the Signal-book, a difference of opinion arose, in the Superb, as to the colour of one of the half-pendants; and as it would have interfered in some degree with our station, I determined to avoid the possibility of mistake (as the opportunity was favourable) to send to the Caesar, and being aware that the admiral had abundance on his hands at the time, I wrote a short note to Captain Brenton, asking the colour of the half-pendant of which we were in doubt. Captain Brenton shewed my note to the admiral, who answered it himself; and I am sorry I did not preserve it, as I think it marked his determination to attack the enemy, at a time when I believe it was not generally thought he could have done it.

As well as I can recollect, and I am sure I am correct in substance, it was as follows:-"My dear sir,-The Spencer's half-pendant was red- you are next to her, and consequently ahead of the Caesar. The mode of attack will probably be on their rear, as we come up; but at all events I shall be glad to have you near my flag".

As soon as we were clear of the Rock, the admiral formed the squadron, in line of battle ahead on the larboard tack. The wind being at east, the line might be called S. by E. and N. by W. But as the signal was made afterwards to wear together, and we stood in on the starboard tack waiting, as it would seem, for the enemy to clear Cabrita, we wore again, without signal, and signals 12, 8, 291, 252, 28, 25, were successively made before we bore up, without signal. The ships appeared to me to be at fault, or doubtful as to the station they were to occupy. In this dilemma, the note of Sir James Saumarez, which I have already noticed, determined me what to do. I closed with the Caesar, and

---

16 **Order of battle** (See Table in the text)
British: Caesar (80), Spencer (74), Venerable (74), Superb (74), Audacious (74), Thames (32), Calpe (14), Louisa (14)
French: Formidable (80), Indomptable (80), Desaix (74), St. Antoine (74), Vautour (14) Muiron (40), Libre (40),[Hannibal 74 and Indienne frigate returned to Algeciras].
Spanish: Real Carlos (112), San Hermenegildo (112), San Fernando (96), Argonauta (80), San Augustin (74), Sabina (34), Clara (Perla) (34).

resolved to remain within hail of her. At this time, we rather more than kept way with the Caesar, under our topsails; though she had her foresail and top-gallant sails set. A little before nine, I was hailed, and ordered to make sail ahead, and attack the stern most of the enemy's ships, keeping in shore of them. At the same time, I was asked if we saw any of them, for that in the Caesar they had lost sight of them. I replied, we saw one, and that the admiral's orders should be obeyed. At this time, I do not imagine the enemy could have been less than four or five miles from us; for at the close of the day it was certainly three miles, and as they bore away some time before we did, it is presumable they had increased their distance a mile or two.

On receiving the admiral's orders, I ordered the foresail and top-gallant sails to be set, and the topmen soon after aloft, to shake out a reef; but the first-lieutenant and master both being of the opinion we should not want wind, I countermanded that order, and soon had reason to be satisfied I had; for it freshened very fast and we had presently plenty of sail. At ten the Caesar, and one other only of our ships, were in sight astern. At eleven we could discern only the Caesar, and she we judged to be three or four miles from us. At this time, it blew very strong, the ship was going upwards of eleven knots, and coming up, hand going, with the enemy, which we regained sight of soon after we made sail. They were now well over on the Barbary shore, running before the wind under a press of sail; and though we had a pretty distinct sight of them, no order of sailing was remarked by any of us, except that the admiral, whose flag we observed to be shifted to a frigate in the afternoon, seemed to lead with a light at his mast-head.

About this time, I ordered the first and second captains of the guns to be assembled on the quarter deck, to whom I addressed myself in a manner I thought suited the occasion, and calculated to give encouragement. I then told them that I had the advantage of having been in action with the enemy by night, and predicted to them what *precisely took place*; namely,- that the Spaniards would blow up, and that we should have more to apprehend from our own carelessness of powder, than from any efforts of the enemy. Being directed by the admiral to make the attack in shore, I concluded, though the hostile squadron was very considerably nearer the African than the Spanish coast, it was his intention I should keep between them and their own shore. To this end, from the time we left the Caesar, and to the time we opened our fire, the course had been regulated accordingly; and when on drawing near, I conversed with Captain Jackson, then first-lieutenant of the Superb, on the mode of attack, he observed, we could get in amongst a cluster a little on the larboard bow. I replied, but that mode would not be in compliance with the admiral's order; and we can, with equal advantage, and in obedience to his direction, make the attack on the wing. I determined so to do.

For some time, the outermost ship to the northward was one of the French ships, with jury topmasts, I believe the Formidable; and I thought, from her position, it would have become my duty to attack her. But, as we approached, she steered more to port, and got within. The northernmost ship was now one of their largest ships. Captain Dickson of the marines was the first that discovered, and mentioned, her to be a three-deck ship. Captain Jackson, and Mr. Pickering, the master, both looked at her, and confirmed her being so. Sutherland M'Beth, a trusty steady seaman (now I hope a master), who, in the Boadicea, and Superb, was the principal look-out man, and the best I ever knew, had been directed by me to stay at my elbow; for it appeared to me his services might be more advantageously employed in this way, in a night action, than at the gun, of which he was captain. This man, who I ordered to look at her, also assured me she was of three decks. I looked at her myself, and was satisfied also. We were now ranging up fast abreast of her, and took in the top-gallant sails, when I went to the larboard gangway. Captain Jackson and the master both came to me. If, before, we had been mistaken in the size of the ship, we had now an opportunity of correcting our judgement; but nothing could be more evident to us, and to all, I believe, that looked at her. The foresail was now hauled, and when we got on her beam, we had two ships nearly in range with her, on her larboard side. I then asked Captain Jackson and Mr Pickering, what distance they thought we were from her. One of them replied, we are very close. I answered, that may mean a cable's length, or a mile. Do you think we are three cables from her? They both replied, certainly not so far. In my opinion, we were little, if any, beyond two. I then said the opportunity is too advantageous to be lost. The officers had been apprised, everything was ready, and in that situation, at twenty or thirty minutes past eleven, we opened our fire.

Extraordinary as it may appear, I am *now* convinced the enemy was not aware of his situation. This fatal security may possibly be ascribed, in part, to an habitual indolence, to confidence in their numbers, to our not having raised suspicion by making signals, or firing on our approach, and to their not suspecting an attack from a single ship. For as the Caesar was seen from the Superb with difficulty at eleven o'clock, and it was afterwards reported to me that she could no longer be kept sight of, and which, on going aft, I found to be the case; it is fairly inferable, [she] had not been seen at all by the enemy. As soon as we could see, after the first broadside, we observed the ship we attacked had put her helm a starboard, for her quarter was to us. We were much surprised we met with no return of fire, and still more so when the ship, towards which she was sheering, and which probably had received some of our broadside, opened fire seemingly at the ship we had fired into. This unfortunate ship now sheered back again towards us, and fired, but more on the starboard-side, and in this situation received a second broadside from us. Confusion seemed now general amongst all of them; for they now began firing in various situations and directions, and evidently at each other. The third broadside had not, I believe, been all discharged from us, when our opponent was evidently on fire. We ceased to molest him. The violence of the wind caused the flames to burst out with great rapidity, and at one time, after we ceased firing, he was so near, that I thought it necessary to order the master to sheer further from her.

The total destruction of that ship no longer doubtful, I ordered the foresail to be set, at thirty-five or forty minutes past eleven - it blew too strong for the top-gallant sails - and the ship to be steered, to close with a ship near and a little on the larboard bow, still keeping in mind the order, in which the admiral had directed the attack to be made, and we availed ourselves of the leisure, which the opportunity afforded, to splice and knot some of the rigging, which had been shot away. The ship on fire continued to run for some time, perhaps for ten minutes after we set the foresail, before the wind, then came suddenly, flew as it were, to the wind, near some of the ships of the enemy, two of which were to the eastward of her; and this must have been the moment when the other first-rate got on board her.

In twenty minutes after the foresail was set, it was again hauled up, at, or very nearly at twelve, [when] we commenced an action with the St. Antoine, at not more than two cables length distance, which ship we remarked, as we approached before the action commenced, to have a broad pendant and her starboard fore-top-mast studding-sail boom rigged out. As soon as we brought her to action, she endeavoured to cross us ahead on starboard. Failing in the attempt, she sheered again to port, steered uncommonly wide. In one of her yaws we were very near on board; after which her helm was put a-starboard, and she came to the wind on the larboard tack. The efforts to shake us off, rendered it impracticable, in a night rather dark and stormy, to support a close steady action.

At one time we became rather widely separated, but the situation was recovered, and the action renewed as expeditiously and as closely as it was in my power to manage, rather on a wind than laying to, for about twenty minutes after she put her helm a-starboard. At thirty-five or forty minutes past twelve, she was completely silenced, hauled down her colours, hoisted and hauled down a light frequently, in token of submission, and hailed repeatedly to say they had struck.

All the time we were in action with the St. Antoine, we had either been steering very widely, to accommodate ourselves to her wild steerage, which was not confined to a range of eight points (from S.W. to N.W.), or we were close hauled with little headway, on the larboard tack. This, of course, afforded the enemy's squadron, which continued its course undeviatingly before the wind, an opportunity of increasing its distance very considerably; and I do not believe any of their ships, at the time the St. Antoine surrendered, could be less than three miles to the westward of us; though at the time she was brought to action, some of them were rather to the eastward of her. It also afforded in the same degree time to the Caesar to approach us, and as from the fore-reaching-way we had, it became necessary for the Caesar to haul up a little, as she drew near to pass ahead, by which some of her foremast guns bore, a few, *four* or *five*, were discharged. The seaman (M'Beth), who I have mentioned before noticed it to me with surprise. [My answer to the man was particular; and if he can be found, will (for I dare say he remembers it) prove that the St. Antoine had struck at this time]. Seeing the admiral determined on passing ahead, I went forward. Capt. Jackson accompanied me, and was, on the rising of the forecastle, forward, with my trumpet, to endeavour to tell the admiral what the prize was; when in crossing we were surprised by a broadside being discharged.

The Venerable following soon after did the same. [When I afterwards met Capt. Hood, I asked him how he came to fire, as I thought he must have been satisfied she had struck. He replied, he was perfectly satisfied himself she had so, but the Caesar discharging her broadside induced him to do so likewise.] I concluded the broad pendant, which was flying some fathoms from the truck, the halyards of which were shot away, and entangled aloft, had led to the mistake. The ensign it seems did also. For, after having hauled it down in token of submission, it seems they intended to have hoisted it again, with an English flag over; but the men having seized on the colour chests, they could not find an English jack or ensign; so, they hoisted an English pendant at the peak, and the French ensign under it. The pendant, though distinctly seen from us, was not perhaps so visible to the Caesar; and yet, as we had been laying for some time peaceably by the prize, we could not expect any doubt of her being so could have been entertained on board the Caesar. When I saw Sir James Saumarez the following day, and we were talking of the transactions of the night, I observed to him that we were surprised at the Caesar's firing at the St. Antoine, as I thought they must have been satisfied she had surrendered. He replied, "I thought we were doing wrong, and said so at the time; but they insisted upon it her colours were flying, and prevailed upon me to fire."

The admiral in the same conversation, expressed to me his surprise at the rate we got from the Caesar after he ordered me ahead, and added, although he should have thought it extremely dangerous from the violence of the wind, to have attempted to set a studding-sail. He nevertheless ordered one to be prepared, if possible, to avoid losing sight of the Superb. I am thus particular, because in my report I considered, as I felt I had the right to do, that the St. Antoine was taken by the Superb alone, and because I think it serves to shew in a strong point of view, the situation of the Superb, relatively with the Caesar at the time the Superb opened her fire on the first-rate. In the report I ought to have given the prize the name St. Antoine, instead of *San Antonio*. She was so named in the Role d'Equipage, and considered by them in every respect a French man-of-war. Her colours were French, her officers were all French; and of the 730 persons, which composed her equipage, only 200 were Spaniards. The rest were either French or foreigners distinguished in the Role d'Equipage as *belonging* to the *French nation*. Not having seen her books at the time my report was made, I was ignorant of these circumstances.

Sensible that there still remained, comparatively with Sir James Saumarez's force, a very formidable body of the enemy together, that the Superb had received no damage to incapacitate her from doing her duty in action, and seeing the admiral still keeping on after the enemy, with the Venerable only near, I determined if possible to join him; and at one time conceiving the services of the Superb, even though purchased at the expense or loss of the St. Antoine, might be advantageous to the public service, I had thought, if no other expedient could be found, of quitting her altogether. For there was too much wind and sea of the worst kind, for boats to do anything effectual in shifting prisoners.

Captain Jackson, to whom I communicated my ideas, and who gave it as his opinion, that it would not be thought right to quit a ship of the line, without somehow destroying her, I doubt not, has a perfect recollection of the circumstance. Whilst ruminating on this subject, the Spencer passed, soon after the Thames, which I hailed *twice*, and ordered to lay by the prize, that I might join the admiral. We thought, at the time, the order was understood, because she hauled her wind under our stern, wore, and stood towards us. I watched her from the poop, till she did so, and when after I hailed the poop to know if she was not near, I was surprised to be informed by the midshipman that she had bore away, and was running before the wind. When afterwards I saw Capt. Holles, he informed me he could not hear what I said. The Thames passed to leeward, but there was a great deal of wind.

The disappointment was lessened, seeing the admiral had brought to, which he did about four miles to leeward of us. But again, it was renewed, when on the Spencer and Thames joining he again bore away. Being now *very close* in with Cape Spartel, we wore. The prize, which had her mainyard shot away, her rigging much cut, and not a single sail left, having still more remnants and shreds of canvas left forward than aft, lay broad off, and forged so much ahead, that it was difficult on that account, independent of the wind and sea, to pass a boat. A small party were thrown on board, and employed in cutting away tattered canvas, &c. Towards day the wind began to abate, when boats were all hoisted out, and employed shifting prisoners.

Prior to this, and whilst it was still dark, our attention was called to loud shrieks and cries of distress to windward; and presently a Spanish launch, filled with men nearly all quite naked, came alongside, and scrambled into the ship. Attracted by the sentinel's light at my cabin door, they huddled aft together, threw themselves on their knees, and with uplifted hands besought our protection, or, in an act of devotion, were returning thanks to their Creator for their deliverance. We then learned that the launch belonged to the Real Carlos, into which all that could, as well from that ship as the Hermenegildo, threw themselves to escape from the conflagration (for those ships were both on fire and on board). Upon examination, we found we had received from this launch, an officer (the second captain), and eighteen men of the Real Carlos, and an officer, an alferez or ensign, and nineteen men of the San Hermenegildo.

Some spirits were given them. The men I ordered to be supplied with slop clothing, the officers reclothed, and I had it explained to them:- "That as, in their distress, they had sought our protection, I would venture to assure them that our admiral would not consider any of them as prisoners;" and they were not treated as such, during the time they remained on board the Superb. As none of them spoke either French or English intelligibly, nor any other language but their own, and we were not very well off for Spanish interpreters, possibly the information we obtained from them may not, in all its parts, be thoroughly correct; but as handed to me, their accounts stated, "That they considered themselves as secure from any attack that night. That some suspicion, as the Superb approached, arose on board the Real Carlos, for on counting their squadron they reckoned one more than their number. That a report was made, but disregarded by the captain, who with several officers, were still at the table smoking after supper, of which number, the second captain, Don Francisco Viscerondo, was one. That captain with some other officers were killed or wounded by our first broadside *in the cabin*, from which none of them moved till we fired. That regarding her destruction, it was said her fore-topmast was shot away in the first broadside, and being almost immediately fired into by a ship on their larboard-side also, their confusion was very great; and in firing, which they did from both sides, the fore-top-sail, which was hanging down, caught fire, and occasioned the conflagration." But my own opinion is, it was occasioned by an explosion of powder pretty general, for I remarked a flash from port to port, which at the moment, I thought a broadside, but heard scarcely any reports. An unusual glare of light was soon after visible, and induced me to observe to Capt. Jackson that I thought she was on fire. The seaman I have already mentioned (M'Beth) almost immediately confirmed my opinion. The officer of the Hermenegildo, and others, as I understood, said that, receiving some shot most unexpectedly, and at a time they had no thoughts of being attacked, they returned, as soon as they could, the fire; and continued so to do, till the ship which had fired into them, was evidently in a blaze:-

"They conceived it was the English admiral; and it was said fore and aft, the English admiral is on fire, let us go under his stern and send 'em all to hell together;" and they believe in that effort they ran foul of the ship on fire, and thus occasioned their own melancholy fate.

At daylight, nothing was seen of either squadron; but the Calpe and Louisa were laying to some distance to windward and came down and joined us. A frigate, half-courses down, appeared to the eastward, which we took for an American. After reconnoitring us, she also came down. It was the Carlotta, Portuguese frigate. Captain Duncan, her commander, sent an officer on board, with a complimentary message, and continued to lay to, seemingly amusing themselves in seeing us shift the prisoners.

When the Calpe and Louisa reached us, I ordered Captain Dundas to put fifteen men into the Antoine, and to take out thirty-five; and Lieutenant Truscott was directed to put in five men, and take out thirty. Captain Dundas received the number of prisoners I ordered, but did not put any men into her, excusing himself on account of being weakly manned, and leaky. Mr. Truscott complied fully with the order. Whilst thus employed, and not more than half the prisoners shifted, a distant cannonade was distinctly heard from our lower gun-deck, though not a single report of a gun could be heard from the quarter deck or poop. It was the Venerable's action with the Formidable, but concluding the action was generally renewing, I called the boats instantly on board, and hoisted them in, and made sail with all possible expedition. I sent the Louisa and the Calpe, with orders for both of them to lay by the prize; and also, to Captain Duncan, of the Portuguese frigate, with my compliments and request that he would also, until I should re-join. Thus, determining rather to trust her to the party I had on board, and the Calpe and Louisa, provided Captain Duncan could *not act*, as I had some reason to believe was the case, than to remain inactive in the sound of guns. I did not wait to receive any answer, but have since known that the Carlotta could not so act.[17] She, however, without even sending a boat to the Antoine, continued at no great distance from her during my absence.

In standing in, we presently lost the strong easterly wind, and the haze clearing away, as we drew in shore, discovered the land to the eastward of Cádiz; the French Formidable running along shore, the Venerable to the southward of her, dismasted, and the Thames frigate near her. Soon after we saw the Caesar and Spencer, and as we were hauling the wind, seeing the action had terminated, to re-join the St. Antoine, the remaining ships of the enemy's squadron were seen, some leagues to the westward of the admiral. This occasioned me to change my plan again, and determined me to run down and join him. It had now fallen little wind, almost calm, so that it was nearly one o'clock before we reached the Caesar.

---

17   Captain Duncan had been advised of a peace having been made between Portugal and France, so he did not participate in any hostilities, beyond carrying dispatches in the aftermath – see Ross, Saumarez Memoirs, Vol2, p14.

The reception I met with was certainly of the most flattering kind. Sir James Saumarez received me himself, at the gangway, and said aloud, "That he could not find the language to express his sense of the services I had rendered my country the last night". He led me into the cabin, when the conversation, which I have already noticed, took place, asked me with some earnestness what the frigate (the Carlotta) was to windward and said he should expect a statement from me of our (the Superb's) services the last night. Having informed him what the frigate was, and the state in which I had left the St. Antoine, and my reason for so doing, I took my leave, and by his direction made the best of my way with the Superb to re-join the prize, which was affected about sunset. At eight o'clock next morning, we joined the Caesar, when I carried on board the statement the admiral has called upon me for. After I had read it, I said to him, "I believe it is correct. I feel that I have said a great deal about the ship I command, but I hope you are not of the opinion I have said too much." He replied, "That is impossible. It differs in nothing material from my own observations, and I will send it with my letter to the Admiralty". I answered, "That I by no means wished him to do so, and that I thought it more properly belonged to himself to make reports of transactions of this nature." Some conversation then ensued regarding the Venerable's action with the Formidable. Sir James Saumarez then opened my letter, took his pen and wrote, I believe, the postscript which appeared in print. I returned immediately afterwards on board, and by his direction made sail, with prize in tow, for Gibraltar. Between eleven and twelve we passed through the melancholy fragments of the Real Carlos and San Hermenegildo, and at 3 p.m. anchored at Gibraltar.

Endnotes

1. *The Shipwrecked Mariner*, Vol XV, No LVII, Old Series, 1868, p.1, at 13.
2. White, C., *Keats*, in LeFevre, P & Harding, R., eds. *British Admirals of the Napoleonic Wars*, Chatham Publishing, London, 2005, p.368
3. Ralfe, J., *The Naval Biography of Great Britain*, Vol II, Whitmore & Fenn, Charing Cross, 1828, p.487-516
4. Clarke J. S & M'Arthur, J, *The Life of Admiral Lord Nelson from his Manuscripts,* Cadell & Davies, London, 1809
5. Somerset Records Office; DD/CPL/30; NMM BGR/K/1
6. Raymond, D. J., *The Royal Navy in the Baltic 1807-1812*, (2010 Ph.D. Thesis) Florida State University Library, p.215
7. *Annual Biography and Obituary*,1835, Vol XIX, Longman, London, p.51
8. *United Services Magazine* 1834, Part 2, Henry Colburn, London, p.217-8
9. *The Naval and Military Remembrancer, 1844*, Maxwell, W.H. (Ed), Henry Bohn, London, p.36
10. See White, *Keats, op. cit.* and contrast Raymond, *op. cit.* p.71
11. Woodman, *The Victory of Sail Power, op. cit.,* p.21, Owen, H., I'll Make Five Sons Of Mine Fight For Their King And Country: The Naval Sons of William IV and Mrs Jordan, *The Mariner's Mirror* , Vol 83, No1, (1997), p.41, at p.42; Parkinson, C.N., *Britannia Rules*; Weidenfeld and Nicolson, London, p.71 and p.183; Woodman, R., *The Sea Warriors*, Constable, London, 200, p.38; Voelcker, T., *Admiral Saumarez versus Napoleon, The Baltic, 1807-12*, Boydell Press, Suffolk, 2008, p.1
12. Ships Instruction No 5, see Appendix II
13. 15 October 1803, Nicolas, N. H., *The Despatches and letters of Vice Admiral Lord Viscount Nelson*, Seven Volumes, Cambridge University Press, 2011, Vol 5, p.248, and 7 December 1803, p.302 (hereinafter referred to as 'Nicolas')
14. Gilbert, C. S., *An Historical Survey of the County of Cornwall*, Vol 2, J. Congdon, London, 1820, p.168. Almost identical wording indicates this information derives from a letter from Rev. Keats to his son, the subject of this memoir, dated 1808 – extracted in a family pedigree annotated by Rev. Keats.

15 The memorial refers to him as a Lieutenant, and although records refer to him as a captain, this appears to be on the basis the promotion had been approved and was to be effective the week after he died – family pedigree, last updated by Admiral Sir R G Keats.
16 Walcott, M.E.C., *William of Wykeham and his Colleges – Roll of Distinguished Wykehamists,* David Nutt, London 1852, p.440, includes a brief biography of Keats. See also Old Wykehamists, *Winchester College 1393-1893,* E. Arnold, London 1893, p.94. Bishop William of Wickham established the college in 1393 (with the motto *Manners Makyth Man*) to prepare boys for his New College School, Oxford. Keats also features in the New College list of distinguished alumni.
17 Great Bridge, 9 December 1775; Norfolk, 1 January 1776; New York, 16 September 1776; Fort Washington, 17 November 1776; Rhode Island, December 1776.
18 NMM AGC/XXIV. See also letter Duke of Clarence to Keats, 28 March 1828.
19 See, for example, Knight, R., *William IV,* Penguin Random House, 2019.
20 Report in *Sheffield and Rotheham Independent,* derived from the Naval and Military Gazette, May 31 1834, p.3.
21 *Annual Biography and Obituary,* 1835, Vol XIX, p.39
22 Letter in possession of Keats family.
23 ADM 6/23, Commission and Warrant Book 1783-1789 August. Kew Archives.
24 Hamilton, R. V., *Letters and Papers of Admiral of the Fleet, Thos. Byam Martin,* Navy Records Society, Vol 1, 1903, p.122; [*Byam Martin Papers*].
25 Knight, R., *William IV, op. cit.* pp.35-7.
26 Hamilton, *Byam Martin Papers, op. cit.,* p.132-3
27 Keats to Stephens, 30 October 1789, and reply 4 November, PRO ADM 80/133.
28 Hamilton, *Byam Martin, Papers, op. cit.,* p.134
29 ADM 1/995; 28 January 1790
30 ADM 51/870.
31 Aspinall, A., *The later Correspondence of George III,* Vol V, Cambridge University Press, 1970 Vol. II, p.66
32 ADM 1/995.
33 King, C., The Russian Armament, *The Mariner's Mirror,* 2013 Vol 24:2, pp.176-183.
34 Hamilton, *Byam Martin Papers,* op. cit., Vol 1, p.14.
35 James, W., *The Naval History of Great Britain* (in six volumes) New Edition, Richard Bentley, London, 1859, Vol I, p 62 *et. seq.* [There are several versions of James's Naval History, in two and six volumes. Future references are to this edition unless otherwise noted]
36 Somerset Records Office DD/CPL/32.
37 Taylor, S, *Commander: The Life and Exploits of Britain's Greatest Frigate Captain,* Faber & Faber, p.58
38 St. Vincent to Markham, 26 October 1806, *Selection from the correspondence of Admiral John Markham,* Naval Records Society, Vol 28, 1905, p.226; [*Markham Papers*].
39 Wareham, T., This disastrous Affair, Sir J.B. Warren and the Expedition to Quiberon Bay, *1795, The Age of Sail,* The International Annual of the Historic Sailing Ship, Conway Maritime Press, Vol 1, p.9
40 Parkinson, C.N., *Britannia Rules,* Weidenfeld and Nicolson, London, p.71 and p.183, Woodman, R., *The Sea Warriors,* Constable, London, 2000, p.38.
41 Parkinson, *ibid*; Woodman, R., *The Sea Warriors,* p.38.
42 *Annual Biography and Obituary,* 1835, Vol XIX, p.42.
43 Taylor, *op. cit.,* p.58

44 Years later Warren passed away suddenly whilst visiting Keats at his apartment at Greenwich; *London Magazine* 5, 1822.
45 Parkinson, C.N., *Sir Edward Pellew Viscount Exmouth, Admiral of the Red*, Methuen, London, 1934, pp.398-9, Pellew years later described then Admiral Smith being "as Gay and thoughtless as ever", Letter Pellew to Keats, 5 March 1814.
46 *London Gazette*, 13919, 6 August 1796 James *op. cit.*, Vol I, p.233
47 James, *op.cit.*, Vol I, p.236
48 Aldous, G., *The Law Relating to the Distribution of Prize Money in the Royal Navy and its relationship to the use of Naval Power 1793-1815*, PhD. Thesis, Kings College London, 2020, p.92; Head money, see p.204
49 Steel's *Prize Pay Lists, new series corrected to 1805*, David Steel, London 1805.p.9, item105.
50 *London Gazette*, 13757, 3 March 1795, p.206
51 *London Gazette*, 13815, 1 September 1795, p.756
52 *London Gazette*, 13773, 25 April 1795, p.379.
53 Steel, *op.cit.*, Item numbers are those used in the reference.
54 Clowes, W.L., *The Royal Navy- A History from the Earliest Times*, Chatham, London, 1997, Vol 4, p.264 *et. seq.*
55 James (Vol 1, p.278) states 1100 of Puisaye's troops plus 2,400 Royalist inhabitants were evacuated, but their arms and stores remained.
56 For a more fulsome description of the role of the Royal Navy in this expedition, see Wareham, *op. cit.*, Vol.1, p.9
57 Clowes, (1997), *op.cit.*, Vol.4, p.495
58 *Annual Biography and Obituary*, 1835, p.43, *United Services Magazine*, 1834, part 2, p.213, Allen, J., Battles of the British Navy, *op.cit.*, Vol1, p 401; Clowes, (1997), *ibid*; James, *op. cit.*, Vol 1, p.355-6
59 Steel, *op.cit., No 250*
60 *Biography and Obituary*, 1835, p.43
61 St. Vincent to Grenville, 18 March 1807, Brenton, *supra*, p.334
62 Brenton, E.P., *Life and Correspondence of John, Earl of St. Vincent*, H. Colburn, London, 1838, p.335
63 Parliamentary Papers; Expedition to the Scheldt, *Cobbett's Parliamentary Debates* Vol XV, 1810, Examination of Keats, p.cclxxiv.
64 See enclosure to St Vincent to Glenville, *Naval Miscellany*, Vol. 92, Naval Records Society, enclosure 7 March 1807, #26, p.489
65 *Annual Biography and Obituary*, 1835, Vol XIX p.43
66 *United Services Magazine*, 1834, part 2, p.214
67 *The Gentleman's Magazine*, Sylvanus Urban, 1796, part 2, p. 953, Debrett, J., *A collection of state papers relating to the war against France*, Picadilly, 1798, Vol V, p.80
68 White, *Keats, op. cit.* p.352
69 *Clark's Battles of England and Tales of the Wars*, Clark, W.M., London, 1848, Vol 4, p.410
70 James *op.cit.*, Vol.1, pp.383-4
71 Seymour to Spencer, 4 January 1796 *The Channel Fleet and the Blockade of Brest, 1793-1801*, Navy Records Society Vol 141, #127 [*The Channel Fleet*].
72 Richmond, H.W. Z, *The Private Papers of George, Earl Spencer*, Vol.4, Navy Records Society, Vol 59 (1924) Contrast his initial thoughts; St. Vincent to Spencer, 5 August 1800, p.18, and this assessment after assuming the post, 23 September 1800, p.19.

73 Bienkowski, L., *Admirals in the Age of Nelson*, Naval Institute Press, Annapolis, Maryland, 2003, pp.203-4
74 *Naval Chronicle*, Bunney & Gold, London, Vol 3, 1800, p.350
75 Correspondence between the men and the Admiralty can be found in *Campbell's Lives of the British Admirals*, H.R. Yorke ed., Bennet, Strand & Harris, London, 1817, Vol 7 p.446 et seq.
76 White, Keats, *op. cit.*, p.352
77 McDougal & Coats (Eds.) *The Naval Mutinies of 1797; Unity and Perseverance*, Boydell Press, 2011, p.7 et. seq.
78 Parker, *Britannia Rules*, p.45 et seq.
79 Le Fevre, P., *Sir John Borlase Warren*, in LeFevre, P. & Harding R, (Eds.), *British Admirals of the Napoleonic Wars*, Chatham, London 2005, pp.227-8.
80 Keats to Warren, 21 April 1897, *The Channel Fleet*, #141.
81 Watt, H. and Hawkins, A. (Eds), *Letters of Seamen in the Wars with France 1793-1815*, The Boydell Press, Suffolk, 2016, Letter B17, p 425. TNA: HO 42/212, fol 129-30.
82 Dugan, J., *The Great Mutiny*, G. P Putnam's, New York, 1966, p.189,
83 Lardas, M., *British Frigate v French Frigate, 1793-1814*, Osprey Publishing, Oxford, 2013, pp.38-9
84 Marshall, J., *Royal Navy Biography*, Longman, Hurst, Rees, Orme & Brown, London, 1823, Vol.1, p.343
85 *The Times*, 4 December 1797, p.2.
86 *London Gazette*, 14065, 14 November 1797, p.1090, *London Gazette*, 15007, p.316
87 Details of the battle can be found in Allen, *op. cit.*, Vol 1, pp.490-3
88 *London Gazette*, 15092, 22 December 1798, p.122
89 *London Gazette*, 15123, p.335
90 *Naval Chronicle* Vol 4, p.161
91 *London Gazette*, 15290, p.1006
92 Outram, B. F., *Memoir of Sir Benjamin Fonseca Outram, Inspector of Naval Hospitals and of Fleets*, Royal College of Physicians of London, 1856
93 Pole to Bridport, 3 July 1799, *The Channel Fleet*, #470
94 James *op. cit.*, Vol 2, p.378 et. Seq.
95 *Ibid.* Vol 3, pp.34-5
96 White, *Keats*, p.353
97 James *op.cit.* Vol 1, p.64
98 See Keats to St. Vincent, 3 May 1800, *The Channel Fleet*, #557, Editor's note 1.
99 Nepean to Bridport, 9 September 1799, *The Channel Fleet*, #496
100 Parkinson, *Edward Pellew, op. cit.*, Ch IX.
101 Mahan, A.T., *Types of Naval Officers, Drawn from the History of the British Navy*, Sampson Low Marston & Co, London, 1902, p.412
102 Gardiner, R (Ed), *The Campaign of Trafalgar, 1803-1805*, Chatham Publishing, London, 1997, p.100-01.
103 Keats to St. Vincent, 3 May 1800, *The Channel Fleet* #557.
104 Berkeley to St. Vincent, 4 May 1800, *ibid.* #559
105 Keats to St. Vincent, 5 May 1800, *ibid,* #562.
106 St. Vincent to Berkeley, 5 May 1800, *ibid.* #565.
107 Keats to St. Vincent, 6 May 1800, *ibid* #567
108 White, *Keats op. cit.*, p.354
109 *Naval Chronicle* Vol 3, p.510

110 Richmond, H. W. Z., *op. cit.* Vol 3, Navy Records Society Vol 58 (1923), p.301.
111 St. Vincent to Keats, 9 July 1800, *The Channel Fleet*, #639.
112 St. Vincent to Keats 17 July 1800, *ibid.* #651
113 *The Times*, 10 November 1800.
114 *Steels Prize Pay Lists*, David Steel, London, 1805, items 522, 550, 720, 780 & 1364; *London Gazette*, No 15300, p.1161; No 1351, p.376; No. 15426, p.1362.
115 Keats to St. Vincent, 31 January 1801, quoted by White, Keats, *op. cit.*, p.362
116 Winfield, R, *British Warships in the Age of Sail*, Seaforth publishing, Yorkshire, 2005. James, *op cit.*, p.114
117 Bienkowski, *op. cit.*, p.182
118 See also *The Mariner's Mirror*, Vol 7, 1921, Issue 10, pp.316-318 and 341-347
119 Cochrane, T., *Remarks on the Conduct of the Naval Administration of Great Britain since 1815*, London, 1847, p.52
120 See generally Duffy, M., *The Gunnery at Trafalgar: Training, Tactics or Temperament. Journal of Maritime Research*,7:1, p.140
121 *United Services Magazine*, 1843, part 3, Vol 43, p.197
122 White, *op.cit.*, citing a letter from Keats to Nelson, 1 April 1805.
123 See McKee, C., *Imitation Is: A plea for Comparative Naval History*, The *Northern Mariner*, XXIV, Nos 3 & 4, 2014, p.1-5
124 Ross, J., *Memoirs and Correspondence of Admiral Lord de Saumarez*, 2 volumes, Richard Bentley, London, 1838, Vol 1, p.327-8
125 Parkinson, C. N., *Britannia Rules*, *op. cit.*, p.72
126 James, *op. cit.*, Vol III, p.110, Clowes, 1997, *op. cit.*, Vol 4, p. 460.
127 Cochrane [Thomas, 10th Earl of Dundonald], *Autobiography of a Seaman*, Richard Bentley, London, 1860, p.130
128 Reproduced at Ekins, C., *Naval Battles of Great Britain*, Baldwin & Cradock, London 1828, p.275
129 Brenton, *op.cit.*, Vol. III, p.35
130 James, op. cit., Vol, III, p.107-9, *Naval Chronicle*, Vol 6, p.246.
131 Collingwood to Carlyle, 24 August 1801; Hughes, E. (Ed) *The Private Correspondence of Admiral Lord Collingwood*, Naval Records Society 1951.
132 Parkinson, *Britannia Rules*, *op. cit.* p.73
133 Saumarez to James Matra, 7 July 1801, PRO (Foreign Office) 174/10, cited in Voelcker, *op.cit.*, p.210.
134 Letter to Richard Saumarez, 6 July 1801, Ross., J., Memoirs, Vol 1, p.389
135 *Ibid.*, p.75.
136 James, *op. cit.*, Vol III, p.97
137 Clowes, (1997), *op. cit.* Vol 4, p.459.
138 Quoted in Ross, *Memoirs, op. cit.*, p.392, and James, *op. cit.*, Vol III, p.109.
139 *The Shipwrecked Mariner*, Vol. XV, 1868, p.4
140 White, Keats *op. cit.* p.354
141 Ross, J., *Memoirs*, p.422
142 Log of the *Superb*, 9-10 July 1801, PRO ADM 51/1598, part 2, cited in Florida State University Ph.D. dissertation, 2005, Musteen, J., *Becoming Nelson's refuge and Wellington's Rock: The Ascendancy of Gibraltar during the Age of Napoleon (1793-1815)*, p.74. Somerset Records Office DD/CPL/30, Journal of the *Superb*. James, Naval History, Vol 3, 124

143 Notes held in Somerset records Office, quoted by White, *op. cit.*, p.354
144 Musteen, J, *Nelson's Refuge; Gibraltar in the Age of Napoleon*, Naval Institute Press, 2011 p.43, and 44, n85. Keith sent the *Généreux* (74), but on her captain hearing of the outcome of the second battle he resumed normal duties and never joined with Saumarez.
145 Saumarez to his wife, Martha, 17 July 1801, Ross, J., *Memoirs, op. cit.*, p.426.
146 Evan Nepean to Saumarez, 4 August 1801, Ross, *Memoirs*, Vol 2, p.27.
147 Proceedings, House of Lords, November 1802
148 Ross, J., *Memoirs op.cit.*, p.403. The approbation of the Admiralty, by letter 4 August 1801, is at Vol II, p.26
149 Ross, *op. cit.*, p.420
150 Laughton, J.K., *Nelson and His Companions in Arms*, Longmans, Green & Co, London, 1896, p.236
151 Admiral Mareno's orders, 11 July 1801, Ross, *Memoirs, op. cit.*, Vol 1, p.437
152 A discussion of the merits of the strategy can be found in Ekins, *Battles of Great Britain, op. cit.*, p.280
153 Warner, O, Richard Keats & the HMS Superb, *Blackwood's Edinburgh Magazine*, 1945, p 193
154 Parkinson, C.N., *Britannia Rules*, p.76
155 Allen, J., *Battles of the British Navy*, Bailey & Co Cornwall, 1842, p.53; Reported also in *The Shipwrecked Mariner*, Vol XV, 1869, p.6
156 Allen, J., *Battles of the British Navy*, H Bohn, London, 1852, p.50
157 Letter 7 October 1801, Ross, J., *Life of Saumarez.*, Vol 2, p.33. The pension was granted in March 1803; Aspinall, *Correspondence of George III, op.cit.*, fol. 2719, Voelcker, *op.cit.*, p.210. He was ultimately raised to the peerage in 1831.
158 Brenton E.P., *The Naval History of Great Britain from 1793-1836*, Rice, London, p.551
159 Ross, *op. cit.*, p.415
160 Ross, *op.cit.*, p.407
161 *Ibid.*
162 Saumarez to Keith, 19 July 1801, *The Keith Papers* Vol II, #18, Navy Records Society, Vol 90.
163 Keats, R.G., *Narrative of the Services of His Majesty's Ship Superb, 74, on the night of the 12 July 1801 and the two following days, by her then Captain, Sir Richard Goodwin Keats G.C.B. &c*, (Appendix III)
164 Brenton, *op. cit.*, p.551
165 Ross, *op. cit.*, Vol II, p.31
166 Thomas, (10th Earl of Dundonald), *The Autobiography of a Seaman*, Richard Bentley, London, 1860, footnote, p.145
167 Keats, R.G., Narrative, *op. cit.* (Appendix III)
168 Outram, B.F., *Memoir, op. cit.*, p.67
169 Earl of Dundonald, *Autobiography of a Seaman, op. cit.*, p.134
170 *Ibid.* p.133
171 Keats, *Narrative*.
172 See correspondence 17 and 18 August 1801, Ross, *The Life of Lord De Saumarez*, Vol 2, p.10 and Thomas, Earl of Dundonald, *op. cit.* p.145
173 Keats, *Narrative*, p.20
174 Pridham, T. L., *Devonshire Celebrities*, Henry S. Eland, London 1869, p.142 *et. seq.* See also *The Quarterly Journal of the Geological Society of London*, Vol.13, 1857, p.67
175 *Naval Chronicle*, 1801, Vol 6, p 162. This is confirmed by the men of the *Hermenigildo*, Narrative, p.21
176 O'Brian, *Master and Commander*, Norton, London, 1994, 411. The novel faithfully records this court

martial as that of Jack Aubrey of the *Sophie*. Surgeon Outram's evidence is repeated verbatim by the fictional Surgeon Maturin. Cordingly, D, *Cochrane the Dauntless: The Life and Adventures of Thomas Cochrane, 1775-1860*, Bloomsbury, 2007, p.66

177 Allen, *op. cit.*, *The Morning Chronicle*, 2 October 1801, p.3.
178 Aldous, *Prize Money, op.cit.*, p.205
179 See letter Tucker to Saumarez, 10 August 1801, Ross, *op.cit*, Vol 2, p.7-8
180 Prizes: *London Gazette*, 15515, 14 September 1802, p.993; Head money, *London Gazette*, 15675, 14 February 1804, p.214.
181 Parkinson, C.N., *Britannia Rules, op. cit.*, p.76
182 *Ibid*, p.9
183 See *Campbells Lives of the British Admirals*, William Stevenson, London, 1817, Vol VII, Appendix, for more details of the size and components of the British navy though its history. Volume VIII includes details of various budget appropriations. Also, Rodger, N.A.M., *The Wooden World: An Anatomy of the Georgian Navy*, Norton, New York, 1986, p.11; *c.f.* Clowes, *op. cit.*, Vol 4, p.153. Various authors put forward slightly different figures, but the differences are not significant for the purpose of general comparison over the years.
184 Taylor, S., *Sons of the Waves*, Yale University Press, London, 2020, p.198, 297, 299 & 373; Knight, R, *Britain Against Napoleon Penguin, 2014*, p.217. Clowes, *op.cit.*, Vol 4, p.153. Parkinson, *Britannia Rules, op.cit.*, p.96 puts the number at 72 sail of the line, 120 frigates and 58 smaller vessels.
185 The *London Gazette*, issue 16186, 24 September 1808, p.1326.
186 15 October 1803, Nicolas, Vol 5, p.248
187 7 December 1803, Nicolas, Vol 5, p.302
188 Nicolas, Vol 5, p.125
189 Nicolas, Vol 5, pp.129-30
190 Nelson to Clarence, 6 September 1803, Nicolas Vol 5, p.197. The *Superb* left the fleet on 28 August and returned on 5 September
191 See Nicolas, Volume VI, p.40, note 6
192 British Library Add Mss 46356 ff88/9, cited in White, C., Nelson's 1805 Battle Plan; *Journal of Maritime Research*, 4:1, 82-88, p.83
193 Nicolas, Vol. 6, p.156
194 Knight, R., *William IV, op. cit.*, p.46
195 Duke of Clarence to Keats, 28 June, Pridham, T. L., *Devonshire Celebrities, op. cit.*, p.138-9. Examples of the medal are in various museum collections, including NMM Greenwich, MEC1191.
196 Laughton, *Nelson, op. cit.*, p.238
197 *Ibid.* pp.247-250
198 *Ibid.*, p.250
199 Mahan, A.T., *The Influence of Sea Power upon History*, Dover Publishing, New York, 1890.
200 *Rear Admiral Bertie, The Naval Chronicle*, Vol 26, July 1811, p.23
201 Nelson to Clarence, 24 May 1804, BL Add. Mss 46356 fol 91/2, quoted in White, C., 'A Man of Business': Nelson As Commander in Chief Mediterranean, May 1803-January 1805, *The Mariner's Mirror*, (2005) 91:2, p.174 at p.176.
202 See Janora, J.J., Analysis Considering The Significance Of The Use Of Naval Blockades During Napoleonic Wars, *The Exposition*, Vol.5 Iss.1, Article 1,

203 Nelson to Dr Moseley, Chelsea Hospital, 11 March 1804, Nicolas Vol 5, p.438
204 Nelson to Alexander Davison (his prize agent) 12 December 1803, Nicolas, Vol 5, p.306; Nelson to Ball, 7 November 1803, Nicolas, Vol V, pp.283-4.
205 Nelson to Ball, 4 October 1804, Nicolas, Vol 6, p.214.
206 Nelson to John Tyson, 12 December 1803, Nicolas, Vol 5, p.308.
207 Keats to Nelson, 3 August 1803, BL Add. Mss 34919fol.376
208 *Report of Superb's Passage through the Straits of Bonifacio,* BL Add. Mss 34919 fol. 355; See also Barritt, M., Agincourt Sound revisited, *The Mariner's Mirror,* (2015) 101:2, p.184 at p.185
209 Keats to Nelson, 19 September 1803, White, *Keats.,* p.358
210 Nelson to Marsden, 12 August 1804, Nicolas, Vol 6, p.150.
211 Gale, C. Piracy & Trade: Barbary and the British Protectorate of Malta; 1800-1813, *2017 United States National Archive paper submission*
212 Admiralty order 7 July 1803, Nicolas, Vol 5, p.181-2.
213 Admiralty Order 26 August Nicolas, Vol 5, p.232.
214 Nelson to the Dey of Algiers, 9 January 1804, Nicolas, Vol 5, p.347.
215 Sugden, J., *Nelson: The Sword of Albion*, Henry Holt, London, 2013, p.646
216 White, C., *Nelson, The New Letters,* Boydell & Brewer, 2005, p.362
217 Nicolas, Vol 5, p.345, and Memorandum at p.349-351
218 Memorandum 9 January 1804; Gale, C.M., *Beyond Corsairs. The British -Barbary Relationship During the French Revolutionary and Napoleonic Wars,* Trinity College, Oxford, Ph.D. Thesis, 2016
219 Nelson to Hobart, 19 January 1804, Nicolas, Vol 5, p.378
220 Nelson to Keats, 17 January 1804, Nicolas, pp.376-7.
221 Nelson to Sir Evan Nepean, Admiralty, 20 January 1804, Nicolas, Vol 5, p.383
222 Nelson to Ball, 16 January 1804, Nicolas, Vol 5, p.373
223 Nelson to Lady Hamilton, 20 January 1804, Czisnik, M., *Nelson's Letters to Lady Hamilton*, Navy Records Society London, 2020, #300
224 Nelson to Hobart, 31 May 1804, Nicolas, Vol 6, p.45.
225 Nelson to Lady Hamilton, *op.cit.;* The Dey of Algiers, Extract from a letter from an officer in Lord Nelson's fleet off Algiers, Jan 18, 1804, *Carlisle Weekly Herald*, 2 May 1804, p.2.
226 Instructions dated 8 March 1804, Nicolas, Vol 6, p.43 *et. seq.*
227 Clarke & M'Arthur, *op. cit.*, Vol 2, p.351
228 *Ibid.*
229 Alluded to in a letter from Ball to Nelson, and conveyed to Lord Hobart by letter of 16 October 1803, Nicolas, Vol V, p.251
230 Instructions 29 October 1804, Nicolas, Vol. 6, pp.295-6.
231 Nelson to Keats, 28 December 1804, Nicolas Vol VI, pp.303-4
232 Gale, *op. cit.*
233 In addition to the comments by Camden, the acting British pro-consul reported Keats conducted himself with great dignity, White, *Keats*, p.358.
234 The Secretary of State for War.
235 Secretary to the Admiralty Board
236 Clarke & M'Arthur, Vol 2, p.350.

237 *Naval Chronicle*, 1805, Vol 15, p.201-3, See also, for example, *Ennis Chronicle & Clare Advertiser*, 13 June 1805, Vol xxii, *Embassy to Algiers*, p.3
238 Nelson to Camden, 16 January 1805, Nicolas, Vol 6, p.333
239 Enclosed with that of Marsden, Admiralty to Nelson, Nicolas, Vol 6, p.295
240 Nelson to Hawkesbury, 29 June 1804, Camden to Nelson, 29 October 1804, Nicolas, Vol 6, p.88 & 298 respectively.
241 Nelson to Lord Camden, 1 April 1805, Nicolas, Vol 6, p.391.
242 *London Gazette*, 16429, 27 November 1810, p.1906, 16246, 11 April 1809, p.506
243 Nelson to Keats 15 January 1805, Nicolas, Vol VI, pp.321-2
244 Sugden, J., *Nelson- the Sword of Albion*, Henry Holt & Co, New York, 2012, p 675.
245 Clowes, (1897) *op.cit.*, Vol 5, p.79.
246 See Note 8, Nicolas, Vol VI, pp.393-5
247 Laughton, J.K., *Nelson, op. cit.*, p.247
248 Nelson to Keats, 8 May 1805.
249 Nelson to Lady Hamilton, Czisnik, *Nelson's Letters, op. cit.*, #341, and see #347, dated 10 October 1804.
250 Nelson to Keats, 3 December 1804, Nicolas *op. cit.* Vol VI, p.283-4, Letter to Lady Hamilton 4 December 1804, Czisnik, *Nelson's Letters, op. cit.* #354
251 *Victory* (100), *Royal Sovereign* (100), *Canopus* (80), *Superb, Spencer, Swiftsure, Belleisle, Conqueror, Tigre, Leviathon* and *Donegal* (74), together with frigates *Active* and *Seahorse*.
252 W. H Smyth, *Sketch of the Present State of the Island of Sardinia*, John Murray, London, 1828, p.249
253 United Services Magazine, Vol 59, 1849, p.488, or as Smyth records it; "it is evident my lord that Providence protects you", Smyth, W.H., *The Mediterranean, A Memoir*, John Parker, London 1845, p.335.
254 Gardiner, *op. cit.*, p.119
255 Nelson, recipient unstated, 1 February, Nicolas, Vol 6, p.334
256 Nelson to Clarence 13 March 1805, White, *New Letters, op. cit.*, p.417
257 See note 8, Nicolas, Vol 6, p.393.
258 Allen, J., *Life of Nelson*, Routledge, London, p.259, and referenced in "*The Old Superb*", below.
259 Southey, R., *The Life of Nelson*, (New Edition), Bell & Daldy, London, 1873, p.339.
260 Nelson to Marsden, 19 April 1805, Nicolas, Vol 6, p.411.
261 Nelson to the Duke of Clarence, Clarke & M'Arthur, op. cit. Vol 2, p.407.
262 Nelson to Simon Taylor, 10 June 1805, Nicolas, Vol 6, p.450.
263 Nelson to Keats, Victory, 8 May 1805
264 Log of the *Canopus*; related in Hubback, J.H. & Hubback, E.C., *Jane Austen's Sailor Brothers*, Cambridge University Press, 1906, p.132 et. seq.; Nelson to Lady Hamilton, 4 June 1805, Czisnik, *Nelson's Letters, op. cit.*, #374.
265 Nelson to Seaforth, Governor of Barbadoes, 8 June 1805, Nicolas, Vol 6, p.449
266 Nelson to Barham, 23 July Nicolas, Vol 6, p.489, and see Nelson to Duke of Clarence, 12 June 1805, Nicolas, Vol 6, p.455.
267 Nelson to the Duke of Clarence, 12 June 1805, Nicolas, Vol 6, p.455.
268 Gardiner, *op. cit.*, p.129
269 Napoleon, 8 September 1805, *The London Literary Gazette*, p.706
270 Lambert, A., *Nelson: Britannia's God of war*, Faber & Faber, *2004*. See also Pope, *England Expects*, Chatham Publishing, London, 1998, chapters 9-14.

271 Nelson to Lady Hamilton, 18 August 1805, Czisnik, *Nelson's Letters, op. cit.*, #381.
272 Nicolas, Vol 7, p.7-letter to Keats, and p.8, Log of Victory, Letter to Marsden, Accounts., £151,763; Letter Nelson to Keats, 19 August Nicolas, Vol 7, p.13. Sugden (*op. cit.*, p.750) puts it at only £32,300.
273 Clarke J.S. & M'Arthur, T, *The Life of Admiral Lord Nelson from his Manuscripts*, Cadell & Davies, London, 1809, Vol 2, p.420.
274 Nelson to St. Vincent 12 December 1803, Nicolas, Vol 5, p.307
275 Sugden, *op. cit.*, p.707
276 Nelson to Marsden, 28 May 1804; Newbolt, Sir J H. *The Year of Trafalgar*, John Murray, London, 1905
277 Nelson to Clarence, 10 May 1805; White, C.S. (Ed.) *Nelson: The New Letters*, Woodbridge, Suffolk, 2005; Nelson to Keats 8 May 1805.
278 Nelson to Keats, 19 May 1805, Nicolas Vol 6, p.442,
279 Newbolt, H.J., *The Year of Trafalgar*, John Murray, London, 1905. See Laughton J.K., Letters and Despatches of Lord Nelson, *The Edinburgh Review*, 1886, Vol 336, Leonard Scott, Philadelphia, p.555-6
280 Reference to the *Majestueux* is curious as she was part of Allemand's Rochefort squadron which sailed on 16 July with orders to cruise south of Cornwall so as to join Villeneuve and Ganteaume as they returned from the West Indies, adding to the strength of the fleet that would ultimately sweep up the Channel. She was not sailing with Villeneuve.
281 Laughton, J.K., *Nelson, op. cit.*, p.274
282 Rose, J. Holland, The State of Nelson's Fleet Before Trafalgar, *The Mariner's Mirror* (1922) Vol 8:3, p.75, at p.76.
283 Nelson to Keats, 19 June 1805, Nicolas, Vol 6, p.463
284 Nelson to Marsden, 25 July 1805, Nicolas Vol 6, p.496
285 Nelson to Cornwallis, 15 August 1805; Holland, *op.cit.*, p.76
286 Including their last interview with Prime Minister William Pitt; see Allen, J, *Life of Nelson,* Routledge, London, p.272
287 BL Add. Mss 34930,f 190, quoted by Stephen Wood, Nelson's Star of the Order of the Bath; Morton & Eden 2015.
288 Letter 24 August 1805, Merton, Nicolas Vol 7, p.15
289 Laughton, *Nelson, op.cit.*, pp.220-227 references Lord Minto and the Duke of Marlborough by way of example.
290 Corbett, J, *Fighting Instructions*, Naval Records Society, 1905, p.291. See also: White, C.; *The Nelson Touch: The Evolution of Nelson's Tactics at Trafalgar, Journal of Maritime Research*, 7;1,123.
291 Pope, *op. cit.,* p120-1. See also Corbett, J.S., *Fighting Instructions 1530-1816,* Vol 29, Navy Records Society, reproduced by Outlook 2018, pp.195-209. See also footnote 9, Nicolas, Vol 7, p.241, which would appear to be the original published source.
292 *Journal of Maritime Research* (2002),4:1, pp.82-88
293 A sketch dated 5 September found on the reverse of a letter intended from Rev. William Nelson to a correspondent at Cambridge University in a scrap book related to the papers of Captain William Layman, who visited Merton on that day has been similarly interpreted as depicting an enemy fleet sailing in line along shore, being attacked by three divisions, sailing faster on a broad reach, cutting the line and engaging from both sides. See auction details: https://www.martyndowner.com/sale-highlights/nelson-a-re-discovered-hand-drawn-plan-of-the-battle-of-trafalgar/

294 Nelson's conversation with Lord Sidmouth, 10 September 1805; Pellew Hon G, *The Life and Correspondence of Henry Addington, First Viscount Sidmouth*, John Murray, London, 1847, Vol 2, p.381

295 Cumberland, R., *The Memoirs of Richard Cumberland*, Lackington & Allen, London, 1807, Vol 1, pp.407-8

296 Wright, G.N. & Watkins., *The Life and reign of William the Fourth*, Fisher, Son & co, London, 1837, pp.73-4; Laughton, *Nelson, op. cit.*, p.289

297 See *Plan of Attack*, said to be drafted on the voyage, Nicolas Vol 6, p.442, Clowes, *op.cit.*, Vol 5, p.103

298 Tildesley, J., The Influence of the Theories of John Clerk of Eldin on British Fleet Tactics, 1782-1805, *The Mariner's Mirror,* 106:2 May 2020, pp.163-174

299 Nicolas Vol 6, p.442, Clowes, *op.cit.,* Vol 5, p.103

300 Locker, E.H., *Memoirs of Celebrated Naval Commanders*, Harding & Leopold, London, 1832, p.12

301 Houghton, 22 March 1824, MS Eng.1965, (133), quoted in Knight, R.; *The Pursuit of Victory*, Penguin, 2006, p.647, and referenced in Corbett, F*ighting Instructions 1530-1816, op. cit.*

302 Corbett, J. S., *The Campaign for Trafalgar-1805,* Vol 2, Pickle Partners, London; Nicolas, Vol 7, p.94

303 Sugden, *Nelson*, p.778; Willis, S., *In the Hour of Victory: The Royal Navy at war in the Age of Nelson*, Atlantic Books, p. 211; Pope, *England Expects*, p.154; Taylor, A.H., (1950) The Battle of Trafalgar, *The Mariner's Mirror*, 36:4, 281, p.283.

304 Pope, *op. cit.*, p 127-8; Tildesley, *op. cit.*, p.171

305 BL Add. Mss. 34931, ff 245-246, quoted in Wood, *Nelson's Star of the Order of the Bath, op. cit.*

306 Nelson to Pitt, 29 August 1805, Nicolas, Vol. 7, p.20; Nelson to Elliot, 30 September 1805, Nicolas, Vol. 7, p.59

307 Nelson to Ball, 15 October 1805, Nicolas Vol 7, p.123

308 Willis *op. cit.* p.255 refers to his favourite musicians.

309 The first-hand account of Edward Trelawny refers to waiting to load the sheep and potatoes, Trelawny, *Adventures of a Younger Son*, Richard Bentley, London, 1835 Vol 1, p.19 Published anonymously; there is no doubt the author was Edward Trelawny.

310 Hill, A., *Trelawny's Family Background and Naval Career,* Keats-Shelley Journal, Vol 5, 1956, p.11, at 16. the author agrees there was a delay from 28th to 2nd.

311 White, *op. cit.*, p.361 refers to his waiting '*long after the ship was ready for sea to enable some of his followers to join him*'.

312 *Ibid.* Willis, S., *op. cit.* p.255-6

313 Pope, D., *England Expects*, p.25 *et. seq.*

314 Some accounts say 'off', not 'after', Trafalgar, but it is clear the interception was off the Scilly Isles, about 60 miles from Falmouth.

315 Trelawny, *op. cit.*, p.18

316 The correspondent is identified only as MM, Naval Club, Bond Street, *The United Services Magazine, 1835*, Part 1, p.547

317 Referenced in Hill, *Trelawny, op. cit.*, p.16

318 *Ibid.* This writer also agrees there was a delay from 28th to 2nd; whilst stores "including thirty-five cases of wine for Vice Admiral Duckworth" were loaded.

319 Pope, D., *op. cit.* pp.22-7

320 *The Barham Papers*, Naval Records Society, 1909, Vol 39, pp.373-7

321 *Ibid.* letter 23 October pp.374-5
322 *Ibid.* pp.375-6
323 Duckworth to Nelson, 14 September 1805, Nicolas, Vol. 7, p.43
324 Duckworth to Nelson, 25 September 1805, Nicolas, Vol.7, p.44
325 Admiral Page's Comments made by hand on his copy of the *Naval Chronicle*, *The Mariner's Mirror*, Vol 53 No.4 (2013), p.377; comment added in Vol XV, 1806, p.255
326 *The Barham Papers, op. cit.*, p.377
327 *The Shipwrecked Mariner*, issue 57-59, Vol XV, P1, George Morrish, London, 1868., at p.7
328 Brenton, *Naval History, op. cit.*, p.104
329 Hill, *Trelawny, op. cit.*
330 See Ralfe, *Naval Biography*, Vol II, Whitmore & Fenn, Charing Cross, 1828
331 Cartel – a ship flying a flag of truce, generally engaged on a humanitarian mission, including, for example, exchange of prisoners.
332 James, *op. cit.* Vol IV, p.92
333 *Ibid.*, p.93
334 Clowes, *op. cit.*, Vol 5, p.187
335 Woodman, *op. cit.*, p.217; Willis *op. cit.* p.255
336 Willis, 2005.
337 Keats to Earl William Nelson, 11 January 1806, Add.Mss.34992, ff. 84-5.
338 *The Shipwrecked Mariner, op. cit.*, p.9
339 Willis *op. cit.*, p.258. See also James, *op. cit.*, Vol. IV, p.194-5. Those who quote a lower figure for the *Impériale* appear to count guns on the upper deck as 12-pounders, where 18-pounders were fitted, and fail to include the 36-pound carronades mounted on the forecastle.
340 Willis *op. cit.*, p.257
341 *Notes and Gleanings; A monthly Magazine Devoted Chiefly to Subjects Connected with the Counties of Devon and Cornwall*, Wm. Pollard, Exeter 1888, p.17
342 Willis *op. cit.*, p.255, the comment made in note 13 thereto.
343 *United Services Magazine*, 1834, part 2, p.216; Marshall, J., *Royal Naval Biography*, Longman Hurst Rees, Orme & Brown, London, 1823, Vol.1, p.346.
344 James describes Brenton as offering a 'panegyric of this kind' to make more of Duckworth's role and of the 'brilliant victory' generally than was deserved. James, *op. cit.* Vol 4, p.108. John Grant, *British Battles on Land and Sea*, Chapter LXXXII, p.338, Cassell, Petter, Golpin, London, agrees, but may be relying upon James.
345 Quoted by Hubback E.C. & J.H., *Jane Austin's Sailor Brothers*, John Lane, London 1906; Chapter XI St. Domingo, and in *Naval Chronicle* 1806, Vol 15, p.450 – the officer concerned is not named.
346 Willis, 2005, note 13, Ch.7I.
347 Brenton, E.P., *The Naval History of Great Britain*, Vol 2, p.109-10, Contrast James, Vol 4, p.103, who considered the victory unremarkable given the relative strengths and states of preparedness of the fleets.
348 *The Shipwrecked Mariner*, 1868, Vol XV, p.9, it would seem quoting Brenton, Vol. 2, p.106
349 Clowes, *op.cit.*, Vol. 5, p.192 (note1).
350 *The Shipwrecked Mariner*, 1868, Vol XV, p.9.
351 Davey, J., *In Nelson's Wake*, Yale University Press, National Maritime Museum, Greenwich, 2017, p.120
352 White, Keats *op. cit.*, pp.361-2

353 James, Vol IV, p.98
354 The Memoir and others confuse the *Brave* of 80 guns captured off Cape Ortegal in November 1805, with the *Brave* of 74 guns which fought at San Domingo
355 The Lloyds Patriotic Fund was established in 1803 in the Lloyds Coffee House, to encourage and reward behaviour above and beyond duty, whether in battle or in protecting trade and merchants. Swords to the value of 100 guineas were presented to the Trafalgar captains and another 35 were issued to various Captains for exceptional services.
356 Long, W.H., *Medals of the British Navy and How They Were Won*, Lancer, New Delhi, 2011, p.433; Southwick, *The Silver vases awarded by the Patriotic Fund*, *The Silver Society Journal*, Winter 1990, pp.27-49
357 *The Shipwrecked Mariner*, 1806, Vol 15, p.10., and Vol XV, 1868, p.9
358 See Duckworth to Marsden 16 February 1806, *The Times* 16 April 1806,
359 Woodman, *Sea Warriors*, Constable, London 2001, p.217
360 Bienkowski, L., *op. cit.* p.184; See also Fraser, E., *The fighting Fame of the King's Ships*, Hutchinson & Co, London, 1910, p.171. Correspondent from the Superb, *Naval Chronicle*, 1806, Vol 15, p.451
361 Clowes, *op.cit.*, Vol 5, p.193; James, *op.cit.*, Vol 4, p.165
362 Morrow, J., *British Flag Officers in the French Wars, 1793-1815*, Bloomsbury, 2018, p.200.
363 Knight, *Britain Against Napoleon, op.cit.*, p.230.
364 The merchants were essentially producers of sugar, which was a source of great wealth both in the West Indies and in Britain. In another context they may be better described as the 'slave owning plantocracy'.
365 Davey, J, *In Nelson's Wake, op. cit.* p.121; White, *op. cit.*, p.362
366 Woodman, *op. cit.*, p.217
367 Arriving after a five-month absence, on 29 April 1806; Willis, *op. cit.*, p.254, *The Shipwrecked Mariner*, Vol XV, 1868, p.10
368 A 'private ship' is one on active service, but not currently as the flagship of a flag officer. It does not entail any notion of private ownership. Having previously been the flagship of Admiral Duckworth, the *Superb* was now under Keats's sole command.
369 *The Shipwrecked Mariner*, Vol XV, 1868, p.11., Allen, J., *Battles of the British Navy* Vol.2, p.173, Henry Bohn, London 1852., Woodman, *Sea Warriors, op. cit.*, pp.222-227, Letter R. D. Oliver to Keats, 29 July 1806, transmitted to Admiral St. Vincent.
370 Keats to St Vincent, 2 August 1806, *Naval Chronicle*, 1806 Vol16, p.172.
371 25 October 1806, Brenton, E.P., *Life and Correspondence of John, Earl of St. Vincent op. cit.* p.319, and then on 3 December 1806, *Naval Miscellany*, Vol 92, Naval Records Society, #12, p.486. Various works incorrectly transcribe this as 'professes' not 'possesses'.
372 Letter dated 3 December 1806 (Brenton, *op. cit.*, p.332).
373 A commodore with a captain under him was effectively a temporary rear admiral. A commodore with broad pendant, but no captain was in charge of a squadron on an *ad hoc* basis and was required to captain his own ship. He did not take a flag officer's share of prize money. Aldous KC, G., *The Law Relating to the Distribution of Prize Money in the Royal Navy and its relationship to the use of Naval Power 1793-1815*, PhD. Thesis, Kings College London, 2020, p.24
374 St. Vincent to Markham, 13 July 1806, *The Papers of Admiral John Markham*, Navy Records Society, 1904, p 58 [*The Markham Papers*]
375 St. Vincent to Markham 18 July 1806, *ibid.* p.58

376 Tucker, J.S., *Memoirs of Admiral the Right Honourable Earl of St. Vincent.*, Richard Bentley, London, 1844, p.308
377 Voelcker, T., op. cit., p.83
378 *The Markham Papers*, p.61
379 St Vincent to Grenville, 5 November 1806, *The Naval Miscellany*, Vol 92, Naval Records Society, #12, p.480
380 St. Vincent to Keats, 9 March 1807, Brenton, E.P., *Life and Correspondence of John, Earl of St. Vincent*, Vol 2, p.333.
381 St. Vincent to Keats, 9 March 1809, Brenton, *op. cit.* p.315
382 St. Vincent to Grenville, 15 March 1807, Brenton, *op. cit.*, p.340
383 Cobbett, *Parliamentary Debates, First session, Third Parliament* Vol IX, 1807, House of Commons, Friday 10 July 1807, [Naval abuses] pp.753-768
384 Those interested in the case for and against and the merits of the various findings are referred to; Thomas, 10th Earl of Dundonald, *The Autobiography of a Seaman*, Richard Bentley, London, 1860, and to a response in Ellenborough, *The Guilt of Lord Cochrane in 1814, A Criticism*, Smith Elder & Co, London 1914.
385 Cobbett, *op. cit.*, p.760
386 Hepper, D. J., *British Warship Losses in the Age of Sail*, Jean Boudroit, 1994, p.117
387 Cobbett, *op. cit.*, p.760
388 St. Vincent to Keats, 9 March 1807, Brenton, *op. cit.*, pp.333-4
389 St. Vincent to Grenville, 18 March 1807, Brenton, *op. cit.*, p.334
390 Bingeman, J., Simpson, P., Tomalin, D., *The Wrecks of HM Frigate Assurance (1755) and Pomone (1811), The Career of Admiral Sir Robert Barrie (1774-1841)*, Oxbow, Oxford, 2021, p.80, See also Marshall, *Naval Biography,* 1832, p.168
391 Marshall, *Naval Biography, op.cit.*, Captain Bowker, Vol III, Part I, p.433
392 Cobbett, *op. cit.*, p.755
393 *Ibid.*, p.761
394 *Ibid.*, p.768
395 Bingeman *et al, op.cit.*, p.80
396 St. Vincent to Grenville 15 March 1807, Brenton, *op. cit.*, p.340
397 Bingeman *et al, op.cit.*, p.80
398 St. Vincent to Keats, 9 March 1806, *ibid.*
399 Keats, R., *Situation of the enemy's squadron under Isle d'Aix (23rd April 1807), with proposed Mode of Attack enclosed*, London, 1807. See Gurney, W.B., *Minutes of a Court martial on the trial of Lord Gambier, Portsmouth 1809.*
400 Instructions to Admiral Lord Gambier, 19 March 1809, (1809) *Naval Chronicle*, Vol 22, p.220
401 Parkinson, *Britannia Rules, op. cit.*, p.149
402 Laughton, J.K., *Oxford Dictionary of National Biography, Sir Eliab Harvey*, p.148
403 Advice from Lord Pembroke, Ambassador to Vienna, to Lord Canning; Glover, G., *The Two battles of Copenhagen 1801 and 1807*, Pen and Sword, Yorkshire, 2018, pp.103-4.
404 Letter Hood, Keats & Stopford to Gambier, 23 July 1807, *The Naval Chronicle*, 1808, Vol 19, p.68; Popham, H., *A Damned Cunning Fellow*, Old Ferry Press, 1991, p.178
405 *Naval Chronicle, ibid.*
406 Hamilton, *Martin Papers*, Vol 1, p.334,
407 Castlereagh to Gambier, 18 July 1807; cited in Ryan, A.N., The Navy at Copenhagen in 1807; *The Mariner's Mirror*, 1953 Vol 39:3, p.201

408   Glover, *op. cit.*, Ch.14.
409   Gambier to Pole 4 August 1807, enclosing instructions to Keats, 27 July and 30 July 1807, Navy Records Society, *Naval Miscellany* Vol V, #16
410   *Ibid*, and see Raymond, D.J., *The Royal Navy in the Baltic*, p.69
411   Keats to Gambier, enclosed with letter Gambier to Pole, 10 August 1807, Naval Miscellany, Vol V, #20.
412   Davey, J., *In Nelson's Wake, op. cit.*, p.153
413   Ryan, *The Navy at Copenhagen in 1807*, *op. cit.*
414   Raymond, *op. cit.*, p.69
415   Glover *op. cit.* p.154 suggests that three hundred and fifty men crossed over undiscovered on 4 September, but were unable to achieve anything of significance
416   Glover, *op. cit.*, p.161.
417   Knight, *Britain Against Napoleon, op .cit.*, p.202.
418   James, *op. cit.*, Vol IV., pp.294-5
419   Nester, W., *Britain's Rise to Global Superpower in the Age of Napoleon*, Pen & Sword, Yorkshire, 2020, p.142
420   Tracy, N., *Who's who in Nelson's Navy,* Chatham, London, p.211. As a result of the public disquiet the work originally described as 'Ships returned from Copenhagen', was renamed by Turner to simply 'Boat's Crew recovering Anchor'; Tate Gallery, London, N00481.
421   Wright, G.N. & Watkins, J., *William the Fourth, op. cit.*, Fisher, Son & Co, London, 1837, p.394
422   Voelcker, *Saumarez, op.cit.,* p.13
423   Wright, G.N. & Watkins, J., *op. cit.*, p.394
424   James, *op. cit.*, Vol IV., p.294, Clowes, *op. cit.*, Vol 5, p.216.
425   *Cobbett's Weekly Political Register,* Vol 12, p.797.
426   James, *op. cit.*, Vol IV., p.211.
427   Ryan, *The Navy at Copenhagen in 1807 op.cit.*
428   James Hunter, Francis Pender, William Otway, George Lumsdaine, (Sir Samuel Hood), Henry Nichols, Herbert Sawyer, and David Gould. Having been appointed flag officer Keats relinquished his Colonelcy of the Royal Marines.
429   *The Shipwrecked Mariner,* Vol XV 1868, p.12.
430   9 March 1807, Brenton, *St. Vincent, op. cit.*, p.333
431   *The Naval Chronicle*, Vol. 22, 1809, p.518 and Vol 29 July 1813, p.172.
432   For example, *Exeter Flying Post*, Thursday 26 November 1807, p.1, *Hampshire Chronicle*, 23 November 1807, p.4, *Public Ledger & Daily Advertiser*, 24 November 1807, p.2.
433   According to Clowes (Vol.5, p.247) there were a total of 14,000 troops in 200 transports. Marsden (2021, p.29) puts the number at 11,000 troops, others refer to 105 transports (*Chronological Retrospect of the History of Yarmouth & Neighbourhood*, Finch-Crisp, W, Yarmouth, 1884 – entry for 1808).
434   Clarence to Keats, Nov 1807, quoted in Owen, H., *I shall make five sons of mine fight for their king and country: The Naval Sons of William IV and Mrs Jordan, The Mariner's Mirror*, Vol 83, Feb 1997, p.42
435   Aspinall, A., *Mrs Jordan and her Family* (1951), 72, letter to George FitzClarence, 4 Dec 1808, quoted in Owen, *op. cit.*, p.42.
436   *Ibid.* p.42
437   Duke of Clarence to Collingwood; May 21 1808, Collingwood, C, *A selection from the Public and Private Correspondence of Vice Admiral Lord Collingwood*, p.120

438 Mulgrave to Saumarez, 20 February, and Saumarez's reply 27 February 1808, Ross, *Memoirs*, Vol 2, p 100.
439 White, *Keats, op. cit.*, p.363, reference NMM KEA6.
440 Saumarez to Hood, Gothenburg, 18 May 1808, Ryan, A.N., *The Saumarez Papers*, Naval Records Society, 1968, [*The Saumarez Papers*], Vol 110, p.18.
441 Voelcker, *op.cit.*, p.41; Knight, R., *Britain Against Napoleon*, Allen lane, London, 2013, p.329
442 Keats to Byam Martin 7 July 1808, Hamilton, *Martin Papers, op. cit.* p.23
443 See Byam Martin letter to Sir Henry Martin 14 July 1808, Hamilton, *Martin Papers*, p.68
444 Admiral Pole to Saumarez, 27 June 1808, *The Saumarez Papers*, #26.
445 Davey, J., *In Nelson's Wake, op. cit.*, p.233.
446 See; Knight, R., *The Achievement and Cost of the British Convoy System, 1803-1815*, in Morgan-Owen, D & Halewood, L, (Eds.) Economic Warfare and the Sea, *Research in Maritime History*, No55, Liverpool University Press, 2020, Knight, R. *Convoys*, Yale University Press, London, 2022, p.186
447 Letter T Byam Martin, Helsingborg, 27 April 1808, Hamilton, *Martin Papers, op. cit.* p.9
448 Keats to Saumarez, 5 August 1808, *The Saumarez Papers*, Vol 110 #15, #36, and footnote.
449 Marshall, J., *op. cit.*, Vol III, Part I, p.43-4
450 James, *op. cit.*, p.369
451 Knight, *Convoys*, 2022, p.191 cites Francis Austen negotiating a reward of £1,500 from the East India Company for successful delivery of a valuable convoy without loss.
452 As CIC Saumarez is said to have earned £12,000 in 1807-08 (Voelcker, op.cit., p.211) and £20,000 over 1808-09, (Morrow, *op.cit.*, p.189). While Keats's share, as commander of one squadron would have been considerably less, it would not have been insubstantial relative to an annual salary of around £500.
453 Davey, J., *War, Naval Logistics and the British State; Supplying the British Fleet*, 1808-1812, Thesis, University of Greenwich, 2009, gala.gre.ac.uk
454 Keats Memorandum, 16 September 1808, see Davey, *In Nelson's Wake op. cit.*, p.79
455 Keats memorandum, 15 September 1808, *ibid*.
456 *Naval Chronicle*, Rear Admiral Bertie, Vol. 26, 1811, p.25.
457 Keats to Pole, 27 November 1808, Ryan, *Saumarez Papers, op. cit.*, #54.
458 Raymond, *op. cit.*, p.169
459 Glover, *op. cit.* (p.196), puts Danish and Norwegian losses at the equivalent of one vessel every other day and 7,000 seamen imprisoned.
460 Davey, *op. cit.* p.248, Knight, *Convoys*, 233 relying on other sources puts the figure at 2,210 ships without loss – but the net effect is clear.
461 Raymond, D. J., *The Royal Navy in the Baltic 1807-1812, op. cit.*, p.71
462 Keats to Byam Martin 7 July 1808, Hamilton, *Martin Papers*, p.23
463 Marsden, J., *Napoleon's Stolen Army*, Helion & Co, Warwick, 2021, p.35
464 Castlereagh to Moore, 30 June 1808, Ryan, *Saumarez Papers, op. cit.*, #30a
465 Thornton to Saumarez, 12 July 1808, Ryan, *Saumarez Papers, op. cit.*, p.28
466 Saumarez to Mulgrave, 28 July 1808, *ibid,*#35 and draft letters, #32.; ADM 1/6 Saumarez to Keats 2 August 1808.
467 Admiralty to Keats; NMM KEA,6/9
468 Saumarez to Mulgrave, 9 August 1808, *The Saumarez Papers*, #39; Davey J., The Repatriation of Spanish troops from Denmark, 1808: The British Government, Logistics, and maritime Supremacy, *The Journal of Military History*, 2010, p.689 at p.699

469 Robertson, J., *Narrative of A Secret Mission to the Danish Islands in 1808*, A.C. Fraser Editor, Longman Green, Longman, Roberts and Green, London, 1863, p.71
470 Robertson *op. cit.*, p.46 & 71, See also Marsden, *Napoleon's Stolen Army, op.cit.*, pp.47-8
471 Saumarez to Mulgrave 28 July 1808, *Saumarez Papers*, #35, see Raymond, *op. cit.*, p.164, *Saumarez Papers*, draft letters #32
472 Robertson, *op .cit.*, p.85 and p.100 *et. seq.*
473 Marsden, *op. cit.*, p.48. John Hookham Frere, Minister Plenipotentiary to the Central Junta in Madrid, provides a different (and less credible) version, whereby Frere provides the means for Robertson to prove his bona fides disguised as a German School teacher, contacts Romana and returns to Heligoland from where McKenzie sets off to Gothenburg to find Moore and failing in this eventually contacts Saumarez; Frere, J.H., *The Works of John Hookham Frere*, Basil Montague Pickering, London, 1874, p.83-7
474 Memoir of La Romana, extracted in Robertson's Narrative, *op. cit.*, pp.159-60
475 Davey, *The Repatriation of Spanish Troops from Denmark,1808*, 2010, Journal of Military History 74, p.689, p.692,n.10; Voelcker, *Saumarez, op. cit.*, p.49; Marsden, *op. cit.*, p.48.
476 *Davey, ibid*, pp.692 & 699.
477 Sparrow, E., *Secret Service, British Agents in France*, John Wiley, London, 1999, p.363.
478 Log of the *Edgar*, 1 August 1808, ADM 51/2336, see Marsden, *op. cit.*, p.65 (spelt Fabragues/ Fabregues in various sources)
479 Marsden, *op. cit.*, p.88.
480 *A Baltic Incident: 1808*, 1954, Naval Review (London) Vol 42, p.78 at p.80, *cf.* Marsden *op. cit.* By way of confirmation it will be noted Keats was apparently uninformed of the events on Zealand when writing to Romana on 5 August and still on 7 August when he proposed collection of the troops in Zealand from point Halskon, which indicates his messenger had not come from that island.
481 Keats to Saumarez, 5 August 1808, *The Saumarez Papers*, # 36.
482 Marsden, *op. cit.*, pp. 67 (Fabregues), 89 (log of the Edgar).
483 Keats to Saumarez, 5 August 1808, *The Saumarez Papers*, # 36. *Ibid.*

484 Keats to Romana, 5 August 1808, Ralfe, J, *The Naval chronology of Great Britain*, Whitmore & Fenn, London, 1820, Vol II, p.83
485 Some sources put it as the night of 5-6 August – but he was certainly onboard the Superb on 5 August and put ashore from the *Edgar* early in the morning of 6 August. He could not have been in Nyborg in the early hours of 6 August.
486 Graves to Keats, 5 August 1808, ADM 1/6/407, TNA, cited by Davey *op. cit.*, p.699, n.43
487 Keats to Saumarez, 4 August 1808, ADM 1/6/403
488 Keats to Romana, 7 August 1808, Ralfe, J, *The Naval chronology of Great Britain*, Whitmore & Fenn, London, 1820, Vol II, p.85
489 Marsden, *op .cit.*, pp.91-2
490 Keats letter to the Admiralty, 11 August 1808.
491 Marsden, op cit., p.73
492 *Ibid.*, p.74
493 *Ibid.*, p.76
494 *Ibid.*, pp.69, 78
495 Keats to the Governor of Nyborg 9 August 1808, ADM 1/6/450, TNA

496 Keats to Saumarez, 11 August 1808, Ralfe, *Saumarez Papers, op. cit.*, pp.81-2. A number of the men were awarded the Naval General Service Medal.
497 Keats to Saumarez, 25 January 1809, Ryan, *Saumarez Papers, op. cit.*, #56
498 Keats to Romana, 9 August Ralfe, *op. cit.,* p.85
499 *A Baltic Incident: 1808*, 1954, Naval Review (London) Vol 42, p.78 at p.81
500 Keats to Governor of Nyborg, 10 August 1808, ADM 1/7/25, TNA
501 Keats to all Captains; *Hound,* off Nyborg, 11 August 1808, ADM80/145, cited at Marsden, *op .cit.,* p.96
502 *A Baltic Incident: 1808*, 1954, Naval Review (London) Vol 42, p78 at p81; Keats to Pole, 11 August 1808, Ralfe *Saumarez Papers, op .cit.,* pp.81-3
503 Keats to Pole, 11 &13 August 1808, Ralfe, *op. cit.,* pp.81 & 86
504 Morrow, J., *British Flag Officers in the French wars, 1793-1815: Admirals' Lives*, Bloomsbury p.22
505 An island off the coast of Funen.
506 Keats to Admiralty, 13 August 1808, ADM 1/6/456, cited in Marsden, *op. cit.,* p.97.
507 Keats to all Captains, cited at Marsden, *op. cit.,* p.100.
508 Marsden, J, *Napoleon's Stolen Army*, Helion & Co, Warwick, 2021, pp.105-106
509 White, Keats, *op. cit.,* p.364
510 LeFevre, *op. cit.,* p.15
511 Marsden, *op. cit.,* p.103 *et. seq.*
512 Keats to Admiralty, 22 August 1808, ADM 1/7/56-59; Davey, *op. cit.* 703. The victualling of these troops and supplying the Baltic fleet more generally is well examined by Davey. J., *War, Naval Logistics and the British state, Supplying the Baltic Fleet, 1808-1812*, Ph.D. thesis, gala.gre.ac.uk, pp.141-5, and more generally in Davey, J., *The Transformation of British Naval Strategy: Seapower and Supply in Northern Europe, 1808-1812*, Woodbridge, Boydell Press, 2012.
513 Keats to Admiralty, 1 September 1808, ADM 1/7/104
514 Barney J., North Sea and Baltic Convoy 1793-1814, *The Mariner's Mirror* (2009) 95:4, p.429 at p.436.
515 Davey, *The Repatriation of Spanish Troops, op. cit.,* p.704
516 Keats to Admiralty 6 September 1808, ADM 1/7/159, cited by Marsden, op. cit., p.112.
517 Hall, C.D., *Wellington's Navy, Sea Power in the Peninsular War, 1807-1814*, p.65
518 Mulgrave to Saumarez, 25 August 1808, Ross, *Saumarez,* Vol 1, p.114.
519 Ralfe, J, *The Naval chronology of Great Britain,* Whitmore & Fenn, London, 1820, Vol II, p.81 *et. seq.*
520 Duke of Portland to the King, 25 August 1808, Aspinall, A., *Correspondence of George III, op. cit.,* p.116.
521 *Ibid.* p.116
522 Lord Mulgrave to Rev. Keats, 22 September 1808
523 Harding, F.G.S., *Historical Memoirs of Tiverton, supra,* Vol.2, pp.116-7. *The London Gazette*, issue 16191, p.1401
524 *Naval Chronicle*, Vol. 26, Dec. 1811, p.24.
525 *The London Gazette,* issue 16275 15 July 1809, p.1097-8.
526 Nicolas, N.H., *History of the Orders of Knighthood of the British Empire*, 1842, Vol 3, p.114. *The London Gazette,* issue 16609, June 1812, p.1053-5, *La Belle Assemblée*, Vol V – New Series, J. Bell London, 1812, p.324
527 Quoted in Sullivan, A., *Man of War: The fighting life of Admiral James Saumarez*, Pen & Sword, Yorkshire, 2017

528 Davey, *op. cit.*, p.702, White, Keats, *op.cit.*, p.364
529 Quoted in *The Shipwrecked Mariner*, Vol XV, 1868, p.12; Brenton, *The Naval History of Great Britain*, Vol 2, p.231 – although in the original version it is incorrectly claimed that the brig and cutter were also restored.
530 Davey, *In Nelson's Wake.*, p.189., Davey, *Repatriation of Spanish Troops*, p.702
531 Raymond, D. J., *op. cit.*, p.165
532 Davey, *op. cit.*, p.705.
533 Pridham, *Devonshire Celebrities*, p.136. Keats's correspondence to The Hon. W. W. Poole, outlining the whole exercise, and the various letters to Marquis de la Romana can be found in Ralfe's *Naval Chronology of Great Britain*, Vol II, p.81 *et. Seq.*
534 St. Vincent to Keats, 2 January 1809, and 9 March 1809; NMM KEA/5
535 Letter to his sister Martha, quoted by Voelcker, *op. cit.*, p.53
536 Ross, *op. cit., Memoirs*, Vol II, p.113; Saumarez to Mulgrave, 9 August 1808, off Bornholm, Ryan, *Saumarez Papers*, #39
537 Sullivan, *op. cit.*, p.161
538 Saumarez to Keats, 15 August 1808, *The Saumarez Papers*, #40
539 See Voelcker, *op.cit.*, p.52 and at 213
540 Hamilton, *Martin Papers* Vol. 2, p.127
541 Cited by Voelcker, *op. cit.*, p.52, note 84.
542 Correspondence 14 October 1808; Aspinall, *Correspondence of George III op. cit.*, Vol V, p.141
543 Keats to Saumarez, 25 December 1808.
544 Correspondence 3 & 4 January 1809, Aspinall, *Correspondence of George III, op. cit.*, Vol V, p.165, # 3779
545 Keats to Navy Board, 30 January, 2 February 1809
546 Keats to Pole, 27 November 1808, *The Saumarez Papers*, #54.
547 Davey, *War, Naval Logistics op. cit.*, pp.164-5
548 Keats to Hood, 6 May 1809, Suffolk RO, HA 93/6/1/548
549 Keats to Merry, 11 March 1809, *The Saumarez papers*, #54.
550 Keats to Hood, 26 March 1809; Voelcker, *op. cit.*, p.82 *et. seq.*
551 Aspinall, *Correspondence of George III op. cit.*, p.249, annotation to Mulgrave's letter.
552 Clarence to Keats, Somerset RO, DD/CPL/35, cited in Owen, *op.cit.*, p.43
553 Brenton, *The Naval History of Great Britain*, Vol 2, p.289
554 Brenton, *ibid.* quoted in Parkinson, *Britannia Rules, op. cit.*, p.153
555 Parkinson, *Britannia Rules, op. cit.*, p.154
556 *Cobbett's Parliamentary Debates Volume* 15, p.573
557 *Letters from Flushing*, By an officer of the 81st Regiment, Richard Phillips, London, 1809, p.24.
558 The illness referred to was often called 'polder fever', a malaria like disease of the swamp lands, which at one time put 14,000 of the 39,000 men on the sick list.
559 The *Scots Magazine* Vol 71, September 1809, p.696.
560 Captain Codrington, letter to his wife, 27 August 180, Bourchier, *Memoir of Sir Edward Codrington*, Longman Green & Co, London, 1873, p 149
561 Howard, M. R., *Walcheren 1809: Scandalous Destruction of a British Army*, Pen & Sword, Yorkshire, 2012,
562 Keats to Strachan, 12 & 15 August. State Papers, *Naval Chronicle*, 1810, p.213

563 Strachan to Pole, 17 August 1808, Ralfe, *op. cit.*, p.211
564 Keats to Rosslyn and reply, 17 August, *ibid.* p216. Brenton, *op. cit.*, pp.302-303
565 Keats to Strachan, 18 August *ibid.* pp.215-6
566 Strachan to W. Pole, Admiralty, 22 August, Brenton, *Naval History of Great Britain*, Vol 2 p.302
567 Brenton, 1825, E.P, *op.cit.*, Vol IV, pp.322-3.
568 *Ibid.*
569 Strachan to Pole, 27 August, *The Scots Magazine*, Vol 71, September 1809, p.697. Some 12,000 soldiers were hospitalised, and 4,000 died -only 106 from wounds, Davey, *In Nelson's Wake, op. cit.* p.201.
570 Chatham to Strachan, 27 August, *ibid.* pp.220-1
571 Strachan to Pole, 27 August, *ibid.* p.219
572 Lanfrey, P. *The History of Napoleon the First*, Macmillan & Co, London, Vol 4, p.202
573 Strachan to Pole, 4 August 1809; *Flowers Political Review and Monthly Register, 1809*, p.143
574 Cobbett's Parliamentary Debates Vol XV, 1810, Papers Relating to the expedition to the Scheldt, p.295
575 Parliamentary Debates – Official Report 1810, Vol 16, p.59
576 Letter 25 August 1809, Bourchier, *Codrington, op.cit.*, p 146
577 Lanfrey, *op. cit.* pp.201-2
578 Keats to Strachan, 12 August 1809, Ralfe, *Naval Chronology, op. cit.* Vol 2, p.211.
579 Woodman, R, *The Victory of Seapower, op. cit.*, p.140
580 *Naval Chronicle*, Vol 23, 1810, Retrospective and Miscellaneous, p.148
581 Cited in Roberts, A., *Napoleon - A life*, Penguin Books, 2015, p.526.
582 *Journal of Joseph Wrangler, Marine*; Yarrow, D, *A Journal of the Walcheren Expedition 1809, The Mariner's Mirror*, 1975, 61.2, p.183 at 184-5. For a more fulsome account, see Bond, G.C.; T*he Great Expedition: The British invasion of Holland 1809,* University of Georgia Press, 1979.
583 Brenton, 1825, Vol IV *op. cit.* p.320
584 Lord Chatham, Report to the King, 14 February 1810, reproduced as Naval Papers, 1810, *The Naval Chronicle*, Vol. 23, p.226.
585 White, Keats *op. cit.*, p.365
586 Owen, *op. cit.*, p.43
587 *Ibid.* p.44
588 *Ibid.* p.45. Henry was deployed to India, where he died aged 22.
589 *London Gazette*, 16327, 1809-12-23, p2041. The Parliamentary Debates from the year 1803 to the present time, Volume 11, p.189
590 Brenton, E. P., *Life and Correspondence of John, Earl of St. Vincent* Vol 1, p.344
591 Davey, *In Nelson's Wake, op.cit.*, p. 205.
592 *The London Chronicle*, 11 June 1810, p.560.
593 Somerset Records Office; DD/CPL/45
594 Extract of a letter from Bideford, *The Exeter Flying Post*, 14 June 1810, p.4.
595 Hall, *op. cit.*, p.157
596 Liverpool to Graham, 12 July 1810, Delavoye, A.M., *Life of Thomas Graham*, Marchant Singer & Co, London, p.393; e.g. *Salopian Journal*, W. Edwards, Shewsbury,18 July 1810.
597 Quoted in Parkinson, *Britannia Rules, op. cit.*, p.136
598 Wellington to Keats, 2 August 1810; Gurwood, *The Dispatches of Field Marshall Duke of Wellington, 1799-1818*, Vol.6, pp.319-22.

599 For a commentary on the unsuccessful attack launched from Gibraltar against Fort Fuengirola in October 1810, see Barker, T.M., A Debacle of the Peninsular War: The British-Led Amphibious Assault Against Fort Feungirola, 14-15 October 1810, *J. of Military History*, 2000, Vol 64 p.9 at p.26
600 Hall, *op. cit.*, p.158, and see note 19.
601 Ralfe, J, *The Naval Biography of Great Britain*, Whitmore and Fenn, London, 1828, Vol III, Edward Codrington, p.198
602 PRO Kew. ADM 1/417, 275 (August 1810). Cited in Barker, *op. cit.*, p.23.
603 Wellington to Keats, 2 August 1810, Gurwood, *op.cit.*, p.321
604 Dispatch of Sir R. G. Keats 5 August 1811.
605 Marshall, *Royal Navy Biography*, op. cit., Smyth, William Henry
606 *Ibid.*
607 *United Services Magazine*, 1844, part 1, p.56 *et seq*. See also, Musteen, *Nelson's Refuge, op. cit.*, pp.111-115.
608 *A Glance on Spain, United Service Magazine* 1844, Vol 1, p.62
609 *Ibid.* p.63. One of these captured howitzers was mounted in St James's Park.
610 White, *Keats,* p366. For a full account of the Battle see Graham, J & Mace, M, *The Battle of Barrosa 1811, Forgotten Battle of the Peninsular War,* Skyhorse, 2014. For more detail on the combined operations off Cádiz, see Hall, *op. cit.*, pp.158-164, and Herson, *supra*.
611 *United Services Magazine*, 1843, part III, *A Glance Upon Spain*, p.488
612 *Ibid.* p.64
613 Davies, H., *Spying for Wellington: British Military Intelligence in the Peninsular War,* University of Oklahoma Press, 2018, p.101, Davies Huw, Naval Intelligence Support to the British Army in the Peninsular War, J. *Society for Army Historical Research*, 86 (2008), pp.34-36.
614 Davies, H, *Naval intelligence op. cit.,* 34, p.40
615 *United Services Magazine*, 1844, part I, *A Glance Upon Spain*, p.58
616 James, *op. cit.*, p.352
617 Herson J. P., *For the Cause, Cádiz & The Peninsular War: Military and Siege Operations 1808-1812,* University of Florida Master's Thesis https://apps.dtic.mil/dtic/tr/fulltext/u2/a252088.pdf
618 Musteen, J.R., *Nelson's Refuge, op. cit.*, pp.116-7.
619 Hall, *op. cit.,* p.163
620 Keats's letter 7 March 1811, A Glance on Spain, *United Service Magazine*, 1844, *op. cit.* p.66
621 See letter R.G. Keats to Sir C. Cotton, 7 March, Ralfe, *The Naval Chronology of Great Britain, 1811,* p.123., Brenton, *op. cit.,* p.398
622 Letter Keats to Sir C. Cotton, 7 March 1811, Ralfe, *The Naval Chronology of Great Britain, The Edinburgh Annual Register for 1811, Vol 4, Part 1, W. Scott,* p.294
623 Herson, *op. cit.*, p.153
624 Smyth, W. H., *Mediterranean; A Memoir, Physical Historical and Nautical*, John W. Parker, London, 1854, p.235-6
625 Voelcker, *op. cit.,* p.83
626 Hall, *op. cit.,* p.156
627 *Ibid.*
628 *A Glance Upon Spain, United Service Magazine,* 1844, *op. cit.,* p 57
629 Raymond, *op. cit.*, p.71
630 Brenton, *op. cit.,* p.332

631 Letter 28 December 1811, Osler, E., *The life of Admiral Viscount Exmouth*, pp.253-4.

632 Parkinson, C. N., *Pellew op. cit.* p.409. Lady Bentinck was a niece of the Duke of Wellington.

633 Taylor, S; *Commander: The life and Exploits of Britain's Greatest Frigate Captain*, Faber & Faber, 2012, pp.194-5

634 Smyth, W. H., *Notices of the Manor and Mansion of Hartwell*, John Boyer, London, 1851, p.379

635 Correspondence in family collection, concerning day to day events, news of acquaintances etc.

636 Parkinson, C.N., *Edward Pellew op. cit.*, p.398-99

637 Taylor, S; *Commander, op. cit.*

638 Raymond, *op. cit.*, p.215

639 St Vincent to Keats, 19 November 1809, Somerset records Office, DD/CPL 43, cited in Morrow, *op. cit.*, p.235

640 Morrow, *op.cit.*, p.241.

641 The Order was modified in January 1815 to recognise more of those who had distinguished themselves in the recent war. Knight Companions of the Order of the Bath (K.B.) of which Keats was one of 36 were elevated to Knight Grand Cross of the Order of the Bath (G.C.B.) of which there could be 72, which became the top tier of three, sitting above Knight Commander (K.C.B.) of which there could be 180 and Knight Companion (K.C).

642 Pengelly, C., *H.M.S. Bellerophon*, Pen & Sword Books, Yorkshire, 2014

643 *Ibid*, p.227

644 *Naval Biographical Dictionary*, Vol.1 (Hawker), O'Byrne, W. R.

645 London Gazette, 1813, p.2167. Bond, A., Cowin, F., and Lambert, A., *Favourite of Fortune, Captain John Quilliam, Trafalgar Hero*, Seaforth Publishing, Barnsley, 2021, p.116

646 Aldous, *op.cit.*, p.108

647 Pengelly *op. cit.*, p.230

648 Bond, A., Cowin, F., and Lambert, *op. cit.*, p.120.

649 Earl William Nelson to Keats, 24 March 1814.

650 Letter Melville to Warren, 24 November 1813, *Naval Miscellany*, Vol 164, Naval Records Society, p.242-3

651 Knight, *Convoys*, 2022, p.260

652 *Ibid*, 58

653 *Journal of the Royal United Services Institute*, Vol 13, W Mitchell & Co London, 1870, p.210-11, *Transactions of the Institution of Naval Architects*, Vol 9, 1868, p.162

654 As related by Knight, *Convoys*, 2022, pp.260-2

655 *The Morning Post*, Saturday 23 July 1814, Letter from St Johns, 12 July, p.3.

656 Correspondence from *Edward Belcher to Journal of the Society for the Arts*, Bell and Daldy, London, 1860 Vol VIII, p.97

657 Pedley, Rev. C., *The History of Newfoundland*, Longman, London, 1863, p.284-5, Mackinnon, R., Farming the Rock: The Evolution of Commercial Agriculture Around St. John's, Newfoundland, to 1945, *Acadiensis*, 1991, Vol 20 (2), 32 at 42.

658 James Macbraine to Keats 18 November 1814, *The Pittsfield Sun*, 23 June 1814, p2.

659 Chappell, Lieutenant. E., *Voyage of His Majesty's Ship Rosamond to Newfoundland*, J Mawman, London, 1818, p.208.

660 Prowse, D.W., *A History of Newfoundland*, MacMillan, London, 1895, p.389

661 Chappell *op. cit.*, pp.209-10

662 *Ibid*, p.49

663 *Ibid*. p.216. Prowse, D.W., *A History of Newfoundland*, MacMillan, London, 1895, p.388.

664 Bond, A., Cowin, F., and Lambert, *op. cit.*, pp.113-4.

665 Dillon, W.H., *A Narrative of my professional adventures, 1790-1839*, Vol 1, Lewis M A (Ed), Naval Records Society London 184., Vol 2, pp.314-8, See introduction, at p.269-70

666 Murphy, T. and Stortz, G, *Creed & Culture: The Place of English Speaking Catholics in Canadian Society*, McGills, Montreal, 1993, p.56.

667 O'Flaherty, P., *Old Newfoundland, A History to 1843*, Long Beach 1999, p.145

668 Howley, J. P., *The Beothuks or Red Indians; the Aboriginal Inhabitants of Newfoundland*, Cambridge University Press, 1915, p.91

669 Marshall, I, *A History and Ethnography of the Beothuk*, McGill-Queens Press, 1998, p.222.

670 Mercer, K, *The Murder of Lt. Lawry; A case study of Naval Impressment in Newfoundland 1794*, (2006), Newfoundland & Labrador Studies 21 (2).https://journals.lib.unb.ca/index.php/NFLDS/article/view/10153/10455

671 Fitzgerald, J; *Ghosts and Oddities*, Jeperson Press, St Johns, 2005, p.102.

672 *The Times*, 21 July 1814.

673 Meeting, St Johns Hall, 27 October 1813; Ingersoll, C.J., *Historical Sketch of the Second War Between the United States of America and Great Britain*, Lea and Blanchard, Philadelphia, 1849, Vol2, p.32.

674 Adams, Quincy, *The Duplicate Letters at the Negotiation of Ghent*, Davies & Force, Washington, 1822., p.220-3

675 Bathurst to Keats, 17 June 1815.

676 Keats - O'Flaherty, in *Dictionary of Canadian Biography*, Vol. 6, University of Toronto, 1987; Ryan, S., *The Ice Hunters: A history of Newfoundland Sealing to 1914*, Breakwater, St Johns, 1994, p.43; Pedley, *op. cit.* p.304

677 North Devon records Office (South West heritage trust) reference B127-6/73-74, attested copy lease accessed at https://discovery.nationalarchives.gov.uk/details/r/5e551f9a-4298-4aee-bd65-a60899388d46 The fields are described as Porthill Lawn, Merrifield Northam, Burgesses Close, lying between Merrifield (or Mary Field) and the highway, Garden Field (formerly Meana Park in Port), Lower Pool, bounded by the turnpike road from Northam to Bideford, five closes called Dallins Ground, formerly part of Over and Lower Port, and a further parcel of ground abutting the turnpike road to the west, summing to approximately 2,700 acres.

678 Somerset Records Office DD/CPL/49

679 Lysons, D & S, *Magna Britannica, A concise topographical account of the several counties of Great Britain*, Vol. 6, Devonshire, Thomas Cadell, London, 1822, pp.310, 365, 602

680 http://www.durranthousehotel.com

681 See The Battle of Algiers, *The Mariner's Mirror*, Society for Nautical Research, No. 27.4, 2013, p.234

682 Osler, E., *The Life of Admiral Viscount Exmouth*, p.317; Taylor, S. *op. cit.* p.237

683 Pridham, *Devonshire Celebrities, op. cit.*, p.147 .

684 Tracey, N., *Who's Who in Nelson's Navy*, Chatham, London 2006, pp.211-2,

685 Johnson, P., *The Board of Longitude; Journal of the Astronomical Association*, 1989, Vol. 99, (2), p63 at p.69.

686 House of Commons, 4 May 1821, pp.519-35.

687 See for example *The Hampshire Telegraph*, 11 May 1818.

688 *The London Gazette*, issue 17505, p.1446

689 *The Morning Chronicle*, Monday 3 May 1819, p.2.

690 *Ibid*, Wednesday 14 April 1819, p.1.

691 *Ibid*, Thursday 13 May 1819, p.1.
692 At least one of William's biographers suggests he made 'earnest recommendations to the Prince Regent' on the matter; Wright, G.N. and Watkins, J, *William the Fourth, op. cit.*, p.457.
693 The Times 15 June 1831, p5.
694 Stansfield, C.H.R., *Memorandum on Greenwich Hospital*, May 1909, Admiralty, London 1909, pp.5-11.
695 Newell, P, *Greenwich Hospital, A Royal Foundation 1692-1983*, Greenwich Hospital, 1984, p.113.
696 *Ibid*, p.122.
697 White, Keats, *op. cit.*, p.367
698 The Times, 1 July 1831, p3, see also; House of Commons, Accounts and Papers, page IV, No 360.
699 See for example letter to *The Times*, 11 July 1831, (p.6) in reply to that of Keats
700 Barrow, J.H. Ed., *The Mirror of Parliament*, second session, 1831, House of Commons p.1232
701 Newell, *op. cit.*, p.150
702 *The Times*, 27 August 1828.
703 *The Times, ibid*; Newell, *op. cit.*, pp.141-147
704 *The Times*, 21 March 1829, p3; Newell *op. cit.*; *The Annual Register* 1828, Baldwin & Cradock, London, 1829, pp.179-182
705 Newell, *op. cit.*
706 *London Gazette*, Issue 18713, 30 July 1830, p.1619-20.
707 Sir James Graham to Rear Admiral Brenton, 24 July 1831, Raike, H. (Ed), *The Life and Services of Sir Jahleel Brenton*, Hatchford & Son, London, 1846, p.633.
708 Letter Charles Adam, Governor, April 1848, Report Sir Richard Bromley, January 1864, The House of Lords, Accounts and Papers, Vol 23, 1864
709 *Smith and Moze v. Keats*, Consistory Court of Rochester, Dr Lushington, *Report of Cases determined in the Ecclesiastical Courts, 1833*, Haggard, J., Butterworth, London 1833, p.275
710 Brockliss, J.C., Cardwell, J., and Moss, M.C., *Nelson's Surgeon: William Beatty, Naval Medicine and the Battle of Trafalgar*, Oxford University Press, 2005, pp.185-6
711 For a detailed examination of the formation of the gallery see; Robinson, C, *Edward Hawke Locker and the Foundation of the National Gallery of Naval Art*, PhD Thesis, University of York, History of Art, 2013.
712 Guidebook item 23, now referenced NMM, BCH0332
713 *Newell, op. cit.* p.152
714 *The Log Book; Or Nautical Miscellany*, J & W Robins, Southwark second issue, No57, p.30
715 Buckingham, J.S. (Chair) *Evidence on Drunkenness presented to the House of Commons*, Thomas Hartley, 30 June 1834, pp.209-10
716 Collins, W.; Speech, *First Public Meeting of the British and Foreign Temperance Society*, S. Bagster, London, 1831.
717 *The Morning Chronicle*, Thursday 21 July 1825, pp.1 & 3.
718 *The New Annual Register*, 1824, p.34.
719 Rev. Samuel Maddock, Hamilton Adam & Co, London, 1825.
721 Mudie, R., *A Historical account of His Majesty's Visit to Scotland 1822*, p.325 *et. Seq.*
722 Letter 2 August 1822, cited by White, *Keats op. cit.*, p.367
723 Tucker, J.S.; *Memoirs of Admiral The Rt. Hon. The Earl St. Vincent*, p.385
724 *The Morning Chronicle*, 5 June 1827.

725 *Hampshire Telegraph*, Monday 7 January 1828, p.2.
726 Wright & Watkins, *op. cit.*, Vol 2, p.625
727 *The Times*, 5 May 1832, p.5, *Naval and Military Register*, 1832, p268-9.
728 *The Times*, 2 May 1832, p.4
729 Taylor, S, *Commander, op. cit.*, p.271
730 Newell, op. cit., p.147
731 *Ibid.* p.164
732 Knight, R, *William IV*, op. cit., p.81
733 Brockliss, *op. cit.*, p.175.
734 King, P.P, *Narrative of a Survey of the Intertropical and Western Coasts of Australia*, Cambridge University Press, p.277; Neville, R., *Colonial Ambition*, State Library of NSW, Magazine for Members, Spring 2010, p.23, at 25 referencing a letter from Roe to his father 22 March 1819.
735 Horden, M.C., *King of the Australian Coast*, MUP, 1997; Fenton, M. *The History and Stories of 39 Radar Port Keats, a RAAF Radar Station in real tribal country*, 1966, radarreturns.net.au
736 Franklin, J., *Narrative of a Second Expedition to the Shores of the Polar Seas in the years 1825, 1826, and 1827*, John Murray, London, 1828, p.242
737 *Reports of the Cambridge Anthropological Expedition to Torres Straits*, Vol 1 General Ethnography, CUP, 1935, pp.5-6
738 Bligh, W., *Captain Bligh's Second Voyage to the South Sea*, Longman Green & Co, London, 1929, p.181, n.4
739 Somerset Records Office DD/CPL/44
740 Bevan, J., *The Infernal Diver: The Lives of John and Charles Deane*, Submex, 1996,
741 *Ibid*, p.49
742 *Ibid*.
743 Hansard, House of Commons, Captain Warner's Invention, Sir F. Burdett, 4 August 1842, Vol 65, cc 1034.
744 *Byam Martin Papers*, Vol 1, p.139.
745 Somerset Records Office DD/CPL/40
746 Society Secretary, reported in *The Sporting Magazine*, Volume 3, p.57
747 *The Sporting Magazine*, 1831, Vol iv, No xix, New Series, p.56
748 *The Times*, 30 June 1832, p5.
749 Pritchett, R.T. *et al, Yachting*, in Watson, A.E., (Ed) *The Badminton Library of Sporting Pastimes*, 1894, Longmans, Green, and Co, London, 1894, Vol 2, Chapter 4.
750 Pritchett, *op. cit.*, p168
751 *The Sporting Magazine*, Vol 1 Second series, p.248
752 *Ibid*
753 *The Sporting Magazine* 1831, Vol 2, New Series, p.295. See generally, Castle, E.W. & Castle, R., *The Royal Thames Yacht Club*, in Watson, A.E., (Ed) *The Badminton Library of Sporting Pastimes*, 1894, Yachting Vol 2, Chapter 4.
754 Pritchett, *op. cit.* p.168.
755 *The Sporting Magazine*, Vol 6, New Series, p.62
756 *The Sporting Magazine* 1834, Vol 9 New Series, p.281; *The Sporting Magazine*, 1842, Vol 7, New Series, p.281
757 Pritchett, *op. cit.*, p.42.
758 *The Sporting Magazine*, Vol XXIV, No 144, September 1829, p.365.

759 *The Sporting Magazine*, Vol XXIV, No 144, September 1829, p.363. Guest, M & Boulton, W.B. *The Royal Yacht Squadron*, John Murray, London, 1903 makes no reference to honorary members prior to 1835. They do include a list of honorary naval members from that date forward, and boat owning members from the date of formation in 1815. The report in *The Sporting Magazine* is however quite specific and includes other verifiable details of membership and boats, including simultaneous with Keats's election, the granting of honorary membership to Charles Day as surgeon and a detailed report of the 1829 regatta.

760 There are many sources for the contention the French had superior ships. What lay behind the British superiority is more contentious; training, discipline, the will to fight encouraged by the prize system, or the system of promotion; See for example Allen, D.W., The British Navy Rules: Monitoring and Incompatible Incentives in the Age of Fighting Sail, 2002, *Explorations in Economic History*, Vol. 39, p.204

761 Guest & Boulton, *op. cit.*, pp.138-40

762 The London Gazette, issue 18709, p.1539

763 Description taken from the Great Exhibition of 1851; Timbs, J., *The Book of Facts,* Extra volume 1851, David Bogue, London, 1851, which quotes from the purported report of Keats and Hardy discussed below.

764 See Walesby, F.P., *Is England's safety or Admiralty interest to be considered,* William Painter, London (pamphlet), pp.9-12. See also Warner's justification in Warner, *Fair Play's a Jewell*, John Oliver, Pall Mall.

765 Sir C. Napier, House of Commons July 31 1844, Hansard, p.1615.

766 Hamilton, R.V. *Martin Papers, op. cit.* Vol 1, p.78

767 *Ibid*, p.134

768 *United Services Magazine*, 1834, Part 2, p.510

769 *The Naval and Military Remembrancer, 1844*, Maxwell, W.H. (Ed), Henry Bohn, London, p.36

770 Harding, *op. cit.* p.95

771 *Annual Biography and obituary*, 1835, Vol XIX, p.51

772 Campbell, J., *Lives of the British Admirals*, W. Stevenson, London, 1817, Vol VII, Appendix, p.144; Clowes, op.cit., Vol 5, p.9 puts the peak man power at 145,000 men, including 31,400 Royal Marines in 1811. He puts the peak number of ships at 728 in 1809. Knight, *Convoys, op.cit.* p.26 puts the peak at 147,000 men in 1813. On any view the Royal Navy was completely transformed its increase being measured by an order of magnitude rather than a percentage.

773 Dillon, Vol 2, p.270

774 *Ibid.* Vol 1, p.46

775 White, *op. cit.*, p.328

776 Taylor, S., *Sons of the Waves*, Yale University Press, London, 2020, p.164.

777 Dillon, *op. cit.* Vol 1, p.52

778 *Ibid.* p. xxxi.

779 Pridham, *op. cit.*, p.144

780 Sir Francis Burdett, Commons 4 August 1842, Hansard Vol 65, cc1034

781 *The Shipwrecked Mariner*, Vol XV, 1868, p.13

782 *Transactions of the Institute of Naval Architects,* Vol 8, 1861, p.221

783 Letter Lt. Gen. Graham to Charles Stuart, 28 July 1810

784 Nelson to Keats, 5 March 1805, Nicolas, Vol 6, pp.386-7

785 ADM 1/17/20, 10 March 1813, quoted in Walker, M. *Mobilising Clothes at Sea: Naval Dress Culture and economy during the French Wars*, 1793-1815, Ph.D. Thesis, University of Alabama, 2020, p.74.

786 Blake, J.L., *General Biographical Dictionary,* 2nd Edition, E. French, New York, 1838, p.513.
787 Random Rambles, *The Naval Chronicle,* 1838, Vol 35, p.463
788 *The Times,* 14 April 1834, p.6
789 *On the State of Vaccination 1810,* Charles McLean, London Vaccine Institution, Covent Garden, 1810.
790 *Rules and Regulations, Royal Naval Annuitant Society,* Congden & Hearle, Devonport, 1823.
791 Warner, O., *op. cit.,* p.95
792 *Ibid.*
793 Sugden, J., *Nelson, The Sword of Albion,* Henry Holt & Co, New York 2012, p.675
794 *Ibid.,* p.195
795 Brenton, *op cit.,* p.340
796 *The Court Journal,* Jan-Dec 1833, Vol 5, p.452, Henry Colburn, London.
797 *Royal Cornwall Gazette,* Saturday 26 October 1833, p.1.
798 Copy Will and associated papers, Derbyshire Records Office. D2538/m/2/60-63
799 *The Times,* 14 April 1834, p.6.
800 Sullivan., p.227; A. Fisher, *The Register of Blundell's School,* J.G. Commin, 1904, p.13
801 *The Times,* 14 April 1834; references the naval officers of the King's Household and the Lords of the Admiralty, but not the King himself.
802 Warwickshire Records Office, *Printed Order of Procession for the funeral of Admiral Sir Richard Goodwin Keats, G.C.B, Governor of Greenwich Hospital.* CR114A/490.
803 *New Monthly Magazine,* Vol 41, p 88, *London and Paris Observer,* Vol 10, p.335
804 Barrow, Sir John, *An Auto-biographical Memoir,* John Murray, London, 1847, p.381-2. See also Sullivan, *op. cit.*
805 *Annual Biography and Obituary,* 1835, Vol XIX, p.37 *et. seq.*; Urban, S.; *The Gentleman's Magazine,* MDCCCXXXIV, Wm. Pickering; John Bowers, London, 1834, p.653-5
806 *Devonshire Celebrities, op. cit.,* p.138; The Ipswich Journal, Saturday 17 October 1835, p.1.
807 Clarke, Henry G, *The Naval Gallery with a Description of the Painted Hall and Chapel, Greenwich Hospital, Guide-book for Visitors,* H.G. Clarke & Co, London, 1842, p.143, item 137, see also Walcott, *op. cit.,* p.441
808 Hatchway, Lt. R.N., *The Greenwich Pensioners,* Henry Colburn, London 1838, p.44
809 Newell, *op. cit.,* p.153. See also, Lt. Col. Harding, F.G.S., *The History of Tiverton, in the County of Devon.* Boyce, Whittaker & Co, 1847, Vol II, p.95
810 Two sources show the inscription as depicted M,DCC,XXXII – Harding, *op.cit.,* p 95 and Hatchway *op.cit.,* indicating it was commissioned during Keats's lifetime in 1832 rather than following his death in 1834.
811 Markham, Sir C. R, *The Story of Majorca and Minorca,* Good Press, 2019.
812 *Ibid.,* p.332
813 Letter 28 December 1811, Osler, E.P, *The Life of Admiral Viscount Exmouth,* Smith Elder & Co, London 1841.
814 Woodman, *The Victory of Sail Power, op.cit.,* p.21; Owen, H, I'll Make Five Sons Of Mine Fight For Their King And Country: The Naval Sons of William IV and Mrs Jordan, *The Mariner's Mirror* , Vol 83, No1, (1997), 41, at p.42; Parkinson, *Britannia Rules, op.cit.,* p.71, Smyth, W.H. *The Mediterranean, A Memoir, op.cit.,* p.99; Voelcker, *Saumarez, op.cit.,* p.1
815 White, Keats *op. cit.,* p.368, Voelcker, *op.cit.,* p82
816 *United Services Magazine* 1834, Part 2, pp.217-8
817 Dillon, W.H., *op. cit.* p.253

818 Obituary, Rear Admiral S. Jackson, CB, *The Gentleman's Magazine*, Vol 177, p.313
819 Raymond, D. J., *The Royal Navy in the Baltic 1807-1812*, p.71
820 Keats to Bridport, 24 August 1799, The Channel Fleet, Vol. 141 #489.
821 Bridport to Admiralty, 31 August 1799, The Channel Fleet, Vol 141, #493
822 Willis, *op. cit.*, p.255
823 Chappell, Lieutenant E., *Voyage of His Majesty's Ship Rosamond to Newfoundland*, J Mawman, London, 1818, p.208
824 Dillon, *op. cit.*, p. xxxi
825 Report of Admiral De Saumarez, July 13 1801, *Field of Mars, An Alphabetical digestion of Naval and Military Engagements*, 1801, Vol 2, p. ALG.
826 Chappell, *op. cit.*
827 *The Naval Chronicle*, I Gold, London, (1805) Vol 14, p.157, written in reporting Calder's action amongst events from July-August 1805, just prior to Nelsons death.
828 Laughton, J.K., *Dictionary of National Biography*, quoted by White, Keats, *supra*. p.347

Select Bibliography

KEATS

Annual Biography and Obituary, Longman Rees Orme, Green & Longman, London,1835, Vol XIX,

O'Flaherty, "Keats" - in *Dictionary of Canadian Biography*, Vol. 6, University of Toronto, 1987.

Marsden, J, *Napoleon's Stolen Army; How the Royal Navy Rescued a Spanish Army in the Baltic*, Helion & Co, Warwick, 20201,

Ralfe, J., *The Naval Biography of Great Britain*, Vol II, Whitmore & Fenn, Charing Cross, 1828, 487

The Gentleman's Magazine, MDCCCXXXIV, Wm. Pickering, John Bowers, London, 1834.

The Mariner's Mirror, Vol 7, 1921, Issue 10, p316-318 and 341-347

The Naval and Military Remembrancer, Maxwell (Ed), Henry Bohn, London 1834.

United Services Magazine, 1834, Part 2.

Warner, O, Keats and the Superb, *Blackwood's Edinburgh Magazine*, W. Blackwood, Edinburgh1945, p193

White, C., *Sir Richard Goodwin Keats*, in *British Admirals of the Napoleonic Wars*, le Fevre & Harding eds., Chatham, London, 2005.

Wood, S, Nelson's Star of the Bath and Awards to the family of Richard Keats, Morton & Eden, https://www.mortonandeden.com/wp-content/uploads/2019/02/45.pdf

OTHER ADMIRALS/BIOGRAPHIES/CORRESPONDENCE

Aspinall, A., *Mrs. Jordan and her Family*, Arthur Baker, London, 1951.

Aspinall, A., *The later correspondence of George III*, Cambridge University Press, 1970

Bienkowski, L, *Admirals in the Age of Nelson*, Naval Institute Press, Annapolis, Maryland, 2003.

Bingeman, J., Simpson, P., Tomalin, D., *The Wrecks of HM Frigate Assurance (1755) and Pomone (1811), The Career of Admiral Sir Robert Barrie (1774-1841)*, Oxbow, Oxford, 2021

Bond, A., Cowin, F., and Lambert, A., *Favourite of Fortune, Captain John Quilliam, Trafalgar Hero*, Seaforth Publishing, Barnsley, 2021 *The Career of Admiral Sir Robert Barrie (1774-1841)*, Oxbow, Oxford, 2021

Brenton, E.P., *Life and Correspondence of John, Earl of St. Vincent* (2 vols.), H. Colburn, London, 1838.

Campbell, J., *Campbell's Lives of the British Admirals*, Vol 7 p446 et seq. (HR Yorke ed., Bennet, Strand & Harris, London, 1817.

Clarke J.S & M'Arthur, J, *The Life of Admiral Lord Nelson from his Manuscripts*, Cadell & Davies, London, 1809

Cochrane [Thomas 10th Earl of Dundonald] *Autobiography of a Seaman*, Richard Bentley, London, 1860.

Collingwood, Adml. Lord C, *A selection from the public and private correspondence of Vice Admiral Lord Collingwood*, Ridgway & Sons, London, 1837.

Cordingly, D, *Cochrane the Dauntless: the life and Adventures of Thomas Cochrane, 1775-1860*, Bloomsbury, 2007.

Dillon, W.H., *A Narrative of my Professional Adventures 1790-1839*, 2 Vols. Lewis M A (Ed), Naval records Society, London, 1841.

Hamilton, R. V., *Letters and Papers of Admiral of the Fleet, Thos. Byam Martin*, Navy Records Society, Vol. 1, 1903, Vol 2 & 3 1898 (Vol. 1, being published last).

Hill, A., *Trelawny's Family Background and Naval Career*, Keats-Shelley Journal, Vol 5, 1956.

Knight, R., *The Pursuit of Victory- the Life and Achievements of Horatio Nelson*, Penguin Books 2005.

Lambert, A., *Nelson: Britannia's God of war*, Faber & Faber, 2004.

Laughton, J.K., *Nelson and his Companions in Arms*, Longmans, Green & Co, London, 1896.

Locker, E.H., *Memoirs of Celebrated Naval Commanders*, Harding & Leopold, London, 1832

Markham, J., *Selections from the Correspondence of Admiral John Markham*, Naval Records Society, Vol 28, 1905.

Marshall, J., *Royal Naval Biography*, Longman Hurst Rees, Orme & Brown, London, 1823

Morrow, J., *British Flag Officers in the French Wars, 1793-1815: Admirals' Lives*, Bloomsbury, 2018.

Nicolas, N. H., *The Despatches and letters of Vice Admiral Lord Viscount Nelson*, Seven Volumes, Cambridge University Press, 2011.

Osler, E., *The life of Admiral Viscount Exmouth*, Smith Elder & Co, London, 1841.

Outram, B. F., *Memoir of Sir Benjamin Fonseca Outram, Inspector of Naval Hospitals and of Fleets*, Royal College of Physicians of London, 1856

Parkinson, C.N., *Edward Pellew, Viscount Exmouth, Admiral of the Red*, Methuen, London, 1934.

Ralfe, J., *The Naval Biography of Great Britain*, Vol II, Whitmore & Fenn, Charing Cross, 1828.

Popham, Hugh, *A Damned Cunning Fellow*, Old Ferry Press, Cornwall, 1991.

Richmond, H.W. Z, *The Private Papers of George, Earl Spencer*, Vol.4, Navy Records Society, Vol 59 (1924)

Ross, J., *Memoirs and Correspondence of Admiral Lord de Saumarez*, 2 volumes, Richard Bentley, London, 1838.

Southey, R., *The Life of Nelson*, (New Edition),Bell & Daldy, London, 1873

Sugden, J., *Nelson: The Sword of Albion*, Henry Holt, London, 2013.

Sullivan, A., *Man of War: The fighting life of Admiral James Saumarez*, Pen & Sword, Yorkshire, 2017

Taylor, S, *Commander: The life and exploits of Britain's greatest frigate captain*, Faber & Faber, London, 2012 (Pellew).

The Barham Papers, Naval Records Society, 1909, Vol 39

The Channel Fleet and the Blockade of Brest, 1793-1801, Navy Records Society Vol 141.

Tracy, N., *Who's who in Nelson's Navy*, Chatham, London 2006.

Trelawny, E., *Adventures of a Younger Son*, Richard Bentley, London, 1835.

Tucker, J.S., *Memoirs of Admiral the Right Honourable Earl of St. Vincent.*, Richard Bentley, London, 1844

Voelcker, T., *Admiral Saumarez v. Napoleon- The Baltic 1807-1812*, The Boydell Press, Martlesham, 2008.

White, C., *Nelson, the New Letters*, Boydell & Brewer, Martlesham, 2005.

Wright, G.N. & Watkins., *The Life and reign of William the Fourth*, Fisher, Son & co, London, 1837.

BALTIC

Davey, J., The repatriation of Spanish troops from Denmark, 1808: The British Government, Logistics, and Maritime Supremacy, *Journal of Military History* 74 (3), 2010, p 689

Davey. J., War, *Naval Logistics and the British state, Supplying the Baltic Fleet*, 1808-1812, Ph.D. thesis, gala.gre.ac.uk

Glover, G., *The two Battles of Copenhagen, 1801 and 1807; Britain and Denmark in the Napoleonic Wars*, Pen & Sword, Yorkshire, 2018, Ch.14.

Marsden, J., *Napoleon's Stolen Army*, Helion & co. Warwick, 2021

Raymond, D. J., *The Royal Navy in the Baltic* 1807-1812 (2010 Ph.D. Thesis) Florida State University

Ryan, A.N., *The Saumarez Papers*, Naval Records Society, 1968, Vol.110

Voelcker, T., *Admiral Saumarez v. Napoleon- The Baltic 1807-1812*, The Boydell Press, Martlesham, 2008.

BATTLES

Adkins, R., *Trafalgar: The Biography of a Battle*, Hachette, London, 2004.

Allen, J., *Battles of the British Navy*, Bailey, Cornwall, 1842, 2 Volumes.

Allen, J., *Battles of the British Navy*, Bohn, London, 1852, 2 Volumes.

Brenton, E.P., *The Naval History of Great Britain from 1793-1836*, Rice, London.

Clark, W. M., *Clark's Battles of England and Tales of the Wars*, Clark, W.M., London 1848, Vol 4

Corbett, J.S., *The Campaign of Trafalgar-1805*, Vol 2, Pickle Partners, London.

Gardiner, R (Ed), *The Campaign of Trafalgar, 1803-1805*, Chatham Publishing, London, 1997

Glover, G., *The Two Battles of Copenhagen, 1801 and 1807; Britain and Denmark in the Napoleonic Wars*, Pen & Sword, Yorkshire, 2018.

James, W., *The Naval History of Great Britain from the Declaration of War by France in February 1793 to the Accession of George IV in January 1820: with an account of the origin and progressive increase of the British Navy (six vols.)* R. Bentley, London, 1837.

Keats, Captain R.G, *Narrative of the Services of Her (sic)Majesty's Ship Superb, 74, on the night of the 12 July 1801 and the two following days, by her then Captain, Sir Richard Goodwin Keats G.C.B.&c*, Ed J.S. Tucker, Longman, 1838

Newbolt, Sir J H. *The Year of Trafalgar*, John Murray, London, 1905.

Ralfe, J., *The Naval Biography of Great Britain*, Vol II, Whitmore & Fenn, Charing Cross, 1828.

Field of Mars, An Alphabetical digestion of Naval and Military Engagements, 1801, Vol 2, p. ALG.

DEVONSHIRE

Harding, F.G.S., *The History of Tiverton, in the County of Devon*. Boyce, Whittaker & Co, Tiverton, 1847, V. II.

Pridham, T. L., *Devonshire Celebrities*, HS Eland, Exeter, *1869*.

GREENWICH HOSPITAL

Clarke, Henry G, *The Naval Gallery with a Description of the Painted Hall and Chapel, Greenwich Hospital, Guide-book for visitors*, H.G. Clarke & Co, London, 1842.

Hatchway, Lt. R.N., *The Greenwich Pensioners*, Henry Colburn, London 1838.

Newell, P., *Greenwich Hospital; A Royal Foundation 1692-1983*, Trustees of Greenwich Hospital, Greenwich, 1984.

NEWFOUNDLAND

Chappell. E., *Voyage of His Majesty's Ship Rosamond to Newfoundland*, J Mawman, London, 1818.

Morrow, J., *The Naval Government of Newfoundland in the French Wars, 1793-1815*, Bloomsbury, 2023.

Pedley, Rev. C., *The History of Newfoundland*, Longman, London, 1863.

Pengelly, C., *HMS Bellerophon*, Pen & Sword, Yorkshire, 1966.

PENINSULA WAR

Davies, H, Naval intelligence support to the British army in the peninsular war, *J of Soc. For Army Historical Research*, 86, (2008), 34.

Davies, H., *Spying for Wellington: British Military Intelligence in the Peninsular War*, University of Oklahoma Press, 2018.

Graham, J & Mace, M., *The Battle of Barrosa 1811, Forgotten battle of the Peninsular War*, Skyhorse, New York, 2014.

Hall, C.D., *Wellington's Navy, Sea Power in the Peninsular War, 1807-1814*, Chatham, London, 2004.

Herson J. P., *For the Cause, Cádiz & The Peninsular War: military and Siege Operations 1808-1812*, University of Florida Master's Thesis https://apps.dtic.mil/dtic/tr/fulltext/u2/a252088.pdf

RELEVANT NAVAL HISTORY

Clowes, W.L., *The Royal Navy- A History from the Earliest Times*, Chatham, London, 1997 (7 Volumes)

Davey, J., *In Nelson's Wake*, Yale University Press, National Maritime Museum, Greenwich, 2017.

Fraser, E., *The fighting fame of the King's ships, Dreadnoughts and Captains of Renown*, Hutchinson, London, 1910.

Gale, C.M., *Beyond Corsairs. The British -Barbary Relationship During the French Revolutionary and Napoleonic wars*, Trinity College, Oxford, Ph.D. Thesis, 2016.

Knight, R, *Convoys – The British Struggle Against Napoleonic Europe and America*, Yale University Press, London, 2022

McDougal & Coats (Eds.) *The Naval Mutinies of 1797; Unity and Perseverance*, Boydell Press, Martlesham, 2011

Musteen, J, *Nelson's Refuge; Gibraltar in the Age of Napoleon*, Naval Investiture Press, 2011

Parkinson, C. N, *Britannia Rules*, Weidenfeld & Nicholson, London, 1977.

Pope, D., *England Expects*, Chatham Publishing, London, 1998.

Pope D., *Life in Nelson's Navy*, Stratus, Cornwall, 1981.

Taylor, S., *Sons of the Waves*, Yale University Press, London, 2020,

Tracy, N., *Who's who in Nelson's Navy*, Chatham, London 2006.

White, C., *The Nelson Touch: The Evolution of Nelson's Tactics at Trafalgar* (Journal of Maritime research, 7:1).

White, C., *Nelson's 1805 Battle Plan*, J. Maritime Research,4:1, 82-88.

Willis, S., *In the Hour of Victory: The Royal Navy at War in the Age of Nelson*, Atlantic Books, 2004y.

Winfield, R., *British warships in the Age of Sail*, Seaforth publishing, Yorkshire, 2005.

Woodman, R., *The Sea Warriors*, Constable, London, 2001.

Woodman, R., *The Victory of Seapower, Winning the Napoleonic War 1806-1814*, Chatham, London 1998.

WALCHEREN

Bond, G.C., *The Great Expedition: The British invasion of Holland 1809*, University of Georgia Press, 1979.

Howard, M. R., *Walcheren 1809: Scandalous Destruction of a British Army*, Pen & Sword, Yorkshire, 2012.

Wareham, T., *This disastrous Affair, Sir J.B. Warren and the Expedition to Quiberon Bay, 1795*, The Age of Sail, The International Annual of the Historic Sailing Ship, Conway Maritime Press, Vol 1, p.9

WARNER'S INVENTIONS

Walesby, F.P., *Is England's Safety or Admiralty Interest to be Considered*, William Painter, London (pamphlet),

Warner, *Fair Play's a Jewell*, John Oliver, Pall Mall.

NOVELS

Bryant, L, *This Blighted Expedition*, 2018, (Walcheren Expedition)

Forester, C.S., *Commodore Hornblower*, Little, Brown & co, New York 1945, (based loosely on Keats exploits in the Baltic).

Goldsworthy, A., *Run Them Ashore*, Weidenfeld & Nicholson, London, 2014 (Cádiz, attack on Fuengirola, battle of Barrosa)

O'Brian, P., *Master and Commander*, Wm Collins, London, 1969, (concludes with the second battle of Algeciras).

Parkinson, C. N., *Touch and Go*, McBooks Press, 1977, (second battle of Algeciras)

Index

A
Acasta 135, 137, 138, 146, 154
Achille 245
Active 50, 115
Adonis 270, 279
Aetna 245, 250
Agamemnon 144, 146, 152, 156
Agincourt 100
Aigle 20, 21
Ajax 17
Alburquerque
   Duke, General Jose Maria de la Cueva (Sp.) 245, 256
Alerte 36
Alexandre 149, 151, 153, 155, 156
Alfred 258
Allemand
   Rear Admiral (Fr) 144, 145
Amazon 118
Amethyst 146, 148
Andromaque 43, 46
Andromeda 26
Ape 107
Arethusa 34, 36, 144
Artois 34, 36, 44
Atalante 166, 167, 168
Atlas 148, 152, 245
Auckland
   Earl George 296, 301, 331
Audacious 73
Austen
   Captain Francis 149
Austin
   Thomas 294

B
Ball
   Alexander 72, 134, 241
Barham
   First Sea Lord 118, 120, 137, 139, 159
Barrie
   Captain Robert 167, 169
Bathurst 303
   Captain 227
   Lord Henry 280
Beatty
   William 303
Belcher
   Admiral Edward 272, 273
Bellerophon 33, 268, 269, 271, 276
Bellona 09, 10
Bernadotte
   Marshal Jean Baptiste (Fr) 194, 198, 200, 201, 211, 212, 213, 214, 220, 221, 341
Berry
   Captain Sir Edward 132, 152, 156
Bertie
   Rear Admiral Thomas 98, 218
Bettesworth
   Commander George 120
Bickerton
   Admiral Sir Richard 93, 95, 196, 286
Bienfaisant 17
Blackwood
   Captain Sir Henry 240

Blake 238, 245
Blayney
   Lt. Col. Lord Andrew 250
Blenheim 182, 183
Bligh
   Captain William 32, 304
Boadicea 49, 50, 51, 53, 54, 58, 144, 170, 332, 341, 367
Bompart
   Admiral Jean-Baptiste (Fr) 52
Bonetta 19, 20, 21
Bounty 32, 304
Brave 152, 153, 155, 156
Brenton
   Captain Jahleel 77, 81, 82, 85, 86, 332, 365
Brereton
   General Thomas 119, 140
Bridport
   Admiral Lord 38, 39, 48, 52, 55, 341, 342
Brisbane
   Captain Charles 144, 145, 148
British and Foreign Temperance Society 297, 327
Brunswick 195, 201, 203, 204, 205, 213, 227
Buchan
   Lieutenant 279
Buck
   Captain Richard 263
   George Stuckley 09
   Lewis 219
Bulley
   Thomas 271

Bulwark 257, 258, 342
Byng
   Vice Admiral George, 6th Viscount Torrington 49

C

Caesar 69, 73, 74, 75, 76, 77, 80, 81, 82, 83, 85, 332, 365, 366, 367, 369, 372, 373
Calcutta 144
Calder
   Vice Admiral Robert 120, 121, 135
Caledonia 262
Calpe 69, 71, 73, 75, 365, 372
Calypso 216
Cambridge 10
Camden
   Marquess 107
Camilla 234
Canning
   Lord George 195, 198, 232
Canopus 148, 149, 152
Captain 10
Carroll
   Lieutenant William 250, 255
Cartwright 108, 109
Castlereagh
   Lord Robert 195, 232, 238
Cathcart
   General Lord Robert 175, 179
Centaur 264
Chappell
   Lieutenant Edward 273, 274
Chatham 240
   General Earl John 232, 235, 237, 239, 243
Chiffonne 138
Clarence
   William, Duke of 08, 14, 25, 26, 30, 32, 58, 76, 95, 96, 97, 117, 123, 181, 182, 183, 221, 262, 289, 291, 299, 301, 306, 307, 313
Clerk
   John, of Eldin 132
Cochrane
   Captain Lord Thomas 71, 85, 86, 87, 90, 166, 167, 168, 170, 171
   Rear Admiral Alexander 118, 148
Cockburn
   Captain George 243, 249, 255
   Lieutenant General James Pattison 247
Codrington
   Admiral Sir Edward 238
Cole,
   Captain Sir Christopher 219
Collingwood
   Admiral Lord Cuthbert 48, 55, 69, 132, 135, 137, 143, 144, 158, 183, 287
Colpoys
   Admiral Sir John 289, 294
Comet 268
Comus 254
Contest 268
Coote
   Magistrate Thomas 279
Cornwallis
   Admiral Sir William 120, 121, 143
Cotton
   Admiral Sir Charles 245
Countess
   Captain George 52
Craig
   General Sir James 219
Crescent 34
   (38) 275
Culloden 17
Cumberland
   HRH Duke of 307
Cumberland Fleet 307
Cumby
   Captain William 279

D

Danaé 54
Dashwood
   Captain Charles 56
Deane
   John & Charles 305
Derwentwater
   Earl James Radclyfe 292
Devastation 205, 207, 210, 245, 250
Dey
   of Algiers 30, 103, 104, 105, 107, 108, 109, 282, 319, 341
Diamond 34, 36, 342
Dickson
   Commander William Henry 292
Dictator 187, 196, 218
Digby
   Rear Admiral Robert 13, 14, 16, 18, 19
Dillon
   Captain William Henry 275, 276, 281, 303, 320, 321, 339, 343
Diomede 149, 151, 153, 155, 156
Diving helmet 305
Donegal 146, 152, 153, 155
Druid 254
Duckworth
   Admiral Sir John 01, 135, 136, 137, 138, 139, 140, 143, 144, 145, 146, 147, 148, 149, 150, 154, 155, 156, 158, 161
Dumanoir
   Admiral, (Fr) 70, 71
Duncan
   Captain Crawfurd (Port) 372
Dundas
   Captain George 91, 372
Dunn,
   Captain 138
Durham
   Captain 132

E

Eagle 138
Edgar 17, 26, 195, 196, 198, 199, 200, 203, 205, 207, 213, 215
Edward
   H.R.H. Prince 26, 27, 28, 29, 30
Elliot
   His Exc. Hugh 96, 122
El Vencedor 250
Emeriau
   Vice Admiral Maxime (Fr) 263
Epervier 149
Episcopal Floating Church 297
Espion 36
Ethalion 52
Étoile 42
Éveillé 42
Excellent
   (74)Br 116

F

Fabregues
  Lieutenant Don Antonio (Sp) 198, 199, 200
Falcon
  Consul, Algiers 103, 104, 105, 107, 109
Fama 205
Felix 168
Fellowes
  Rear Admiral Sir Thomas 250, 256
Ferris
  Captain Solomon 69
Fidele 240
Fielding
  Captain Charles 64
FitzClarence
  Captain Lord Adolphus 331
  Henry 182, 183, 240, 322
Fleeming
  Captain Charles 257, 258, 301
Fooks
  Captain William 19
Formidable (Fr) 372, 373
Fox
  Captain William 20
Franchise 263
Franklin
  Captain Sir John 304

G

Galatea 33, 34, 35, 36, 37, 38, 40, 41, 42, 44, 47, 48, 49, 50, 332
Gambier
  Admiral Sir James 64, 133, 170, 171, 173, 174, 179, 180, 181, 264
Ganges 173, 174
Ganteaume
  Admiral Joseph (Fr) 113, 121
Gardiner
  Admiral Lord Alan 165
Gloire 20
Gorgon 213
Graham
  Admiral Sir James 293, 294, 307, 331, 332
  General Thomas 243, 253, 254, 255, 256, 323
Graves
  Captain Sir Thomas 205, 227
Gravina
  Admiral Federico Carlos (Sp.) 117
Grenville
  First Lord Thomas 43, 162, 164, 165, 181
Gustav
  King, of Sweden 184, 226

H

Haesingeland 36
Halifax 10
  Earl of 09
Halket
  Captain Peter 173
Hall
  Captain Robert 249, 250
Hamilton
  Admiral 332
Hannibal 68, 73, 78, 87, 365
Hardy
  Admiral Sir Charles 18
  Rear Admiral Sir Thomas 132, 133, 301, 308, 313, 314
Harrison
  John 285
Hawker
  Captain Edward 268, 276
Hawkesbury
  Lord Robert 107
Hibernia 08, 161, 261, 264
Hobart
  Lord Robert 106, 109
Holles (Hollis)
  Captain Askew P 370
Hood
  Admiral Viscount Samuel 31, 32
  Rear Admiral Sir Samuel 02, 67, 77, 83, 85, 164, 165, 166, 167, 168, 174, 180, 184, 189, 213, 224, 264, 369
Horatio 275, 303
Hotham
  Admiral William 332
Hound 205, 206, 210, 245, 256
Howe
  Admiral Lord 32, 33, 48
Hydra 161
Hyperion 279

I

Impériale 148, 149, 151, 152, 155, 158
Implacable 08, 194, 243, 245, 247, 255
Indienne 73

J

Jackson
  Captain Samuel 76, 87, 176, 210, 341, 366, 367, 369, 370, 371
Jordan
  Mrs. 182, 183, 322
Jupiter 152, 155, 156

K

Keats
  Lady Mary (nee Hurt) 327, 328
  Rev. Richard (Snr) 08, 218, 264
  Rev. Richard (Jnr) 223, 332, 337
  William Abraham 08, 322
Keith (Viscount)
  Admiral George Elphinstone 57, 73, 83, 342
Keppel
  Admiral Viscount Augustus 13
King
  Captain Phillip 303
Kingfisher 10, 148
Kite 205, 207, 210
Kittoe
  Captain Edward 247, 255, 261

L

Laforey
  Admiral Sir Francis 118, 332
La Meillerie
  Captain (Fr) 161
Langara
  Admiral Don Juan de (Sp.) 15, 17, 132
Langford
  Captain 144
La Pena
  General Manuel (Sp.) 254
Lark 144

Lascy
  General Luis (Sp.) 249
Lavie
  Captain Sir Thomas 169
Le Bon Francois
  (privateer, Fr) 249
Le Curieux 120
Legge
  Rear Admiral Arthur 261
Leissegues
  Admiral Corentin (Fr) 143, 145, 148
Le Ray
  Commodore Julien (Fr) 75
Leveson-Gower
  Rear Admiral John 26
Linois
  Admiral Charles-Alexandre (Fr) 68, 71, 72, 90, 144
Lion 20, 21
Lobo
  Envoy Don Raphael (Sp.) 196, 198, 199, 200
Locker
  Edward Hawke 130, 292, 296, 301
Lockhart-Ross
  Rear Admiral Sir John 16
Lockyer
  Captain Nicholas 210
Loire 161, 268
London 32, 33
Louis
  Rear Admiral Sir Thomas 149, 158
Louisa 73, 75, 365

M

MacNamara
  Captain James 203, 205
Magicienne 148, 154
Majestueux 125
Malcolm
  Admiral Pulteney 152, 158, 310
Markham
  Admiral Lord 164, 165, 167
Marlborough 17
Mars 161, 162, 182, 183
Martin
  Admiral Sir George 331
  Admiral Sir Thomas Byam 26, 27, 32, 194, 223, 244, 306, 309, 318, 332, 339

Maskelyne
  Royal Astronomer 286
Mazarredo
  Admiral Don-Joseph (Sp) 71, 87
Medina 271, 272, 310
Melville
  (Robert Dundas) Viscount 289, 309
Mercury 10
Mermaid 303
Merry
  Anthony 225
Milford 08, 247, 252, 253, 255, 261, 263, 332
Minorca 138
Minx 210
Missiessy
  Admiral Edouard (Fr) 113, 121, 238, 239
M'Kenzie
  Commodore 13
Montagu
  Admiral George 121
  Captain James 10
  Captain John 09, 13
Moore
  General Sir John 182, 184, 195, 243
Moreno
  Admiral Juan(Sp.) 71, 73
Mosquito 176, 196, 198, 199
Muiron 71
Mulgrave
  Admiral Lord Henry 174, 180, 217, 218, 224, 225, 228
Murray
  Rear Admiral Sir George 323, 324

N

Nagle
  Captain Sir Edmund 34, 35, 44
Napoleon
  Bonaparte, Emperor (Fr) 57, 92, 98, 113, 118, 121, 132, 143, 171, 173, 179, 193, 194, 195, 217, 231, 232, 240, 244, 245, 256, 268

Nelson
  Charles 147, 322
  Earl William 147, 271, 322
  Vice Admiral Viscount Horatio 02, 03, 64, 76, 91, 95, 96, 97, 98, 100, 103, 104, 105, 107, 108, 109, 110, 111, 114, 115, 116, 117, 118, 119, 120, 121, 122, 123, 125, 126, 129, 130, 131, 132, 133, 134, 135, 136, 137, 138, 140, 147, 149, 150, 166, 213, 262, 263, 317, 321, 322, 324, 326, 339, 341, 342, 343, 344
Nepean
  Sir Evan 45, 55, 109
Niger 26, 31, 275, 320, 332
Niobe 268
Norge 178, 245
Northesk
  Admiral Earl 135
Northumberland 118, 148, 151, 152, 154

O

Outram
  Benjamin Fonseca, Surgeon 53, 89

P

Pasley 71
Pellew
  Sir Edward, (Admiral Viscount Exmouth) 33, 34, 35, 36, 56, 69, 99, 100, 261, 262, 263, 264, 282, 293, 300, 326, 339, 343
Perseus 271
Phillips
  Captain Charles 304, 325
Phoebe 117
Pickle 135, 137
Pickmore
  Admiral Francis 243, 246, 323
Pike 271, 272
Plumper 304
Pole
  Rear Admiral Sir Charles 53, 167
  William Wellesley (Lord Mornington) 171, 224
Pomone 44, 48

Pompée 61, 68, 73, 90, 174
Popham
   Captain Sir Home 158, 174
Powerful 137, 146, 148
Prince George 14, 15, 16, 17, 18, 19, 334
Proby
   Captain Lord 54
Prothee (Protée) 18
Providence 304
Pym
   Captain Sir Samuel 148

Q

Quartidi 36
Quilliam
   Captain John 269, 275

R

Racoon 20, 21, 22, 216
Rambler 249
Ramillies 13
Real Carlos 53, 78, 79, 81, 86, 87, 371, 373
Revolutionnaire 36, 64
Rhin 162
Rhinoceros 19
Richards
   Captain George 304
Robertson
   Rev. James 195, 197, 198
Rodney 245, 248, 250
   Admiral Sir George 15, 16, 17, 132
Roe
   John Septimus 303
Romana
   Marquis General Pedro de La (Sp.) 194, 195, 198, 201, 203, 207, 209, 217, 219, 221, 244, 253, 335
Romney 13
Rosamond 270, 273
Rosily
   Admiral Francois (Fr) 245
Ross
   Captain John 304, 325
Rosslyn
   General Earl 236
Royal George 16, 135
Royal Sailing Society 306, 327

Royal Thames Yacht Club 307, 308, 327
Royal Yacht Club 309
Royal Yacht Squadron. 309
Ryves
   Rear Admiral George 100

S

Sabrina 233
Sacorman 205
Salisbury 269
Salsette 227, 233
Saltren-Willett
   Augustus 281
San Fiorenzo 53
San Hermenegildo 78, 79, 80, 81, 86
San Julien 15
Saumarez
   Admiral Sir James 02, 34, 36, 46, 67, 68, 69, 70, 71, 72, 73, 74, 76, 80, 81, 82, 83, 85, 91, 182, 184, 185, 196, 200, 210, 212, 218, 220, 222, 223, 224, 228, 264, 304, 307, 332, 365, 369, 370, 373
Sawyer
   Admiral Sir Herbert 271
Seahorse 105, 115
Seymour
   Admiral Sir George 331, 332
   Vice Admiral Lord Hugh 45
Sidmouth
   Lord Henry 132
Smith
   Admiral Sir Sidney 34, 35, 36, 264
Smyth
   Captain W.H. 116, 263
Snape-Douglas
   Captain Sir Andrew 34
Snipe 204, 208, 210
Sophie 20, 22
Sotheron
   Admiral Frank 332
Southampton 26, 28, 29, 30, 31, 306, 318
Sparrowhawk 250
Speedy 71, 87, 90
Spencer 73, 75, 146, 151, 303, 365, 370
   Earl George 45, 46, 48
Spranger
   Captain John William 255

Standard 255
Stanhope
   Vice Admiral Henry 174
St. Antoine
   (San Antoine) 75, 76, 80, 81, 82, 83, 85, 87, 90, 91, 368, 369, 370, 372, 373
Stately 254
Stopford
   Admiral The Hon. Robert 151, 154, 159, 164, 174, 308, 332
Strachan
   Admiral Sir Richard 144, 169, 170, 231, 235, 236, 237, 239, 339
St. Vincent
   Admiral Earl 34, 55, 56, 57, 58, 64, 76, 77, 91, 98, 99, 122, 161, 162, 164, 165, 166, 167, 168, 169, 181, 190, 222, 241, 265, 286, 326, 339, 340, 343, 363
Superb 08, 63, 64, 67, 68, 69, 71, 72, 73, 74, 75, 76, 77, 79, 80, 81, 82, 83, 85, 86, 87, 88, 89, 90, 95, 96, 101, 104, 105, 108, 111, 114, 115, 121, 122, 123, 125, 126, 129, 133, 135, 136, 137, 138, 139, 143, 144, 146, 147, 149, 150, 151, 152, 155, 161, 165, 166, 176, 181, 182, 195, 199, 205, 207, 210, 213, 218, 227, 240, 322, 324, 332, 340, 341, 351, 363
Sutton
   Admiral Sir John 61, 166
Sylph 44, 52, 56
Symonds
   Captain Sir William 310

T

Temeraire 133
Terrible 13
Thames 67, 71, 73, 75, 370, 372
Thompson
   Admiral Sir Boulden 295
   Vice Admiral Charles 46
Thornbrough
   Vice Admiral Edward 165
Thornton
   Envoy Edward 203
Thunder 245, 250, 256
Tigress 187, 196

Tobin
  Captain George 148
Tonnant 245
Topaze 250
Touche-Treville
  Vice Admiral Comte Louis-Rene de La (Fr) 20, 21, 22, 27, 78, 79, 99
Towry
  Captain George 51
Trelawny
  Edward 135, 136, 137, 139
Troubridge
  Captain Thomas 80, 164, 182
Turbulent 187

U

Uranie 51, 57, 341

V

Varlo
  Captain Weston 10
Vencedor 247
Venerable 67, 71, 73, 75, 77, 83, 85, 90, 91, 369, 370, 372, 373
Vernon 300, 310
Vestal 20, 21
Victor
  Marshal Claude (Fr) 245, 253, 254, 257
Victory 105, 111, 114, 121, 133, 134, 197, 214, 222, 303, 360
Villeneuve
  Admiral Pierre-Charles (Fr) 99, 113, 116, 117, 119, 120, 121, 125, 132, 140, 144, 323
Vives
  Lt.Col. Don Dionisio (Sp) 198, 200
Voiture 240
Volontaire 36

W

Warner
  Captain Samuel Alfred 313, 314, 315
Warren
  Admiral Sir John Borlase 33, 34, 36, 38, 41, 42, 44, 45, 46, 47, 48, 49, 52, 144
Warrior 255
Warwick 20, 21
Wasp 144
Wellington
  General Arthur Wellesley, Duke of 197, 244, 256, 322, 336
White
  Captain John Chambers 44, 52
Willaumez
  Admiral Jean-Baptiste (Fr) 143, 145, 147, 148, 158
William
  King, IV 314, 332, 339
Wolverine 271

Y

Yarmouth 10

Z

Zealous 245

RICHARD GOODWIN KEATS

Author

Peter Hannah BSc, LLB (Hons) is a lawyer and amateur historian with a family connection to Admiral Keats and an interest in the Age of Sail. A project to transcribe a handwritten memoir of the Admiral's naval career led to further enquiry and a more significant undertaking examining the totality of his career and seeking a more detailed understanding of the character of Nelson's favourite captain.

He regularly sails a restored gaff rigged Couta Boat – a traditional craft that developed for the barracouta fishery supplying Melbourne in the late 1800's and has co-edited *The Tradition Lives On – A Register of the Historic Couta Boats*.

Milton Keynes UK
Ingram Content Group UK Ltd.
UKHW031824151223
434437UK00013B/594

9 781923 088030